DESIGNING
PASCAL SOLUTIONS

A CASE STUDY APPROACH

PRINCIPLES OF COMPUTER SCIENCE SERIES

Series Editors
Alfred V. Aho, Bellcore, Morristown, New Jersey
Jeffrey D. Ullman, Stanford University, Stanford, California

Alfred V. Aho and Jeffrey D. Ullman
Foundations of Computer Science

Egon Börger, Editor
Trends in Theoretical Computer Science

Michael J. Clancy and Marcia C. Linn
Designing Pascal Solutions: A Case Study Approach

Ruth E. Davis
Truth, Deduction, and Computation: Logic and Semantics for Computer Science

A. K. Dewdney
The Turing Omnibus: 61 Excursions in Computer Science

Vladimir Drobot
Formal Languages and Automata Theory

Narain Gehani
C: An Advanced Introduction, ANSI C Edition

Eitan M. Gurari
An Introduction to the Theory of Computation

David Maier
The Theory of Relational Databases

Martti Mäntylä
An Introduction to Solid Modeling

Shamim Naqvi and Shalom Tsur
A Logical Language for Data and Knowledge Bases

Christos Papadimitriou
The Theory of Database Concurrency Control

Gregory J. E. Rawlins
Compared to What? An Introduction to the Analysis of Algorithms

Stuart C. Shapiro
LISP: An Interactive Approach
COMMON LISP: An Interactive Approach

Richard Snodgrass
The Interface Description Language: Definition and Use

James A. Storer
Data Compression: Methods and Theory

Steven Tanimoto
Elements of Artificial Intelligence
Elements of Artificial Intelligence using COMMON LISP

Jeffrey D. Ullman
Computational Aspects of VLSI
Principles of Database and Knowledge-Base Systems, Vol. I: Classical Database Systems
Principles of Database and Knowledge-Base Systems, Vol. II: The New Technologies

DESIGNING PASCAL SOLUTIONS

A CASE STUDY APPROACH

Michael J. Clancy
University of California, Berkeley

Marcia C. Linn
University of California, Berkeley

COMPUTER SCIENCE PRESS

AN IMPRINT OF W. H. FREEMAN AND COMPANY

NEW YORK

Library of Congress Cataloging-in-Publication Data

Clancy, Michael, 1950-
    Designing Pascal solutions: a case study approach / Michael J.
Clancy, Marcia C. Linn
        p.   cm.
    Includes index.
    ISBN 0-7167-8258-8
    1. Pascal (Computer program language) I. Linn, Marcia C.
II. Title
QA76.73.P2C54 1992
005.13'3--dc20   91-48079
                                                  CIP

Chapter illustration credits on page 439.

Printed in the United States of America

Computer Science Press
An imprint of W. H. Freeman and Company
The book publishing arm of *Scientific American*
41 Madison Avenue, New York, NY 10010
20 Beaumont Street, Oxford OX1 2NQ, England

1 2 3 4 5 6 7 8 9 0 KP 9 9 8 7 6 5 4 3 2

To our parents,
who inspired and encouraged us
to learn and to teach.
MJC
MCL

Contents

CHAPTER 1   *Check That Number!*   1

More and more activities are controlled by numbers every day. Now we have numeric codes to get money, to register for class, to access a phone company, to arm an alarm system, or to use a copy machine. Computers often validate these numbers. This case study describes a program that validates numbers for a copy machine.

CHAPTER 2   *Banners With CLASS*   21

From ancient times banners have proclaimed events and advertised opportunities. Computers allow individuals to create personalized banners of varied sizes and styles. This program prints block versions of six letters in user-specified sizes using the letters PASCL. It can be altered to create banners with such messages as PASS PASCAL CLASS.

CHAPTER 3   *The Calendar Shop*   *45*

Keeping track of time is a major industry. Historically, calendars have defined weeks and months quite differently from today. This program will create a calendar for any given year. It can be altered to create fantasy calendars without Mondays and historical calendars with 10-day weeks or 28-day months.

CHAPTER 4 *Roman Calculator Construction* *73*

Calculators have revolutionized mathematics, making hand computation of square roots obsolete. This program will control a calculator that takes a Roman numeral and converts it to its decimal equivalent.

CHAPTER 5 *Is It Legal?* *95*

How should programs respond to illegal data? Assuming that data will be legal asks for trouble: What if users mistype? What if users want to confuse the program? This case study describes how to guard against illegal data in the *Check That Number!*, *Banners With CLASS*, *Calendar Shop*, and *Roman Calculator Construction* programs.

CHAPTER 6   *Space Text*   147

Computers now make desktop publishing possible. Publishing software allows users to display text in much the same way as it is displayed in books. This case study describes the development of a procedure that could be inserted into a word-processing program to display text flush with the right and left margins.

CHAPTER 7   *You Are What You Eat*   183

The current enthusiasm for choosing a healthy diet motivates people to keep track of the calories, fat, and cholesterol they consume. Suppose you were asked to design a program to help. This case study describes how a programmer might respond.

CHAPTER 8 *You Forgot What You Ate* **217**

The user of the *You Are What You Eat* program has more trouble recalling what he ate than anticipated. He also wonders if the computer can keep track of the fat and calories in each thing he eats so that he only has to enter it once. This case study describes how a programmer might respond to problems encountered by users. What does "user-friendly" really mean?

CHAPTER 11   *Roman Calculator Repair*   *341*

How do you know that a program works? Julius Caesar Enterprises has constructed a program they claim will convert Roman numerals to their decimal equivalents. See if it works, fix it if it fails, and submit a bill for consultant services.

CHAPTER 12   *The Eating Club*   *361*

Whole groups of people want to keep track of what they eat and to compare progress. This case study describes extensions to the *You Are What You Eat* and *You Forgot What You Ate* programs to handle a complex food list, multiple users, and several reporting formats. The program should be able to sort foods and entries and do it quickly.

To Instructors

Why Case Studies?

Designing Pascal Solutions engages students as "apprentices" to expert programmers to extend and reinforce skill in designing solutions to programming problems. Students actively participate in solving problems, solution programs to some of which have several hundred lines of code, yet never get bogged down in the syntax details. Students using this book learn more and are better prepared for advanced courses than students who rely only on traditional textbooks.

Are you covering more but enjoying it less?

Introductory courses are often so packed with details that students lose sight of the big picture, gain only superficial understanding of program design, and fail to appreciate the problem solving power of a programming language. As introductory books get bigger and bigger, many instructors find that they are covering more technicalities but neglecting the design of problem solutions.

Moreover, although program design and problem solving really make sense to students only in the context of big, complex programs, typical textbooks neglect these topics. In contrast, the case studies in *Designing Pascal Solutions* make big, complex problems accessible and understandable to students by engaging students as apprentices.

How can students learn program design?

To teach program design, the ultimate goal of programming courses, we have developed the case studies in *Designing Pascal Solutions*. The case studies focus on the *process* of program design and development rather than the end product. Using case studies, students actively participate in designing solutions to problems they could not solve alone. The concepts of design are illustrated in the context of large, complex programs, where these ideas make sense. The case studies engage the student as an apprentice who contributes to the program design. They feature hundreds of self-test questions as well as hundreds of exercises that can be assigned as homework, discussion questions, and computer laboratory activities. Students learn powerful programming templates and useful programming principles as they read the cases, answer the self-test questions, and do the exercises. They learn to rely on the templates and principles to generate and compare problem solutions and to determine when to postpone the details of a design.

Do case studies help students learn?

Empirical studies[*] show the power of case studies for teaching Pascal. Pascal case studies have been tested at the University of California, Berkeley, in several courses at other colleges and universities, and in 25 high school Advanced Placement courses.

What were the results of class tests?

Only the fittest case studies survived the scrutiny of students. Students rejected many problems as "nerdy" or uninteresting. They refused to read long paragraphs. They demanded clear, concise explanations. They asked for, and got, more questions and exercises. They wanted case studies not just about writing programs, but about writing modules, designing interfaces, and debugging. This collection is the result.

Case Study Features

How do students use case studies?

Case studies engage students in the process of program design in the context of a program that is larger than those they design on their own. In each case study of *Designing Pascal Solutions*, students first read and analyze a Problem Statement. Then they use the Commentary on the design to guide their own knowledge construction. They answer self-test questions while reading the Commentary. At appropriate intervals they extend their understanding by doing on-line and off-line exercises. They consolidate their knowledge using the Review section, doing exercises to link their ideas to related problems and issues. As they engage in these activities they read the Pascal Code for each problem solution and work with it on-line in a computer laboratory.

What are templates?

Case studies help students organize their knowledge into patterns that we call **templates**. Templates are reusable abstractions of programming knowledge constructed by students. Examples are such actions as "input, process, output," "process until done," and "insert into an array." All the templates introduced in *Designing Pascal Solutions* are described in the Template Appendix. To communicate their generality, we represent templates with verbal descriptions and pseudocode as well as with code examples. To communicate their reusability, we reuse templates in case studies after they are introduced.

Case studies illustrate how templates are used to plan problem solutions. Using the case studies helps students learn when to use a given template,

---

[*] Linn and Clancy, "The Case for Case Studies of Programming Problems," *Communications of the ACM*, March 1992, vol. 35, no. 3, pp. 121–132; Linn and Clancy, "Can Experts' Explanations Help Students Develop Program Design Skills?" *International Journal of Man-Machine Studies* (in press).

how to test the template, and what bugs to expect when they implement the template.

How do case studies help avoid the "illusion of comprehension"?

As apprentices using case studies, students answer both self-test questions and exercises. They continuously assess their comprehension, solve parts of the problem themselves, test and debug parts of the solution, and reflect on alternative ways to approach the problem. As a result students get regular feedback on their understanding. They avoid the "illusion of comprehension" that sometimes comes from superficial understanding of problem solutions.

Which students benefit most?

Passive readers are often lulled into the illusion of comprehension. These students have difficulty applying information in textbooks because they do not integrate it with their other ideas. In contrast, students who actively try out ideas as they are introduced are likely to understand the material presented and to connect what they read with their own experience. The best students spontaneously test their ideas and reflect on their experiences; for them, case studies are a natural extension of their approach to studying. Case studies encourage this disposition toward integrated understanding in other students, giving all students the power to be successful in programming courses.

How can students test their understanding of the material?

Research shows that self-test questions can increase learning from text by allowing students to assess their own progress. These questions encourage students to actively evaluate the decisions and actions of the expert rather than to passively read the information. The case studies include several hundred *stop-and-think* questions that students can use to test their comprehension.

The stop-and-think questions in the Commentary ask students to:

- *Stop & Help* solve the problem.

- *Stop & Predict* what the experts will do.

- *Stop & Consider* alternatives.

Answers to all the *Stop & Help* and *Stop & Predict* questions are available in the Commentary and Pascal Code sections, so they serve as a *self-test* for students. Students who test themselves as they read the case study will be able to determine when they understand and when they are confused. Thus students using the questions can allocate their study time effectively, focusing on difficult material. In contrast, those who read passively may assume they understand when in fact they are confused.

How do the exercises help students gain integrated understanding?

Exercises at the end of each section and at the end of each case study can be used for homework, laboratory assignments, or discussion activities. The questions ask students to identify connections and integrate their ideas. They are called *making sense* questions because they require more complex applications of the case material and take longer to answer than stop-and-think questions.

Making sense questions fall into six categories.

- *Modification* questions ask students to modify the program in the case study to make it better or different.

- *Application* questions ask students to apply the ideas from the case study solution to a related problem.

- *Analysis* questions ask students to compare and evaluate different solutions or approaches to a particular problem.

- *Debugging* questions ask students to identify bugs in a program, diagnose a bug from a symptom, anticipate bugs, or test for bugs.

- *Testing* questions ask students to interrogate their operating system or the program in the case study.

- *Reflection* questions ask students to assess programming practices and problem solving strategies especially in terms of their own experience. One purpose of reflection questions is to help students identify helpful and unproductive programming habits.

Which exercises work in computer laboratories?

The *making sense* questions are marked with icons that identify which ones require computer activities, which require on-line code from the case study, which are mathematical, and which are difficult.

⌨ indicates that students need to write or run Pascal code on-line.

💾 indicates that students need an on-line version of the case study solution.

Σ indicates that students will be applying mathematical concepts. Students do not need to know college mathematics to use the case studies. However, for those who are interested, there are a few study questions that ask students to apply case study ideas to mathematical concepts or that ask students to analyze an outcome mathematically.

★ indicates a question that is difficult or time consuming.

What problems do case studies solve?

In the Problem section, each case study is introduced with a Problem Statement. Many of the cases illustrate how programmers make sense of terse and abstract problem specifications. Some cases present a problem as a discussion between a client and a programmer. Still others ask the programmer to test and debug programs that are supposed to work.

How is the solution explained?

The Commentary section provides a decision-by-decision description of the problem solution. It describes the solution from the vantage point of an expert but with the details appropriate for a student. To show how visualizing helps solve problems, the Commentary uses drawings and tables. The Commentary describes alternative views of the solution to meet the needs of students who learn better with diagrams, verbal descriptions, pseudocode, or some combination of these approaches.

How do the margin questions help?

The Commentary lists design and development questions in the left margin that are answered by the text on the right. The questions identify all the decisions that are necessary to solve the problem. If students already know the answer to a question they can skip the answer. If they do not understand the question, reading the answer may help. If they do not read the question, interpreting the answer will be more challenging. The efficient student will read the marginal questions (these are the students who read headings in textbooks).

What does the Review section contain?

The Review section summarizes the case study. Design and development questions from the Commentary are listed in outline form. Students can use the outline to organize their reading, to guide review of the case, and to select parts of the case for further study.

The Programmers' Summary identifies the main points introduced in the case study and connects them to more general issues in program design. In particular, the summary describes how principles of program design are applied in the solution. It also summarizes the main decisions in the case study.

What are the principles of program design?

The eight principles listed in the table on page xx govern the design of each program in the case studies. Expert programmers follow these principles to devise good problem solutions. For example, the Literacy principle says that code should be self-documenting. Implementing this principle helps programmers remember what a program does when it later needs to be modified. The Recycling principle says that code should be abstracted into templates and that templates should be recycled. Implementing this principle gives the programmer the power of cumulative knowledge. Taken together the programming principles help programmers integrate their ideas. Integrated ideas are linked and connected; programmers with integrated ideas create cohesive programs.

Using Case Studies

How many case studies should students use?

Case studies are like chocolate—more is always better. Case studies are especially effective as the topic for regularly scheduled discussion sections, as the source of computer laboratory assignments, and as the basis for examinations.

How can case studies be used in lectures?

Most instructors prefer to introduce case studies in lectures. Often students come to their first programming course with the idea that they will learn programming solely by writing code. They are shocked to discover

Literacy	Produce code that is self-documenting so that it is easy to understand, modify, and debug. Use self-documenting code to make the purpose of each section clear and to automatically update documentation while modifying the program.
Divide and Conquer	Code and test complex programs a piece at a time to isolate program bugs and reduce the time spent searching for problems. Use this process of incremental development to reduce the cognitive demands of programming by concentrating on one component at a time.
Recycling	Reuse ideas, especially design templates, that worked before. Elaborate on a known template to solve a new problem rather than attempting to design new code from scratch for every problem encountered.
Alternative Paths	Generate and evaluate alternative designs for programming solutions. Develop processes for finding alternatives and criteria for selecting among alternatives.
Multiple Representations	To gain robust understanding of templates, represent them in multiple ways. Promising representations include natural language, pseudocode, diagrams, and dynamic illustrations.
Persecution Complex	Adopt a persecution complex to test computer programs. Test for all possible weaknesses in the program using typical and extreme cases. List all the cases that should be tested and regularly consider whether additional cases should be tested.
Fingerprint	Develop effective debugging skills by associating symptoms of bugs (their "fingerprints") with the appropriate bug. Knowledge of common bugs and their associated fingerprints—symptom-bug associations—facilitates debugging.
Reflection	Reflect on alternative designs for programming problems and on problem solving processes. Develop skill in monitoring progress and in diagnosing unproductive activities. Anticipate personal weaknesses and guard against them.

Principles of program design

that programmers also read books on algorithms, study programs written by others, and even review research articles. Case studies provide an opportunity to communicate this important learning strategy to programming students from the beginning. An effective strategy is for instructors to discuss the things they read to become better computer scientists and to describe how they learned about programming from reading code written by others.

In lectures instructors can help students make sense of a case study by asking students which of the solutions described in the Commentary they preferred, by encouraging students to say why one solution would be easier to debug than another, and by discussing the principles that are illustrated in each solution. Lectures are an opportunity to connect the case study to other class activities, discussing how the templates introduced in the case can be used to solve problems assigned as homework or presented in class.

Instructors can also use the lecture to introduce solutions to case study problems not covered in the book. Some instructors use this opportunity to point out solutions they consider better (or worse) than those in the book. We expect to hear about these solutions; instructors can expect us to comment.

How can case studies be used in discussion sections?

Discussion is most effective when students can contribute diverse perspectives and expertise. Thus, brainstorming is almost always a successful group activity. Discussion can also be effective if students are assigned to solve *Analysis* or *Application* questions in advance and then compare their approaches in class. Often *Reflection* questions are appropriate for discussion because students are likely to have different points of view.

Another way to ensure that students contribute diverse expertise is to ask subgroups of students to report on different case studies. Students tend to study material carefully if they expect others to ask them questions about it during the discussion.

How do case studies work in computer laboratories?

Exercises appropriate for computer laboratories are indicated by an icon, as mentioned earlier. We find that laboratories are most successful when students are asked to come to the session with a plan for solving the assigned problems. Students' laboratory grades might be determined, in part, by whether or not they bring plans to the sessions.

Not all the program solutions are polished to perfection. Polishing would have led in some cases to overly obscure code, and in other cases to extra explanation whose inclusion, we felt, would detract more from the presentation than it would add. We also intend, however, that students have opportunities for program polishing; many of the exercises provide such opportunities. We believe our programs to be bug-free—the commentaries describe the process with which we tested them—but a bug that escaped our notice should also provide an occasion for a useful lab activity.

How can case studies provide questions for examinations?

We have found that examinations based on case studies are excellent indicators of students' ability to solve complex problems. Once students have digested a case study, it provides a context for questions more sophisticated than those that commonly appear on class examinations. End-of-section questions provide examples of good examination questions. (Examinations, scoring criteria, and potential student responses have been developed for each case study and are available in the Instructor's Manual.)

If I already use case studies, do I need these?

Some instructors already use case studies in lectures. *Designing Pascal Solutions* will augment and reinforce ideas about problem solving introduced in lectures. Moreover, the case studies will actively engage all the students, not just those who raise their hands and participate in class.

What Pascal concepts do students need to know for each case study?

The Pascal constructs required and introduced in each case study are listed in the table on page xxiii. Students will learn most if the *required* constructs are covered before using the case study. The Pascal sections in the Template Appendix will help students review them. The *introduced* concepts can be understood in the context of the case study without being covered in class. The Pascal sections in the Template Appendix give the details necessary for interpreting the case study. Students who first encounter these Pascal elements in case studies will be well prepared when they are subsequently covered in class.

Which templates are introduced in each case study?

Each case study introduces or elaborates several templates, listed in the table on page xxiii. The required Pascal constructs are sequenced so that the cases can be used with any Pascal textbook. (See the Instructor's Manual for specific suggestions.) As noted, the required Pascal constructs should be covered before using the case study, but the Pascal constructs introduced can be understood in the context of the case study.

Can some of the case studies be skipped?

The case studies build on one another, but students need not do them all. Students will get the most out of the book if they examine the Outline of Design and Development Questions, Programmers' Summary, and Template Appendix for the case studies they skip. By reviewing these sections students will still benefit from the continuity between cases in *Designing Pascal Solutions*.

What dialect of Pascal is used?

All solution programs are written in Standard Pascal. Turbo Pascal solutions and on-line versions of the solutions are available from the publisher to adopters of the text.

Acknowledgments

We could not have written this book without the many helpful, argumentative, and insightful comments supplied by students, instructors, family members, pets, and colleagues.

We would like to thank the many people who read the case studies before they were class-tested and who tried the cases in programming courses, along with all the students in our courses who read and reviewed the cases.

Chapter	Templates introduced or elaborated	Pascal constructs required	Pascal constructs introduced
1 *Check That Number!*	prompt, then read; input, process, output.	program heading; variable declarations; writeln and readln	comments; integer, real, and char types; begin and end; arithmetic operators, including mod and div; assignment statement; write and read; ord and chr; if statement
2 *Banners With CLASS*	input one, process one; do something a specified number of times; select from alternatives	for loop	const definition; procedures and value parameters; case statement,
3 *The Calendar Shop*	input and process until done; process in cycles		boolean type; functions; repeat loop; not, and, and or
4 *Roman Calculator Construction*	accumulate values until done; fill an array	type definition; one-dimensional arrays	var parameters, while loop, eoln
5 *Is It Legal?*	process every element of a one-dimensional array; search a one-dimensional array		
6 *Space Text*	insert into a one-dimensional array; copy a segment of a one-dimensional array; insert while copying a one-dimensional array		
7 *You Are What You Eat*	process elements of a file until done; insert into a file	files	records, reset, rewrite, eof
8 *You Forgot What You Ate*			enumerated types, pred, succ
9 *Chess Challenges*	process a two-dimensional array until done; process the diagonal of a two-dimensional array		two-dimensional arrays
10 *The Shuffler's Dilemma*			
11 *Roman Calculator Repair*	read forward, process backward		recursion
12 *The Eating Club*	divide and process elements		

Templates and Pascal constructs introduced in each chapter

We especially appreciate the many San Francisco Bay area high school Pascal instructors who were the first intrepid users of our case studies. It is appropriate that our first case study was a program that played *Mad Libs*. Our project motto of "try and trash" summarizes the kinds of changes that were necessary as the result of feedback on the materials.

The following high school teachers provided much helpful feedback: Suzanne Antink, Dennis Barbata, Tim Brown, Al Cooper, Michael Descilo, William Ferrero, Claudia Fort, Sarah Johnson, Paul Juarez, Rosanne Krane, John Liu-Klein, Ray Louie, Bob Macartney, Chris Maters, Harold Nay, Armando Picciotto, Gary Porter, Don Proia, Brian Stoll, and Gary Triebwasser.

David Barton, Claire Bono, Oliver Grillmeyer, Brian Harvey, and Mark Tuttle class-tested our materials in university courses. Their feedback was also invaluable.

We would like to thank members of and consultants for the Computer Science Advanced Placement Test Development Committee for much philosophical debate and constructive criticism on the AP case study and on case studies in general: Owen Astrachan, Stephen Cook, Tim Corica, Sarah Fix, Stephen Garland, Mark Hoover, Susan Horwitz, Sharon Lee, Stuart Reges, Fred Schneider, Frances Trees, and Jeff Wadkins.

More personal thanks go to Caryn Dombroski for modeling the debugging process for *Roman Calculator Repair*, and to Joe Faletti for careful reading and many excellent suggestions in evenings of discussion.

We are extremely appreciative of the support and encouragement we received from the National Science Foundation. Grants for research enabled us to investigate the teaching and learning of computer science. Meetings of project directors organized by Andrew Molnar and Ray Hannapal at NSF helped to build a community of scholars concerned with technology and instruction. These collegial interactions have been invaluable. We especially appreciate suggestions from Hal Abelson, John Anderson, Carl Berger, Andy di Sessa, Erik Decorte, Ed Dubinsky, Karl Frey, Richard Mayer, Phil Miller, Rich Pattis, Roy Pea, Alan Schoenfeld, and Elliott Soloway.

We also want to thank all the participants in the research projects that laid the groundwork for this book. Special thanks go to John Bell, Charles Fischer, Freda Husic, Michael Katz, Ellen Mandinach, Lydia Mann, Rafaela Marco, David Rogosa, William D. Rohwer, Patricia Schank, Kathryn Sloane, and John Thomas.

Donald Knuth has long inspired us, first as a model of effective teaching and a great person to work for as a teaching assistant, and more recently as a missionary for "literate programming." The case studies are our contribution to this tradition.

We owe a debt of gratitude to Caryn Dombroski and C. Bruce Tarter for patience, sacrifice, and humor. We know that Mort also played a key role in the creation of this book.

We would also like to thank all those involved in the production of this book including editors, designers, and reviewers. Nola Hague encouraged and supported us through all phases of the production of this book. Megan Higgins provided a creative design and resourceful solutions to unique problems. Penny Hull provided careful editing, patience, and humor. Ann Di Fruscia supplied help with FrameMaker, our document production system, exactly when we most needed it.

We are especially grateful to artist Joan Berger Siem who actually read several case studies and created the artwork on the cover.

This book was produced with the FrameMaker program by Frame Technology Corporation on an Apple Macintosh computer, using Caslon, Futura, Serif Gothic, Courier, Symbol, and Zapf Dingbats typefaces by Adobe Systems Incorporated and the Apple Pi typeface by Hank Gillette.

MJC
MCL

To Students

How to Use Case Studies

Is your view of programming an accurate one?

Does programming seem to consist entirely of memorizing details and forgetting where to put the semicolon? Does it seem as if solving complex problems is always postponed until the next course? These case studies involve you in solving complex problems as "apprentices" to an expert. (For more information about how the case studies are constructed, consult To Instructors. You might as well find out what the instructor thinks you will learn from this book.)

Is apprenticeship with case studies like the Sorcerer's Apprentice?

The Sorcerer's Apprentice turned a reasonable project into an impossible task. Case studies do the opposite. As an apprentice you will be answering lots of questions conveniently placed between paragraphs and at the end of sections. Answering these questions as you go along will help you learn to program better.

We have research to back up this statement. If you are skeptical of research, however, just reflect on your own experience. Do you ever complete an entire chapter and then realize that you cannot remember anything? Do you ever listen to instructions and believe that you know how to get to East Grinstead or operate the tape player or interpret the symbolism in a play only to discover when you actually try to do it that you did not understand at all? It's not premature Alzheimer's disease; the problem is that you were lulled into the *illusion of comprehension*.

The questions in the case study will help you detect this illusion long before it becomes a habit. Trust us, the questions are there to help you.

What is different about case studies?

Using case studies, you will solve complex problems, apply these solutions to other complicated problems, and also find out how programmers turn seemingly impossible tasks into reasonable projects.

What if you can already solve the problem?

There will be times when you suspect that you already understand the material in the case study. In these circumstances, the questions in the left margin will really be helpful.

If you suspect that you know how the case study will go, try answering the questions in the margin. If they seem easy, try answering the stop-and-think questions inserted in the text and the questions at the end of each section and at the end of the chapter. If you can answer these, then skip the related parts of the Commentary.

If the problem solved by the case study sounds easy, try writing down your solution before reading the Commentary. Warning: Resist the illusion of comprehension. Compare your predictions to the programs in the Pascal Code section. If the code for any of the solutions does not make sense, then review the Commentary. Make sure to examine all the solutions to the problem.

Isn't one solution to a problem enough?

There are many problems—like poverty—for which even one solution would be terrific. In programming, though, several solutions often have to be considered to find one that is best or even really good enough.

In our class tests, students who came up with their own solutions sometimes ignored other solutions. They missed the opportunity to compare solutions and figure out which one was best. They also missed many questions on the examinations.

Keep in mind that programming involves both finding a solution to a problem and being able to say why the solution is as good as or better than other solutions. All the case studies compare several different solutions to the same problem. To be honest, when we were solving these problems sometimes one author came up with a solution that the other author was able to improve—substantially. We also learned a great deal about diplomacy from these encounters.

What if you have a better solution to a case study?

Not all of our solution programs are polished to perfection. We wrote the programs so that they would be easy to explain and understand. Some improvements or extensions are left for you to do in exercises; others you may discover on your own.

We like suggestions and criticism. If you have a better solution, try explaining it to your instructor or to a classmate. Use apprenticeship and ask lots of questions. If your instructor or classmate understands your solution, send it to us—be sure to include the questions.

Formatting and Coding Conventions

Within each case study, we use this typeface to present pseudocode set off in its own paragraphs and Pascal code within text paragraphs. Pascal program segments are presented in `this fixed-width typeface`. Terms in boldface are defined in the Glossary section of the book.

Our Pascal code adheres to several conventions. Each subprogram is accompanied by a comment that describes the parameters and return values, along with any preconditions on which the subprogram depends. Sometimes, in a comment for a boolean function, we use the phrase "returns true exactly when" some condition holds; this means that the function returns false when the condition doesn't hold. Comments generally do not accompany statements within subprograms; we rely on variable and subprogram names and the Commentary section of the case study to provide detailed information about how a given subprogram works.

Our variable names begin with lower-case letters. Where a name consists of the concatenation of two or more English words, we capitalize all words after the first, for instance, numToInsert. We capitalize names of types and subprograms, for instance, ReadTrimmedLine, and use all capitals for names of Pascal constants.

Loop bodies of for and while loops, along with the bodies of if...then...else statements, are always bracketed with begin and end, even if the begin and end enclose only one statement. Within each loop of if body, we indent each statement and terminate it with a semicolon. This convention clearly displays the boundaries of the loop or if body; it also eliminates both the need to decide whether or not to include a begin and end, and the errors that result from adding a statement to a one-statement loop without also enclosing the pair of statements with begin and end. Here's an example:

```
for date := startOfWeek to startOfWeek+6 do begin
    if (date > 0) and (date <= monthLength) then begin
        write (date: 3);
    end else begin
        write (BLANK: 3);
    end;
end;
```

This convention may offend instructors or programmers who view a semicolon as a statement *separator* rather than a *terminator*. To us, the more easily modified programs that result are more important.

CHAPTER 1 *Check That Number!*

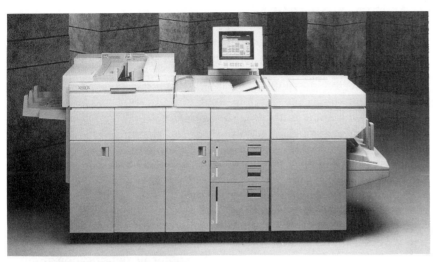

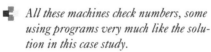
All these machines check numbers, some using programs very much like the solution in this case study.

More and more activities are controlled by numbers every day. Now we have numeric codes to get money, to register for class, to access a phone company, to arm an alarm system, or to use a copy machine. Computers often validate these numbers. This case study describes a program that validates numbers for a copy machine.

Problem Statement

Write a program that determines whether identification numbers typed by users of a photocopier are valid, and prints appropriate messages.

The program should assume that the input consists of one line containing (only) a four-digit identification number. For testing purposes, the program should prompt for input and print the output. Assume that the tested program, with input and output procedure calls appropriately replaced, will become the processor for a photocopier whose display panel is similar to the illustration.

The program should prompt the user for a four-digit identification number, read the number, and determine whether it is valid. Valid numbers have a correct "check digit." The check digit for an identification number is its rightmost digit; a correct check digit is equal to the remainder of the sum of the other three digits divided by 7.

The program should print one of the following messages after verifying the number:

```
The number is valid. Ready to make copies.
```

or

```
*** The number is not valid for this copy machine.
```

The asterisks printed in the case of an invalid number are intended to make the message more noticeable to the user.

Analysis 1.1 Does the identification number 4150 have a correct check digit?

Σ *Analysis* 1.2 Suppose a correct check digit were determined by dividing the sum of the first three digits by 3 rather than 7. Determine a four-digit value whose check digit would be correct in either system.

★ *Application* 1.3 How does the inclusion of a check digit in the identification number help protect against illegal use of the copier? Do some research to determine if commonly used identification numbers, like credit card numbers or Social Security numbers, include a check digit.

Preparation

The reader is expected to be familiar with the heading for a Pascal program, variable declarations, and the writeln and readln procedures. This case study introduces the use variables of type integer and char, the ord function, the div and mod operators, assignment statements, the write procedure, and the if statement.

Understanding the Problem

How do programmers start to make sense of problem statements?

Understanding a programming problem involves at least making sense of the problem statement, identifying the input and output behavior of the desired program, and designing an algorithm that solves the problem.

Stop & Predict ➤ *What words in the problem statement seem to have special meanings for programmers?*

What aspects of the problem statement are important?

Interpreting a problem statement or specification often requires understanding special programming terms that may have different meanings from their standard English usage. For example, the *Check That Number!* problem statement uses the term **prompt**, which in computer jargon means to print a message that asks for a response from the user.

To understand a problem statement it often helps to restate the problem in more familiar language. For example, the *Check That Number!* program should print a message asking the user for a four-digit identification number, read in the number that the user types, determine the check digit, compare it to what the check digit is supposed to be, and print a message saying whether or not the number is valid.

What will the program input and output?

Translating the problem specification into the desired **input-output behavior** clarifies what the program accomplishes. It involves answering three questions: What input for the program is legal? What output is desired for legal input? What behavior is desired for illegal input?

The problem statement indicates that the input will be a nonnegative four-digit number. That means values like –1437, 28, ABC, and 3P0 will not be input, so the program need not check for them. It is not clear whether a value less than 1000 qualifies as a four-digit number. 0012 has four digits and would be punched into the keyboard in that way; however, 0012 has the same value as 12. We will infer from the intended use of the program that 0012 is allowable input and 12 is not.

As for the output, it will be one of the two messages given in the problem statement. The output will be determined by examining the input value, viewed as a two-piece value, as shown below.

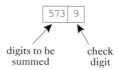

digits to be   check
summed   digit

Stop & Predict ➤   *What form should the input and output messages take?*

Note that the problem statement has not specified the exact format of the prompt. It makes sense, however, for the request for input and the user's input itself to be on the same line and for the output message to be on the line that immediately follows. The request for input should also tell the user as precisely as possible what he or she is supposed to type.

Here are some sample interactions with the program, with the user's input shown in boldface:

```
Please type a four-digit identification number:  5739
*** The number is not valid for this copy machine.
Please type a four-digit identification number:  5731
The number is valid. Ready to make copies.
```

How are algorithms designed? Solving the problem involves designing an **algorithm** for the solution, namely a solution outline that can be straightforwardly translated into a Pascal program that satisfies the specifications.

Reflection   1.4   How would *you* benefit from restating the problem and specifying the input and output before starting to write the code for the solution? To answer this question, consider how well you have done in situations where you had to interpret a specification and produce an answer based on the specification. How much clarification did you need? Did you ever misinterpret the question?

Analysis   1.5   Try to convince a fellow programmer that a value like 28 is a four-digit number and should be allowable input.

Application, Analysis   1.6   In what ways is the output specification incomplete? Describe a situation in which deviating from the desired output format in subtle ways could have serious consequences.

Analysis   1.7   What could be the consequences of producing *extra* output beyond what is requested in the specification?

Solution That Uses Only Integer Variables

How is the Pascal program designed?

Terms used in the problem statement suggest Pascal constructs to use in the solution:

"prompts the user"	write or writeln
"reads the number"	read or readln, with some variable representing the number
"print one of the ... messages"	write or writeln
"checks whether"	if

Stop & Predict ➤   *Are we ready to write the code?*

Trying to combine the constructs into some sort of program means dealing with both Pascal details and the steps of the solution at the same time. We might end up wasting time writing useless Pascal code. To reduce confusion, we postpone the details of Pascal code until the main steps in the solution are worked out. A good way to identify the steps is to outline the solution.

Outlining a problem solution before turning it into Pascal is like outlining an essay before turning it into English prose: one arranges the big ideas without getting bogged down in the details. By dividing the problem into parts and **refining** each part of the outline in turn, there are never too many things to consider at once. Many people call this approach **divide and conquer**.

Stop & Consider ➤   *Give an example of a problem that is easier to solve with a "divide and conquer" strategy than with an "all at once" strategy.*

What are the steps in the solution?

The problem statement describes these steps in the solution:

- Prompt the user for the identification number.
- Read the number.
- Determine if the identification number is valid.
- Print a message saying if the number is valid.

Since prompting and reading generate the input for the program, it makes sense to treat these steps as a single component of the outline:

Input: Get the identification number from the user by (a) prompting the user and (b) reading the value.

Process: Determine if the identification number is valid.

Output: If the number is valid, print an appropriate message; if it is invalid, print an appropriate message.

These steps are an example of a common programming pattern: input of data values, processing of that data, and output of associated information.

Stop & Help ➤ | *What details are being postponed?*

What are the variables in the program?

Identifying and naming variables as soon as possible during program design makes it easier to devise and keep track of further steps in the solution. Variables should have names that express their purpose so that they are easy to identify in the code. Two obvious choices for variables in this program are the identification number, which we'll call idNumber, and the check digit, which we'll call checkDigit. Since both are numbers, it makes sense for both to be represented by integer variables.

Using these variables, we rewrite the outline as follows:

Input: Get the identification number from the user.

```
write ('Please type a four-digit identification number:  ');
readln (idNumber);
```

Process: Determine whether the three leftmost digits in idNumber, when summed and divided by 7, have a remainder equal to checkDigit.

Output: If checkDigit is equal to the remainder, then

```
writeln ('The number is valid. Ready to make copies');
```
otherwise
```
writeln ('*** The number is not valid for this copy machine.');
```

Stop & Help ➤ | *Why were* write *and* readln *used for input rather than* writeln *and* read*? Why was* writeln *used for output rather than* write*?*

How is the identification number validated?

To validate the identification number we need to figure out the check digit, sum the remaining digits, and compare the remainder when the sum is divided by 7 to the check digit.

How is the check digit computed?

The problem statement says that the check digit is the rightmost digit of the identification number. The best technique for isolating this digit is to use the Pascal mod operator, computing the remainder when dividing the identification number by 10. In Pascal, this computation may be done with the statement

```
checkDigit := idNumber mod 10;
```

Stop & Consider ➤ | *What if the leftmost digit were the check digit? How would it be separated?*

How are the remaining digits summed?

The problem statement says that a valid identification number has a check digit that is equal to the remainder of the sum of the other three digits in the identification number divided by 7. Thus these three digits must be separated, then added. That suggests that four more variables will be needed:

digit1, the leftmost digit of idNumber
digit2, the second digit
digit3, the third digit
remainderDigit, the remainder when the sum of the three digits is divided by 7

The process and output steps in the outline then become

Process: Separate checkDigit. Separate digit1, digit2, and digit3. Compute remainderDigit.

Output:
```
if remainderDigit = checkDigit then begin
    writeln ('The number is valid. Ready to make copies.');
end else begin
    writeln ('*** The number is not valid for this copier.');
end;
```

How are the digits of the identification number separated? We move on to separate the digits. We already determined the rightmost digit. The leftmost digit of a four-digit value is the number of "thousands" the value contains. In Pascal, we find this by using the div operator:

```
digit1 := idNumber div 1000;
```

The middle digits are harder to separate.

Stop & Predict ➤ *How could determining the middle digits become just like determining the leftmost and rightmost digits?*

A good approach is to determine some quantity for which the digit we want is the first or last digit. This is called **reducing the problem to a problem previously solved**. Then we can repeat the approach we just took to find digit1 and checkDigit. The second digit in idNumber is the rightmost digit of the number of hundreds in idNumber, that is, the rightmost digit of idNumber div 100. Thus in Pascal we have

```
digit2 := (idNumber div 100) mod 10;
```

Similarly,

```
digit3 := (idNumber div 10) mod 10;
```

What does the program look like? We can put all this together into the following program.

```
program verifyId (input, output);
var
    idNumber, checkDigit, digit1, digit2, digit3,
        remainderDigit: integer;
begin
    write ('Please type a four-digit identification number:  ');
    readln (idNumber);
```

```
checkDigit := idNumber mod 10;
digit1 := idNumber div 1000;
digit2 := (idNumber div 100) mod 10;
digit3 := (idNumber div 10) mod 10;
remainderDigit := (digit1+digit2+digit3) mod 7;
if remainderDigit = checkDigit then begin
    writeln ('The number is valid. Ready to make copies.');
end else begin
    writeln ('*** The number is not valid for this copy machine.');
end;
end.
```

Does the program work?

One way to get evidence about whether or not a program works is to **test** it, that is, run it, provide some input, and observe the output. All programmers make errors, so testing is always necessary.

Stop & Predict ➤

What might go wrong with this program?

Errors that tests might expose include typographical errors and incorrect computations. Tests can show that even straightforward programs like this one have **logical errors**.

Can tests guarantee that a program works?

Tests can also provide evidence that a program works correctly, if the program's output matches the result of hand calculations on sufficiently well chosen values. Even seemingly convincing evidence, however, can have flaws. Sometimes complicated programs run for years before errors are detected in an unusual situation.

Stop & Consider ➤

How could a program flaw go undetected during program testing?

What are good test values?

Tests should collectively execute all the code in the program. If a section of code isn't executed, there's no way (other than proofreading it) to tell if it works as intended. In the test runs for this program, data should include both valid and invalid identification numbers, so that both output messages get printed.

What attitude towards a program helps in testing it?

A helpful attitude to adopt when testing a program is to imagine oneself as an opponent, trying to break it. Of course "typical" numbers should be tested. To break a program, however, the best values are usually those that push it to its limits in some way. Such values are called **extreme values** or **boundary values**. Examples for this program would be values where one or more of the digits are 0 or 9.

Whatever the test values, it is good to figure out ahead of time what answers to expect, so discrepancies stick out.

How can errors be isolated?

Errors tend to occur in the complicated parts of the program. It helps to print **intermediate results** to see how the computation is going. Here, the code in which the digits are separated is the most complicated. Thus the values of digit1, digit2, and digit3 should be printed.

Stop & Help ➤ *Should the value of* remainderDigit *and* checkDigit *also be printed? Why or why not?*

To produce this output, we add writeln statements to the program before the if statement. The output is labeled clearly as intermediate debugging results. Before releasing a "production" version of the program, we would either remove the intermediate output code (in general, not a good idea) or surround it by an if statement that only prints debugging output if a debugging variable has an appropriate value.

The complete program, including the statements that produce debugging output, appears in the Pascal Code section.

Stop & Help ➤ *Type in, run, and test the first program in the Pascal Code section. Did it run correctly? If not, what were the symptoms of the error?*

Reflection 1.8 How did postponing the details make this problem easier to solve?

Reflection 1.9 What parts of the solution helped you understand how to solve programming problems? What parts would you do differently?

🖻 *Analysis* 1.10 Are the parentheses necessary in the digit separation code in the program? Are there other correct ways to parenthesize the expressions on the right-hand side of the assignments to digit2 and digit3?

🖾 *Analysis* 1.11 Suppose that one of your fellow programmers misparenthesized the expression assigned to digit2 as idNumber div (100 mod 10). What would be the consequences of this mistake?

🖾 *Analysis* 1.12 Suppose that one of your fellow programmers omitted an assignment statement to one of the digit variables, so that it is uninitialized. What error message, if any, does your Pascal environment provide when the program is run?

Modification 1.13 Write a Pascal expression that uses digit1 to convert idNumber into a three-digit number whose first digit is digit2.

Improving the Integer Program

What more work does the program need?

The program now runs, probably correctly. Can we rest on our laurels? No. We should analyze how easily the program can be understood by others who might need to modify it later.

Stop & Predict ➤ *Why might this program need to be modified in the future?*

Typically, programs are used by a number of people. Often users point out problems that were not anticipated by the programmer. In addition, this program may need to be changed if the copy machine is redesigned.

Thus a program should be written as clearly as possible, so that modifications are easy to make. Both the original programmer and a new programmer who might work on the program will have an easier time if the program is written to communicate its purpose and design clearly.

Stop & Help ➤   *Why might the original programmer benefit from a clearly written program?*

How can the clarity of the program be improved?

The most complicated part of the program is the section where the digits are separated. This code uses combinations of mod and div that any programmer would have to examine closely. Perhaps it can be simplified.

One way to simplify code is to break it into smaller pieces. Another way is to make the pieces as similar as possible. With similar pieces, if one of the pieces is understood, then the others are too.

Stop & Predict ➤   *What parts of the program resemble one another?*

How can the other digits be separated?

Thus one way to make the code clearer is to make the digit separation as similar as possible for the four digits. We noticed that separating the last digit of an integer value was easy. To find the second and third digits of idNumber, we first made them the last digit of some value, then we separated the digit. To make this process more transparent, it would help to isolate the computation of the value whose last digit is useful. We could call this variable idPart. Here's how it might be used.

First compute checkDigit as before.

Then store the first three digits of the value into idPart, using the statement

```
idPart := idNumber div 10;
```

The last digit of the value in idPart is the third digit of idNumber, so we can separate and store it in digit3 as follows:

```
digit3 := idPart mod 10;
```

Now we turn to the second digit in idNumber by removing the third digit from idPart:

```
idPart := idPart div 10;
```

The last digit of idPart is now the second digit of idNumber, which can be stored in digit2:

```
digit2 := idPart mod 10;
```

We remove idPart's last digit again:

```
idPart := idPart div 10;
```

Its current last digit is the first digit of idNumber, so it gets stored in digit1:

```
digit1 := idPart mod 10;
```

Here's how this process would work, applied to the identification number 5738.

Statement	Contents of relevant variables

```
checkDigit := idNumber mod 10;
```
| 8 |
| checkDigit |

```
idPart := idNumber div 10;
```
| 573 |
| idPart |

```
digit3 := idPart mod 10;
```
| 3 | | 573 |
| digit3 | | idPart |

```
idPart := idPart div 10;
```
| 57 |
| idPart |

```
digit2 := idPart mod 10;
```
| 7 | | 57 |
| digit2 | | idPart |

```
idPart := idPart div 10;
```
| 5 |
| idPart |

```
digit1 := idPart mod 10;
```
| 5 | | 5 |
| digit1 | | idPart |

The code, collected, appears below.

```
checkDigit := idNumber mod 10;
idPart := idNumber div 10;
digit3 := idPart mod 10;
idPart := idPart div 10;
digit2 := idPart mod 10;
idPart := idPart div 10;
digit1 := idPart mod 10;
```

Note the similarities of the code in the boxes. Had the first assignment to idPart been replaced by the pair of statements

```
idPart := idNumber;
idPart := idPart div 10;
```

the boxed code would have been even more similar.

What intermediate values should be printed in the revision?

As in the first solution, intermediate output should be included. The key to the separation of digits is the sequence of values that the idPart variable takes on, so we add writeln statements to print these values. The complete program appears in the Pascal Code section.

Stop & Help ➤   *Type in, run, and test the "Improved Integer Solution" program in the Pascal Code section. Did it run correctly? If not, what were the symptoms of the error?*

Analysis   1.14   What are the advantages of using the variable idPart rather than using separate variables to store the pieces of idNumber?

💾 *Analysis*   1.15   The revised solution just described has several different checks of the debug variable. Can all the debugging output be combined and produced with just one test of the debug variable? Why or why not?

💻 💾 *Debugging*   1.16   After typing in the program, you run it and get the following output:

```
Please type a four-digit identification number: 1234
DEBUG: First value of idPart is    123
DEBUG: Second value of Idpart is    12
DEBUG: Third value of idPart is    1
DEBUG: Individual digits are    1    0    3    4

The number is valid. Ready to make copies.
```

Is there an error? If so, and assuming that you made an error typing *one* of the statements, which one is it?

Solution That Uses Character Variables

Are further simplifications possible?

Is it really necessary to take the identification number apart? Why not read each digit separately?

Stop & Predict ➤   *How could each digit be read separately?*

If the digits of the number were read as single characters rather than as an integer they would already be separated. Of course, the problem then would be to convert the character values to integers in order to compute their sum.

Stop & Predict ➤   *Will reading the digits as characters simplify the program?*

How will character values be input, processed, and output?

Since the identification number has four digits, a straightforward solution will use four character variables. We will call these d1, d2, d3, and d4 respectively, suggesting that they are almost digits. An outline of the program is then:

Input: Get the identification number from the user by prompting the user as in the previous solutions and by reading the number's digits into d1, d2, d3, and d4.

Process: Convert d1, d2, and d3 into the corresponding integer values and store them in digit1, digit2, and digit3 respectively; convert d4 into the corresponding integer value and store it in checkDigit; compute remainderDigit.

Output: Compare remainderDigit with checkDigit and print the appropriate message as in the previous solutions.

How is a character digit converted to the corresponding integer value?

The characters '0', '1', ..., '9' are represented differently from the integers 0, 1, ..., 9. The Pascal function ord, given a character as argument, returns an integer. For the characters '0', '1', ..., '9', however, the returned values will not be the integers 0, 1, ..., 9. Instead, ord returns the position of the argument character in the computer's **character sequence**. (Typically, punctuation characters, not digits, are the first few characters in the sequence.)

Stop & Help ➤ *Write and run a program that prints the values of* ord('0'), ord('1'), *and* ord('9').

The Pascal Standard guarantees that the digits '0' through '9' will occur consecutively in the computer's character sequence. That is, ord('1') will be 1 plus ord('0'), ord('2') will be 1 plus ord('1'), and so on. This fact allows the computation of the integer value for a given digit character. It's just the distance that digit character is from '0'; equivalently, it's the difference between ord of that character and ord('0').

Here is code that reads the characters in the identification number and computes the corresponding digit values.

```
readln (d1, d2, d3, d4);
digit1 := ord(d1) - ord('0');
digit2 := ord(d2) - ord('0');
digit3 := ord(d3) - ord('0');
checkDigit := ord(d4) - ord('0');
```

Stop & Predict ➤ *How is this an improvement over the integer solution?*

How does the character solution compare with the integer solutions?

The code for the character solution is simpler than that for the integer solutions. The character solution also has similar pieces, just like the final integer version.

The only complexity is the conversion of character variables to integers. This seems to be something that will come up again and again, so it's worth understanding.

Are there any changes in the testing procedure?

To guard against typographical errors, we could retain the intermediate output of all the digit values. However, since all the digits are being processed in exactly the same way, printing one value might be enough. The similarities in the code for these computations enhance our confidence in the program's correctness.

The program that uses this approach appears in the Pascal Code section.

Stop & Help ➤ *Type in, run, and test the program. Did it run correctly? If not, what were the symptoms of the error?*

◄

Analysis 1.17 Explain the difference between the values '1' and 1.

🖥 *Analysis* 1.18 What output does the statement writeln(ord('2')) produce?

🖫 *Analysis* 1.19 What does the program just described do if a numeric value of fewer than four digits is input? Explain.

🖥 🖫 *Modification, Reflection* 1.20 The program just described computes ord('0') three times. Someone might argue that the program would be more efficient if an additional variable were used to store the value of ord('0'), then used in each character-to-integer conversion. Make this modification to the program. Is the revised version noticeably faster? How much does the change affect how easy it is to understand the program?

Outline of Design and Development Questions

These questions summarize the main points of the commentary.

Understanding the Problem
How do programmers start to make sense of programming problems?
What aspects of the problem statement are important?
What will the program input and output?
How are algorithms designed?

Solution That Uses Only Integer Variables
How is the Pascal program designed?
What are the steps in the solution?
What are the variables in the program?
How is the identification number validated?
    How is the check digit computed?
    How are the remaining digits summed?
    How are the digits of the identification number separated?
    What does the program look like?
Does the program work?
    Can tests guarantee that a program works?
    What are good test values?
    What attitude towards a program helps in testing it?
    How can errors be isolated?

Improving the Integer Program
What more work does the program need?
How can the clarity of the program be improved?
How can the other digits be separated?
What intermediate values should be printed in the revision?

Solution That Uses Character Variables
Are further simplifications possible?
How will character values be input, processed, and output?
How is a character digit converted to the corresponding integer value?
How does the character solution compare with the integer solutions?
Are there any changes in the testing procedure?

Programmers' Summary

This case study presents three solutions to the problem of verifying an identification number. Two of the programs read the identification number as an integer, then take it apart to perform the verification computation. The other program reads the digits of the identification number separately as characters, then converts them to an integer to verify the identification number.

The programs are designed via **stepwise refinement**, that is, writing an outline of the program and expanding each step of the outline in turn. This allows the programmer to effectively manage the program complexity and avoid having to deal with all the details of the program at once.

The three programs provide successively better examples of organizing code into similar pieces. In the first program, the second, third, and fourth digits are separated by first determining a value whose *last* digit is the one to be stored. In the second program, digits are separated using a sequence of "store the rightmost digit, then remove that digit" steps. The third program separates the digits during input, then applies exactly the same operation to each one to compute its integer representation. Similarities among code segments provide more confidence in the correctness of the code; if one works, the others are more likely to work as well.

All the solutions illustrate the power of the Divide and Conquer principle.[*] When in doubt about how to proceed, one should select a part of the problem that seems straightforward, and solve it; often the remainder of the problem seems easier as a result.

Reading the code is not sufficient for determining correctness. The collection of tests executes every part of each program. In addition, **bound-**

---

[*] Principles are described in To Instructors, page xx.

ary values for the quantities are tested according to the Persecution Complex principle. Since the programs deal with digits whose extremes are 0 and 9, values with 0 or 9 as digits are used as test data. (Thorough tests are typically not sufficient for determining correctness either.)

All three programs also provide examples of two common programming patterns, or **templates**. One is "prompt the user for a value, then read the value." The other is "input values, process them, then output the results." A third common operation, used in the character solution, is that of determining the integer value a given character represents.

Early in the design, the program's input-output behavior is analyzed. This is reflected in the program comments. Descriptive names are chosen for the variables to indicate their purpose and to make it easier to remember what each part of the program does. This choice of names illustrates the Literacy principle and makes it easier to modify versions of the program.

■ Making Sense of *Check That Number!*

Reflection 1.21 Which of the three programs is easiest for you to understand? Why?

🖫 *Analysis* 1.22 In the first and third program solutions, the digits were separated left to right. In the second revised solution, the digits were separated in the opposite order. In which of the programs could the assignment statements have been rearranged to separate the digits in the opposite order? Briefly explain.

🖥 🖫 *Reflection, Debugging* 1.23 Have one of your fellow programmers make a minor change to one of the statements in one of the programs in the Pascal Code section, and see how long it takes you to find the change. Do the same for each program. For which of the program did you find the change most quickly?

🖥 🖫 *Modification* 1.24 Change each version of the program to accommodate the following change in the problem statement: "A correct check digit is equal to the remainder of the sum of the other three digits divided by 9."

Σ *Analysis* 1.25 Which of the three programs could be substantially shortened under the conditions of question 1.24? Briefly explain.

🖥 🖫 *Modification* 1.26 Question 1.24 suggests that one might wish to have versions of the program that compute different remainders. Pascal provides a way to define **named constants** with the const construct to make program modification easier. In order to change the divisor—which in a larger program might be used more than once—one simply changes the definition. Modify each version of the program to include the definition and use of a named constant for the divisor.

☒ ☐ *Modification*   1.27   The problem specification promises that the identification number input by the user will be an actual four-digit number. In general, however, it is not reasonable to assume that users will provide legal data. Add code to each program that checks the identification number for legality as extensively as possible. Which program allows you to incorporate the most extensive checks?

☒ *Application*   1.28   Design and test a program that reads a three-digit number from the user, and prints the four-digit value that results from computing the check digit as done in this case study and appending it to the right of the input value.

Solution Using Integer Variables

```pascal
program verifyId (input, output);
{
    Read in a four-digit identification number, and determine
    whether or not its check digit--the rightmost digit--is
    correct.  A correct check digit is equal to the remainder
    when dividing by 7 of the sum of the other three digits.
    Input from the user is assumed to be error-free.
}
var
    {the identification number read from the user}
    idNumber: integer;
    {the individual digits of the identification number}
    digit1, digit2, digit3, checkDigit: integer;
    {the remainder when dividing the digit sum by 7}
    remainderDigit: integer;
    {a debugging variable: 0 if not debugging, nonzero otherwise}
    debug: integer;
begin
    debug := 1;   {indicate that we're debugging}

    write ('Please type a four-digit identification number:  ');
    readln (idNumber);

    checkDigit := idNumber mod 10;
    digit1 := idNumber div 1000;
    digit2 := (idNumber div 100) mod 10;
    digit3 := (idNumber div 10) mod 10;
    if debug <> 0 then begin
        writeln ('DEBUG: Individual digits are ',
            digit1, digit2, digit3, checkDigit);
        writeln;
    end;
    remainderDigit := (digit1+digit2+digit3) mod 7;
```

```
        if remainderDigit = checkDigit then begin
            writeln ('The number is valid. Ready to make copies.');
        end else begin
            writeln ('*** The number is not valid for this copier.');
        end;
end.
```

Improved Integer Solution

```
program verifyId (input, output);
{
    Read in a four-digit identification number, and determine
    whether or not its check digit--the rightmost digit--is
    correct.  A correct check digit is equal to the remainder
    when dividing by 7 of the sum of the other three digits.
    Input from the user is assumed to be error-free.
}
var
    {the identification number read from the user}
    idNumber: integer;
    {the individual digits of the identification number}
    digit1, digit2, digit3, checkDigit: integer;
    {the remainder when dividing the digit sum by 7}
    remainderDigit: integer;
    {a debugging variable: 0 if not debugging, nonzero otherwise}
    debug: integer;
    {a variable for storing pieces of the identification number}
    idPart: integer;
begin
    debug := 1;   {indicate that we're debugging}

    write ('Please type a four-digit identification number:  ');
    readln (idNumber);

    checkDigit := idNumber mod 10;
    idPart := idNumber div 10;
    if debug <> 0 then begin
        writeln ('DEBUG: First value of idPart is ', idPart);
    end;
    digit3 := idPart mod 10;
    idPart := idPart div 10;
    if debug <> 0 then begin
        writeln ('DEBUG: Second value of idPart is ', idPart);
    end;
    digit2 := idPart mod 10;
    idPart := idPart div 10;
    if debug <> 0 then begin
        writeln ('DEBUG: Third value of idPart is ', idPart);
    end;
    digit1 := idPart mod 10;
    if debug <> 0 then begin
        writeln ('DEBUG: Individual digits are ',
            digit1, digit2, digit3, checkDigit);
```

```
        writeln;
    end;
    remainderDigit := (digit1+digit2+digit3) mod 7;

    if remainderDigit = checkDigit then begin
        writeln ('The number is valid. Ready to make copies.');
    end else begin
        writeln ('*** The number is not valid for this copy machine.');
    end;
end.
```

Solution Using Character Variables

```
program verifyId (input, output);
{
    Read in a four-digit identification number, and determine
    whether or not its check digit--the rightmost digit--is
    correct.  A correct check digit is equal to the remainder
    when dividing by 7 of the sum of the other three digits.
    Input from the user is assumed to be error-free.
}
var
    {the character digits of the identification number
     read from the user}
    d1, d2, d3, d4: char;
    {the individual digits of the identification number}
    digit1, digit2, digit3, checkDigit: integer;
    {the remainder when dividing the digit sum by 7}
    remainderDigit: integer;
    {a debugging variable: 0 if not debugging, nonzero otherwise}
    debug: integer;
begin
    debug := 1;  {indicate that we're debugging}

    write ('Please type a four-digit identification number:  ');
    readln (d1, d2, d3, d4);

    digit1 := ord(d1) - ord('0');
    digit2 := ord(d2) - ord('0');
    digit3 := ord(d3) - ord('0');
    checkDigit := ord(d4) - ord('0');
    if debug <> 0 then begin
        writeln ('DEBUG: Individual digits are ',
            digit1, digit2, digit3, checkDigit);
        writeln;
    end;
    remainderDigit := (digit1+digit2+digit3) mod 7;

    if remainderDigit = checkDigit then begin
        writeln ('The number is valid. Ready to make copies.');
    end else begin
        writeln ('*** The number is not valid for this copy machine.');
    end;
end.
```

CHAPTER 2

Banners With CLASS

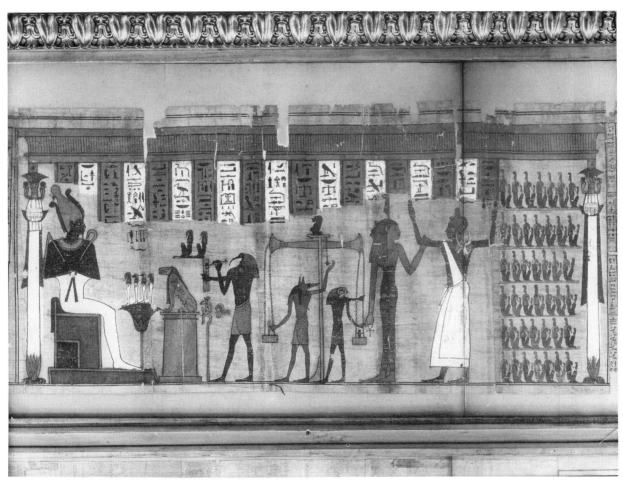

◀ *Getting the word out in Egypt: Banners have been popular from ancient times. Imagine the frustration of early banner writers when they made an error. On-line banners are much easier to correct.*

From ancient times banners have proclaimed events and advertised opportunities. Computers allow individuals to create personalized banners of varied sizes and styles. This program prints block versions of six letters in user-specified sizes using the letters PASCL. It can be altered to create banners with such messages as PASS PASCAL CLASS.

Problem Statement

Write a Pascal program that reads letters supplied by the user and prints them down the screen in a block format. The program should first prompt the user for a value—the *letter size*—that specifies the number of printed lines and columns that will be used to print each letter. After reading the letter size, the program should prompt the user for six letters chosen from P, A, S, C, and L. Finally, it should read and print the six letters on the terminal screen in a block format.

You may assume that the user will provide a letter size value between 5 and 24, and that he or she will provide only letters chosen from P, A, S, C, and L.

For example, here is how the program might work. The user input is indicated in boldface.

```
Type a size for the letters between 5 and 24?  9
Type six letters, chosen from PASCL:  ACLASP

        ********
        ********
        **    **
        **    **
        ********
        ********
        **    **
        **    **
        **    **


        ********
        ********
        **
        **
        **
        **
        **
        ********
        ********
```

(Block versions of L, A, S, and P are then printed.)

The program should be easy to modify, to add more letters and eventually to print banners.

Assume also that this program is being written as part of a collection of programs intended to display letters on a variety of output devices (terminal screens, printers, or plotters). Thus instead of printing with write or writeln, the program should make calls to three procedures, DrawBar, DrawIndentedBar, and DrawTwoBars, to create the letters. The parameters for these procedures include the number of lines—the *height*—and the number of columns—the *width*—needed to draw the corresponding figure. Here are descriptions of the procedures.

- DrawBar, given height and width values, prints a bar composed of asterisks of the specified height and width. Its heading is

```
procedure DrawBar (height, width: integer)
```

A sample call,

```
DrawBar (3, 5);
```

would produce the following output.

```
*****
*****
*****
```

- DrawIndentedBar, given values for height, width, and the number of columns to indent, prints a bar indented by the specified amount. Its heading is

```
procedure DrawIndentedBar (height, width, indentAmt: integer);
```

A sample call,

```
DrawIndentedBar (3, 5, 8);
```

would produce the following output. (Eight blanks precede each line of asterisks.)

```
        *****
        *****
        *****
```

- DrawTwoBars, given values for height, width, and amount of separation, prints two bars of the specified height and width, separated by the specified number of columns. Its heading is

```
procedure DrawTwoBars (height, width, separation: integer);
```

A sample call,

```
DrawTwoBars (3, 5, 8);
```

would produce the following output. (Eight blanks separate each sequence of asterisks.)

```
*****          *****
*****          *****
*****          *****
```

You may choose how to use these procedures to print attractive-looking letters.

Reflection 2.1 Which of the following is more attractive to you? Briefly explain.

```
*******        *******
*     *        *     *
*     *        *     *
*******        *     *
*     *        *******
*     *        *     *
*     *        *     *
```

Reflection 2.2 Design block versions of the letters P, S, C, and L for letter size 9. Keep track of the decisions you make.

Analysis 2.3 What other letters can be drawn using the procedures DrawBar, DrawIndentedBar, and DrawTwoBars?

Analysis 2.4 Name five letters that cannot be drawn easily using DrawBar, DrawIndentedBar, and DrawTwoBars. What extra procedures would be needed to draw these letters?

Application 2.5 Write a sentence composed completely of words made out of the letters P, S, C, A, and L.

Preparation

The reader is expected to be familiar with the for statement and the readln, write, and writeln procedures. This case study introduces the use of procedures and the case statement.

Initial Design Steps

How should one start
solving this problem?

As in *Check That Number!* this solution involves breaking or **decomposing** the problem into smaller subproblems, figuring out solutions for the smaller problems, and putting the solutions together.

Stop & Predict ➤   *What are the main subproblems that will need to be solved?*

One set of subproblems focuses on the letters: first figure out how to draw each letter and then combine the solutions for the letters. This does not sound much easier than the original problem.

Another set of subproblems focuses on what has to be done to design each letter: read the size, read the letter, draw the letter, and so on. This sounds a little easier than the original problem.

A good way to approach a solution is to design **top-down**, from the least detailed part of the program to the most detailed. This would involve starting at the main program, then designing the procedures that the main program calls, and so on. The top-down approach is usually preferred because it is easier to keep track of the structure of the program and how its parts fit together.

What are the big steps for the top-down design of the program? Often a problem statement provides the main steps in the top-down design of the solution.

Stop & Predict ➤   *What steps are given in the problem description for* Banners With CLASS?

The problem statement for *Banners With CLASS* lists three steps: ask for and read a number saying how large the letters should be drawn, ask for six letters, and read and draw the letters.

What decomposition of these steps makes sense? The problem statement suggests three big steps for the decomposition. However, these steps are not really parallel. One deals with the letter size and two deal with the letters. We decide to start with two steps: one dealing with the letter size, the other with the letters themselves. Asking for letters goes with reading and printing them in the same way that asking for the letter size goes with reading it. We outline the high-level decomposition as follows:

block letter program:
     ask the user for the letter size, then read it;
     ask the user for the letters, and read and draw them.

We will gradually expand the points in the outline to more closely approximate Pascal code.

What quantities need names? Assigning names to quantities used in a program as soon as they are identified helps keep them straight and also makes it easier to talk about the problem solution. The best name for a quantity is one that describes it well. Thus, we will represent the letter size in a variable and call it letterSize .

How does the program ask for and read a value for letterSize? As in *Check That Number!* we group the two tasks of asking for and reading a value for letterSize. The program should print a prompt like "Enter a size for the letters between 5 and 24." and then use a Pascal readln statement to store the answer typed by the user.

Stop & Help ➤ *Will a letter drawn in 24 lines fit on your terminal screen? What is the size of the largest letter that will fit?*

How does the program ask for, read, and draw the letters?

What steps are involved in asking for, reading, and drawing the letters? We continue to describe big steps and to postpone the details.

Stop & Predict ➤ *How can the task of drawing the letters be divided into steps just like those selected for getting the letter size?*

This task can be split into the same sort of steps used to ask for and read the letter size. One step "asks for," and the other "reads and draws." An outline of the decomposition so far appears below.

block letter program:
    ask the user for the letter size, and read it;
        ask for the letter size;
        read the letter size;
    ask the user for the letters, and read and draw them;
        ask the user for the letters;
        read and draw them;

How is the task of reading and drawing the letters decomposed?

There are two choices for decomposing the task of reading and drawing the letters. One is to read all six characters and then print the block versions of all six characters. We'll call this the "read all, print all" decomposition. Another decomposition is to read a letter, print it, read another letter, print it, and so on until all the letters are printed. We'll call this the "read one, print one" decomposition. In pseudocode these options look like this:

"Read all, print all:"

read all six letters;
print the block versions of all six letters;

"Read one, print one:"

do the following six times:
    read a letter;
    print the block version of the letter;

These decompositions are outlined below.

The "read all, print all" decomposition:
    read and draw the letters
        read all six letters
            do the following six times: read a letter
        draw all six letters

do the following for each letter read: draw the letter

The "read one, print one" decomposition:
    read and draw the letters
        do the following six times:
            read a letter;
            draw the letter;

What templates do these decompositions use?

The first decomposition employs a template that appeared in *Check That Number!* and will appear again and again. The "read all, print all" decomposition uses the "input, process, output" template:

input a value or set of values;
process the value(s);
output the value(s).

The "read one, print one" decomposition uses a variation of the "input, process, output" template that inputs, processes, and outputs one item at a time:

read a single value, process it, and output results until there aren't any more values to read.

The "read all, print all" decomposition deals with the input values as a "batch." The "read one, print one" decomposition deals with them item by item.

What other factors affect the choice of decomposition?

Factors that influence the choice of decomposition include the ease of implementing the solution and the chance of making errors. In *Check That Number!* we chose bulk processing. In the first two solutions to that problem, there was only one piece of information to handle, the integer identification number. In the third solution, four character variables were used to store the digits of the input number; while this approach simplified the rest of the program, using four separate variables was somewhat clumsy.

The problem of clumsiness arises with the "read all, print all" decomposition here. How will the letters be stored while they are being drawn? We would have to use six character variables; this is even clumsier than four, and keeping track of six variables would probably be a source of errors.

How does the programming environment affect the choice of decomposition?

A system consideration may affect the choice of decomposition. Some Pascal programming environments read a character and send it to the program immediately after the character is typed (**immediate input**), while others wait for the user to type a carriage return before sending any of the characters on the line to the program. If the programming environment uses immediate input, it is possible to get the output mixed up on the screen with the characters being typed by the user.

Stop & Help ➤   *Which input method does your system use?*

Stop & Predict ➤	*For systems with immediate input, which decomposition is best? For systems without immediate input, which decomposition is best? Why?*
Which decomposition will be used in this solution?	To avoid the clumsiness of storing six different character values at once, we will choose the "read one, print one" decomposition. This may cause problems in an environment where immediate input is used, since a block letter may get printed before the remaining letters are input.
What progress has been made on the solution so far?	Progress so far is outlined below.

block letter program:
    ask the user for the letter size, and read it;
        ask for the letter size;
        read the letter size;
    ask the user for the letters, and read and draw them;
        ask the user for the letters;
        read and draw them;
            do the following six times:
                read a letter;
                draw the letter;

Stop & Predict ➤   *What Pascal construct will carry out the "do six times" action?*

The main program has the following outline:

```
request letterSize from the user;
ask the user for six letters;
for letterNum := 1 to 6 do begin
    read a letter;
    draw the letter in block form;
end;
```

We have introduced a variable called letterNum along with a for statement to implement the "do six times" step in the decomposition. In general, a for loop is the easiest way to code the action of "doing something a specified number of times."

What are ways to decompose the "draw the letter" task?

For the "draw the letter" task, we again identify big steps and postpone the details. Recall that the program must be able to draw five letters: P, A, S, C, and L.

One step is to figure out which of the five letters the user has entered, so as to produce a block P when the user types P, a block A when the user types A, and so on. Thus the decomposition will have to include a test to determine which letter has been entered.

Another step is to print the letter. One decomposition is letter by letter. In this approach, the letter is treated as a unit. The letter-by-letter approach reflects the purpose of the program which is to print block letters. The pseudocode decomposition for the letter-by-letter approach is

if the letter is P, draw a block P;
if the letter is A, draw a block A;
if the letter is S, draw a block S;
if the letter is C, draw a block C;
if the letter is L, draw a block L.

Another decomposition is line by line. In this approach the lines are treated as units. The line-by-line approach takes advantage of similarities among the letters. The pseudocode decomposition for the line-by-line approach is

draw the first line or component of the letter, whatever it is;
draw the second line or component of the letter, whatever it is;

$$\vdots$$

draw the last line or component of the letter, whatever it is.

Stop & Predict ➤   *Which approach is best: letter by letter or line by line? Why?*

Which decomposition makes sense for this problem?

To choose between these alternatives it is useful to consider the purpose of the program, the ways in which it is likely to be modified, the implementation of the solution, and the chance of making errors.

We already mentioned that the letter-by-letter approach is closer to the purpose of the program. It is likely, knowing what we know about the alphabet, that our program will eventually be modified to add the capability of drawing other letters. The problem statement suggested that that will be the case. It will be easier to add the code to draw another letter if the program is already organized around letters rather than in some other way.

Furthermore, a decomposition around lines or components is likely to be complicated. The number of lines used to draw a letter is input by the user and therefore not known in advance. The number of components *is* known in advance, for example two for L, five for S, but it varies greatly among letters. A program organized around components is likely to be harder to keep track of, and therefore it is more likely to contain errors.

Thus we choose the letter-by-letter decomposition.

How is each letter handled separately?

A Pascal procedure will draw each letter: DrawP to draw a P, DrawA to draw an A, and so on. Each procedure needs to know how big its letter should be, so letterSize should be passed to each one as a value parameter.

How does the program decide which letter procedure to call?

There are only five possibilities for letters. Since each possibility is a single character, a case statement is most appropriate for selecting among the letter-drawing procedures. A descriptive name for the character variable that holds a letter is letter. This yields the following pseudocode:

case letter of
    'P': draw all lines of P;

```
        'A': draw all lines of A;
        'S': draw all lines of S;
        'C': draw all lines of C;
        'L': draw all lines of L;
    end;
```

How is the main program coded in Pascal?

The main program, with some refinement, now looks like this.

```
write ('Enter a size for the letters between 5 and 24:');
readln (letterSize);
write ('Type six letters, chosen from PASCL: ');
for letterNum := 1 to 6 do begin
    read (letter);
    case letter of
    'P':   DrawP (letterSize);
    'A':   DrawA (letterSize);
    'S':   DrawS (letterSize);
    'C':   DrawC (letterSize);
    'L':   DrawL (letterSize);
    end;
end;
```

Analysis 2.6 In the decompositions considered so far, the task of reading the letters was grouped with the task of drawing the letters rather than with the task of asking for them. Would grouping the actions of prompting for and reading the letters fit better into the "read all, print all" approach or the "read one, print one" approach? Explain.

Reflection 2.7 An outline was used as an aid to keep track of details in the design. What aids have you used to keep track of details in solving a complex problem?

Application 2.8 Design a program that will allow you to determine whether or not the Pascal environment in which it is run uses immediate input.

Application 2.9 Use a case statement to generate pseudocode for the line-by-line decomposition or for the component-by-component decomposition.

Designing the Letters

What will the letters look like?

The problem statement says that the letters will have the same number of rows (lines) as columns, and that they will have bars, indented bars, and bar pairs. It says to design "attractive" letters.

Stop & Predict ➤ *What is a good way to figure out the characteristics of attractive letters?*

To figure out what a letter will look like, we select a typical letter and try some options. The problem statement provides the letter A as an example, so we start with it.

The A shown in the problem statement has a top bar, a pair of bars (the "walls" of the A), another bar, and a longer pair of bars (the "legs" of the A). These components of the letter vary in size depending on letterSize. To determine how they vary, we construct these samples:

```
size 5          size 6          size 7          size 8

*****           ******          *******         ********
*   *           *    *          *     *         ********
*****           *    *          *     *         **    **
*   *           ******          *******         **    **
*   *           *    *          *     *         ********
                *    *          *     *         ********
                                *     *         **    **
                                                **    **


size 9              size 10             size 11

********            **********          ***********         ◀——— bar
********            **********          ***********
**    **            **      **          **       **         ◀——— walls
**    **            **      **          **       **
********            **      **          **       **
********            **********          ***********         ◀——— bar
**    **            **********          ***********
**    **            **      **          **       **
**    **            **      **          **       **         ◀——— legs
                    **      **          **       **
                                        **       **
```

Stop & Help ➤   *Draw the letter* S *in sizes 5 to 11.*

Stop & Help ➤   *Figure out the dimensions for the letters* S *and* C. *What is the smallest size possible for the letter* S? *Why?*

How are the dimensions for the letter A determined?

We note that the first two components of the letter A are about half of the letter, the bar size is about one quarter of the letter, and the width of each leg is the same as the bar height. These dimensions are shown in Table 2.1.

Size of letter	Height of both bars	Height of walls	Width of walls, legs	Height of legs
5	1	1	1	2
6	1	2	1	2
7	1	2	1	3
8	2	2	2	2
9	2	2	2	3
10	2	3	2	3
11	2	3	2	4

Table 2.1 *Dimensions for various sizes of the letter* A

How are the dimensions represented in Pascal?

In Pascal, we choose a variable for each quantity. Values for the dimensions for the letter A can be computed in terms of letterSize as follows:

```
topHalfHeight := letterSize div 2;
barHeight := letterSize div 4;
wallHeight := topHalfHeight - barHeight;
wallWidth := barHeight;
legHeight := letterSize - topHalfHeight - barHeight;
legWidth := barHeight;
```

Stop & Help ➤ *Compute the dimensions for each part of the letter* S.

How do these dimensions apply to drawing an A?

The problem statement requires that the letters be drawn using the Draw-Bar, DrawIndentedBar, and DrawTwoBars procedures. One way to decompose the drawing of the letter is to draw each line individually with these procedures. Loops that draw the components of the A are shown below.

```
for lineNum := 1 to barHeight do begin
    draw a line with height = 1 and width = letterSize;
end;
for lineNum := 1 to wallHeight do begin
    draw two bars with height = 1, width = wallWidth,
    and letterSize–2*wallWidth columns in between;
end;
for lineNum := 1 to barHeight do begin
    draw a line with height = 1 and width = letterSize;
end;
for lineNum := 1 to legHeight do begin
    draw two bars with height = 1, width = wallWidth,
    and letterSize–2*wallWidth columns in between;
end;
```

Stop & Help ➤ *Write loops using code and pseudocode to draw the components of the letter* S.

Must loops be used to draw the letter?

Each loop, however, can be rewritten as a single call to DrawBar or Draw-TwoBars, since each of the two procedures can take an arbitrary height value as an argument. This yields the following code:

```
DrawBar (barHeight, letterSize);
DrawTwoBars (wallHeight, wallWidth, letterSize-2*wallWidth);
DrawBar (barHeight, letterSize);
DrawTwoBars (legHeight, legWidth, letterSize-2*legWidth);
```

Stop & Help ➤ *Convert the loops for* DrawS *into calls to procedures.*

What will DrawBar look like in Pascal?

DrawBar is also yet to be written. A "bar" is just a rectangle of asterisks. This sounds like a nested loop: each iteration of the outer loop prints a single line, and each iteration of the inner loop prints a single asterisk on the line. Here's the code.

```
procedure DrawBar (height, width: integer);
var
    lineNum, colNum: integer;
begin
    for lineNum := 1 to height do begin
```

```
                        {draw a line of the bar}
                        for colNum := 1 to width do begin
                            write ('*');
                        end;
                        writeln;
                    end;
            end;
```

The procedures for DrawIndentedBar and DrawTwoBars are similar. The differences are in the printing of characters on each line; the body of the outer loop must contain additional code to print the blanks for indenting or the blanks between bars. Here is the code for DrawIndentedBar; the extra for statement (boxed) is the main addition.

```
procedure DrawIndentedBar (height, width, indentAmt: integer);
const
    BLANK = ' ';
var
    lineNum, colNum: integer;
begin
    for lineNum := 1 to height do begin
        {draw a line of the bar}
        for colNum := 1 to indentAmt do begin
            write (BLANK);
        end;

        for colNum := 1 to width do begin
            write ('*');
        end;
        writeln;
    end;
end;
```

For ease of understanding, the new inner loop was intentionally written to be similar to the old one, even though Pascal allows a shorthand way to write sequences of blanks. The constant BLANK is used to avoid any confusion between the blank character and other nonprinting characters.

Stop & Help ➤   *Code the* DrawTwoBars *procedure in Pascal.*

What does DrawA look like in Pascal?   Substituting calls to procedures for the pseudocode results in the following DrawA procedure:

```
procedure DrawA (letterSize : integer);
var
    topHalfHeight, barHeight,
    wallHeight, wallWidth,
    legHeight, legWidth : integer;
begin
    barHeight := letterSize div 4;
    topHalfHeight := letterSize div 2;
    wallHeight := topHalfHeight - barHeight;
    wallWidth := barHeight;
    legHeight := letterSize - topHalfHeight - barHeight;
    legWidth := barHeight;
```

```
        DrawBar (barHeight, letterSize);
        DrawTwoBars (wallHeight, wallWidth, letterSize-2*wallWidth);
        DrawBar (barHeight, letterSize);
        DrawTwoBars (legHeight, legWidth, letterSize-2*legWidth);
    end;
```

Stop & Help ➤   *Code the* DrawP *procedure in Pascal.*

💾 *Modification*   2.10 Redesign the A so that the walls are always longer than the legs.

Analysis   2.11 DrawIndentedBar contains the loop

```
    for colNum := 1 to width do begin
        write ('*');
    end;
```

Why can't that loop be rewritten as a single write statement?

Reflection   2.12 What makes letters attractive? What might a programmer do to make the letters even more attractive? Why is it difficult to figure out how to make letters attractive?

💾 *Analysis*   2.13 A proposal is made to code DrawA as follows, so that the height of the walls is the same as the height of the legs:

```
    wallHeight := letterSize div 4;
    legHeight := wallHeight;
    barHeight := (letterSize - wallHeight - legHeight) div 2;
    wallWidth := barHeight;
    legWidth := barHeight;
    DrawBar (barHeight, letterSize);
    DrawTwoBars (wallHeight, wallWidth, letterSize-2*wallWidth);
    DrawBar (barHeight, letterSize);
    DrawTwoBars (legHeight, legWidth, letterSize-2*legWidth);
```

Evaluate this proposal.

Development

How should the program be assembled?

The program is now designed and must be **developed**, that is, turned into a program that runs. Once assembled, it will be a relatively large program: five letter-drawing procedures, plus three shape-drawing procedures. If it were typed in and tested all at once, and produced incorrect output, it could be difficult to localize the source of the errors. **Incremental development**—coding and testing the designed program piece by piece, in isolation—is a good development strategy. It allows us to debug the pieces of the program without having bugs from the various pieces interfere with each other.

How can incremental development be applied to this problem?

Incremental development is often done in a **bottom-up** fashion, that is, testing and debugging the lowest-level subprograms, then those that call them, and so forth. This is best shown in a **call diagram**:

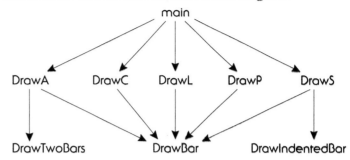

The "nodes" in this diagram are the procedures in the program, with the more abstract procedures—those involving less detail—drawn at the top of the diagram. A line is drawn from one procedure to another if the first procedure calls the second.

In the call diagram above, each level corresponds to a level of detail. The second level represents letters. The third level represents shapes. A well-organized program has a call diagram in which the levels of abstraction can be easily separated.

It is clear from the call diagram that DrawBar is an important procedure. All the letter-drawing procedures call it. Thus, it makes sense to test DrawBar by itself, to get as much evidence as possible that it works correctly, before adding the routines that call it.

In general, a bottom-up approach to development starts with routines at the bottom of the call diagram—those called by more abstract procedures. These routines are tested and debugged in isolation before being combined with routines that depend on them. This is analogous to the process of building a house or a bridge; one wants to know that the foundation is secure before adding the walls, girders, and so on to it.

What extra code should be written to help test the procedures?

Extra code must typically be written to test a procedure like DrawBar in isolation from the rest of the program. This involves a **driver program**, whose sole purpose is to provide a convenient way to test a procedure. Such a program in this case might ask the user for a height and a width, and call DrawBar with the input values, as follows:

```
program test (input, output);
var
    height, width: integer;

procedure DrawBar (...);
    code for DrawBar;
```

```
begin
    write ('Type a height and a width:');
    readln (height, width);
    writeln ('12345678901234567890');
    DrawBar (height, width);
end.
```

This program would then be run several times to gather evidence that DrawBar works as intended. Note the output of a line containing column numbers. This makes it even easier for us to see whether the program's output is correct or incorrect. (We included this output for the same reason we included debugging output in *Check That Number!*)

The amount of code we test and debug for each increment varies depending on our experience with the programming constructs and templates we are using. Since the idea is to make bug-finding easy, however, each increment should be small enough to be able to pin down any errors immediately. For this problem, it makes sense to test and debug the shape-drawing procedures first, then add each letter-drawing procedure one by one.

Thus, by starting with the DrawBar, DrawTwoBars, and DrawIndentedBar procedures, we can code and test DrawA. (DrawIndentedBar perhaps could be delayed.) Once these are running, we can add DrawP. Once these are running, we can add the routines for the other letters and test the whole program. The Pascal Code section contains the result.

What tests provide the best evidence that the program works?

In general, test data should be sufficient at least to exercise all statements in the program. One problem with this program is that exercising each statement in the program isn't enough; the statements interact in complicated ways. Referring to Table 2.1, we see that we can get a reasonable picture of the program's correctness only by testing a group of at least four values, one for each possible value of letterSize mod 4.

We tested each letter in sizes 5 through 11, the cases in our table. Some of the letters looked weird because the horizontal spacing differed from the vertical spacing on the terminal screen; adjacent characters on a line are closer together than adjacent characters on different lines. We fixed the ratios to get more attractive letters.

Stop & Help ➤   *Generate test data for the rest of the letter-drawing procedures.*

🖫 *Debugging*   2.14   Suppose that, after you type in the program just described, it prints an A as shown on the right. Which procedure most likely contains the bug? Explain.

```
*****
*   *
*****
*   *
*   *
```

🖫 *Testing*   2.15   Describe how to get DrawC running after DrawA without finishing the program.

Outline of Design and Development Questions

These questions summarize the main points of the commentary.

Initial Design Steps

How should one start solving this problem?
  What are the big steps for the top-down design of the program?
  What decomposition of these steps makes sense?
  What quantities need names?
How does the program ask for and read a value for letterSize?
How does the program ask for, read, and draw the letters?
  How is the task of reading and drawing the letters decomposed?
    What templates do these decompositions use?
    What other factors affect the choice of decomposition?
    How does the programming environment affect the choice
        of decomposition?
    Which decomposition will be used in this solution?
  What progress has been made on the solution so far?
  What are ways to decompose the "draw the letter" task?
    Which decomposition makes sense for this problem?
  How is each letter handled separately?
  How does the program decide which letter procedure to call?
How is the main program coded in Pascal?

Designing the Letters

What will the letters look like?
  How are the dimensions for the letter A determined?
  How are the dimensions represented in Pascal?
  How do these dimensions apply to drawing an A?
  Must loops be used to draw the letter?
What will DrawBar look like in Pascal?
What does DrawA look like in Pascal?

Development

How should the program be assembled?
How can incremental development be applied to this problem?
What extra code should be written to help test the procedures?
What tests provide the best evidence that the program works?

Programmers' Summary

Banners With CLASS presents a single program to print block letters, designed using stepwise refinement. It involves several *levels* of decomposition:

- the main program, which reads a letter size, then repeatedly reads a letter and calls the appropriate procedure to draw it

- the letter-drawing procedures, which combine calls to shape-drawing procedures to draw the various letter components

- the shape-drawing procedures, which print asterisks in various rectangular patterns

The solution also involves two *choices* of decomposition. The first choice is to solve the problem of reading and drawing the letters: should they all be read first, then drawn, or should they be handled letter by letter by reading, then drawing, then reading, then drawing, and so on? We decided to handle the letters one by one, to avoid the clumsiness of managing six variables. (This choice would cause problems, however, in a Pascal environment that provides only the facility for *immediate* input, that is, input without waiting for a carriage return.)

The second choice comes when deciding how to decompose the task of drawing letters: should decomposition be in terms of letters, or lines of output, or components of letters? The important concern here is ease of understanding and modification; since the program's purpose is to print letters, it should be organized around procedures that deal with letters.

Designing individual letters involves some planning on paper. Sample letters are sketched out, a table made of the dimensions of their components (applying the Multiple Representations principle), and code inferred from the table. The div operator shows up again—*Check That Number!* uses it also—in computing the dimensions.

Banners With CLASS illustrates the power of the Divide and Conquer principle. The program sounds difficult at first, but by dividing it into pieces and implementing each piece it turns out that the solution is just a sequence of templates that are either familiar or similar to familiar templates.

Three templates likely to be of use in future programming are introduced. One is a variant of "input, process, output," namely "input one, process one" to do item-by-item processing. Another, "select from alternatives," is used to decide which procedure to call to draw the letter just read. Finally, the template of "do something a specified number of times" is used to design the procedures to draw components of each letter.

The *Banners With CLASS* program is much larger than any of the *Check That Number!* programs, and, once designed, must be put together carefully. The strategy of **incremental development** is used to test and debug it. The increments are chosen from the **call diagram** illustrating how the procedures call one another: the bottom-level procedures are tested first, then the procedures that call them, added one by one. **Driver programs** are used early in the development process to provide values for testing the procedures. Applying the Persecution Complex principle as in the *Check That Number!* programs, the test programs used here include debugging output to allow easy detection of errors in the code.

Compared to the *Check That Number!* program, this program is easier to test since the output is displayed directly on the screen, requiring fewer hand calculations. Design of test data requires somewhat more thought, however. The relative sizes of letter components vary with the overall letter size, and a sufficient set of test data must include examples of all possible patterns.

Making Sense of *Banners With CLASS*

Debugging 2.16 Suppose a "friend" of yours who often deletes lines from programs used the *Banners With CLASS* program three times. Each time you got the program back, it had a different bug. Where would you look for these bugs?

- Every time a letter was input, the program printed block versions of P, A, S, C, *and* L.

- The block version of the letter C was too short.

- The letter S had a space in it.

Modification 2.17 Design block versions of the letters S, C, and L. Compare your versions with those produced by the *Banners With CLASS* program. Explain how yours differ. Change the *Banners With CLASS* program to produce letters your way.

Application 2.18 Design and test procedures to print the block digits 0 through 9.

Application 2.19 Suppose the *Banners With CLASS* program were going to run on a terminal where the columns were close together but the lines were far apart. What would be necessary to get the program to produce attractive block letters? Implement your idea.

Application 2.20 Write a procedure to draw a block letter E on a terminal with columns close together and lines far apart.

Analysis 2.21 Suppose a version of Pascal allowed the user to move the print cursor anywhere on the screen. How would this add to the power of the *Banners With CLASS* program? What new primitives (procedures like DrawBar, DrawLandR, etc.) would be useful?

☑ 🖫 *Application* 2.22 Modify the *Banners With CLASS* program so that it prints a word of any length. The program should ask the user for the length and then print the word.

☑ 🖫 *Application* 2.23 Modify the *Banners With CLASS* program so that it will print a series of words rather than just one word. The program should keep asking the user for words until the user enters the letter E (for end). Design a banner using words that can be written with the letters P, A, S, C, and L and print the banner. An example might be "SC SAPS CAL."

Reflection 2.24 Compare your design and development decisions to those described in the commentary. What, if anything, would you do differently?

Reflection 2.25 What problems in a program other than bugs might incremental development help detect?

Reflection 2.26 What ideas in the *Banners With CLASS* solution will you use in designing future programs? What ideas seem wrong or unnecessary for designing programs in the future?

◼◼ Linking to Previous Case Studies

Reflection 2.27 Compare the design process for *Banners With CLASS* and *Check That Number!* What techniques were successful for both?

Analysis 2.28 Compare the use of the "input, process, output" template (programming pattern) in *Banners With CLASS* and *Check That Number!* Explain why templates are helpful.

☑ 🖫 *Modification* 2.29 Rewrite the character variable version of the *Check That Number!* program to ask the user how many digits the identification number is supposed to contain, and then to read and process the specified number of digits. (The last digit read will then be the check digit.)

Complete *Banners With CLASS* Program

```
{
        This program asks the user for letters and the size to draw the
        letters, then prints the letters in block style down the page.
}
program blockLetters (input, output);
```

```
var
    letterSize, letterNum: integer;
    letter: char;

{
    Draw a bar of the given height and width.
}
procedure DrawBar (height, width: integer);
var
    lineNum, colNum: integer;
begin {Draw Bar}
    for lineNum := 1 to height do begin {draw a line of the bar}
        for colNum := 1 to width do begin
            write('*');
        end;
        writeln;
    end;
end; {Draw Bar}


{
    Draw two bars of the given height and width, separated by the given
    amount. The thickness of each portion is about 1/4 of the width.
}
procedure DrawTwoBars (height, width, separation: integer);
const
    BLANK = ' ';
var
    lineNum, colNum: integer;
begin {Draw Two Bars}
    for lineNum := 1 to height do begin
        for colNum := 1 to width do begin
            write('*');
        end;
        for colNum := 1 to separation do begin
            write(BLANK);
        end;
        for colNum := 1 to width do begin
            write('*');
        end;
        writeln;
    end;
end; {Draw Two Bars}


{
    Draw an indented bar of the given height and width, indented by the
    given amount. The thickness of the right side is about 1/4 of the
    width.
}
procedure DrawIndentedBar (height, width, indentAmt: integer);
const
    BLANK = ' ';
var
    lineNum, colNum: integer;
begin {Draw Indented Bar}
    for lineNum := 1 to height do begin
        for colNum := 1 to indentAmt do begin
```

```
                        write(BLANK);
                    end;
                    for colNum := 1 to width do begin
                        write('*');
                    end;
                    writeln;
            end;
    end; {Draw Indented Bar}


    {
        Draw a block P of the given size. The top bar should be roughly 1/4 of
        the P's height, and the middle bar should be at the top of the bottom
        half.
    }
    procedure DrawP (letterSize: integer);
    var
        topHalfHeight, barHeight,
        wallHeight, legHeight, wallWidth, legWidth: integer;
    begin {Draw P}
        {each bar should be around 1/4 of the P}
        barHeight := letterSize div 4;
        topHalfHeight := letterSize div 2;
        {stuff that isn't bar is "walls" of the P}
        wallHeight := topHalfHeight - barHeight;
        wallWidth := barHeight;
        legHeight := letterSize - topHalfHeight - barHeight;
        legWidth := barHeight;
        DrawBar(barHeight, letterSize);
        DrawTwoBars(wallHeight, wallWidth, letterSize - 2 * wallWidth);
        DrawBar(barHeight, letterSize);
        DrawBar(legHeight, legWidth);
    end; {Draw P}


    {
        Draw a block A of the given size. The top bar should be roughly 1/4 of
        the A's height and the middle bar should be at the top of the bottom
        half.
    }
    procedure DrawA (letterSize: integer);
    var
        topHalfHeight, barHeight,
        wallHeight, wallWidth, legHeight, legWidth: integer;
    begin {Draw A}
        {each bar should be around 1/4 of the A}
        barHeight := letterSize div 4;
        topHalfHeight := letterSize div 2;
        {stuff that isn't bar is "walls" of the A}
        wallHeight := topHalfHeight - barHeight;
        wallWidth := barHeight;
        legHeight := letterSize - topHalfHeight - barHeight;
        legWidth := barHeight;
        DrawBar(barHeight, letterSize);
        DrawTwoBars(wallHeight, wallWidth, letterSize - 2 * wallWidth);
        DrawBar(barHeight, letterSize);
        DrawTwoBars(legHeight, legWidth, letterSize - 2 * legWidth);
    end; {Draw A}
```

```
{
    Draw a block S of the given size. The bars should be roughly 1/4 of
    the S 's height, with the middle bar roughly at the middle (slightly
    above if necessary).
}
procedure DrawS (letterSize: integer);
var
    barHeight, firstWallHeight, secondWallHeight, wallWidth: integer;
begin {Draw S}
    barHeight := letterSize div 4;
    {three bars and two walls in an S}
    firstWallHeight := (letterSize - 3 * barHeight) div 2;
    wallWidth := barHeight;
    {want lower wall to be a bit taller}
    secondWallHeight := letterSize - firstWallHeight - 3 * barHeight;
    DrawBar(barHeight, letterSize);
    DrawBar(firstWallHeight, wallWidth);
    DrawBar(barHeight, letterSize);
    DrawIndentedBar(secondWallHeight, wallWidth, letterSize - wallWidth);
    DrawBar(barHeight, letterSize);
end; {Draw S}

{
    Draw a block C of the given size. The top and bottom bars should be
    roughly 1/4 of the C's height.
}
procedure DrawC (letterSize: integer);
var
    barHeight, middleHeight, wallWidth: integer;
begin {Draw C}
    barHeight := letterSize div 4;  {each bar should be around 1/4 of the C}
    {height of the rest of the C}
    middleHeight := letterSize - barHeight - barHeight;
    wallWidth := barHeight;
    DrawBar(barHeight, letterSize);
    DrawBar(middleHeight, wallWidth);
    DrawBar(barHeight, letterSize);
end; {Draw C}

{
    Draw a block L of the given size. The bottom bar should be roughly 1/
    4 of the L's height.
}
procedure DrawL (letterSize: integer);
var
    barHeight, legHeight, legWidth: integer;
begin {Draw L}
    barHeight := letterSize div 4;  {the bar should be around 1/4 of the L}
    legHeight := letterSize - barHeight;  {height of the rest of the L}
    legWidth := barHeight;
    DrawBar(legHeight, legWidth);
    DrawBar(barHeight, letterSize);
end; {Draw L}
```

```
begin {main program}
    write('Enter a size for the letters between 5 and 24: ');
    readln(letterSize);
    write('Type six letters, chosen from PASCL: ');
    for letterNum := 1 to 6 do begin
        read(letter);
        case letter of
            'P', 'p':  DrawP(letterSize);
            'A', 'a':  DrawA(letterSize);
            'S', 's':  DrawS(letterSize);
            'C', 'c':  DrawC(letterSize);
            'L', 'l':  DrawL(letterSize);
        end;
        writeln;
    end;
end.
```

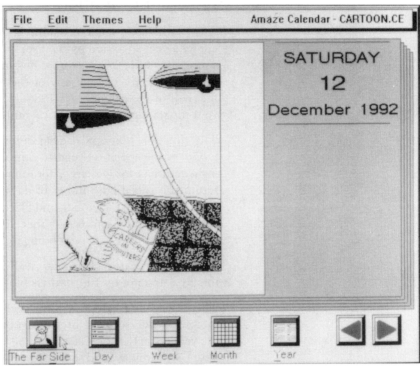

Create your own calendar with illustrations from popular cartoonists. The Calendar Shop *program shows how it can be done.*

Keeping track of time is a major industry. Historically, calendars have defined weeks and months quite differently from today. This program will create a calendar for any given year. It can be altered to create fantasy calendars without Mondays and historical calendars with 10-day weeks or 28-day months.

Problem Statement

The Pascal Code section contains an incomplete program to print a calendar for a year specified by the user. An integer function, NumberOfDaysIn, and a procedure, PrintMonth, are missing. Add the code for the missing subprograms. Don't change any of the existing code. Sample output—the first half of the calendar for 1986—appears on the next page. Verify that your program produces identical output for the given months.

The function NumberOfDaysIn determines the number of days in each month of the specified year. It requires two integer arguments representing a month (1 for January, 2 for February, and so on) and a year. It should return the specified number of days in the month. For January, March, May, July, August, October, and December, it should return 31. For April, June, September, and November, it should return 30. For February, it should return 28 or 29, depending on whether the year is a leap year.

Recall that a year is a leap year (its February has 29 days) when it is divisible by 4 and not by 100, or divisible by 400.

The procedure PrintMonth prints each month of the year as shown in the sample output. It takes three integer arguments: the month to be printed, the year (as in NumberOfDaysIn), and the first day of the month (0 for Sunday, 1 for Monday, and so on). Exactly one blank line is to be printed between successive months.

Analysis   3.1   Which of the following years are leap years: 1900, 1990, 1991, 1992, 2000?

Analysis, Reflection   3.2   What are aspects of the problem specification that potentially will lead to bugs in the code?

Preparation

This case study introduces repeat loops, functions, and boolean variables; it also uses if and case statements, procedures, and value parameters.

Output for the First Half of 1986

```
January    1986

S  M  T  W  T  F  S
            1  2  3  4
5  6  7  8  9 10 11
12 13 14 15 16 17 18
19 20 21 22 23 24 25
26 27 28 29 30 31


February      1986

S  M  T  W  T  F  S
                     1
2  3  4  5  6  7  8
9 10 11 12 13 14 15
16 17 18 19 20 21 22
23 24 25 26 27 28


March     1986

S  M  T  W  T  F  S
                     1
2  3  4  5  6  7  8
9 10 11 12 13 14 15
16 17 18 19 20 21 22
23 24 25 26 27 28 29
30 31


April     1986

S  M  T  W  T  F  S
         1  2  3  4  5
6  7  8  9 10 11 12
13 14 15 16 17 18 19
20 21 22 23 24 25 26
27 28 29 30


May      1986

S  M  T  W  T  F  S
                  1  2  3
4  5  6  7  8  9 10
11 12 13 14 15 16 17
18 19 20 21 22 23 24
25 26 27 28 29 30 31


June     1986

S  M  T  W  T  F  S
1  2  3  4  5  6  7
8  9 10 11 12 13 14
15 16 17 18 19 20 21
22 23 24 25 26 27 28
29 30
```

Understanding the Program

How should one start modifying the program?

Since this problem requires the completion of a program, a good first step is to try to understand what the program is supposed to do. In particular, it will help to understand the **algorithm** the program implements—the sequence of steps it uses to solve the problem—and the variables that it manipulates. We also need to understand the program's style in order to make modifications consistent with the existing code.

Stop & Predict ➤ *What are the first steps in figuring out how a program works?*

What parts of the program tell about the algorithm and the variables?

To understand the algorithm implemented by a program, one starts by reading the main program, which ideally provides the major steps in the decomposition. To find out about the variables being manipulated, one inspects the constant and type definitions and variable declarations.

In a Pascal program, the main program appears at the end, since it must appear *after* all subprograms that it calls. In contrast, since variables must be declared *before* they are used in the main program or its subprograms, they come at the beginning of the program.

Stop & Help ➤ *How does one go about understanding individual procedures and functions in a Pascal program?*

Should the algorithm or the variables be inspected first?

In this program, the algorithm is likely to be more complicated than the variables used, so reading the main program is a good place to start. Here is the main program:

```
begin
    ReadYearInfo (year, dayForFirst);
    for month := JAN to DEC do begin
        PrintMonth (month, year, dayForFirst);
        dayForFirst := (dayForFirst + NumberOfDaysIn (month, year)) mod 7;
    end;
end.
```

What is the algorithm for this program?

It appears that ReadYearInfo reads some information from the user. Since year and dayForFirst have no values before the program calls ReadYearInfo, we assume they receive values from that procedure as *var* parameters.

Stop & Predict ➤ *Is it best to check out the details or continue with determining the algorithm?*

Rather than checking ReadYearInfo to find out exactly what it does, we continue to examine the main program to get the "big picture" of the algorithm. Here we postpone looking at the details to avoid getting confused. In designing solutions, we postpone thinking about the details for the same reason.

What is the for statement doing?	Most for loops are indexed by integers, so the JAN and DEC come as a surprise. Examining the beginning of the program reveals that the integers 1, 2, ..., 12 have been given names as Pascal constants. This use of one of Pascal's naming facilities provides valuable information; MAY is a much more meaningful term than 5 in this program.

It looks as if the loop is doing something for each month. This becomes clear when we examine the loop body. The program is printing the month and updating the variable dayForFirst. |
| **What is the purpose of dayForFirst?** | The comment accompanying dayForFirst says that it is the index of the first day of month. The comment accompanying the calling procedure, ReadYearInfo, gives more information: 0 stands for Sunday, 1 for Monday, and so on, and the value is computed by using a formula from a book. The value stored in dayForFirst thus tells how many "blank days" to print at the start of the first week of a month. (We note, as anticipated, that ReadYearInfo's parameters are both var parameters.) |
| **How is dayForFirst updated?** | To update dayForFirst (that is, to find the first day of the next month), the program adds the number of days in the current month to dayForFirst, then eliminates all full weeks (that is, "mods" by 7).

We consider an example. Suppose that January starts on a Wednesday, as it did in 1986. Then dayForFirst for 1986 would be 3. We determine what day February of 1986 starts on by adding 31, the number of days in January, to 3 to get 34, and taking the remainder of 34 after division by 7, to get 6. Thus February starts on a Saturday. |
| *Stop & Help* ➤ | *Determine the day on which March 1986 starts, given that February 1986 starts on Saturday.* |
| **What else does ReadYearInfo do?** | Examining the rest of ReadYearInfo (starting at the end again), we find a loop that reads values from the user until one is "legal." Legality is defined by a boolean function, which in this case merely checks if the year is positive. Here is another instance of using a name to convey additional information. A test for year > 0 in ReadYearInfo could mean many things, but a test for the legality of a year clearly indicates that the code is checking that the program can handle the year.

The code to check for legal values is an instance of a variation of the "read one, process one" template introduced in *Banners With CLASS*. It can be called an "input and process until done" template and looks like this: |

```
repeat
    ask the user for input and read values for variables;
    if not Legal (variables) then begin
        print an error message;
    end;
until Legal (variables);
```

"Processing" here consists of checking for legality.

What is the program decomposition? By reading the program starting at the end, we have figured out what it does. The outline below provides a summary of what we know so far. Missing parts are boxed.

Stop & Predict ➤ *Write down the decomposition before looking at the outline.*

Produce a calendar.
    Read the year and find what day it starts on.
        Read a legal year from the user.
            Repeat the following until we have a legal year:
                Ask the user for a year.
                Read the response.
                Check the response.
        Find the day of the week of January 1 of that year.
    Produce the calendar for the given year.
        For each month, do the following:
            | Print the calendar entry for the month. |
            Determine the starting day of the next month.
                | Find the number of days in the month just printed. |
                Add it to the old starting day, and mod by 7.

Stop & Help ➤ *Write the function header for* NumberOfDaysIn *and the procedure header for* PrintMonth.

Should PrintMonth **or** NumberOfDaysIn **be designed first?** In deciding which routine to design first, the main concern is that the design of one routine does not interfere with a good design for others. In addition, some people prefer to do hard things first, and others start with easy things.

PrintMonth at first glance looks more complicated than NumberOfDaysIn. Furthermore, PrintMonth will probably need to call NumberOfDaysIn to determine how many days to print for the month. Thus we start with NumberOfDaysIn.

Reflection 3.3 Compare the approach to reading code described so far to your own approach to reading code. What techniques mentioned in the commentary will you use in the future?

Reflection 3.4 Read a fellow programmer's code, and keep track of what is easy to understand and what is difficult.

Reflection 3.5 How would you have written the main program? What aspects of the code in the program framework were especially clear or especially confusing for you?

Σ *Analysis* 3.6 Derive the "magic" formula for computing the day on which January 1 falls.

▣ *Analysis* 3.7 Explain why PrintMonth will never be given a nonnegative value for its year parameter.

▣ *Analysis* 3.8 Why should dayForFirst be updated in the main program rather than in PrintMonth?

Reflection 3.9 Given a collection of tasks to perform, do you prefer to do the hard tasks first or the easy ones? Why?

Designing and Developing NumberOfDaysIn

What does NumberOfDaysIn do?

Given a month, NumberOfDaysIn is supposed to return the number of days it has. There are thirteen possibilities: two for February and one for each of the other months.

Stop & Predict ➤

What Pascal construct will be best for the body of NumberOfDaysIn*?*

This function could be implemented with a sequence of if...then...else tests. It returns essentially the same thing—a number of days—for each month, however. A better way to show this **parallelism** is to use a case statement:

```
case month of
    JAN, MAR, MAY, JUL, AUG, OCT, DEC:
        NumberOfDaysIn := 31;
    FEB:
        the right thing for February;
    APR, JUN, SEP, NOV:
        NumberOfDaysIn := 30;
end;
```

How should the case for February be coded?

The decision for February could also be coded as an if statement. Better, however, would be code that's more similar to the other cases, namely an assignment statement. One way to do this is with a function that returns the number of days in February:

```
FEB:
    NumberOfDaysIn := FebDays (year);
```

An even better way to communicate the exceptional nature of the leap year is the following:

```
FEB:
    NumberOfDaysIn := 28 + LeapDay (year);
```

where LeapDay is an integer function returning 1 or 0 according to whether or not the year is a leap year.

How is LeapDay coded?

Determining the value of LeapDay requires several tests. In general, people understand positive tests better than negative tests, so LeapDay appears as follows:

```
if (year mod 4 = 0) and (year mod 100 <> 0) then begin
    LeapDay := 1
end else if year mod 400 = 0 then begin
    LeapDay := 1
end else begin
    LeapDay := 0;
end;
```

The code for the complete NumberOfDaysIn appears in the Pascal Code section.

When and how should NumberOfDaysIn be tested?

NumberOfDaysIn should be tested all by itself, so that any bugs within it will be easy to locate. We can wait until the rest of the program is designed to test NumberOfDaysIn. We can also test it now. What we gain by not waiting is a feeling of accomplishment once the code works and some encouragement to tackle the rest of the task.

To test NumberOfDaysIn all by itself, we create a simple main program that asks for a month and a year and prints what NumberOfDaysIn returns.

Stop & Help ➤

Write a simple main program to test NumberOfDaysIn, *identify good test values, and test the function.*

What are good test cases?

As with any code, test values should be chosen at least to exercise all statements at least once. One cannot be really sure that a statement works correctly without executing it. Thus test values should be chosen that (a) exercise each part of the case statement in NumberOfDaysIn, and (b) exercise each part of the if statement in LeapDay. Thus the test values should include at least one of the months with 30 days, at least one of the months with 31 days, and several different years for February. (One might reasonably argue that test values should include *every* month.)

Stop & Predict ➤

List all the leap year cases that need to be tested.

We make a table to help clarify the purpose of each test for February:

Test year	Leap year?	Reason
1986	no	not divisible by 4
1988	yes	divisible by 4 and not by 100
1900	no	divisible by 4 and 100, but not by 400
2000	yes	divisible by 400

Modification

3.10 Write and test the FebDays function mentioned in the commentary.

☐ ☐ *Debugging*   3.11   Insert a bug into the NumberOfDaysIn function, let a fellow programmer test it without being able to read the code, and see how long he or she takes to find the bug. What kinds of bugs are easy for a tester to overlook?

☐ *Analysis*   3.12   Suppose that LeapDay were rewritten as a four-part if...then...else as follows, with each if condition being a single equality test involving year and the mod operator.

```
if ____ then begin
    LeapDay := ____ ;
end else if ____ then begin
    LeapDay := ____ ;
end else if ____ then begin
    LeapDay := ____ ;
end else begin
    LeapDay := ____ ;
end;
```

In which order(s) may the tests for year mod 4 = 0, year mod 100 = 0, and year mod 400 = 0 be made? Explain.

Designing and Developing PrintMonth

The first step in designing PrintMonth is to break the problem into more manageable pieces by identifying the big steps in the decomposition. The sample output accompanying the problem statement suggests some ways to decompose the printing of a month: title and days or title and weeks. These are illustrated in Figure 3.1.

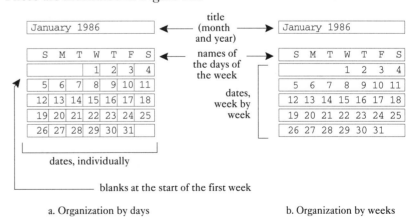

a. Organization by days   b. Organization by weeks

Figure 3.1 *Diagram of ways to decompose* PrintMonth

A month of the printed calendar can be decomposed into headings followed by the dates of the month. PrintMonth can thus be two procedure calls, one to a procedure called PrintHeading to print the headings, the other to a procedure called PrintDates to print the dates. The dates will be printed with a loop. One choice for the loop, corresponding to Figure 3.1a, would print a single date in each iteration; the other, corresponding to Figure 3.1b, would print a whole week in each iteration.

How should PrintHeading be designed?

PrintHeading prints the name of the month, the year, and S M T W T F S. It needs the month and year as parameters, and it must translate the integer value of month into the printed name of the month.

Stop & Predict ➤   *What Pascal construct is most appropriate for printing the month names?*

We could code PrintMonth with a sequence of if...then...else statements. A case statement, however, is more concise. In addition, a case statement clearly communicates the similar nature of the action for each month: printing a month name.

A case statement using the already defined names for the month values results in the following code:

```
procedure PrintHeading (month, year: integer);
begin
    case month of
        JAN:  write ('January ');
        FEB:  write ('February ');
        MAR:  write ('March ');
        APR:  write ('April ');
        MAY:  write ('May ');
        JUN:  write ('June ');
        JUL:  write ('July ');
        AUG:  write ('August ');
        SEP:  write ('September ');
        OCT:  write ('October ');
        NOV:  write ('November ');
        DEC:  write ('December ');
    end;
    writeln (year);
    writeln;
    writeln ('  S  M  T  W  T  F  S');
end;
```

Stop & Help ➤   *Why are there two spaces before S M T W T F S?*

Which decomposition is better?

Figure 3.1 showed two ways to decompose a month. Since both sound promising, we examine them both before making a decision.

Stop & Predict ➤   *What are the main parts of each choice for the decomposition of PrintDates?*

How should the day-by-day PrintDates be designed?

Figure 3.1a shows a day-by-day decomposition of the printing of dates in a month. The program first prints the blanks at the start of the first week, then prints each date.

Stop & Predict ➤   *Write the Pascal code for printing a single date on the calendar.*

The sample output shows that each date is printed in a three-space field. The code for printing the dates will use some sort of loop around the statement write(date:3).

How is the blank space before day 1 printed?

The value of dayForFirst tells how many blank dates to print (0 for Sunday, 1 for Monday, and so on). One can use a loop that runs from 1 to dayForFirst to print the blank dates.

Standard Pascal also allows printing the blank space before the first day all at once in a single write statement:

```
write (' ':3*dayForFirst);
```

Stop & Help ➤   *What does the statement above print if* dayForFirst *has value 4? For six blank characters to be printed, what value must* dayForFirst *have?*

Stop & Predict ➤   *Is this statement always appropriate for printing the blank spaces before the first day of the month?*

This statement has a flaw, however; the expression after the colon has to have a positive integer value, and an error would occur in months that start on Sunday. If the single write statement is used, the program must either have a special test for Sunday or indent the whole month by one extra space.

What loop prints the days?

The loop to print the days is straightforward:

```
for date := 1 to the number of days in the month do
    write (date:3);
    if at the end of the week, print a carriage return;
end;
```

This is an instance of the template "do something a specified number of times" introduced in *Banners With CLASS*, where the "something" is printing a date and possibly a carriage return.

How can the program detect the end of a week?

To figure out how to detect the end of a week (Saturday), we look for a pattern. Consider a sample month, January 1986, from Figure 3.1. The Saturdays are the 4th, the 11th, the 18th, and the 25th. For each week 7 days are added, so the remainder when each of these dates is divided by 7—the "mod 7" value—is the same: 4.

The "mod 7" values for the dates representing Saturdays will be different in every month. If, however, there were some expression that always had a fixed value on a Saturday, say 0, the test for the end of the week could merely be a comparison of that expression with 0. We notice, for example, that the second week starts when the number of blank dates printed, plus the date, is equal to 7. In Pascal this becomes dayForFirst + date = 7. The next carriage return should be printed when dayForFirst + date = 14, then when dayForFirst + date = 21.

Aha! This pattern reveals that a new line starts when (dayForFirst+date) mod 7 = 0. The code looks like this:

```
for date := 1 to the number of days in the month do begin
    write (date:3);
    if (dayForFirst + date) mod 7 = 0 then begin
        writeln;
    end;
end;
```

Under what conditions is a carriage return needed after the loop?

With any loop, one should think about the **invariant conditions**, those that are true at the beginning and the end of each iteration. The key condition to look for here is whether or not a full line of dates has been printed at the end of the loop. The problem statement includes an explicit warning that "exactly one blank line is to be printed between successive months." For some months, the loop will end in the middle of a line, and two writeln statements will be necessary after the loop; for other months, the loop will end at the beginning of a line, and only one writeln will be necessary. Thus the following code will need to come after the loop:

```
writeln;
if the loop has ended in the middle of a line then begin
    writeln;
end;
```

Stop & Predict ➤ *Describe as carefully as you can the months for which the loop ends at the beginning of a line.*

Stop & Consider ➤ *Why will the loop never end at the end of a line?*

The way to determine if the loop has ended at the start of a line is merely to repeat the test that caused the writeln, as follows:

```
writeln;
if (dayForFirst + the number of days in the month) mod 7 <> 0 then begin
    writeln;
end;
```

What's left?

All that's left to compute, and all that the PrintDates procedure really needs to know other than the month name, is the number of days in the month. The function NumberOfDaysIn provides this value, so we can call it and pass the resulting value to PrintDates to complete the PrintMonth procedure. The Pascal Code section contains the result; an outline of the decomposition appears below.

Print the calendar page for the month.
    Print the month name and the heading for the weeks.
    Print the "body" of the month.
        Print blanks to start the first week.

Print the dates.
> For each date from 1 to the number of days in the month,
> do the following:
> > Print the date.
> > If it's a Saturday, print a carriage return.
> Print one or two blank lines.

Stop & Predict ➤ *How will the week-by-week decomposition differ from the day-by-day decomposition?*

How are dates printed week by week? Figure 3.1b illustrates week-by-week printing of the dates of the month. This decomposition first determines how many weeks are to be printed, then uses a for loop that goes from 1 to the number of weeks to print the weeks. In pseudocode, we have

```
numWeeks := the number of weeks in the month;
for weekNumber := 1 to numWeeks do begin
    print the weekNumber'th week;
end;
```

Stop & Predict ➤ *Figure out the pattern for determining the number of weeks in a given month. What types of months create special problems?*

How many weeks are there in a month? Figuring out the number of weeks that need to be printed requires the same sort of searching for a pattern as we did to determine when a new week started in the day-by-day version of PrintDates. The number of weeks depends on the total number of dates in the month plus the number of blank dates at the beginning of the first week. To determine the number of weeks (groups of seven days) the month spans, we want to divide the sum of the blank dates plus the number of days by 7. But what if there is a remainder? The arithmetic is somewhat tricky, since the number of weeks is usually—but not always—one more than the result from dividing by 7. As in *Banners With CLASS*, a table is helpful.

Stop & Predict ➤ *How many entries should the table contain?*

dayForFirst + month length	Number of weeks	(dayForFirst + month length) div 7	dayForFirst + month length	Number of weeks	(dayForFirst + month length) div 7
28	4	4	35	5	5
29	5	4	36	6	5
30	5	4	37	6	5
...	5	4			

Entries in the table go from the minimum number of days, corresponding to a February that starts on Sunday, to the maximum number, for a 31-day month that starts on Saturday.

We note that the last column in the table is six days ahead of the desired result, and thus produce the following code:

```
numWeeks := (dayForFirst + monthLength + 6) div 7;
```

Stop & Consider ➤ *What is another way to compute the number of weeks using both* div *and* mod?

What code prints the week?

Printing a "typical" week (one in the middle of the month) is easy. If we know where to start, we can just loop seven times, from the starting date to 6 plus the starting date, printing the date. After printing a carriage return, we're finished. The code below would handle a typical week.

```
for date := startOfWeek to startOfWeek+6 do begin
    write (date:3);
end;
writeln;
```

What about the first and last weeks of the month?

The first and last weeks of the month often have leading or trailing blanks. PrintWeek could do one thing for the first week, another for typical weeks, and a third thing for the last week. If the first and last weeks are treated as special cases, almost half the weeks printed will be special.

If the dates are thought of as either blanks or numbers—two different types of data—special code will be necessary to handle each possibility. However, if we view the blanks as special kinds of numbers, then we need merely include a test to check for the "blank numbers" and print blanks for them instead of numeric values. It is easy to determine when blanks appear. Dates past the end of the month are blank. Dates before the beginning of the month are blank. Other dates are printed normally. Using this scheme, January 1986 looks like this:

```
-2 -1  0  1  2  3  4
 5  6  7  8  9 10 11
12 13 14 15 16 17 18
19 20 21 22 23 24 25
26 27 28 29 30 31 32
```

Stop & Help ➤ *Explain why the leading blanks in a month can be thought of as zero or negative dates.*

Fixing the code for the typical case to include printing blank dates appropriately involves inserting tests for negative dates and for dates larger than the last day of the month. After filling in the details, the following code for printing a single week results:

```
procedure PrintWeek (startOfWeek, monthLength: integer);
var
    date: integer;
begin
    for date := startOfWeek to startOfWeek + 6 do begin
        if (date > 0) and (date <= monthLength) then begin
            write (date: 3);
        end else begin
```

```
            write (BLANK: 3);
        end;
    end;
    writeln;
end;
```

How does the program know where to start each week?

All that's left is to compute the starting "date" for the month for the initial call to PrintWeek. To start the first week, we count back from 1 for each blank date. That means the first week starts on date 1 – dayForFirst. Once we know the first date, we can just add 7 to get the start of the next week.

We fill in the details, and arrive at the code in the Pascal Code section. An outline of the decomposition appears below.

Print the calendar page for the month.
    Print the month name and the heading for the weeks.
    Print the "body" of the month.
        Set numWeeks to the number of weeks in the month.
        Determine the starting date of the first week.
        Print the weeks.
            For weekNumber := 1 to the number of weeks,
            do the following:
                Print the dates in the weekNumber'th week.
                    For date := start to start+6, do the following:
                        If the date is legal, then print it,
                            otherwise print a blank.
                Print a carriage return.
                Find the starting date of the next week.

How is each version of PrintMonth tested?

Testing the two versions of PrintMonth may proceed in two ways, **black-box testing** and **glass-box testing**. The two approaches describe how the test data are chosen.

In black-box testing, the program is regarded as a "black box" whose interior—the program code—is invisible. Black-box test data is derived only from the problem specification; it consists of **typical values**, well within the program specification, and **extreme** or **boundary values**, those near the boundaries of some aspect of the program specification. Sometimes it is also appropriate to test **illegal values** as well.

Glass-box testing was applied to the NumberOfDaysIn function and in the earlier case studies. In this approach, one chooses test data that sufficiently exercise all statements in the code to be executed.

Neither method is sufficient to *prove* that the program works correctly in all cases, since testing can only display errors, not prove that no errors exist. Evidence of correctness or incorrectness is what we're looking for, however, and one of the approaches to testing can often provide evidence of errors that would be overlooked if the other approach were used alone.

Stop & Predict ➤

What test data does the black-box approach suggest?

What could go wrong with this program?

We start with the black-box approach and examine the kinds of errors that could arise in printing a calendar:

- Problems within a month. These include the wrong number of days in the month, the wrong number of days in a week, and a badly formatted heading.

- Problems from one month to the next. An example is a month that starts on a day other than the one following the day on which the previous month ended. Another example is two months with the wrong number of blank lines between them.

- Problems with the year. A February with the wrong number of days or a January starting on the wrong day fall into this class.

Test data should expose all these errors.

How much test data are needed?

A complete test would include every possible year. We would need to test 14 years, one with each possible starting day, each tested in a leap year and in a normal year. Obviously, this would take too long to analyze. Can advance planning reduce the task?

Stop & Predict ➤

What cases should be tested?

Let's start with potential problems with a year. If the program correctly prints a year in which January 1 starts on a Wednesday, it will probably work for Tuesday and Thursday as well. If the program is going to fail, it will probably do so at the *extreme* points in the week, that is, Saturday or Sunday. Similarly, if the program prints February correctly for the year 1982, it will probably do so for 1981 and 1983 as well. Extreme values here are leap years.

Stop & Help ➤

Generate a set of test years that includes (a) all possibilities for leap years and (b) years in which January 1 falls on a Sunday, a weekday, and a Saturday.

This kind of analysis can be used to narrow down the tests needed to detect errors between printing two consecutive months and errors within a month. An advantage of this program is that it prints all twelve months in the year, so it will be relatively easy to think of a year that tests both typical and extreme conditions.

Stop & Help ➤

What extreme situations are not *tested in the year 1986?*

What test data does the glass-box approach suggest?

Applying the glass-box approach involves looking at each version of the code. As with the NumberOfDaysIn function and the *Banners With CLASS* program, we choose values that exercise each part of a case or if statement. Loops introduce a complication. It's easy to pick test values that cause a loop body to be executed *once*, but that usually doesn't provide much information. More convincing test data will cause a loop to be executed the **minimum number of times**, and the **maximum number of times**.

The day-by-day version of PrintMonth contains two loops, one that prints the blanks at the start of the month, the other that prints the days. The blank-printing loop should be tested with months that have no leading blanks and on months that start on Saturday. The date-printing loop goes from 1 to the month length; thus it should be tested on months that are as short as possible (a February of 28 days) and as long as possible.

Similarly, the loop in the week-by-week version should be tested on months with as few weeks as possible and as many weeks as possible. Some months span six weeks. Some Februarys span only four.

Stop & Help ➤   *Select test cases for each version of* PrintMonth *and test the program.*

How should the two versions be compared?   We now have two versions of PrintMonth. How do we decide which is preferable? Programs may be compared in various ways. An obvious way is efficiency—which one runs fastest and uses the least memory? However, efficiency is rarely as important as **understandability** and **modifiability**. Understandable programs make sense to others. Modifiable programs can be debugged or extended by other programmers.

The day-by-day solution seems understandable in that its decomposition reflects a fairly natural way to think of a calendar month: as a heading followed by a sequence of days. It is also the shorter of the two.

The week-by-week solution seems less understandable. It uses the rather obscure idea of a negative date. Its decomposition of a month into a sequence of weeks is at first glance somewhat unnatural.

But consider modifiability. A real calendar may have Sundays printed in a special typeface. It may have the dates printed in block numerals. The calendar may be printed in the center of the page rather than against the left margin. For months where the 31st falls on a Sunday, it may print something like 24/31. All of these embellishments would be relatively easy to add to the week-by-week solution.

Thus, there are advantages to each approach. The choice depends on the expected uses for the program.

💾 *Testing*   3.13 Write Pascal code to test PrintMonth in isolation from the rest of the *Calendar Shop* program.

💾 *Reflection*   3.14 Which decomposition do you prefer, the day-by-day decomposition or the week-by-week decomposition? Why?

🖫 *Reflection* 3.15 Suppose every month were to start on a Sunday. How would this change allow the week-by-week version of PrintMonth to be coded more clearly?

🖫 🖫 *Modification,* 3.16 Change each version of PrintMonth to make every month start on
Reflection Sunday, and decide again which decomposition you prefer.

🖫 🖫 *Modification,* 3.17 Change each version of PrintMonth so that an extra blank space is
Reflection printed between weekend days and weekdays. For example, the modified PrintMonth should produce the following output for January 1986.

```
January    1986

S   M  T  W  T  F    S
            1  2  3    4
5   6  7  8  9 10   11
12 13 14 15 16 17   18
19 20 21 22 23 24   25
26 27 28 29 30 31
```

Which version of the procedure is easier to modify? Why?

🖫 🖫 *Debugging* 3.18 Insert a bug into either version of the PrintMonth function, let a fellow programmer test it without being able to read the code, and see how long he or she takes to find the bug. What kinds of bugs are easy for a tester to overlook?

Reflection 3.19 Explain how the design of PrintMonth followed the principles of top-down design. Describe how the details were postponed to simplify the process.

Outline of Design and Development Questions

These questions summarize the main points of the commentary.

Understanding the Program
How should one start modifying the program?
What parts of the program tell about the algorithm and the variables?
Should the algorithm or the variables be inspected first?
What is the algorithm for this program?
What is the for statement doing?
What is the purpose of dayForFirst?
How is dayForFirst updated?

What else does ReadYearInfo do?

What is the program decomposition?

Should PrintMonth or NumberOfDaysIn be designed first?

Designing and Developing NumberOfDaysIn

What does NumberOfDaysIn do?

How should the case for February be coded?

　　How is LeapDay coded?

When and how should NumberOfDaysIn be tested?

　　What are good test cases?

Designing and Developing PrintMonth

How should PrintHeading be designed?

Which decomposition is better?

How should the day-by-day PrintDates be designed?

　　How is the blank space before day 1 printed?

　　What loop prints the days?

　　　　How can the program detect the end of a week?

　　　　Under what conditions is a return needed after the loop?

　　What's left?

How are dates printed week by week?

　　How many weeks are there in a month?

　　What code prints the week?

　　What about the first and last weeks of the month?

　　How does the program know where to start each week?

How is each version of PrintMonth tested?

　　What test data does the black-box approach suggest?

　　How much test data are needed?

　　What test data does the glass-box approach suggest?

How should the two versions be compared?

Programmers' Summary

In this case study, code is added to an existing program framework to produce a program to print a calendar for a year input by the user. The first part of the solution involves understanding the program framework; the rest describes the design and development of the missing code.

Pascal programs have a standard form. Variable declarations and constant and type definitions come at the beginning; subprograms come afterward, with called subprograms preceding the routines that call them. Thus if one wishes to learn about the algorithms used in a program, one reads from back to front. If one wants to know about the data on which the program operates, one reads from front to back. Understanding the algorithm implemented in the program framework was our first task for this problem, so we started with the main program at the end of the code.

The existing code illustrates an interesting use of Pascal constants to stand for month values. The numeric values 1, 2, ..., 12 could stand for things like clock numbers or grades up through high school, but the names JAN, FEB, and so on say clearly what they mean. In reading the main program, we are able to infer actions of procedures it calls without reading the procedures; this is a characteristic of well-written code. Writing code that is easy to understand and self-documenting follows the Literacy principle.

Design of one of the missing subprograms, a function to return the number of days in a given month in a given year, involves the use of a case statement. Pascal provides two conditional constructs, case and if. The form of the case statement highlights the **parallelism** of similar case actions, and thus it seems most appropriate for this application. To increase the information communicated by the case statement, we write the code for the various cases to be as similar as possible.

The other missing subprogram prints the dates in a calendar month. Two decompositions are possible for the code to print the dates in the month. The day-by-day approach involves a loop from 1 to the month length. The week-by-week approach involves a nested loop. The outer loop goes from 1 to the number of weeks; the inner loop prints the days in the selected week. This choice between looping over individuals (dates) and looping over groups (weeks) is a common one in programming problems. Considering two reasonable approaches to solving this problem illustrates the Alternative Paths principle.

The main considerations in the day-by-day approach concern the loop body and its **invariant** and **termination conditions**: what's true after each iteration? what's true at the end? Design of the week-by-week loop mainly focuses on the beginning and end of the loop. Analysis of these characteristics of a loop are important in program design and verification.

In general, it is good to avoid special cases in programming. The design of the week-by-week version of PrintMonth avoids special handling of the first and last weeks of the month by introducing the concept of a "negative date," and translating it into a blank when printing.

Both versions use the mod operator. In *Check That Number!* integer arithmetic is used to "take apart" a numeric value. In *Banners With CLASS*, it is used to compute the size of components of a letter. Here, it is used to represent the *cyclic* behavior of weeks within a month. We will see other uses in later case studies.

Given two solutions, how can they be compared? The commentary suggests several ways:

- conciseness (shorter code is usually easier to understand)
- naturalness (computer algorithms that are closer to people algorithms are usually easier to understand)
- modifiability

The problem statement does not mention any potential modifications to be accommodated in the design, so we really don't have grounds for choosing between the two versions on the basis of modifiability. We do mention a few possible modifications that would be easier to make in the week-by-week solution, however.

As in previous case studies, we devise test data that exercise all statements in the code. This solution, however, introduces the approach of **black-box testing**, the inventing of test data solely from the problem specification. The test data is used to check for the following kinds of errors:

- errors within components (months)
- coordination errors between components (alignment of the end of one month with the beginning of the next, or spacing between months)
- errors in the component collection (the year)

Finally, in keeping with the Recycling principle, several variants of templates from earlier case studies are used in this solution:

- reading and processing until done (a variation on "read one, process one")
- doing something a given number of times, in cycles
- doing something a given number of times, accumulating as we go
- doing something over a given range of values

By reusing templates we are familiar with we save time on design, implementation, and debugging. Recycling templates also helps in program design. Thinking about how to combine templates to solve a problem is often more effective than thinking about how to combine individual elements of the syntax to come up with a solution.

 ## Making Sense of *The Calendar Shop*

Application 3.20 Think of another application in which the NumberOfDaysIn function would be useful.

Reflection 3.21 List the templates introduced in *The Calendar Shop*. Indicate at least two other problems each template could help solve.

Reflection 3.22 Critique the design decisions in the *Calendar Shop* solution. Which would you do differently? Which ones seemed most important? Which ones will you try to remember for the future?

Reflection   3.23 How do you design solutions to complicated problems? How far ahead do you think before you get started?

💾 *Reflection*   3.24 Suppose that the PrintHeading procedure used numeric values for the months rather than the constants defined in the original program, as follows:

```
case month of
    1:  write ('January ');
    2:  write ('February ');
    3:  write ('March ');
```

How would that be inconsistent with the style of the original program? How do the other additions to the program maintain the style of the original program?

🖳💾 *Debugging*   3.25 After a fellow programmer modifies the day-by-day version of the program, you find that it prints every month with an extra day but with the correct starting day for the month, as shown below:

```
January     1986

   S  M  T  W  T  F  S
            1  2  3  4
   5  6  7  8  9 10 11
  12 13 14 15 16 17 18
  19 20 21 22 23 24 25
  26 27 28 29 30 31 32


February     1986

   S  M  T  W  T  F  S
                     1
   2  3  4  5  6  7  8
   9 10 11 12 13 14 15
  16 17 18 19 20 21 22
  23 24 25 26 27 28 29
```

The programmer, when confronted with the error, insists that only one line was changed but can't remember which one. Where could the bug be?

🖳💾 *Modification*   3.26 Change the *Calendar Shop* program so that it prints only one month of a given year rather than the whole calendar. Make as few changes to the original program as possible.

🖳💾 *Modification*   3.27 The Gregorian reform to the calendar in 1582 involved the deletion of ten days in October of that year; October 15 was the day after October 4. In order to print October 1582 correctly, which subprograms would have to be modified, and which should not be modified? Explain your answer.

Application 3.28 Write a program that asks the user for a year and two dates (month + day) in the year, and that prints the two given dates and the number of days between them.

Linking to Previous Case Studies

Reflection 3.29 Compare the process of top-down design described in the first three case studies. Identify similarities and differences.

Reflection 3.30 Compare the cases used to test the programs in the first three case studies. Describe typical cases and extreme cases in a general way.

Application 3.31 Write and test a program that prints a calendar using block digits.

Modification 3.32 Replace the nested loop in the DrawBar procedure in the *Banners With CLASS* program by a single loop that calls the writeln procedure at appropriate intervals within the loop.

Analysis 3.33 Would an if statement be better or worse than a case statement in the main program of *Banners With CLASS?* Briefly explain your answer.

Modification 3.34 In the letter-drawing procedures in the *Banners With CLASS* program, integer arithmetic is used to determine the size of the various components. A different approach is to determine an approximate size, then test to see if it's off by one line. For example, one might write the following code for the DrawA procedure:

```
legHeight := letterSize div 4;
if odd(letterSize) then begin
    legHeight := legHeight + 1;
end;
```

Rewrite the letter-drawing procedures to use this approach. Is the result easier to understand? Why or why not?

Incomplete Program Framework

Names of missing procedures appear in boldface.

```
{
    This program asks the user for a year,
    and prints a calendar for that year.
}
program calendar (input, output);
```

```
const
    JAN = 1;
    FEB = 2;
    MAR = 3;
    APR = 4;
    MAY = 5;
    JUN = 6;
    JUL = 7;
    AUG = 8;
    SEP = 9;
    OCT = 10;
    NOV = 11;
    DEC = 12;
    BLANK = ' ';

var
    month,   {the index of the month we're printing}
    year,    {the year we're printing the calendar for}
    dayForFirst: integer;  {the index of the first day of month}

{
    We will only deal with years AD.
}
function Legal (year: integer) : boolean;
begin {Legal}
    Legal := (year > 0);
end; {Legal}

{
    Read the year from the user, and compute (using a magic formula)
    the day on which its January 1 falls. Sunday is 0, Monday 1, etc.
    The formula to find the first day of the given year was found in
    the book A Collection of Programming Problems and Techniques, by
    H.A. Maurer and M.R. Williams (Prentice-Hall, 1972).
}
procedure ReadYearInfo (var year, dayForFirst: integer);
var
    y : integer;
begin {Read Year Info}
    repeat
        write ('Please type the year for which you want a calendar: ');
        readln (year);
        if not Legal (year) then begin
            writeln ('Can''t make a calendar for that year.');
        end;
    until Legal (year);
    y := year - 1;
    dayForFirst := (36 + y + (y div 4) - (y div 100) + (y div 400)) mod 7;
end; {Read Year Info}

begin {main program}
    ReadYearInfo (year, dayForFirst);
    for month := JAN to DEC do begin
        PrintMonth (month, year, dayForFirst);
        dayForFirst := (dayForFirst+NumberOfDaysIn(month, year)) mod 7;
```

```
        end;
end    {main program}.
```

NumberOfDaysIn

```
{
    Return 0 to represent no leap day, or 1 if it's a leap year.
}
function LeapDay (year: integer): integer;
begin {Leap Day}
    if (year mod 4 = 0) and (year mod 100 <> 0) then begin
        LeapDay := 1;
    end else if year mod 400 = 0 then begin
        LeapDay := 1;
    end else begin
        LeapDay := 0;
    end;
end; {Leap Day}


{
    Return the number of days in the given month in the given year.
}
function NumberOfDaysIn (month, year: integer): integer;
begin {Number Of Days In}
    case month of
        JAN, MAR, MAY, JUL, AUG, OCT, DEC:
            NumberOfDaysIn := 31;
        FEB:
            NumberOfDaysIn := 28 + LeapDay (year);
        APR, JUN, SEP, NOV:
            NumberOfDaysIn := 30;
    end;
end    {Number Of Days In};
```

Day-by-Day PrintMonth

```
{
    Print the month name, year, and the week heading.
}
procedure PrintHeading (month, year: integer);
begin {Print Heading}
    case month of
        JAN: write ('January ');
        FEB: write ('February ');
        MAR: write ('March ');
        APR: write ('April ');
        MAY: write ('May ');
        JUN: write ('June ');
        JUL: write ('July ');
        AUG: write ('August ');
        SEP: write ('September ');
```

```
                OCT:  write ('October ');
                NOV:  write ('November ');
                DEC:  write ('December ');
        end;
        writeln (year);
        writeln;
        writeln ('  S  M  T  W  T  F  S');
    end   {Print Heading};


{
    Print the dates of the month in nice calendar form.
    First print the blanks in the first week, then print the days
    of the month, adding a carriage return at the end of each week.
}
procedure PrintDates (dayForFirst, monthLength: integer);
var
        date: integer;
begin {Print Dates}
        if dayForFirst > 0 then begin
            write (BLANK: dayForFirst * 3);
        end;
        for date := 1 to monthLength do begin
            write (date: 3);
            if (date + dayForFirst) mod 7 = 0 then begin
                writeln;
            end;
        end;
        if (monthLength + dayForFirst) mod 7 <> 0 then begin
            writeln;
        end;
        writeln;
    end   {Print Dates};


{
    Print the dates of the given month in the given year,
    with a nice heading.  dayForFirst is the day (SUN=0, MON=1, ...)
    of the first of the month.
}
procedure PrintMonth (month, year, dayForFirst: integer);
begin {Print Month}
        PrintHeading (month, year);
        PrintDates (dayForFirst, NumberOfDaysIn (month, year));
    end   {Print Month};
```

Week-by-Week PrintMonth

```
{
    Print a week's worth of dates.
    The date starting the week we're working on is in startOfWeek.
    It may be negative for the first week of a month.
}
procedure PrintWeek (startOfWeek, monthLength: integer);
var
        date: integer;
```

```
begin {Print Week}
    for date := startOfWeek to startOfWeek + 6 do begin
        if (date > 0) and (date <= monthLength) then begin
            write (date: 3);
        end else begin
            write (BLANK: 3);
        end;
    end;
    writeln;
end   {Print Week};


{
    Print the dates of the month week by week in nice calendar form.
    Do this by first computing how many weeks the month spans.
    Then find the "date" representing Sunday of the first week.
    Then call PrintWeek for each week.
}
procedure PrintDates (dayForFirst, monthLength: integer);
var
    numWeeks, startOfWeek, weekNum: integer;
begin {Print Dates}
    numWeeks := (dayForFirst + monthLength + 6) div 7;
    startOfWeek := 1 - dayForFirst;
    for weekNum := 1 to numWeeks do begin
        PrintWeek (startOfWeek, monthLength);
        startOfWeek := startOfWeek + 7;
    end;
    writeln;
end   {Print Dates};


{
    Print the dates of the given month in the given year,
    with a nice heading.  dayForFirst is the day (SUN=0, MON=1, ...)
    of the first of the month.
}
procedure PrintMonth (month, year, dayForFirst: integer);
begin {PrintMonth}
    PrintHeading (month, year);
    PrintDates (dayForFirst, NumberOfDaysIn (month, year));
end   {PrintMonth};
```

CHAPTER 4

Roman Calculator Construction

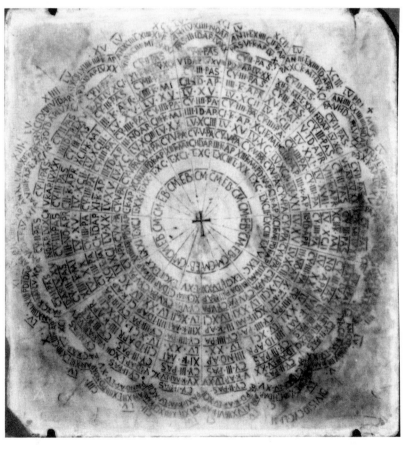

The Roman calculator described in this case study would really have helped the ancient Romans who depended on this sort of calendar.

Calculators have revolutionized mathematics, making hand computation of square roots obsolete. This program will control a calculator that takes a Roman numeral and converts it to its decimal equivalent.

Problem Statement

Write and test a program that reads a Roman numeral expressed in Roman digits and prints the corresponding decimal value.

The program should assume that the input consists of one line, containing (only) a legal Roman numeral less than 3999. For testing purposes, the program should prompt for input and print the output. Assume that the tested program, with input and output procedure calls appropriately replaced, will become the processor for a Roman numeral translator. The translator will resemble a calculator and is pictured on the right.

Description of Roman Numerals

Values less than 3999 in the Roman numeral system are written using "digits" whose decimal equivalents are given in the table. (Additional conventions for writing values larger than 3999 are not discussed here. See, for instance, *The World of Mathematics*, by J. R. Newman, Simon and Schuster, 1956, for further information.)

Roman "digit"	Decimal equivalent
M	1000
D	500
C	100
L	50
X	10
V	5
I	1

Roman numerals are composed using the following rules.

Digit order: Roman digits are written in nonascending order, and digit values are added to produce the represented value, except for prefixes as mentioned below.

Number of occurrences: No more than three occurrences of M, C, X, or I may appear consecutively, and no more than one D, L, or V may appear at all.

Prefixes: The digits C, X, and I can be used as prefixes, and their value is then *subtracted from* rather than added to the value being accumulated, as follows:

- One C may prefix an M or a D to represent 900 or 400; the prefixed M is written after the other M's, as in MMMCM. The digits following the M or D represent a value no more than 99.
- One X may prefix a C or an L to represent 90 or 40; the prefixed C is written after the other C's. The digits following the C or L represent a value no more than 9.
- One I may prefix an X or a V to represent 9 or 4. The prefixed digit must appear at the end of the numeral.

Some examples:

Decimal number	Roman numeral
1987	MCMLXXXVII
1999	MCMXCIX
339	CCCXXXIX

Analysis 4.1 What is the decimal value of each of the following Roman numeral values: MCMLII, MMCDV, CXCIX?

Analysis 4.2 How is each of the following decimal values written using Roman numerals: 1988, 1000, 1349?

Analysis 4.3 For each of the following, determine its value if it's a legal Roman numeral, or describe which of the rules listed in the problem statement that it violates: XMICVC, XLIX, IIX, XIXIV.

Preparation

The reader is expected to be familiar with one-dimensional arrays, functions, procedures, and if and case statements. This case study introduces var parameters, the while statement, a char array indexed by integers, an integer array indexed by characters, and the eoln function.

Preliminary Planning

What should the
program do?

The program should read in the "digits" of a Roman numeral and store them somehow, then compute the corresponding decimal value and print it out. The computation seems to be the hardest part of the solution, since input and output are easy.

What problems have
decompositions similar to
this one?

The decomposition sounds similar to those in previous case studies. Two templates seem possible for processing the Roman digits. One, used in *Banners With CLASS* and *The Calendar Shop*, is "read one, process one":

read a value and process it until there aren't any more values

The "values" here are the Roman digits; "processing" a digit means incorporating it into the decimal value we're building. This template yields a "digit-by-digit" approach, as illustrated in the pseudocode below.

read and translate the Roman numeral, by doing the following until
    there are no more Roman digits:
        read a Roman digit;
        translate and accumulate the digit;
print the result.

Another template, used in *Check That Number!* was

input a value or sequence of values;
process the value(s);
output the result.

This template yields an "entire-numeral" approach since all the Roman digits are input before they are translated. Here is the pseudocode:

read all the Roman digits;
translate the Roman numeral to decimal;
print the result.

Stop & Predict ➤

What operations will these two decompositions have in common?

How should the information
used in the program be
represented?

Either approach involves reading in the Roman digits and writing out a decimal value. The Roman digits M, D, C, L, X, V, and I are letters, which we'll represent as *character* values. We'll represent the corresponding decimal value as an *integer*.

How can Roman digits be
translated into decimal digits?

In either approach, we need to translate the individual Roman digits into their decimal equivalents. Thus, M becomes 1000, D becomes 500, and so on. A function is more appropriate than a procedure because it's intended for the situation where a single value is being returned. The function takes a character argument and returns an integer. An informative name is

DecimalTrans. DecimalTrans is easy to design, so we will postpone working on it until later.

Reflection 4.4 Does the digit-by-digit or the entire-numeral approach sound easier to design and develop? Why?

Application, Reflection 4.5 Describe another problem whose solution involves a choice between (a) processing information incrementally and (b) collecting all the information before starting to process it. Which approach seems more productive in everyday problems? What are weaknesses of the two approaches?

Digit-by-Digit Approach

What sort of loop will the digit-by-digit approach use?

The *Banners With CLASS* program used a for loop to read and process its input, since it knew how much input to expect. For this problem, the number of Roman digits the input will contain is not known, and thus a for loop is inappropriate.

Stop & Predict ➤ *What kind of loop will be appropriate for reading and processing Roman digits?*

A while loop and a repeat loop both handle situations where the number of iterations cannot be specified in advance. The body of a while loop is executed 0 or more times, and a test for whether or not to *continue* occurs before each iteration. The body of a repeat loop is executed 1 or more times, and a test for whether or not to *stop* occurs after each iteration.

The problem statement guarantees that the input Roman numeral is legal—that is, it has at least one digit. Also, the condition for exiting the loop—reaching the end of the line—is somewhat easier to state than the condition for continuing the loop. Thus we choose to code the loop using repeat. If the program were required to worry about empty input lines or other errors, we would use while instead.

The problem statement suggests that the loop will be adding up values determined by the input, so it will look something like the following:

```
ask the user for a Roman numeral;
initialize a "sum" variable to 0;
repeat the following:
    read a Roman digit;
    add the decimal value of the Roman digit into the sum;
until the end of the line is encountered.
```

The pseudocode can easily be converted to Pascal. The eoln function is used to check if all the Roman digits have been read. A variable of type char called romanDigit stores each Roman digit. An integer variable sum accumulates the sum.

Stop & Predict ➤   *What modifications are needed to make this loop work?*

How can prefixes be handled?

This loop does not handle prefixes (the C in CMXI or the I in IV). Prefixes must be subtracted from the decimal value being accumulated. A prefix cannot be detected until the character it prefixes has been processed.

The loop could be modified to check, after reading a digit, whether that digit might be a prefix, and then to immediately read the next digit. This program would probably be confusing and hard to debug.

Stop & Consider ➤   *What cases must be handled within a loop that tries to read a prefix and the prefixed digit in the same iteration?*

To be understandable, a loop should be written to do *exactly one thing*. In this situation, a good solution is a loop that reads exactly one character in each iteration.

To figure out how the loop should work, we try solving the problem by hand, by "playing computer" on the input CXIV. (Remember that the loop processes one Roman digit at a time.) The loop initializes sum to 0, reads C, and adds 100 to sum. Then it reads X, and adds 10 to sum. Next it reads I, and adds 1 to sum. sum now contains 111, the correct decimal value for CXI. Next the loop reads V. To get the right answer of 114 in sum, the program should first add 5, the value for V (sum now contains 116), then subtract the value for I *after undoing the previous addition* (which incorrectly added the value for I into sum).

Doing this requires that the loop keep track of the Roman digit previously read as well as the one currently being processed. We use a char variable called prevDigit to hold potential prefixes.

What is the precise definition of the loop action?

The action of the loop body can be concisely described as adjusting the value of sum to account for the most recently read Roman digit. Thus, at the end of every iteration sum will contain the decimal value of the Roman digits read so far. (We include the description as a comment in the code.)

The resulting code looks like this:

```
{
    Read each Roman digit, and adjust the value of sum to account for it.
    At the end of each iteration, the value in sum will be the decimal
    value of all the Roman digits read so far.
    If the previous Roman digit is a prefix--i.e. its value is
    less than the value of the current Roman digit--we have to undo
    it along with adding in the value of the current digit.
}
repeat
    read (romanDigit);
```

```
        if DecimalTrans (romanDigit) <= DecimalTrans (prevDigit) then begin
            sum := sum + DecimalTrans (romanDigit);
        end else begin
            sum := sum + DecimalTrans (romanDigit)
                - DecimalTrans (prevDigit) - DecimalTrans (prevDigit);
        end;
        prevDigit := romanDigit;
    until eoln;
```

What code must precede and follow the loop?

In order to get a value to translate, the program must prompt the user for input before the loop and print the translated value after the loop. Before entering the loop, the program also needs to initialize prevDigit and sum. A common way to do this is to separate the first iteration of the loop, as follows:

```
write ('Type a Roman numeral followed by RETURN: ');
read (romanDigit);
sum := DecimalTrans (romanDigit);
prevDigit := romanDigit;
(the loop follows here)
```

Stop & Predict ➤ *What changes in the loop are necessitated by separating the first iteration?*

Since the input is assumed to be correct, there will always be at least one Roman digit to read in the initialization code. However, by separating the first iteration, we invalidate the assumption that there will always be at least one digit to read within the loop itself. We need to recode the repeat loop as a while loop:

```
while not eoln do begin
    read (romanDigit);
    if DecimalTrans (romanDigit) <= DecimalTrans (prevDigit) then begin
        sum := sum + DecimalTrans (romanDigit);
    end else begin
        sum := sum + DecimalTrans (romanDigit)
            - DecimalTrans (prevDigit) - DecimalTrans (prevDigit);
    end;
    prevDigit := romanDigit;
end;
```

The pattern represented in the while loop involves reading values and processing them until all the values have been read. This seems to be a pattern that will appear over and over again.

A more concise way to initialize sum is the following:

```
write ('Type a Roman numeral followed by RETURN: ');
read (prevDigit);
sum := DecimalTrans (prevDigit);
while not eoln do begin ...
```

Stop & Help ➤ *Why doesn't romanDigit need to appear in an assignment statement in the "concise" initialization code?*

How should DecimalTrans be written?

Recall that DecimalTrans is a function that takes a character as argument and returns an integer. Code for selecting from alternatives and processing the alternative selected is similar to that used in *The Calendar Shop* program. This application of the template should select a character from M, D, C, L, X, V, and I. Here's the code:

```
function DecimalTrans (romanDigit: char): integer;
begin
    case romanDigit of
        'M':  DecimalTrans := 1000;
        'D':  DecimalTrans :=  500;
        'C':  DecimalTrans :=  100;
        'L':  DecimalTrans :=   50;
        'X':  DecimalTrans :=   10;
        'V':  DecimalTrans :=    5;
        'I':  DecimalTrans :=    1;
    end;
end;
```

Can the code be simplified?

Reviewing the rest of the code before we type it in, we notice that we can shorten the loop by saving the values returned by DecimalTrans(roman-Digit) and DecimalTrans(prevDigit) rather than recomputing them. We define two more variables, currentValue and prevValue, for this purpose. The first program in the Pascal Code section results.

Stop & Predict ➤ *What are important test cases for this program?*

How should the program be tested?

As in *The Calendar Shop*, test data should be chosen using both the glass-box and the black-box approaches. The glass-box approach suggests values that cause every statement to be executed, and that cause the loop to execute as few and as many times as possible.

Stop & Help ➤ *Produce a set of test data that causes every statement in the digit-by-digit program to be executed, and that causes the loop to be repeated as few and as many times as possible.*

The black-box approach yields a more extensive set of test data. It suggests easy as well as trickier cases, and typical as well as extreme cases. Easy cases include single digits and groups of digits without prefixes. Typical cases include combinations with prefixes. Extreme cases include Roman numerals that are as short as possible, and that start with a prefix.

Stop & Help ➤ *Produce a set of test data that will test the digit-by-digit program.*

Stop & Consider ➤ *Should a Roman numeral that ends with a prefix be tested as another boundary case? Why or why not?*

How can the process of testing be simplified?

Running the program once for each test case is inefficient. Testing will be more convenient if, when the program is run, it keeps processing values rather than processing just one. Thus, we add a main program with a loop that asks for, reads, and converts a Roman numeral each time through. (We'll take out the loop for the final program.) We package these actions into a procedure called ConvertRoman. The following main program results:

```
begin {main program}
    while true do begin
        ConvertRoman;
    end;
end.
```

Stop & Help ➤ *The main program above contains an infinite loop. How do you interrupt a program running in your programming environment?*

The loop could instead include a statement to ask if we wish to continue testing. This would require us to enter both a Roman numeral and an answer to the "continue?" prompt each time through the loop, however.

What bugs were encountered? In the actual tests of this program, we had a bug. The program converted the first Roman numeral correctly, then crashed in the case statement in DecimalTrans. We had forgotten the readln at the end of ConvertRoman, so the end-of-line character was read as a blank and assumed to be part of a Roman numeral.

🖫 *Debugging* 4.6 Suppose the program gave a negative value for the outcome. Where would you look for the error?

🖫 🖫 *Debugging* 4.7 One of your fellow programmers, while reading the digit-by-digit version of the program, accidentally changes a line. The modified result apparently ignores prefixes instead of handling them correctly. Thus XL is evaluated as 50, XLIV as 55, and so on. What line was changed, and how?

🖫 🖫 *Reflection* 4.8 What bugs would *you* expect to encounter using the digit-by-digit approach?

🖫 🖫 *Modification* 4.9 Rewrite the while not eoln loop as a repeat loop preceded by an if statement.

🖫 🖫 *Modification* 4.10 Rewrite the loop in the main program to ask the user whether or not to continue, and to continue only if the character 'y' is entered.

🖫 🖫 *Modification, Reflection* 4.11 Rewrite the function DecimalTrans using a sequence of if...then...else statements rather than a case statement. Why is the original version clearer than the rewritten version?

🖫 🖫 *Analysis* 4.12 What will occur if a non-Roman digit is sent to DecimalTrans?

Entire-Numeral Solution

What does the entire-numeral solution involve?

The entire-numeral approach separates the input, the processing, and the output.

The input step stores the Roman numeral by reading its digits into an *array* of characters. We define a type called StringType to use to store the input and will use a procedure called ReadRoman to do the input.

The process step translates the Roman numeral to a decimal value. Since the process step produces a single result—the decimal value of the Roman numeral—we use a function called DecimalValue.

The output step prints the result. A procedure called PrintDecimal will do the output.

How is the array declared?

Declaring an array involves specifying the type of the array and the size of the array. Arrays of characters are typically called **strings**, so we define a type called StringType to store the characters. We use a constant, MAXSTRLEN, to define the size of the array. By using a constant we can change the size of the array easily if necessary.

Stop & Help ➤ *What is the longest possible legal Roman numeral that represents a value less than 3999? Based on this information, assign a value to MAXSTRLEN.*

Stop & Consider ➤ *What is the longest possible Roman numeral that uses the digits M, D, C, L, X, V, and I?*

What does the input step look like?

Reading a line of text into an array is a common action. We can recycle the input-handling template used in the digit-by-digit approach (being sure to remember the readln at the end!). The body of the loop reads each character and stores it into the next array cell. The loop must also count the characters it reads and use the counter variable to index the array. We'll call the counter variable length. Both the characters and the count are passed back to the main program in order to simplify subsequent processing of the array. We use var parameters because the variables are updated in the procedure. Here's the code:

```
const
    MAXSTRLEN = 20;

type
    StringType = array [1..MAXSTRLEN] of char;

         .
         .
         .

procedure ReadRoman (var roman: StringType; var length: integer);
var
    ch: char;
begin
```

```
write ('Type a Roman numeral followed by RETURN: ');
length := 0;
while not eoln do begin
    read (ch);
    length := length + 1;
    roman [length] := ch;
end;
readln;
end;
```

What are the advantages of the array approach?

An array significantly simplifies the conversion of the Roman numeral. Using an array, the program can *look ahead* at the next Roman digit to see whether to add or subtract its value from the sum, since all the digits have been stored in the array beforehand. Thus the loop can go digit by digit through the array, as follows:

```
function DecimalValue (roman: StringType; length: integer): integer;
var
    sum, k: integer;
begin
    sum := 0;
    for k := 1 to length-1 do begin
        if DecimalTrans(roman[k]) >= DecimalTrans(roman[k+1]) then begin
            sum := sum + DecimalTrans(roman[k]);
        end else begin
            sum := sum - DecimalTrans(roman[k]);
        end;
    end;
    DecimalValue := sum + DecimalTrans(roman[length]);
end;
```

What about the output step?

Printing is easy. PrintDecimal consists of a single writeln. The final program appears in the Pascal Code section.

Stop & Predict ➤ *Will the same tests used in the digit-by-digit version work for this program? Why or why not?*

How is the program tested?

Most of the test data for the first version of the program was chosen according to the black-box approach, derived only from the problem specification, not from the code itself. Thus the same set of data can be used to test the current version. The glass-box approach suggests another boundary case, a Roman numeral as long as possible. We first test the routines that use arrays (ReadRoman and DecimalValue) to get the bugs out of them before combining them with other routines.

Stop & Predict ➤ *How can the parts of the program that use arrays be tested separately?*

How can the parts be tested?

For a program patterned on the "input, process, output" template, there are typically two ways to test it in smaller pieces. One way is to test the input routine first, and merely have a writeln statement or some other such **stub** routine for the processing. The other way is to include assignment statements in the program to initialize some variables, and then process those. Either way requires an output routine, so we can see the results of the testing.

Testing the ReadRoman procedure by itself uses the first way. An output routine to print the result of the input could be called WriteRoman. The main program would look something like the following:

```
begin {main program}
    while true do begin
        {Read the Roman numeral and its length.}
        ReadRoman (roman, length);
        {Print both out to make sure we've read them correctly.}
        WriteRoman (roman, length);
    end;
end.
```

Testing the DecimalValue function by itself requires using assignment statements to set up a Roman numeral without doing input. In some versions of Pascal, this may be done as follows:

```
roman := 'CXIV';
length := 4;
WriteDecimal (DecimalValue (roman, length));
```

Stop & Predict ➤

How does the entire-numeral solution compare with the digit-by-digit solution?

How does the entire-numeral version compare with the digit-by-digit version?

The entire-numeral approach, though slightly longer than the digit-by-digit approach, is easier to split into smaller pieces, which can in turn be easily understood, tested, and debugged. Basing the entire-numeral solution on the "input, process, output" template forces us to use an array to store the Roman numeral. Storing the values in the array make it possible to *look ahead* at the next Roman digit and thus simplifies the task of converting the Roman numeral to decimal. In general, when processing a sequence of data items that depend on each other, it is much easier to read them all into an array, if possible, before processing than to try to process the items "on the fly" without storing them.

🔖 *Debugging*

4.13 A common bug in a program is an off-by-one error. Suppose that, on entry to the DecimalValue function, its length argument is either one too high or one too low. Explain what would happen, and how a programmer would notice the bug from the output.

🔖 *Reflection*

4.14 What bugs would *you* expect to encounter using the entire-numeral approach?

🔖 *Modification*

4.15 The loop in DecimalValue can be rewritten as follows:

```
for k := 1 to length-1 do begin
    sum := sum + ValueToAccum(...);
end;
```

Write the ValueToAccum function.

Another Use for an Array

An alternative solution uses an array to replace the DecimalTrans function. An array defines an association between an index value and the contents of the corresponding array cell, and in this way acts as a function that takes the index as an argument and returns the indexed value. (In some programming languages, the notation for accessing an array is exactly the same as that for calling a function.)

How can the DecimalTrans function be replaced by an array?

This suggests that a function whose single argument is a value of type integer, char, or boolean (a legal type for an array index) may be converted to a one-dimensional array instead. DecimalTrans is such a function, and it may be replaced by an array whose index values are characters and whose contents are integers. Thus, the values of the array would be as follows:

decimalTrans ['M'] = 1000,
decimalTrans ['D'] = 500,

and so on. These values could be assigned at the start of the main program or in an initialization procedure.

Pascal doesn't allow arrays indexed *only* by the characters 'M', 'D', 'C', 'L', 'X', 'V', and 'I'; the index set must include all the characters in between as well. What do we do with decimalTrans['E'], decimalTrans['F'], and all the others? With correct input, they won't be used. If they're somehow used as a result of a bug, they should have values that produce obviously incorrect output. A reasonable choice is maxint, predefined in Pascal as the largest value of type integer.

This array acts just like a Pascal constant. After its values are assigned at the start of the program, they don't change. Pascal unfortunately doesn't allow the use of arrays in const declarations, so the array must be declared in the var section and initialized with assignment statements. To show the array's role in the program, however, we use all capital letters for its name just as we do for Pascal constants. For the same reason, we do not pass it as a parameter to DecimalValue, but instead use it globally. The result appears in the Pascal Code section.

🖫 *Debugging* 4.16 Suppose that, on entry to the rewritten DecimalValue function, its length argument is either one too high or one too low. Explain what would happen, and how a programmer would notice the bug from the output.

📓 🖫 *Application* 4.17 Write and test a loop that, for every element of the decimalTrans array, prints either the element's value if it's less than maxint or the word illegal if the value is equal to maxint.

Outline of Design and Development Questions

These questions summarize the main points of the commentary.

Preliminary Planning
What should the program do?
What problems have decompositions similar to this one?
How should the information used in the program be represented?
How can Roman digits be translated into decimal digits?

Digit-by-Digit Approach
What sort of loop will the digit-by-digit approach use?
    How can prefixes be handled?
    What is the precise definition of the loop action?
    What code must precede and follow the loop?
How should DecimalTrans be written?
    Can the code be simplified?
How should the program be tested?
    How can the process of testing be simplified?
    What bugs were encountered?

Entire-Numeral Solution
What does the entire-numeral solution involve?
    How is the array declared?
    What does the input step look like?
    What are the advantages of the array approach?
    What about the output step?
How is the program tested?
    How can the parts be tested?
How does the entire-numeral solution compare with the digit-by-digit solution?

Another Use for an Array
How can the DecimalTrans function be replaced by an array?

Programmers' Summary

This case study introduces arrays as a problem-solving tool and illustrates programming templates that use arrays. The case compares two solutions to Roman numeral translation: one without arrays, the digit-by-digit solution, and another with arrays, the entire-numeral solution. The introduction of the array illustrates the Multiple Representation principle: several representations of the array concept are presented. Arrays are verbally described, illustrated, and diagrammed.

The digit-by-digit solution introduces the template

read and process input until no more values.

Following this template, each Roman digit is translated into an integer, then added into a running sum as it is read.

The entire-numeral solution uses the "input, process, output" template introduced in *Check that Number!* Following this template, all the Roman digits are read into an array before any of them are processed.

The array used in the entire-numeral solution provides more than just a convenient storage area. It simplifies the processing of the Roman digits, too, by making it easy to look ahead at the next Roman digit when encountering a possible prefix. In general, arrays make it easier to solve problems that require accessing more than one value in a set.

A suggested modification to the entire-numeral solution illustrates an interesting interchangeability between program structure and data structure. Where a case statement is used to associate an integer value with a given Roman digit, the modification makes use of an array of integer values, indexed by possible Roman digits.

Implementing the digit-by-digit solution requires finding a clear way to handle prefixes. Ideally the template loop reads one value during each iteration. However, prefixes cannot be evaluated without considering two values in sequence. Rather than reading two values during some iterations and none during others, a variable is added that keeps track of the previous digit read. Processing then involves handling two situations within the loop, one for a prefix and the other for a nonprefix.

Template applications to fill an array and to process the array in the entire-numeral solution are straightforward. The pattern

while not eoln do begin
    read input value;

      ...

end;
readln;

is useful in both solutions.

This case also provides a good example of the Divide and Conquer principle in that each of the solutions involves dividing most of the action of the program into familiar templates. By dividing the program into parts that can be implemented with familiar templates, the details and complex parts are postponed. Often, as a result, the parts that are postponed turn out to be easier than expected.

As in *The Calendar Shop*, test data are selected via both the glass-box and black-box approaches; the latter approach suggests a wider range of tests, useful to exercise both versions of the program. Extreme test values include Roman numerals as large and as small as possible and numerals with prefixes occurring at the ends of the data sequence. A main program that repeatedly reads and evaluates Roman numerals is added for testing. (To conform to the problem statement, the main program will be replaced by a program that reads just one value.)

This case study illustrates the Fingerprint principle by associating common array bugs with their symptoms. For example, the off-by-one bug can be detected when a program accesses an out-of-range location in an array.

Incremental development of the entire-numeral solution is easy because we can split the program into pieces and test them individually. We use a **stub** procedure—one that handles only a small part of its intended purpose—for the processing step while testing the input step. We also use an assignment statement as a stub for the input procedure while testing the processing step.

Making Sense of *Roman Calculator* Construction

Application 4.18 Think of other problems whose solution would be simplified by using arrays.

Reflection 4.19 Suppose you had taken the digit-by-digit approach and attempted to create a loop that, on encountering a possible prefix, read another Roman digit. There are several cases to analyze in such a solution. Would you try to analyze all the cases? If not, at what point would you give up and look for a better solution?

Analysis 4.20 The loop in ConvertRoman in the digit-by-digit version of the program contains the statement

```
sum := sum + currentValue - prevValue - prevValue;
```

Why isn't the corresponding statement in the loop in DecimalValue in the other two versions written as follows?

```
sum := sum - DecimalTrans(roman[k]) - DecimalTrans(roman[k]);
```

Analysis 4.21 We claim in the commentary on the digit-by-digit solution that sum will contain the value of the Roman numeral represented by the digits read so far at the end of each iteration of the loop. But what if the digits so far do not represent a legal Roman numeral? More generally, if the first few digits of a legal Roman numeral are considered by themselves, do they also represent a legal Roman numeral?

Modification 4.22 Rewrite ConvertRoman as a function that returns the decimal value of the Roman numeral. Update the main program so that it prints the value returned by the function. (This use of a function that does input is somewhat controversial; input is a side effect, and functions by convention avoid side effects.)

Application 4.23 Write and test a "Roman Numerals Quiz" program that asks the quizmaster for a Roman numeral, asks the participant for the decimal equivalent, and then tells the participant if the answer is correct.

Application 4.24 Write and test a calculator program that prints the sum of two Roman numerals input by the user.

Modification 4.25 Modify each version of the program to handle two more Roman digits, T, meaning 10,000, and F, meaning 5000. M can prefix T to represent 9000 or F to represent 4000. No more than three occurrences of T may appear consecutively, and no more than one occurrence of F may appear at all. What is the longest Roman numeral that can be formed with these and the other Roman digits?

Application 4.26 Write and test a program that reads a hexadecimal numeral (base 16) and prints its base 10 value. Hexadecimal numerals use the letters A, B, C, D, E, and F to represent the values 10, 11, 12, 13, 14, and 15. Digits in a hexadecimal numeral represent successively higher powers of 16; for instance, 3E9 represents 3*256 + 14*16 + 9 = 768 + 224 + 9 = 1001.

Linking to Previous Case Studies

Modification 4.27 Rewrite the character variable version of the *Check That Number!* program so that it reads an identification number of up to twenty digits into an array of characters, then checks the result. The last digit of the value read will be the check digit, computed as in the original problem.

Modification 4.28 Rewrite the *Banners With CLASS* program to read a line of letters into an array, then print block versions of every letter in the line.

Modification 4.29 Rewrite *The Calendar Shop* main program to produce a calendar for each of a sequence of years provided by the user.

Reflection 4.30 Describe similarities and differences between the translation of Roman digits to decimal values in this case study and the translation of characters to digit values in *Check That Number!*

Digit-by-Digit Program

```pascal
program RomanNumerals (input, output);

{
    Given a legal Roman digit, return its decimal value.
}
function DecimalTrans (romanDigit: char): integer;
begin {Decimal Trans}
    case romanDigit of
        'M': DecimalTrans := 1000;
        'D': DecimalTrans :=  500;
        'C': DecimalTrans :=  100;
        'L': DecimalTrans :=   50;
        'X': DecimalTrans :=   10;
        'V': DecimalTrans :=    5;
        'I': DecimalTrans :=    1;
    end;
end {Decimal Trans};


{
    Ask for and read a Roman numeral, then print its decimal value.
}
procedure ConvertRoman;
var
    sum, prevValue, currentValue: integer;
    romanDigit: char;
begin {Convert Roman}
    write ('Type a Roman numeral followed by RETURN: ');
    read (romanDigit);
    prevValue := DecimalTrans (romanDigit);
    sum := prevValue;
    {
        Read each Roman digit, and adjust the value of sum to account
        for it. At the end of each iteration, the value in sum will be the
        decimal value of all the Roman digits read so far.
        If the previous Roman digit is a prefix--i.e. its value is
        less than the value of the current Roman digit--we have to undo
        it along with adding in the value of the current digit.
    }
    while not eoln do begin
        read (romanDigit);
        currentValue := DecimalTrans (romanDigit);
        if currentValue <= prevValue then begin
            sum := sum + currentValue;
        end else begin
            sum := sum + currentValue - prevValue - prevValue;
        end;
        prevValue := currentValue;
    end;
    readln;
    writeln (sum);
end {Convert Roman};
```

```
begin {main program}
    while true do begin
        ConvertRoman;
    end;
end.
```

Entire-Numeral Program

```
program RomanNumerals (input, output);

const
    MAXSTRLEN = 20;

type
    StringType = array [1..MAXSTRLEN] of char;

var
    roman: StringType;   {the Roman numeral read from the user}
    length: integer;     {how many Roman digits it contains}

{
    Given a legal Roman digit, return its decimal value.
}
function DecimalTrans (romanDigit: char): integer;
begin {Decimal Trans}
    case romanDigit of
        'M': DecimalTrans := 1000;
        'D': DecimalTrans :=  500;
        'C': DecimalTrans :=  100;
        'L': DecimalTrans :=   50;
        'X': DecimalTrans :=   10;
        'V': DecimalTrans :=    5;
        'I': DecimalTrans :=    1;
    end;
end {Decimal Trans};

{
    Given a Roman numeral and the number of Roman digits it contains,
    return its value in decimal.
}
function DecimalValue (roman: StringType; length: integer): integer;
var
    sum, k: integer;
begin {Decimal Value}
    sum := 0;
    for k := 1 to length-1 do begin
        if DecimalTrans(roman[k])>=DecimalTrans(roman[k+1]) then begin
            sum := sum + DecimalTrans(roman[k]);
        end else begin
            sum := sum - DecimalTrans(roman[k]);
        end;
    end;
    DecimalValue := sum + DecimalTrans(roman[length]);
end {Decimal Value};
```

```
{
    Request and read a Roman numeral from the user.
    Also return the number of Roman digits in the numeral.
}
procedure ReadRoman (var roman: StringType; var length: integer);
var
    ch: char;
begin {Read Roman}
    write ('Type a Roman numeral followed by RETURN: ');
    length := 0;
    while not eoln do begin
        read (ch);
        length := length + 1;
        roman [length] := ch;
    end;
    readln;
end {Read Roman};


{
    Print the decimal value of a Roman numeral.
}
procedure PrintDecimal (n: integer);
begin {Print Decimal}
    writeln (n);
end {Print Decimal};

begin {main program}
    while true do begin
        ReadRoman (roman, length);
        PrintDecimal (DecimalValue (roman, length));
    end;
end.
```

Program Using an Array of Decimal Equivalents for Roman Digits

```
program RomanNumerals (input, output);

const
    MAXSTRLEN = 20;

type
    StringType = array [1..MAXSTRLEN] of char;

var
    roman: StringType;   {the Roman numeral read from the user}
    length: integer;     {how many Roman digits it contains}
    c: char;
    DECIMALEQUIV:  array ['C'..'X'] of integer;
                    {decimal equivalents to Roman digits}
```

```
{
    Given a Roman numeral and the number of Roman digits it contains,
    return its value in decimal.
}
function DecimalValue (roman: StringType; length: integer): integer;
var
    sum, k: integer;
begin {Decimal Value}
    sum := 0;
    for k := 1 to length-1 do begin
        if DECIMALEQUIV[roman[k]] >= DECIMALEQUIV[roman[k+1]] then begin
            sum := sum + DECIMALEQUIV[roman[k]];
        end else begin
            sum := sum - DECIMALEQUIV[roman[k]];
        end;
    end;
    DecimalValue := sum + DECIMALEQUIV[roman[length]];
end {Decimal Value};


{
    Request and read a Roman numeral from the user.
    Also return the number of Roman digits in the numeral.
}
procedure ReadRoman (var roman: StringType; var length: integer);
var
    ch: char;
begin {Read Roman}
    write ('Type a Roman numeral followed by RETURN: ');
    length := 0;
    while not eoln do begin
        read (ch);
        length := length + 1;
        roman [length] := ch;
    end;
    readln;
end {Read Roman};


{
    Print the decimal value of a Roman numeral.
}
procedure PrintDecimal (n: integer);
begin {Print Decimal}
    writeln (n);
end {Print Decimal};

begin {main program}
    {Initialize "constant" array of decimal equivalents.}
    for c := 'C' to 'X' do begin
        DECIMALEQUIV [c] := maxint;
    end;
    DECIMALEQUIV ['M'] := 1000;
    DECIMALEQUIV ['D'] :=  500;
    DECIMALEQUIV ['C'] :=  100;
    DECIMALEQUIV ['L'] :=   50;
    DECIMALEQUIV ['X'] :=   10;
    DECIMALEQUIV ['V'] :=    5;
```

```
        DECIMALEQUIV ['I'] :=    1;

    {Read and translate Roman numerals.}
    while true do begin
        ReadRoman (roman, length);
        PrintDecimal (DecimalValue (roman, length));
    end;
end.
```

CHAPTER 5

Is It Legal?

Claiming legality is popular today. This case study could lead to gainful employment.

How should programs respond to illegal data? Assuming that data will be legal asks for trouble: What if users mistype? What if users want to confuse the program? This case study describes how to guard against illegal data in the *Check That Number!*, *Banners With CLASS*, *Calendar Shop*, and *Roman Calculator Construction* programs.

Problem Statement

The problem statements for *Check That Number!*, *Banners With CLASS*, *The Calendar Shop*, and *Roman Calculator Construction* all make assumptions about the nature of the input. Such assumptions are rarely justified. What if users mistype? What if the user tries to confuse the program? A better approach is to make sure that only legal input is processed. This case study explores general ways to check input for errors as well as specific solutions for the programs encountered up to now.

Modify the programs for *Check That Number!*, *Banners With CLASS*, *The Calendar Shop*, and *Roman Calculator Construction* so that they handle invalid input appropriately. They should prompt for input, read a value or values from the user without crashing, analyze the values, and repeat this process until the user provides legal input.

Recall the legal input for the four earlier case studies:

Check That Number!	a line containing only a four-digit identification number
Banners With CLASS	a line containing a legal letter size (an integer between 5 and 24, inclusive), possibly preceded by blanks; a line containing exactly six characters, all chosen from P, A, S, C, and L
The Calendar Shop	a line containing a legal year, possibly preceded by blanks
Roman Calculator Construction	a line containing a legal Roman numeral

Analysis 5.1 Why was it initially reasonable to assume that the data for the *Check That Number!* and *Roman Calculator Construction* programs would be legal? Why would this assumption not be appropriate for the *Banners With CLASS* or *Calendar Shop* programs?

Reflection 5.2 How susceptible are you to making typing errors? If you are an inaccurate typist, how do you catch errors?

Reflection 5.3 Which programs, when you run them, have left you unsure about what to type at a given point? What improvements that would help might be incorporated in these programs?

📖 *Testing* 5.4 Think of ways to crash the programs produced in earlier case studies. Catalog the error messages or crash situations that result.

Preparation

Solutions in this case study use one-dimensional arrays, loops, the eoln function, procedures, and functions.

Checking for Legal Input

What changes are needed to guard against illegal data?

The problem statement outlines several changes that must be made to the programs in earlier case studies to handle invalid input. First, each program is to print a prompt before reading, to alert the user to what kind of input is requested. Second, it must read the input without crashing, and analyze it. Third, the program must reprompt as long as the input is illegal.

Stop & Predict ➤ *What parts of the input-handling code will be common to all the programs?*

Thus all the programs will need code that prompts for input; only the contents of the prompt will differ between programs. All the programs will contain some sort of loop that continues to prompt, read, and analyze the input until it's legal. The analysis that must be performed on the input will probably differ from program to program. We will start by concentrating on the code that is similar among all four programs, and postpone the program-specific code.

Stop & Predict ➤ *Did any of the programs from earlier case studies involve a check for legal data?*

The *Calendar Shop* program already includes a check that its input is legal. Here is its input loop:

```
repeat
    write ('Please type the year you want a calendar for: ');
    readln (year);
    if not Legal (year) then begin
        writeln ('Can''t make a calendar for that year.');
    end;
until Legal (year);
```

| How can the code from *The Calendar Shop* be recycled? | The code in *The Calendar Shop* suggests a framework for the loop that reads legal values from the user: |

```
repeat
    prompt for input;
    read a set of input values;
    if the values aren't legal then print an error message;
until the values are legal;
```

Stop & Consider ➤ *Why is* repeat *more appropriate for the above loop than* while?

| What template is represented in this decomposition? | This is another example of the "input one, process one" template: |

Input: Prompt for input, then read a set of input values.
Process: Check for legality, and print an error message if necessary.

| What type of variable should be used for input? | Trying to read a nonnumeric value into an integer or real variable will cause an error. However, any input can be read into a *character* variable without error. Thus the input step should read the values as characters and convert them to a numeric representation if necessary. (The template for converting characters to numeric values was introduced in *Check That Number!*) |

Stop & Predict ➤ *How should the character variables be stored?*

To read a numeric value in this way, each digit will have to be stored as a character. This argues for the use of an *array* of characters to store the input. Use of an array will allow values that are too long or too short to be easily detected.

| How much should be read at a time? | In all these programs the input is on a single line, so reading one line at a time and checking if the information is legal will work. In particular, *Check That Number!* and *The Calendar Shop* each expect one numeric value on the line, *Banners With CLASS* expects a numeric value on one line and six letters on the next, and *Roman Calculator Construction* expects one string of characters. |

| What definitions and declarations are used? | To read values into an array we use the "fill an array" template introduced in the *Roman Calculator Construction* program. |

Using a constant to specify the maximum line length for convenience in adapting to the four different applications yields the following definitions and declarations:

```
const
    LINELENGTH = some positive integer ;

type
    LineType = array [1..LINELENGTH] of char;

var
    line: LineType;
```

How is a line read? We can recycle code to read values into an array from the entire-numeral version of the *Roman Calculator Construction* program:

```
length := 0;
while not eoln do begin
    read (ch);
    length := length + 1;
    roman [length] := ch;
end;
readln;
```

Stop & Predict ➤ *What can go wrong with array input?*

What if the line is longer than the array? The code will crash if enough input is provided to overflow the array. We can guard against this error with a test:

```
length := 0;
while not eoln do begin
    read (ch);
    length := length + 1;
    if length <= LINELENGTH then begin
        line [length] := ch;
    end;
end;
readln;
```

Stop & Consider ➤ *What would be wrong with code that assigned a value to* length *only if* length *was smaller than* LINELENGTH, *as follows?*

```
while not eoln do begin
    read (ch);
    if length <= LINELENGTH then begin
        length := length + 1;
        line [length] := ch;
    end;
end;
```

What is the right length for LINELENGTH? To detect a value that is too long, LINELENGTH should be one more than the length of the longest legal line. This will allow us to store any legal line and to detect lines that have too many characters.

How does detecting legal values fit into a procedure? Just as we used the procedure ReadRoman in *Roman Calculator Construction*, we package the input code here into a procedure ReadLine:

```
procedure ReadLine (var line: LineType; var length: integer);
var
    ch: char;
begin
    length := 0;
    while not eoln do begin
        read (ch);
        length := length + 1;
        if length <= LINELENGTH then begin
            line [length] := ch;
        end;
    end;
```

```
        readln;
    end;
```

What happens if the input is illegal?

If the input is illegal the program should print an error message. We decide to test legality in a boolean function called IsLegal, similar to that used in *The Calendar Shop* program, and update the main loop as follows:

```
repeat
    prompt for input;
    ReadLine (line, length);
    if not IsLegal (line, length) then begin
        print an error message;
    end;
until IsLegal (line, length);
```

❧

■ *Testing* 5.5 What error message does your Pascal environment produce if, when running a program, you type a letter when an integer is expected?

■ *Testing* 5.6 Does the text editor on your system impose a limit on the length of a line? If so, how does it handle a line that's too long?

■ ▤ *Modification* 5.7 The input-handling loop includes two calls to IsLegal, where only one is necessary. Modify the code to save the result of the first call to IsLegal in a boolean variable, and then to check the saved result when determining whether or not to continue looping.

Analysis 5.8 What is the advantage of using a boolean function in the input loop?

Modifying the *Check That Number!* Program

**What are illegal inputs to *Check That Number?*

The program for *Check That Number!* has an input of exactly four digits and nothing else. The IsLegal function can thus check length, then check each of the four characters to make sure they are digits.

```
function IsLegal (line: LineType; length: integer): boolean;
var
    k: integer;
begin
    IsLegal := true;
    if length <> 4 then begin
        IsLegal := false;
    end else begin
        for k := 1 to 4 do begin
            if not IsDigit (line[k]) then begin
                IsLegal := false;
            end;
        end;
    end;
end;
```

What template is used for checking the digits?

Checking for digits is an instance of the template "process every element of an array." Here the "processing" is making sure it's a digit. Making Is-Digit a function with an informative name communicates that it performs a well-defined activity and makes the code clearer as well.

Stop & Predict ➤ *Write the* IsDigit *function. Recycle code from* Check That Number!

What are good test cases?

Testing for illegal data requires a comprehensive set of illegal data, best generated using the black-box approach. For this program we start with typical cases with four digits to make sure that the program still works. Then we try extreme cases.

To find the extremes, it helps to consider numeric quantities associated with the input, and to choose data for which these quantities are as small and as large as possible. One such quantity is the *length* of the input. Thus the extremes are an input line that's as long as possible and another that's as short as possible. Since we're worried about illegal data, we must also check lines that are 1 character too long and 1 character too short. with incorrect numbers of digits. These are cases with 0, 3, and 5 digits.

Two other quantities associated with the input are the *position in the line* at which an error can occur, and the *number of digits* in the line. We need test cases with the position as small and as large as possible, i.e. with nondigits at the front, at the back, and as the only input. We should also test lines containing all digits (that's the typical case) and with no digits.

The complete *Check That Number!* program, with error checking, appears in the Pascal Code section.

Stop & Help ➤ *Devise test data in the categories just described, and test the program.*

◄

🖫 *Analysis* 5.9 Why should the length check precede the digit-checking loop?

🖬🖫 *Debugging* 5.10 What is wrong with the following code for the digit-checking loop?

```
for k := 1 to 4 do begin
    Legal := Digit (line[k]);
end;
```

Explain the circumstances under which it would cause a different answer to be returned.

🖬🖫 *Modification* 5.11 On many Pascal systems, it is possible to signal end-of-input from the keyboard. The program just designed will crash or enter an infinite loop if this is done. Using Pascal's eof function, modify the program to detect and handle end-of-input signaled by the user.

🖬🖫 *Modification* 5.12 The code that checks that if characters in the line are digits need not check all the characters, since it is an error if *any* nondigits appear in the line. Recode the loop as a while or repeat loop that stops executing when a nondigit is encountered in the line.

📘 💾 *Modification* 5.13 Modify the code to print, for each nondigit in the line, a message informing the user of the position of the nondigit.

Modifying *Banners With CLASS* and *The Calendar Shop*

What are illegal inputs to *Banners With CLASS* and *The Calendar Shop*?

The *Banners With CLASS* program has two inputs. One is a "bounded" integer—an integer bounded by specified values. The other is a set of six letters. We'll start with the latter.

How can the letters in *Banners With CLASS* be checked?

One line of input to *Banners With CLASS* should contain exactly six letters chosen from the set 'P', 'A', 'S', 'C', and 'L'. Checking this line is just like checking the input to *Check That Number!*

Stop & Help ➤ *Write a boolean function called* IsLegalLine *that checks a line of letters to see that there are exactly six characters on the line and that they all are either* 'P', 'A', 'S', 'C', *or* 'L'.

The Calendar Shop program also reads a bounded integer. A general subprogram that returns a legal integer will thus be useful in both programs and probably in others as well. Its code can be altered if necessary to check that the integer is in the valid range. We will design a procedure called ReadInInteger— consistent with Pascal's readln—that returns a legal integer value in its single parameter.

How can bounded integers be checked?

To be legal, a bounded integer needs to be composed of digits and in the specified range. To be consistent with integer input in Pascal, the program should ignore blanks that appear before the integer.

What are alternatives for decomposing the input and testing of an integer?

Alternatives for reading and testing integers include the following.

Ignoring the leading blanks in the line:
    read a line, ignoring leading blanks;
    check that it consists entirely of digits;
    if so, then
        convert it to an integer value;
        check if the integer value is in range;

Storing the leading blanks in the line:
    read a line;
    check that it consists entirely of blanks followed by digits;
    if so, then
        convert it to an integer value;
        check if the integer value is in range;

Storing, then removing leading blanks in the line:
read a line;
remove the leading blanks;
check that it consists entirely of digits;
if so, then
convert it to an integer value;
check if the integer value is in range;

Since there are several ways for an input not to represent an integer, each of the alternatives requires that extra code be added to the error-checking loop designed in the previous section.

Stop & Predict ➤   *Which of the three alternatives seems best? Why?*

Stop & Predict ➤   *In which alternative can the user provide a sequence of blanks followed by a sequence of digits that results in the program not returning the numeric value? How can this happen?*

Which decomposition should be chosen? The easiest alternative to implement is the "storing and removing blanks" decomposition because each step is an easy array operation. To use an array, however, we must know its length in advance. No matter what length we choose, an obnoxious or obtuse user can provide more blanks than the array can hold. If the line array is not long enough to store all the blanks, the program may crash, or at least not be able to store all the digits.

It seems better to ignore the leading blanks, so we choose the first decomposition above.

How are the nonblank characters in a line read? The input step should skip leading blanks and read the remaining characters into an array. Leading blanks are easily detected. However, there are two ways for the blank-skipping loop to terminate: either a nonblank is read or the end of the line is encountered.

Stop & Predict ➤   *How can tests for blanks and for end-of-line be combined?*

How can a while loop be used to test for blanks and end-of-line? The problem with using a while loop to skip leading blanks is that eoln must be tested *before* input is done, whereas blanks can only be detected *after* a character is read. Combining these tests will be complicated and hard to understand. To test for both eoln and for blanks, we instead use a boolean variable done along with a while not done loop.

Within the loop, the various conditions for termination are tested in sequence, and the done variable is set appropriately. We alter the ReadLine code from the previous section as follows:

```
done := false;  {not done yet}
while not done do begin
    if eoln then begin
        done := true;
    end else begin
```

```
        read (ch);
        if ch <> BLANK then begin
            done := true;
        end;
    end;
end;
```

A constant called BLANK, already used in *The Calendar Shop* program, is a more descriptive way to represent a blank character than an unnamed quoted blank.

Stop & Consider ➤   *Explain why the above loop is sure to terminate.*

Stop & Predict ➤   *When the loop terminates, what do you know about the contents of* ch*?*

How is the rest of the line read into the line **array?**   To finish designing code that reads the line, we must analyze its **postcondition**, the condition that is true at the end of the loop just written. When the blank-skipping loop terminates, either ch contains the first nonblank character on the line, or eoln is true.

Stop & Predict ➤   *Can the array-filling code come right after the blank-skipping code?*

Appending the array-filling code immediately after the loop would give the following result:

```
length := 0;
while not eoln do begin
    read (ch);
    length := length + 1;
    if length <= LINELENGTH then begin
        line [length] := ch;
    end;
end;
```

What must be done to the array-filling code to make it usable?   The **preconditions** of the array-filling code—the conditions that must be true immediately before the code for it to work correctly—do not match the postconditions of the blank-skipping code.

Postcondition of blank-skipping code: eoln or (ch <> BLANK)
Precondition of input-and-store loop: No characters have yet been read from the line.

If ch were known to contain a nonblank character, then it and the rest of the line could be stored as follows:

```
line [1] := ch;
length := 1;
while not eoln do begin
    read (ch);
    length := length + 1;
    if length <= LINELENGTH then begin
        line [length] := ch;
    end;
end;
```

This loop would then be the same as the loop from ReadLine, except that it would fill the second and following characters of line rather than the first and following characters.

This code works only if ch contains a nonblank. So now the problem is to determine if ch contains a nonblank. Can we test it? No, since it wasn't initialized. Can we check eoln instead? No, because it may happen that eoln is true *and* ch contains a nonblank.

Stop & Help ➤   *Under what conditions will* eoln *be true and* ch *contain a nonblank?*

To determine whether to add elements to line, we could modify the blank-skipping code in two ways, either by initializing ch to a blank or by setting length to 1 when a nonblank is first encountered. Code that skips blanks will probably be useful in the future, so we initialize ch. References to a variable—length—that really has nothing to do with the blank-skipping would clutter the code and make it more difficult to recycle in other programs.

How is line checked to consist only of digits?

Once line is filled, it must be checked to make sure that its characters are all digits. We did this already for the *Check That Number!* program, and we recycle that code:

```
for k := 1 to length do begin
    if not IsDigit(line[k]) then begin
        IsLegal := false;
    end;
end;
```

How are the digits in line converted to an integer?

Converting the digits in line to a single integer value involves extracting the numeric digit values and computing the integer. First we convert characters to integers, as done in the *Check That Number!* program.

Stop & Help ➤   *Using the code from* Check That Number! *as a model, write a function called* DigitValue *that returns the numeric value of a character digit.*

How are digit values combined to get an integer?

Combining the various digit values into an integer value requires an accumulation loop similar to that used in *Roman Calculator Construction*. The accumulation loop will use a sum variable and add each digit value in turn. Each time through the loop, one more digit will be "attached" to the accumulated value.

We consider an example, 5193. These characters will be stored in the line array as follows:

line   length

        1 2 3 4 5 6   4

       | '5' | '1' | '9' | '3' | ? | ? | ... | ? |

We want a loop that successively accumulates the first character in line, then the second character, and so on into an integer value, as shown in the following sequence of values:

Number of times through loop	Digit to accumulate	Accumulation value
1	5	5
2	1	51
3	9	519
4	3	5193

As noted in *Check That Number!* each digit in a decimal numeral represents a power of 10. Thus, to get from one accumulation value to the next, the first value should be multiplied by 10, then the new digit value should be added. Here's the code:

```
sum := 0;
for k := 1 to length do begin
    sum := sum * 10 + DigitValue (line[k]);
end;
```

Stop & Help ➤

Code the conversion of digits to an integer as a function called IntegerValue.

How are the various code segments combined?

All steps of the decomposition of the process of reading and error checking an integer have now been coded. The only remaining design decision concerns the arrangement of the code into subprograms.

Subprograms should be easy to reuse and should help make the code readable. Thus, each subprogram should perform one easily described action and should not perform actions that would inhibit use in another context.

These criteria suggest four subprograms: ReadTrimmedLine, IsAllDigits, IntegerValue, and IsInRange. Since there are several ways for the input to be illegal, we code the body of the read-and-error-check loop in similar fashion to the blank-skipping loop, using a boolean variable called error.

```
procedure ReadInteger (var n: integer);
var
    error: boolean;
    line: LineType;
    length: integer;
begin
    repeat
        error := false;
        write (prompt message);
        ReadTrimmedLine (line, length);
        if (length = 0) or (length > LINELENGTH) then begin
            error := true;
        end else if not IsAllDigits (line, length) then begin
            error := true;
        end else begin
```

```
                    n := IntegerValue (line, length);
                    if not IsInRange (n) then begin
                        error := true;
                    end;
                end;
                if error then begin
                    writeln (error message);
                end;
            until not error;
    end;
```

At the end of this loop, the parameter n contains the integer value typed by the user.

Stop & Help ➤ *Add the prompt message, the in-range check, and the error message appropriate for the* Banners With CLASS *program.*

Stop & Help ➤ *Add the prompt message, the in-range check, and the error message appropriate for the* Calendar Shop *program.*

How is the code summarized? The various error checks focus increasingly specifically on the input. Their narrowing action is represented by the diagram below. A check is made to see if there are any nonblanks in the input, then another to see if the nonblanks represent a number, then (after conversion) a third to make sure the number is in the specified range.

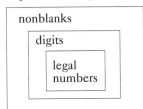

The Pascal Code section displays the use of the error-checking code along with arrays in the *Banners With CLASS* program. Error checking may be similarly included in the *Calendar Shop* program.

How should the code be tested and debugged? As in previous programs, we test and debug the code a piece at a time. We start with a main program that repeatedly calls ReadlnInteger and prints the result:

```
begin
    while true do begin
        ReadlnInteger (n);
        writeln ('value read is ', n);
    end;
end.
```

Alternatively, we could use a for loop to call ReadlnInteger a specific number of times, or use a test for a specific input value as an indication to stop.

ReadInteger calls four subprograms, ReadTrimmedLine, IsAllDigits, Integer-Value, and IsInRange. IsAllDigits and IsInRange are short, and the code for Is-AllDigits was tested in the previous section, so we decide not to test them individually. That leaves ReadTrimmedLine and IntegerValue.

What code should be tested first?

One might test these two subprograms individually in a variety of ways. We choose to test ReadTrimmedLine by calling it from ReadInteger, to code IntegerValue initially as a stub that always returns 0, and to code In-Range always to return true. For debugging output, we add a statement that prints the line and the length after returning from ReadTrimmedLine.

What test values should be used?

As before, we consider numeric quantities associated with the input to generate extreme cases. The number of leading blanks and the number of nonblanks in the line are two such quantities. Thus we test ReadTrimmed-Line on lines with 0, 1, and 2 leading blanks, in combination with lines containing 0 nonblanks, 1 nonblank, the maximum allowed number of nonblanks, and 1 more than the maximum allowed number of nonblanks.

Stop & Help ➤   *Generate a set of test data for* ReadTrimmedLine.

How should the remaining code be tested?

Once ReadTrimmedLine is tested and debugged, we can replace the stubs for IntegerValue and InRange. Test data for these routines should involve input with one digit, input with a maximum number of digits, and input at both sides of the boundaries of the legal range of values.

Stop & Help ➤   *Identify typical and boundary cases for testing the letter size input to the* Banners With CLASS *program. Use them to test the program in the Pascal Code section.*

Stop & Help ➤   *Identify typical and boundary cases for the* Calendar Shop *program.*

🔲 *Testing*   5.14   Run some experiments to find out if your Pascal environment limits the number of blanks that may precede integer input; if it does limit the number of leading blanks, determine the maximum number it allows.

🔲 *Analysis*   5.15   One might argue that the loop in IsAllDigits should stop when it detects a character in line that's not a digit, and that therefore the loop should be coded as a while or repeat. What do you think? Justify your choice.

🔲 *Analysis*   5.16   The IntegerValue function does not guard against constructing a value greater than maxint. What other part of the program can be used to ensure that no attempt is made to construct an integer that exceeds maxint?

🔲🔲 *Modification*   5.17   Fix IntegerValue to return maxint if the contents of line represents a larger value.

🖥 💾 *Modification* 5.18 Reorganize the code to check, before calling IntegerValue, that the characters of line represent a value at most maxint.

Application 5.19 Describe how blank-skipping code could be used in a program that identified words in text.

One Way to Modify *Roman Calculator Construction*

What should be the first step of the modified ReadRoman?

Error checking the *Roman Calculator Construction* program involves modifying its ReadRoman procedure to return only legal Roman numerals. As with the other programs, this should start with a call to ReadLine to read the Roman numeral into a character array.

Stop & Help ➤

How long should the line array be? That is, what is the longest Roman numeral whose value is less than 4000?

What are illegal Roman numerals?

Illegal Roman numerals are those that violate the rules for Roman numerals. Recall the description of a legal Roman numeral:

- All its characters are Roman digits (M, D, C, L, X, V, I).

- No more than three occurrences of M, C, X, or I may appear consecutively, and no more than one D, L, or V may appear at all.

- C may prefix M or D; the digits following the prefixed digit represent a value no more than 99. X may prefix C or L but not both; the following digits represent a value no more than 9. I may prefix X or V; the prefixed digit must end the numeral.

- Roman digits are written in nonascending order (except for prefixes).

What are the alternatives for testing the legality of a Roman numeral?

Two possible ways of approaching this problem might be called the **rule-violation approach** and the **rule-confirmation approach**. We can test the legality of a string either by making sure it has all the characteristics of a Roman numeral or by describing each step of its construction using rules of building Roman numerals. With the rule-violation approach, we list a number of characteristics of legal Roman numerals and check to see if any of them are violated. With the rule-confirmation approach, we try to *build* a legal Roman numeral with the same digits as the one in question; if we succeed, then the Roman numeral is legal. The rule-violation approach is appropriate when the set of characteristics to be checked covers all possible cases. The rule-confirmation approach is appropriate when the rules for construction are well specified.

The rule-violation approach starts with the conditions listed above. They describe a legal Roman numeral, but they don't tell us how to build one.

If the conditions are complete, however—and we think they are—any sequence of Roman digits that satisfies them all is legal.

How is the rule-violation version of IsRoman designed?

The structure of the checking function, which we'll call IsRoman, is merely a sequence of tests:

```
if not IsLegalRomanDigits(line, length) then begin
    IsRoman := false;
end else if not IsLegalCounts(line, length) then begin
    IsRoman := false;
end else if not IsLegalPrefixes(line, length) then begin
    IsRoman := false;
end else if not LegalOrder(line, length) then begin
    IsRoman := false;
end else begin
    IsRoman := true;
end;
```

Note that all the functions return a *positive* result. We code them all the same for consistency; we return positive results because people find them easier to understand than functions that return negative results. The code is clearer as a result.

Stop & Consider ➤ *How would IsRoman be coded as a single assignment statement whose right side is a boolean expression that uses the and operator? What would be a potential problem with coding it in this way?*

How is IsLegalRomanDigits coded?

The IsLegalRomanDigits function merely checks to see if all the characters in the line are 'I', 'V', 'X', 'L', 'C', 'D', or 'M'. This is almost the same as checking that all the characters in the line are 'P', 'A', 'S', 'C', or 'L'. We can copy the code from the revised *Banners With CLASS* program and modify it appropriately.

Stop & Help ➤ *Write IsLegalRomanDigits.*

The remaining checks look more complicated. There are two sets of rules for Roman digits, one for I, X, C, and M, another for V, L, and D. Even counting the occurrences of a Roman digit is not straightforward; for example, both XXXIX and XXXX contain four X's, but only one of them is legal. A numeral containing X as a prefix can contain only one other X. The other rules about prefixes complicate matters still further.

Stop & Consider ➤ *List the Roman numerals up to 49 and describe the rules governing legal placement of X.*

How can the prefix tests be simplified?

In earlier case studies, we applied the principle of reducing the problem to problems that are easier to solve. Here, we apply this principle to the analysis: we convert the line to something that's easier to analyze. One approach is to replace each pair consisting of a prefix and the prefixed digit by a single new character. The rule for I, X, C, and M in the new representation is simpler; each can occur at most three times, and occurrences must be consecutive.

The following code results:

```
if not IsLegalRomanDigits(line, length) then begin
    IsRoman := false;
end else begin
    ReplacePrefixes(line, length);
    if not IsLegalCounts(line, length) then begin
        IsRoman := false;
    end else if not IsLegalOrder(line, length) then begin
        IsRoman := false;
    end else begin
        IsRoman := true;
    end;
end;
```

Will it work to substitute single digits for prefix combinations?

Before starting on the design of ReplacePrefixes, we need to make sure that this idea will work. Thus we move to IsLegalCounts and IsLegalOrder, assuming tentatively that the digit pairs IV, IX, XL, XC, CD, and CM have been replaced by the characters '1', '2', '3', '4', '5', and '6' respectively. (Any six characters that aren't Roman digits would be appropriate.)

How do the new digits behave compared with the original Roman digits?

The replacement characters act like V, L, and D in that each can appear only once. They differ from V, L, and D in that the digits that may follow them are constrained. For instance, VI is legal, but 1I and 2I (the transformed versions of IVI and IXI) aren't. Moreover, pairs of replacement characters are also limited. The numbers 1 and 2 can't occur together; nor can 3 and 4 or 5 and 6. We summarize the conditions on all the digits in Table 5.1. Where multiple occurrences of a digit are allowed, they must be consecutive.

How should the error-checking functions be separated?

Ideally, we can split error checking into a number of small steps that correspond either to templates or to short, easily designed code segments. The table suggests one such step. IsLegalCount can be coded to count the occurrences of each digit, but shouldn't worry about whether or not multiple occurrences are consecutive. Nonconsecutive occurrences will be caught by the order checking; for instance, MMXM will be flagged as illegal because an M may not follow an X.

How can an array be used to see if two digits are correctly ordered?

Table 5.1 also suggests a way to use arrays to check that digits are correctly ordered. The first column forms an array in which the original Roman digits precede every Roman digit they are allowed to follow. Thus if we look up two consecutive digits in the array

1	2	3	4	5	6	7
'I'	'V'	'X'	'L'	'C'	'D'	'M'

and the second digit occurs earlier in the array than the first, the two digits are in correct order in the Roman numeral.

Digit	Number of times it may occur	Digits that may follow it
I	3	none
1 (formerly IV)	1	none
V	1	I
2 (formerly IX)	1	none
X	3	I, 1, V, 2
3 (formerly XL)	1	I, 1, V, 2
L	1	I, 1, V, 2, X
4 (formerly XC)	1	I, 1, V, 2
C	3	I, 1, V, 2, X, 3, L, 4
5 (formerly CD)	1	I, 1, V, 2, X, 3, L, 4
D	1	I, 1, V, 2, X, 3, L, 4, C
6 (formerly CM)	1	I, 1, V, 2, X, 3, L, 4
M	3	I, 1, V, 2, X, 3, L, 4, C, 5, D, 6

Table 5.1 *Legal orderings of Roman digits*

The next step is to figure out how the new digits fit into this scheme. First, we notice that for the purposes of checking for legality, the digits representing IV and IX act *exactly alike*, and only one can occur in a given Roman numeral. Thus we only need one digit to represent both IV and IX. The same holds for XL and XC and for CD and CM. That means that only three new digits are needed, not six, which should simplify the code somewhat.

Stop & Help ➤ *Verify that XL and CL cannot both occur in the same Roman numeral.*

Stop & Help ➤ *Rewrite Table 5.1 using the character '1' to represent IV and IX, the character '2' to represent XL and XC, and the character '3' to represent CD and CM.*

Second, we observe that placing the new digits in the array as shown below allows them to be checked in almost the same way as the original Roman digits.

```
 1   2   3   4   5   6   7   8   9  10
['I'|'V'|'1'|'X'|'L'|'2'|'C'|'D'|'3'|'M']
```

Stop & Help ➤ *Can V appear in a Roman numeral that has IX or IV in it?*

The exception is that each new digit can precede only those digits that occur *two or more places* before it in the array. The algorithm for checking the original Roman digits works correctly with the new digits added. We identify two conditions to apply to each pair of digits in the Roman numeral:

either the first digit is one of the original Roman digits, or it's one of the prefix pairs represented by a 1, 2, or 3.

How is ReplacePrefixes coded?

Satisfied that the scheme of replacing pairs that contain a prefix and the prefixed digit with single characters will yield a reasonable design, we return to the ReplacePrefixes procedure. ReplacePrefixes consists merely of looking at every character in the line, checking if it is a prefix, and if so replacing the pair of characters by the appropriate single character.

What template is applicable to the problem of replacing prefixes?

The template "process every element of an array" would seem to be applicable here. The "process" is to check if the element is a prefix and to replace it and its successor element if so. The template suggests the following code:

```
for k := 1 to length-1 do begin
    if line[k] is a prefix then replace line[k] and line[k+1] by a new single digit;
end;
```

Stop & Help ➤ *Why does the loop variable not go from 1 to* length?

Stop & Predict ➤ *The code has a flaw. What is it?*

How must the code suggested by the template be modified?

A problem with the code is that replacing a pair of Roman digits with a single character reduces the length of line. As written, the code checks characters past the end of the transformed Roman numeral, since changes to length within the loop do not affect the number of times the loop is executed. One can either code the replacing procedure carefully so that characters past the end of the numeral cause no harm, or code the loop in such a way that the problem does not arise. We choose the latter approach and code a while loop that simulates the for-loop code.

```
k := 1;
while k < length do begin    {length will be evaluated at every iteration}
    if line[k] is a prefix then replace line[k] and line[k+1] by a new single digit;
    k := k+1;
end;
```

How are prefixes detected?

There are three possibilities for a possible prefix, I, X, and C; the "select among alternatives" template suggests coding the body of the loop as a case statement.

```
k := 1;
while k < length do begin
    case line[k] of
        'I': if (line[k+1]='V') or (line[k+1]='X') then begin
                Replace(line, length, k, '1');
            end;
        'X': if (line[k+1]='L') or (line[k+1]='C') then begin
                Replace(line, length, k, '2');
            end;
        'C': if (line[k+1]='D') or (line[k+1]='M') then begin
                Replace(line, length, k, '3');
            end;
```

```
          'V', 'L', 'D', 'M': ; {don't do anything for these}
      end;
      k := k+1;
  end;
```

How are prefixes replaced?

The code uses the name Replace for the digit replacement procedure. This procedure will have to receive the line, its length, the position at which the replacement is to occur, and the new character as arguments. After storing the replacement character in the specified position, it must move the subsequent elements down one position. The processing of the replacement of the first prefix in MCMXXIV is illustrated below, with the array cells or variables that change in each step outlined in bold.

Storing the new character:

Shifting subsequent elements down one position:

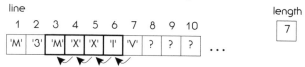

Contents of line and length after replacement:

line

1	2	3	4	5	6	7	8	9	10
'M'	'3'	'X'	'X'	'I'	'V'	'V'	?	?	?	...

length

6

Storing the new character and decrementing the length are easy. Shifting the elements down one position results from tailoring the "process every element of an array" template; the action performed is "copy the next element into the current position," and it's applied not to the entire array but only to the elements from the specified position to the next-to-last. Here's the code for Replace:

```
procedure Replace(var line: LineType; var length: integer;
    pos: integer; replacement: char);
var
    k: integer;
begin
    line[pos] := replacement;
    for k := pos+1 to length-1 do begin
        line[k] := line[k+1];
    end;
    length := length-1;
end;
```

How are the digit counts determined?

We move on to IsLegalCounts. Tallying every Roman digit in the line is another application of the "process every element of an array" template.

IsLegalCounts could be organized as ten loops, one to count the occurrences of each Roman digit. There is a better way, however, that uses an array of counts indexed by characters, in the same way as the third version of the *Roman Calculator Construction* program did. The counting is done by a loop that, for each element of line, adds 1 to the corresponding element of the count array:

```
for k := 1 to length do begin
    counts[line[k]] := counts[line[k]] + 1;
end;
```

Here line[k] is used both as an *element* of an array (line) and as an *index* into another array (counts).

How is IsLegalCounts coded?

The loop is preceded by initialization of the counts array (only ten elements need be initialized, since line is known to contain only legal Roman digits when IsLegalCounts is called) and followed by testing the counts to make sure they don't exceed the limits. The following code, though somewhat inelegant, is straightforward:

```
function IsLegalCounts (line: LineType; length: integer): boolean;
var
    k: integer;
    counts: array[char] of integer;
begin
    counts['I'] := 0;  counts['V'] := 0;
    counts['X'] := 0;  counts['L'] := 0;
    counts['C'] := 0;  counts['D'] := 0;  counts['M'] := 0;
    counts['1'] := 0;  counts['2'] := 0;  counts['3'] := 0;
    for k := 1 to length do begin
        counts[line[k]] := counts[line[k]] + 1;
    end;
    IsLegalCounts := (counts['I'] <= 3) and (counts['V']<=1)
        and (counts['X'] <= 3) and (counts['L'] <= 1)
        and (counts['C'] <= 3) and (counts['D'] <= 1)
        and (counts['M'] <= 3) and (counts['1'] <= 1)
        and (counts['2'] <= 1) and (counts['3'] <= 1);
end;
```

Stop & Consider ➤ *What makes the code inelegant? Suggest a way to improve it.*

How is the order of the digits checked?

Finally, we consider IsLegalOrder. Here's the pseudocode for this function:

```
for k := 1 to length-1 do begin
    if line[k+1] can't legally follow line[k], then IsLegalOrder := false;
end;
```

The digit line[k+1] can legally follow one of the original Roman digits in line[k] if line[k+1]'s position in the array of all the Roman digits precedes line[k]'s position in that array. A digit can follow '1', '2', or '3' if its position in the array of all the Roman digits is at least three before the '1', '2', or '3'.

How is the position of a digit in the array of digits located?

A function to search an array of characters for a particular character is required. A straightforward implementation uses the "process every element of an array" (again!):

```
function Location (ch: char; line: LineType; length: integer): integer;
var
    k: integer;
begin
    for k := 1 to length do begin
        if line[k] = ch then begin
            Location := k;
        end;
    end;
end;
```

What's wrong with examining every array element?

One problem with applying the "process every element of an array" template is that it may not be desirable to process *every* element, especially in long arrays. The Location function just coded will continue to check characters in the string, even after it has found what it's looking for. The operation of searching an array appears frequently, and it is likely that we will be able to recycle Location's code in future programs. For long strings, however, we will want a more efficient version, so we choose to invest a bit more time here to produce it.

What code searches only as far in the array as necessary?

The code will include a loop that checks elements of the string argument. The loop should keep going either until the desired value is found or until all elements of the array have been checked. The situation is similar to the blank-skipping process we encountered in the previous section: there were two ways to end the loop, either by finding a nonblank or by encountering the end of the line. Here is that code:

```
done := false;
while not done do begin
    if eoln then begin
        done := true;  {no more line to check}
    end else begin
        read (ch);  {get next character}
        if ch <> BLANK then begin
            done := true;  {found what we're looking for}
        end;
    end;
end;
```

And here is how we modify it:

```
done := false;
k := 1;
while not done do begin
    if k > length then begin
        done := true;  {no more array elements to check}
    end else if line[k] = ch then begin
        done := true;  {found what we're looking for}
    end else begin
        k := k + 1;  {move to next array element}
```

```
      end;
  end;
```

In both code segments, the first thing to check is whether there were more elements to compare. Subsequent steps were rearranged because there is no need to "read" the next element of an array.

Both ways of exiting the search loop should be accounted for before the Location function returns; something will have to be returned if the specified value is not found in the array. This should not happen in this program, since earlier code has ensured that all the elements of the Roman numeral are Roman digits. As a debugging aid, however, we'll add code to print an error message if the character isn't in the string.

How is IsLegalOrder coded?

If LineType is declared as a *packed array* of characters, Standard Pascal allows the use of a string constant as the LineType argument. (Most versions of Pascal allow somewhat more flexible use of strings.) We take advantage of this shorthand notation and package the code into functions as follows:

```
function InOrder (romanDigit1, romanDigit2: char): boolean;
const
    ALLDIGITS = 'IV1XL2CD3M            ';
begin
    if (romanDigit1 = '1') or (romanDigit1 = '2')
        or (romanDigit1 = '3') then begin
        InOrder := Location(romanDigit1, ALLDIGITS, 10)
            >= Location(romanDigit2, ALLDIGITS, 10) + 3;
    end else begin
        InOrder := Location(romanDigit1, ALLDIGITS, 10)
            >= Location(romanDigit2, ALLDIGITS, 10);
    end;
end;

function IsLegalOrder (line: LineType; length: integer): boolean;
var
    k: integer;
begin
    IsLegalOrder := true;
    for k := 1 to length - 1 do begin
        if not InOrder(line[k], line[k + 1]) then begin
            IsLegalOrder := false;
        end;
    end;
end;
```

Note that IsLegalOrder checks all consecutive pairs of elements in the array, even though it could stop early if there's an error. The difference between this situation and that of searching an array is that (a) we *expect* to check the whole array if the Roman numeral is legal—inefficiency only appears in the error case—and (b) this is a special-purpose routine intended for handling relatively short Roman numerals, so straightforward coding is more important than efficiency.

The complete set of functions appears in the Pascal Code section.

How is the code for the rule-violation version tested?

All the functions can easily be tested individually and in combination. We include if DEBUGGING then ... code in the more complicated routines to print information about the values they return: the line with prefixes removed by RemovePrefixes, the contents of the count array in IsLegalCounts, the position of out-of-order digits in IsLegalOrder, and the error check that failed in IsRoman. A less experienced programmer may wish to add debugging output to the other functions as well.

The search and replace functions can be tested with data that deal with the typical situation, involving something in the middle of the array, and the extreme situations, involving the ends of the array. IsLegalCounts should be tested with Roman numerals that contain all the digits, with the maximum number and one greater than the maximum number of occurrences.

Why are test results not so convincing for this code?

Once we've tested the individual functions, what then? In this problem, knowing that the various components of the program work is not as encouraging as it was in the other case studies. We have certainly eliminated a collection of illegal Roman numerals—we've caught those with illegal digits, those with too many of a particular digit, and those in which consecutive pairs of digits are out of order—but there still remains the possibility that we forgot to check some subtle illegality, perhaps involving digits that are two or more positions apart in the Roman numeral. The application of a spelling check is analogous; with a complex system of rules such as those for English spelling, it is not always possible to list every special case. Our situation is represented in diagram form (similar to an illustration earlier in this case study) as follows:

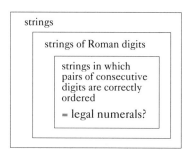

The flaw inherent in the rule-violation solution to the problem is that the resulting program is only as good as the description, which may itself be incomplete. We see that straightforward code alone is not sufficient evidence of correct code. The alternative approach to checking a Roman numeral, to be discussed next, will shed some light on how to generate a good set of test data.

🖫 *Reflection* 5.20 What test results would be sufficient to convince you that the function detected all illegal Roman numerals?

🖫 *Reflection* 5.21 What test results would be sufficient to convince you that the function correctly identified a legal Roman numeral as legal?

⬛ 🖫 *Debugging* 5.22 Insert a bug in the code that causes the function to identify an illegal Roman numeral as legal, and get a fellow programmer to find the bug. Do the same with a bug that causes the function to identify a legal Roman numeral as illegal. Which bug is easier to find?

Another Way to Modify *Roman Calculator Construction*

What are the benefits of the rule-confirmation approach?

The rule-confirmation approach to checking a Roman numeral is potentially more encouraging. A program based on the rules for constructing a Roman numeral could reveal either the rule that was violated by an illegal numeral or the steps by which the Roman numeral was legally constructed. The latter is much more convincing evidence that no subtle error conditions were overlooked. We turn now to this approach to the design of IsRoman, focusing on the rules for building Roman numerals.

What are the rules for constructing Roman numerals?

The digits of a Roman numeral can be grouped into sequences of the same digit, prefix combinations, and single digits. For example, suppose that a Roman numeral representing a value of 3999 or less starts with some number of M's. Then the M's can be grouped, and what follows them has to represent a value of 999 or less. Continuing the process, a value of 999 or less might start with the prefix combination CM. Those two Roman digits can be grouped, and what follows them must represent a value of 99 or less. The diagram below shows the digit grouping for the numeral MMMCMLXIV:

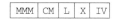

Table 5.2 contains an analysis of all the cases.

How can the rules help with the design?

One way to use these rules as a basis of a program is to design a collection of boolean functions that, when given a line and a position in the line, return true exactly when the contents of the line starting at the given position represent a certain kind of Roman numeral. One might, for instance, have thirteen procedures, one for each rule, named IsLegalAtMost3999, IsLegalAtMost999, IsLegalAtMost899, and so on.

How do the rules suggest a state-based design?

Another way is to organize the program as a loop that moves from state to state as it advances through the line, depending on what characters the

A value at most	either is	or is
3999	one, two, or three M's, perhaps followed by a value at most 999	a value at most 999
999	CM, perhaps followed by a value at most 99	a value at most 899
899	D, perhaps followed by a value at most 399	a value at most 499
499	CD, perhaps followed by a value at most 99	a value at most 399
399	one, two, or three C's, perhaps followed by a value at most 99	a value at most 99
99	XC, perhaps followed by a value at most 9	a value at most 89
89	L, perhaps followed by a value at most 39	a value at most 49
49	XL, perhaps followed by a value at most 9	a value at most 39
39	one, two, or three X's, perhaps followed by a value at most 9	a value at most 9
9	IX	a value at most 8
8	V, perhaps followed by a value at most 3	a value at most 4
4	IV	a value at most 3
3	one, two, or three I's	

Table 5.2 *Rules for constructing Roman numerals*

line contains. A **state** is a situation. In this program, a state might represent the situation "I'm looking for a Roman numeral representing a value at most 89." In a state-based program, the contents of a variable indicates what state the program is in. The loop body is essentially a *case* statement, one case for each state, in which the next character in the line is examined and the state updated. In pseudocode, using variables named state and linePos (the position in line), it looks like this:

```
state := the start state;
linePos := 1;
while state isn't the "done" state or the "error" state, do the following:
    case state of
        "looking for a value at most 3999":
            examine line[linePos] and set state to a new state value;
        "looking for a value at most 999":
            examine line[linePos] and set state to a new state value;
            ⋮
        "looking for a value at most 3":
            examine line[linePos] and set state to a new state value;
        end;
end;
```

One may view a state-based program as similar to a house. Rooms in the house are analogous to states in the program; wandering from room to room is like changing the state variable from one value to another.

Neither one of these approaches looks too encouraging at first glance; the idea of a large collection of boolean functions or a large case statement seems intimidating, involving too much "brute force" and not enough "elegance." Sometimes, however, it is possible to exploit commonalities in code through clever use of subprograms and arrays. Table 5.2 suggests that several of the state processing segments will resemble one another. Thus, we will attempt to use a state-based framework as a basis for Roman numeral checking.

How can a collection of states and state transitions be pictured?

When working with a state-based program, it helps to create a **state diagram** to keep track of all the possible situations and paths between them. The state diagram represents the different states by boxes and the ways to get from state to state—the **transitions**—by labeled arrows. Analogously, players of computer adventure games create maps of the various "rooms" of the adventure and the ways to get from room to room. The state diagram for the Roman numeral checker appears in Figure 5.3.

How is a value of 3999 or less checked?

Back to the program design. To start, we pick a state—the first one, "looking for a value at most 3999," seems as good as any—and see how the associated code might look. According to the table, checking if a Roman numeral represents a value of 3999 or less involves first isolating the leading M's, then analyzing the remaining Roman digits via one of the other rules. In pseudocode, we have

```
Count the leading M's;
If number of M's > 3, then state := "error detected",
     since the Roman numeral isn't legal.
If the Roman numeral is all M's, then return true.
Otherwise, return the result of checking whether
     the rest of the Roman numeral represents a value at most 999.
```

How is the number of leading M's found?

Determining the number of leading M's is the same as finding the position of the first non-M. We've already written code that does almost exactly that: the Location function in the previous section. Here's the code, modified for the purposes of the current application:

```
k := linePos;  nonMfound := false;
while not nonMfound do begin
    if k > length then begin
        nonMfound := true;
    end else if line[k] <> 'M' then begin
        nonMfound := true;
    end else begin
        k := k + 1;
    end;
end;
```

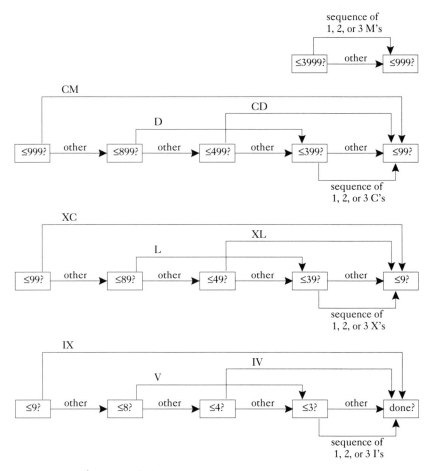

Figure 5.3 *State diagram for the Roman numeral checker*

How is the result of the M-skipping loop used?

Once the loop terminates, the variable k contains the position of the first non-M, so the expression k – linePos represents the number of leading M's. This should be at most 3. If the Roman numeral is all M's, it is legal; otherwise, the state "looking for a value at most 999" is entered to check the Roman numeral that starts at position k. The following code implements these steps.

```
if k - linePos > 3 then begin
    state := "the error state";
end else if k > length then begin
    state := "the success state";
end else begin
    linePos := k;
    state := "looking for a value at most 999";
end;
```

Stop & Help ➤   *What other states will be handled in a similar way?*

How should states be
represented in Pascal?

It makes sense here to pick a representation for states. One choice is to have a state be an integer value: "looking for a value at most 3999" would be 1, "looking for a value at most 999" 2, and so on. It would be difficult for someone reading the code to keep track of how states and integers were associated, however. A better idea is to refer to states somehow by names.

Recall that in *The Calendar Shop* Pascal's const facility allowed months to be referred to by name instead of by number. We can do the same thing here, defining constants ERROR, SUCCESS, ATMOST3999, ATMOST999, and so on down to ATMOST3. The main loop body is then

```
state := ATMOST3999;
linePos := 1;
while (state<>SUCCESS) and (state<>ERROR) do begin
    case state of
        ATMOST3999:
            examine line[linePos] and set state to a new state value;
        ATMOST999:
            examine line[linePos] and set state to a new state value;
          ⋮
        ATMOST3:
            examine line[linePos] and set state to a new state value;
    end;
end;
```

and the code for handling state ATMOST3999 will be

```
k := linePos;
nonMfound := false;
while not nonMfound do begin
    if k > length then begin
        nonMfound := true;
    end else if line[k] <> 'M' then begin
        nonMfound := true;
    end else begin
        k := k + 1;
    end;
end;
if k - linePos > 3 then begin
    state := ERROR;
end else if k > length then begin
    state := SUCCESS;
end else begin
    linePos := k;
    state := ATMOST999;
end;
```

How is a value of 999
or less checked?

We move on to design code to handle the next state, ATMOST999. Table 5.2 indicates that either such a Roman numeral starts with CM, or it represents a value of 899 or less.

The code is easy. First it checks that there are at least two Roman digits left in the line; if not, then the numeral doesn't represent anything in the 900's, but it may represent a smaller value. If the first is C and the next is M, the rest must represent a value at most 99. Otherwise, we look for a value at most 899.

```
if linePos + 1 > length then begin
    state := ATMOST899;
end else if (line[linePos]='C') and (line[linePos+1]='M') then begin
    state := ATMOST99;
    linePos := linePos + 2;
end else begin
    state := ATMOST899;
end;
```

Stop & Help ➤

How is a value of 899 or less checked?

What would happen if the check for two remaining digits was omitted?

Next, we handle ATMOST899. The code should check for a leading D after making sure there are Roman digits remaining in the line. (No more remaining means success.) The digits following a D must represent a value of 399 or less; if there is no leading D, the existing digits must represent a value of 499 or less. The code is similar to that for ATMOST999:

```
if linePos > length then begin
    state := SUCCESS;
end else if (line[linePos] = 'D') then begin
    state := ATMOST399;
    linePos := linePos + 1;
end else begin
    state := ATMOST499;
end;
```

How are the other states coded?

Continuing with the remaining functions, we find that the code to handle ATMOST499, ATMOST49, and ATMOST4 are all very similar. We also find close similarities among ATMOST3999, ATMOST399, ATMOST39, and ATMOST3, among ATMOST999, ATMOST99, and ATMOST9, and among ATMOST899, ATMOST89, and ATMOST8.

The only tricky part comes in ATMOST9 and ATMOST4, when the sequences IX and IV must be the last characters on the line. We handle this by adding a state called ATMOST0. Code to handle this state consists merely of checking that linePos is equal to length + 1; if so, state := SUCCESS, otherwise state := ERROR.

Stop & Help ➤

How can the code be simplified?

Write the code for ATMOST3.

We now have a lot of code. We'd like to have less. First, we examine the similarities among the code for ATMOST3999, ATMOST399, ATMOST39, and ATMOST3. The search for a non-M or non-C or whatever can be packaged in a function, in the same way the Location code was packaged in the previous section. We'll call the function PositionOfNon; it takes as arguments the line, its length, the current position, and the character to search for something other than. After inserting a call to that function, we have the following pattern:

```
k := PositionOfNon(line, length, linePos, ①);
if k - linePos > 3 then begin
    state := ERROR;
end else if k > length then begin
    state := SUCCESS;
end else begin
    linePos := k;
    state := ②;
end;
```

① stands for a Roman digit; ② stands for a state name. The table below indicates what should be substituted for ① and ② in each case.

Current state	To be substituted for ①	To be substituted for ②
ATMOST3999	'M'	ATMOST999
ATMOST399	'C'	ATMOST99
ATMOST39	'X'	ATMOST9
ATMOST3	'I'	ATMOST0

How can the code pattern be represented in a procedure?

Thus we can make a procedure called Update3x, called whenever we are looking for a value at most 3999, 399, 39, or 3:

```
procedure Update3x(line: LineType; length: integer;
    var linePos: integer; digit: char;
    var state: StateType; newState: StateType);
var
    k: integer;
begin
    k := PositionOfNon(line, length, linePos, digit);
    if k - linePos > 3 then begin
        state := ERROR;
    end else if k > length then begin
        state := SUCCESS;
    end else begin
        linePos := k;
        state := newState;
    end;
end;
```

Similar procedures called Update9x, Update8x, and Update4x can be written to unify the code for states ATMOST999, ATMOST99, and ATMOST9, for ATMOST899, ATMOST89, and ATMOST8, and for ATMOST499, ATMOST49, and ATMOST4. The main loop is then coded as follows:

```
state := ATMOST3999;
linePos := 1;
while (state<>SUCCESS) and (state<>ERROR) do begin
    case state of
        ATMOST3999:Update3x(line,length, linePos, 'M', state, ATMOST999);
```

```
ATMOST999: Update9x(line, length, linePos, 'C', 'M',
               state, ATMOST99, ATMOST899);
ATMOST899: Update8x(line, length, linePos, 'D',
               state, ATMOST399, ATMOST499);
ATMOST499: Update4x(line, length, linePos, 'C', 'D',
               state, ATMOST99, ATMOST399);
ATMOST399: Update3x(line, length, linePos, 'C', state, ATMOST99);
ATMOST99: Update9x(line, length, linePos, 'X', 'C',
               state, ATMOST9, ATMOST89);
ATMOST89: Update8x(line, length, linePos, 'L',
               state, ATMOST39, ATMOST49);
ATMOST49: Update4x(line, length, linePos, 'X', 'L',
               state, ATMOST9, ATMOST39);
ATMOST39: Update3x(line, length, linePos, 'X', state, ATMOST9);
ATMOST9: Update9x(line, length, linePos, 'I', 'X',
               state, ATMOST0, ATMOST8);
ATMOST9: Update8x(line, length, linePos, 'V',
               state, ATMOST3, ATMOST4);
ATMOST4: Update4x(line, length, linePos, 'I', 'V',
               state, ATMOST0, ATMOST3);
ATMOST3: Update3x(line, length, linePos, 'I', state, ATMOST0);
   end;
end;
```

How can procedure parameters be eliminated?

Next we notice that the "at most" value corresponding to a given state can be *computed* from the value for the previous state, and that furthermore the Roman digit(s) to be checked for can be computed from that value. Table 5.4 shows the possibilities for going from one "at most" value to the next.

Table 5.4 suggests that a state should be represented not by a word, but by the maximum value to be found in that state. Its digits can be counted

First digit	Possibilities for next value	Roman digits to look for
3	the former "at most" value without its first digit	M, C, X, or I, depending on whether the number of digits in the "at most" value is 4, 3, 2, or 1
9	the former "at most" value with the first digit removed or changed to 8	the pair C and M, the pair X and C, or the pair I and X, depending on whether the number of digits in the "at most" value is 3, 2, or 1
8	the former "at most" value with the first digit removed or changed to 3 or 4	D, L, or V, depending on whether the number of digits in the "at most" value is 3, 2, or 1
4	the former "at most" value with the first digit removed or changed to 3	the pair C and D, the pair X and L, or the pair I and V, depending on whether the number of digits in the "at most" value is 3, 2, or 1

Table 5.4 *Computation of state transitions*

and separated using techniques similar to those described in *Check That Number!* We still need a state variable, but now it will have only three values: INPROCESS, SUCCESS, and ERROR.

How can an array be used to associate the "at most" value with a Roman digit?

Furthermore, two arrays of Roman digits can be used to look up the digits to search for. One array, which we'll call TENDIGITS, will store powers of 10: 'I', 'X', 'C', and 'M'. The other, which we'll call FIVEDIGITS, will store digits representing 5 times the corresponding power of 10: 'V', 'L', and 'D'. The code for Update3x is then

```
procedure Update3x (line: LineType; length: integer;
    var linePos: integer; var maxValue: integer; var state: StateType);
var
    k: integer;
begin
    k := PositionOfNon (line, length, linePos,
        TENDIGITS[NumDigits(maxValue)]);
    if k - currentNdx > 3 then begin
        state := ERROR;
    end else if k > length then begin
        state := SUCCESS;
    end else begin
        linePos := k;
        maxValue := AllButFirstDigit(maxValue);
    end;
end;
```

In fact, we can avoid the need for functions to count and remove digits by splitting maxValue into two components: its first digit and the number of digits it has. We incorporate the first digit back into the state variable to get the final set of subprograms in the Pascal Code section.

How is the code tested?

We now proceed to test the program. LocationOfNon can of course be tested separately. The various state-handling routines are probably best tested together, since they are so closely connected.

How can the state diagram help generate test data?

To test the state-based code, we return to the black-box approach. Test data that exercise every statement in the code will be data that test all **transitions**, or movements, from state to state. Thus tests for all possible transitions from state to state must be invented. As we test Roman numerals, we can check off the transitions they exercise on the state diagram to make sure we've covered them all.

This set of data is also useful for testing the Roman numeral checking function designed using the rule-violation approach. Since these data essentially cover all the ways to build a legal Roman numeral, they may reveal checks that were overlooked in designing that program.

Stop & Help ➤ *Generate a set of test data, and test both versions of* IsRoman *with it.*

As in previous programs, we install if DEBUGGING then ... code to provide debugging output. Here, the interesting information is the sequence of states that the program runs through to check the numeral, and the pieces of the Roman numeral being checked at each state.

🖼 🖫 *Analysis*   5.23   Trace the execution of IsRoman on XLIX, XIXI, and XAXII.

🖫 *Analysis*   5.24   Would adding a check that the string consists solely of Roman digits allow the code for the rest of IsRoman to be simplified? Explain.

🖼 🖫 *Debugging*   5.25   Insert a bug in the code that causes the rule-confirmation version of IsRoman to identify an illegal Roman numeral as legal, and get a fellow programmer to find the bug. Do the same with a bug that causes the function to identify a legal Roman numeral as illegal. Which bug is easier to find?

🖼 🖫 *Modification*   5.26   Modify the rule-confirmation version of IsRoman to enter an error state immediately on encountering a character that's not a Roman digit.

🖫 *Analysis*   5.27   In what other situations is it possible to detect an error before processing the entire string?

Analysis   5.28   PositionOfNon is perhaps not the best name for a function that finds the position of an element not equal to a given value. Invent a better name for this function.

Outline of Design and Development Questions

These questions summarize the main points of the commentary.

Checking for Legal Input
What changes are needed to guard against illegal data?
How can the code from *The Calendar Shop* be recycled?
     What template is represented in this decomposition?
What type of variable should be used for input?
How much should be read at a time?
What definitions and declarations are used?
How is a line read?
     What if the line is longer than the array?
     What is the right length for LINELENGTH?
     How does detecting legal values fit into a procedure?
What happens if the input is illegal?

Modifying the *Check That Number!* Program
What are illegal inputs to *Check That Number!*
What template is used for checking the digits?
What are good test cases?

Modifying *Banners With CLASS* and *The Calendar Shop*
What are illegal inputs to *Banners With CLASS* and *The Calendar Shop*?
How can the letters in *Banners With CLASS* be checked?
How can bounded integers be checked?
    What are alternatives for decomposing the input and testing
     of an integer?
    Which decomposition should be chosen?
    How are the nonblank characters in a line read?
       How can a while loop be used to test for blanks and end-of-line?
    How is the rest of the line read into the line array?
       What must be done to the array-filling code to make it usable?
    How is line checked to consist only of digits?
    How are the digits in line converted to an integer?
       How are digit values combined to get an integer?
    How are the various code segments combined?
    How is the code summarized?
How should the code be tested and debugged?
    What code should be tested first?
    What test values should be used?
    How should the remaining code be tested?

One Way to Modify *Roman Calculator Construction*
What should be the first step of the modified ReadRoman?
What are illegal Roman numerals?
What are the alternatives for testing the legality of a Roman numeral?
How is the rule-violation version of IsRoman designed?
    How is IsLegalRomanDigits coded?
    How can the prefix tests be simplified?
       Will it work to substitute single digits for prefix combinations?
       How do the new digits behave compared with the original
        Roman digits?
       How should the error-checking functions be separated?
       How can an array be used to see if two digits are correctly
        ordered?
    How is ReplacePrefixes coded?
       What template is applicable to the problem of replacing prefixes?
       How must the code suggested by the template be modified?
       How are prefixes detected?
       How are prefixes replaced?
    How are the digit counts determined?
    How is IsLegalCounts coded?

How is the order of the digits checked?

How is the position of a digit in the array of digits located?

What's wrong with examining every array element?

What code searches only as far in the array as necessary?

How is IsLegalOrder coded?

How is the code for the rule-violation version tested?

Why are test results not so convincing for this code?

Another Way to Modify *Roman Calculator Construction*

What are the benefits of the rule-confirmation approach?

What are the rules for constructing Roman numerals?

How can the rules help with the design?

How do the rules suggest a state-based design?

How can a collection of states and state transitions be pictured?

How is a value of 3999 or less checked?

How is the number of leading M's found?

How is the result of the M-skipping loop used?

How should states be represented in Pascal?

How is a value of 999 or less checked?

How is a value of 899 or less checked?

How are the other states coded?

How can the code be simplified?

How can the code pattern be represented in a procedure?

How can procedure parameters be eliminated?

How can an array be used to associate the "at most" value with a Roman digit?

How is the code tested?

How can the state diagram help generate test data?

Programmers' Summary

This entire case study is an application of the Persecution Complex principle, a realization that nasty or confused users are liable to type just about anything as input to a program, and that a well-written program is able to handle such illegal input gracefully. Error-checking code is added to the programs for each of the earlier case studies, to ensure that a numeric value is provided in *Check That Number!*, *Banners With CLASS*, and *The Calendar Shop*, a correct set of letters is provided in *Banners With CLASS*, and a correct Roman numeral is provided in *Roman Calculator Construction*.

Error checking in all cases begins with reading a line of input into an array of characters. Two straightforward tests are then made, ensuring that the length of the input is appropriate and that it consists solely of relevant characters. For integer input, there is a complication and an extra step: to be consistent with Pascal's input procedures, our program has to ignore blanks before the integer. After making sure that the nonblank characters are all digits, it then has to convert the characters to an integer value and check that the value is within specified bounds.

Detecting errors in a Roman numeral is more complicated, due to the assortment of rules defining the structure of a Roman numeral. Two alternatives for error checking are explored: a *rule-violation* approach, in which the code checks successively for a number of different characteristics of an illegal numeral; and a *rule-confirmation* approach, in which the code attempts to construct a legal Roman numeral with the same digits as the input and signals error if it can't. The rule-violation approach decomposes the error-checking process into a number of tests that apply common array templates, and it employs the technique of *transforming the input into something easier to handle.* The result is a program that is relatively easy to understand and develops incrementally. However, the approach has a flaw: one really can not be sure that *all* characteristics of an illegal Roman numeral have been checked by the code.

The rule-confirmation approach is based on a set of thirteen rules for constructing Roman numerals. From these rules, a *state-based* program is designed that moves from state to state as it recognizes Roman numerals in successive segments of the input line. The design starts with code segments for each rule; by noticing similarities in the code, we are able to design four state-processing procedures that can be repeatedly called to recognize the numeral. The *state diagram*, an example of an alternate representation, is used to devise a comprehensive set of test data that display all the ways a Roman numeral can be built.

Testing of the code mostly uses the black-box approach. Extreme cases are determined by finding numeric quantities associated with the input, such as its length and the number and position of interesting characters (digits, nondigits, leading blanks, or nonblanks) it contains. Test data are chosen that maximize or minimize legal and illegal values of these quantities. In the rule-violation version of the Roman numeral checker, test data are derived from the state diagram, chosen to exercise all *transitions* from state to state. In all the programs, the Persecution Complex principle is applied by adding debugging output that displays the values of relevant variables.

Applying the Recycling principle, the case study displays many examples of code reuse and template application. The main error-checking loop is copied from *The Calendar Shop.* Conversion of characters to numeric values is copied from *Check That Number!* The "process every element of an array" template, introduced in *Roman Calculator Construction*, is applied in several ways: checking that the input characters are all digits or all letters drawn from 'P', 'A', 'S', 'C', and 'L'; accumulating the numeric value of a string of digits; shifting array elements down one position; tallying each array element in a counts array; and checking that each consecutive pair of Roman digits is properly ordered. A second array template, "searching an array," is derived from the code that reads a line into an array and then is applied to find the location of a particular Roman digit and to skip through a sequence of M's, C's, X's, or I's. The line-reading code is also recycled to produce the code that skips through blanks in the input and the code used to construct and check an integer value. Finally, the "select from alternatives" template was recycled to produce code that handles the various Roman digits in different ways.

On several occasions a choice is made between code that perhaps needlessly checks every element of an array and more complicated code that terminates when an array element with specified properties is found. Two criteria guide the choice: Is efficient code really necessary? Is the extra effort in designing the more complicated code likely to pay off in future applications?

Arrays are used in interesting ways. One use is to represent precedence constraints on Roman numerals: two Roman digits are correctly ordered if one precedes the other in a special array of Roman digits. Another pair of arrays is used to compute, from the number of digits in the argument to one of the state-handling procedures, the Roman digits to look for in that procedure.

Design of the integer input procedure involves a choice from three decompositions. Template application suggests one choice; the desire to be consistent with Pascal's handling of integer input leads to another. The two-part input routine, which first skips blanks and then fills the line array with nonblank characters, requires careful attention to matching up the *postcondition* of the blank-skipping loop with the *precondition* of the array-filling loop.

The Literacy principle appears throughout in our choice of informative variable and procedure names. It is applied in the use of the const facility to give names to states in the rule-confirmation Roman numeral checker. This principle is also applied in the rule-violation Roman numeral checker and in code derived from the "search an array" template, by using *positive* rather than *negative* boolean values to make the code more understandable.

 # Making Sense of *Is It Legal?*

Analysis   5.29 What categories of test cases are necessary to determine whether checks for illegal data are successful?

Reflection	5.30	Why are there so many opportunities to recycle other solutions in this case study?
Analysis	5.31	What categories of illegal data are detected by the procedures in this case study?
Application	5.32	Provide a real-world situation in which errors are sometimes checked with the rule-violation approach and sometimes with the rule-confirmation approach.
Application	5.33	Which method makes more sense for checking that a Pascal program is syntactically correct, the rule-violation method or the rule-confirmation method?
🖫 *Reflection*	5.34	Which version of IsRoman do you find easier to understand? Which version of IsRoman do you find easier to believe is correct?
💻 🖫 *Modification*	5.35	Modify each version of IsRoman to handle two more Roman digits, T, meaning 10000, and F, meaning 5000. M can prefix T to represent 9000 or F to represent 4000. In other ways, T is similar to M, C, X, and I, and F is similar to D, L, and V.
💻 🖫 *Modification*	5.36	The problem statement specifies that errors be detected in input to the programs of the earlier case studies. However, it does not ask that the errors be *diagnosed*. Quality software will not only inform the user that an error has occurred, but it will also try to explain the circumstances of the error. Identify opportunities in which more details could be provided about illegal input in each of the earlier programs, and modify the programs to produce diagnostic output.
💻 🖫 *Application*	5.37	Write a program called GuessMyNumber that asks the user to guess a number between two randomly generated values. Check for illegal (for example, out of bounds) input, and print informative messages.

▨ PASCAL CODE **PASCAL CODE**

Revised *Check That Number!* Program

```
program validate (input, output);

const
    LINELENGTH = 5;

type
    LineType = array[1..LINELENGTH] of char;
```

```
var
    line: LineType;
    length: integer;   {length of the input line}

{
    Read and return a line of up to LINELENGTH characters.
    The length of the line will be returned in length;
    if more than LINELENGTH characters are provided on the line,
    excess characters are discarded.
}
procedure ReadLine (var line: LineType; var length: integer);
var
    ch: char;
begin {Read Line}
    length := 0;
    while not eoln do begin
        read(ch);
        length := length + 1;
        if length <= LINELENGTH then begin
            line[length] := ch;
        end;
    end;
    readln;
end; {Read Line}

{
    Return true exactly when c is a digit.
}
function IsDigit (c: char): boolean;
begin
    IsDigit := (c >= '0') and (c <= '9');
end;

{
    Return true exactly when line represents
    a legal identification number.
}
function IsLegal (line: LineType; length: integer): boolean;
var
    k: integer;
begin {Is Legal}
    IsLegal := true;
    if length <> 4 then begin
        IsLegal := false;
    end else begin
        for k := 1 to 4 do begin
            if not IsDigit(line[k]) then begin
                IsLegal := false;
            end;
        end;
    end;
end; {Is Legal}

{
    Validate the id number in line by checking that
    its check digit is correct.
```

```
}
procedure Validate (line: LineType; length: integer);
var
    digit1, digit2, digit3, checkDigit: integer;
    {the components of the id number}
begin {Validate}
    checkDigit := ord(line[4]) - ord('0');
    digit1 := ord(line[1]) - ord('0');
    digit2 := ord(line[2]) - ord('0');
    digit3 := ord(line[3]) - ord('0');
    if (digit1 + digit2 + digit3) mod 9 = checkDigit then begin
        writeln('The number is valid.');
    end else begin
        writeln('*** The number is invalid.');
    end;
end; {Validate}

begin
    repeat
        write('Please type the four-digit number to be validated: ');
        ReadLine(line, length);
        if not IsLegal(line, length) then begin
            writeln('You must type a four-digit identification number.');
        end;
    until IsLegal(line, length);
    Validate(line, length);
end.
```

Revised *Banners With CLASS* Program

```
program blockLetters (input, output);

const
    NUMLETTERS = 6;
    LINELENGTH = 7;
    BLANK = ' ';

type
    LineType = array[1..LINELENGTH] of char;

var
    letterSize, letterNum, length: integer;
    line: LineType;

{
    Read a line after skipping leading blanks.
    Nonblank characters beyond the LINELENGTH'th nonblank read
    after the initial sequence of blanks are discarded.
}
procedure ReadTrimmedLine (var line: LineType; var length: integer);
var
    done: boolean;
    ch: char;
begin {Read Trimmed Line}
```

```pascal
            done := false;
            ch := BLANK;
            length := 0;
            while not done do begin   {skip blanks}
                if eoln then begin
                    done := true;
                end else begin
                    read(ch);
                    if ch <> BLANK then begin
                        done := true;
                    end;
                end;
            end;
            if ch <> BLANK then begin
                length := 1;
                line[1] := ch;
                while not eoln do begin
                    read(ch);
                    length := length + 1;
                    if length <= LINELENGTH then begin
                        line[length] := ch;
                    end;
                end;
            end;
            readln;
        end; {Read Trimmed Line}


        {
            Return true exactly when line contains only digits.
        }
        function IsAllDigits (line: LineType; length: integer): boolean;
        var
            k: integer;
        begin {Is All Digits?}
            IsAllDigits := true;
            for k := 1 to length do begin
                if not (line[k] in ['0'..'9']) then begin
                    IsAllDigits := false;
                end;
            end;
        end; {Is All Digits?}


        {
            Return the integer value of the given digit.
        }
        function DigitValue (ch: char): integer;
        begin
            DigitValue := ord(ch) - ord('0');
        end;


        {
            Return the integer value of the contents of line,
            which must consist of all digits.
        }
        function IntegerValue (line: LineType; length: integer): integer;
        var
```

```
        k, value: integer;
begin {Integer Value}
    value := 0;
    for k := 1 to length do begin
        value := value * 10 + DigitValue(line[k]);
    end;
    IntegerValue := value;
end; {Integer Value}


{
    Return true exactly when n is in the range 5, …, 24.
}
function IsInRange (n: integer): boolean;
begin {Is In Range?}
    IsInRange := (n >= 5) and (n <= 24);
end; {Is In Range?}


{
    Read and return an integer between 5 and 24;
    keep prompting until the user supplies one.
}
procedure ReadInteger (var n: integer);
var
    error: boolean;
    line: LineType;
    length: integer;
begin {Read Integer}
    repeat
        error := false;
        write('Type a size for the letters between 5 and 24 : ');
        ReadTrimmedLine(line, length);
        if (length = 0) or (length > LINELENGTH) then begin
            error := true;
        end else if not IsAllDigits(line, length) then begin
            error := true;
        end else begin
            n := IntegerValue(line, length);
            if not IsInRange(n) then begin
                error := true;
            end;
        end;
        if error then begin
            writeln('You must type an integer between 5 and 24.');
        end;
    until not error;
end; {Read Integer}


{
    Read and return a line of up to LINELENGTH characters.
    The length of the line will be returned in length;
    if more than LINELENGTH characters are provided on the line,
    excess characters are discarded.
}
procedure ReadLine (var line: LineType; var length: integer);
var
    ch: char;
```

```
begin {Read Line}
    length := 0;
    while not eoln do begin
        read(ch);
        length := length + 1;
        if length <= LINELENGTH then begin
            line[length] := ch;
        end;
    end;
    readln;
end; {Read Line}

{
    Return true exactly when c is a digit.
}
function IsDigit (c: char): boolean;
begin
    IsDigit := (c >= '0') and (c <= '9');
end;

{
    Return true exactly when c is one of PASCL.
}
function IsInPASCL (c: char): boolean;
begin
    IsInPASCL := (c = 'P') or (c = 'p')
        or (c = 'A') or (c = 'a')
        or (c = 'S') or (c = 's')
        or (c = 'C') or (c = 'c')
        or (c = 'L') or (c = 'l');
end;

{
    Return true exactly when line represents a legal identification
    number.
}
function IsLegal (line: LineType; length: integer): boolean;
var
    k: integer;
begin {Is Legal}
    IsLegal := true;
    if length <> NUMLETTERS then begin
        IsLegal := false;
    end else begin
        for k := 1 to NUMLETTERS do begin
            if not IsInPASCL(line[k]) then begin
                IsLegal := false;
            end;
        end;
    end;
end; {Is Legal}

{
    Read a line consisting of the right number of PASCL.
    Keep prompting until the user provides such a line.
}
```

```
procedure ReadLetters (var line: LineType; var length: integer);
begin {Read Letters}
    repeat
        write('Type ', NUMLETTERS : 1, ' letters, chosen from PASCL: ');
        ReadLine(line, length);
        if not IsLegal(line, length) then begin
            writeln('Either you haven''t typed ', NUMLETTERS : 1,
                ' characters, or one of them isn''t PASCL.');
        end;
    until IsLegal(line, length);
end; {Read Letters}

{letter drawing procedures go here}

begin
    ReadInteger(letterSize);
    ReadLetters(line, length);
    for letterNum := 1 to NUMLETTERS do begin
        case line[letterNum] of
            'P', 'p': DrawP(letterSize);
            'A', 'a': DrawA(letterSize);
            'S', 's': DrawS(letterSize);
            'C', 'c': DrawC(letterSize);
            'L', 'l': DrawL(letterSize);
        end;
        writeln;
    end;
end.
```

Code for the Rule-Violation Approach

```
{
    Return true exactly when all the digits in the line are
    legal Roman digits.
}
function AllLegalRomanDigits (line: LineType; length: integer): boolean;
var
    k: integer;
begin {All Legal Roman Digits?}
    AllLegalRomanDigits := true;
    for k := 1 to length do begin
        if not (line[k] in ['I', 'V', 'X', 'L', 'C', 'D', 'M']) then begin
            AllLegalRomanDigits := false;
        end;
    end; {All Legal Roman Digits?}
end;


{
    Replace the *two characters* in the line starting at the given position
    by the *single* replacement character. The length of the line is
    reduced by 1 as a result.
    Precondition: pos < length.
}
```

```
procedure Replace (var line: LineType; pos: integer; var length: integer;
    replacement: char);
var
    k: integer;
begin {Replace}
    line[pos] := replacement;
    for k := pos + 1 to length - 1 do begin
        line[k] := line[k + 1];
    end;
    length := length - 1;
end; {Replace}

{
    Replace each pair of Roman digits that starts with a prefix by a
    single character. {IV and IX are replaced by 1; XL and XC are replaced
    by 2; CD and CM are replaced by 3.
}
procedure ReplacePrefixes (var line: LineType; var length: integer);
var
    k: integer;
begin {Replace Prefixes}
    k := 1;
    while k < length do begin
        case line[k] of
            'I': if (line[k + 1] = 'V') or (line[k + 1] = 'X') then begin
                    Replace(line, k, length, '1');
                end;
            'X': if (line[k + 1] = 'L') or (line[k + 1] = 'C') then begin
                    Replace(line, k, length, '2');
                end;
            'C': if (line[k + 1] = 'D') or (line[k + 1] = 'M') then begin
                    Replace(line, k, length, '3');
                end;
            'V', 'L', 'D', 'M': ;
        end;
        k := k + 1;
    end;
    if DEBUGGING then begin
        write('*** After prefix substitution: ');
        WritelnLine(line, length);
    end;
end; {Replace Prefixes}

{
    Return true exactly when there are at most 3 occurrences of
    I, X, C, and M, and at most 1 occurrence of V, L, D, 1, 2, and 3
    in the given line. {1 represents the pair IV or IX; 2 represents
    the pair XL or XC; 3 represents the pair CD or CM.
    Precondition: line consists only of Roman digits, 1, 2, and 3.
}
function LegalCounts (line: LineType; length: integer): boolean;
var
    k: integer;
    counts: array[char] of integer;
begin {Legal Counts?}
    counts['I'] := 0;  counts['V'] := 0;
```

```
        counts['X'] := 0;   counts['L'] := 0;
        counts['C'] := 0;   counts['D'] := 0;
        counts['M'] := 0;
        counts['1'] := 0;   counts['2'] := 0;   counts['3'] := 0;
        for k := 1 to length do begin
            counts[line[k]] := counts[line[k]] + 1;
        end;
        LegalCounts := (counts['I'] <= 3) and (counts['X'] <= 3)
            and (counts['C'] <= 3) and (counts['M'] <= 3)
            and (counts['V'] <= 1) and (counts['L'] <= 1)
            and (counts['D'] <= 1) and (counts['1'] <= 1)
            and (counts['2'] <= 1) and (counts['3'] <= 1);
end; {Legal Counts?}


{
    Return the position in the line of the given character.
    Precondition: ch occurs somewhere in line.
}
function Location (ch: char; line: LineType; length: integer): integer;
var
    k: integer;
    done: boolean;
begin {Location}
    done := false;
    k := 1;
    while not done do begin
        if k > length then begin
            done := true;   {no more array elements to check}
            Location := 0;
            if DEBUGGING then begin
                writeln('*** character ', ch, ' not found in line!');
            end;
        end else if line[k] = ch then begin
            done := true;   {found what we're looking for}
            Location := k;
        end else begin
            k := k + 1;   {move to next array element}
        end;
    end;
end; {Location}


{
    The two Roman digits occur consecutively in a Roman numeral
    being checked for legality, whose prefixes (along with the digits
    they prefix) have been replaced by the digits 1, 2, and 3.
    Return true exactly when the two Roman digits are in the correct
    order. {M, if it occurs, must precede all other digits; 3 (meaning
    CM or CD), if it occurs, must come next; and so on.
}
function InOrder (romanDigit1, romanDigit2: char): boolean;
const
    ALLDIGITS = 'IV1XL2CD3M           ';
begin {In Order?}
    if (romanDigit1 = '1') or (romanDigit1 = '2') or (romanDigit1 = '3')
      then begin
        InOrder := Location(romanDigit1, ALLDIGITS, 10)
```

```
                            >= Location(romanDigit2, ALLDIGITS, 10) + 3;
            end else begin
                InOrder := Location(romanDigit1, ALLDIGITS, 10)
                    >= Location(romanDigit2, ALLDIGITS, 10);
            end;
    end; {In Order?}


    {
        Return true if consecutive Roman digits in line are ordered correctly.
    }
    function LegalOrder (line: LineType; length: integer): boolean;
    var
        k: integer;
    begin {Legal Order?}
        LegalOrder := true;
        for k := 1 to length - 1 do begin
            if not InOrder(line[k], line[k + 1]) then begin
                LegalOrder := false;
            end;
        end;
    end; {Legal Order?}


    {
        Return true exactly when line contains a legal Roman numeral.
    }
    function IsRoman (line: LineType; length: integer): boolean;
    begin {Is Roman?}
        if not AllLegalRomanDigits(line, length) then begin
            if DEBUGGING then begin
                writeln('*** failed digit check');
            end;
            IsRoman := false;
        end else begin
            ReplacePrefixes(line, length);
            if not LegalCounts(line, length) then begin
                IsRoman := false;
                if DEBUGGING then begin
                    writeln('*** failed count check');
                end;
            end else if not LegalOrder(line, length) then begin
                IsRoman := false;
                if DEBUGGING then begin
                    writeln('*** failed order check');
                end;
            end else begin
                IsRoman := true;
            end;
        end;
    end; {Is Roman?}


    {
        Read a Roman numeral from the user.
        Keep prompting until the user supplies a legal Roman numeral.
    }
    procedure ReadRoman (var roman: LineType; var length: integer);
    begin {Read Roman}
```

```
    repeat
        write('Please type a Roman numeral: ');
        ReadLine(roman, length);
        if not IsRoman(roman, length) then begin
            writeln('*** What you typed isn''t a valid Roman numeral.');
        end;
    until IsRoman(roman, length);
end; {Read Roman}
```

Code for the Rule-Confirmation Approach

```
const
    MAXSTRLEN = 20;
    DEBUGGING = true;
    STATE3 = 1;
    STATE9 = 2;
    STATE4 = 3;
    STATE8 = 4;
    ERROR = 5;
    SUCCESS = 6;

type
    DigitTable = array[1..4] of char;
    LineType = array[1..MAXSTRLEN] of char;
    StateType = integer;

var
    TENDIGITS, FIVEDIGITS: DigitTable;
    roman: LineType;
    length: integer;

procedure Initialize;
begin {Initialize}
    TENDIGITS[1]  := 'I';
    TENDIGITS[2]  := 'X';
    TENDIGITS[3]  := 'C';
    TENDIGITS[4]  := 'M';
    FIVEDIGITS[1] := 'V';
    FIVEDIGITS[2] := 'L';
    FIVEDIGITS[3] := 'D';
end; {Initialize}
{
    Return the position of the first character in line starting at
    position pos that is not the same as ch. If all characters in line
    starting at position pos are the same as ch, return length+1.
}
function PositionOfNon (line: LineType; length, pos: integer;
    ch: char): integer;
var
    done: boolean;
begin {Position of Non}
    done := false;
    while not done do begin
        if pos > length then begin
```

```
                      done := true;
              end else if line[pos] <> ch then begin
                      done := true;
              end else begin
                      pos := pos + 1;
              end;
          end;
          PositionOfNon := pos;
end; {Position of Non}

{
    Check for a Roman numeral representing at most 3999, 399, 39, or 3;
    state should have the value STATE3. maxDigits will be 4, 3, 2, or 1
    depending on which of the Roman numerals is being checked for.
    Proceed by looking for a sequence of M's, C's, X's, or I's, depending
    on maxDigits; if there are four or more in the sequence, there is an
    error, otherwise the state and the position within the line are
    updated. The next thing to look for will be either 999, 99, 99, or the
    end of the numeral.
}
procedure Update3x (var maxDigits: integer; var state: StateType;
    line: LineType; length: integer; var linePos: integer);
var
    k: integer;
begin {Update 3x}
    k := PositionOfNon(line, length, linePos, TENDIGITS[maxDigits]);
    if k - linePos > 3 then begin
        state := ERROR;
    end else if k > length then begin
        state := SUCCESS;
    end else begin
        linePos := k;
        state := STATE9;
        maxDigits := maxDigits - 1;
    end;
end; {Update 3x}

{
    Check for a Roman numeral representing at most 999, 99, or 9;
    state should have the value STATE9. maxDigits will be 3, 2, or 1
    depending on which of the Roman numerals is being checked for.
    Proceed by looking for one of CM, XC, or IX, depending on maxDigits.
    If it is found, the next thing to look for will be 99, 9, or the end
    of the numeral; if not, the next thing to look for will be 899, 89,
    or 8.
}
procedure Update9x (var maxDigits: integer; var state: StateType;
    line: LineType; length: integer; var linePos: integer);
begin {Update 9x}
    if linePos + 1 > length then begin
        state := STATE8;
    end else if (line[linePos] = TENDIGITS[maxDigits])
      and (line[linePos + 1] = TENDIGITS[maxDigits + 1]) then begin
        linePos := linePos + 2;
        maxDigits := maxDigits - 1;
    end else begin
```

```
                   state := STATE8;
            end;
end; {Update 9x}


{
    Check for a Roman numeral representing at most 499, 49, or 4;
    state should have the value STATE4. maxDigits will be 3, 2, or 1
    depending on which of the Roman numerals is being checked for.
    Proceed by looking for one of CD, XL, or IV, depending on maxDigits.
    If it is found, the next thing to look for will be 99, 9, or the end
    of the numeral; if not, the next thing to look for will be 399, 39,
    or 3.
}
procedure Update4x (var maxDigits: integer; var state: StateType;
    line: LineType; length: integer; var linePos: integer);
begin {Update 4x}
    if linePos + 1 > length then begin
        state := STATE3;
    end else if (line[linePos] = TENDIGITS[maxDigits])
      and (line[linePos + 1] = FIVEDIGITS[maxDigits]) then begin
        linePos := linePos + 2;
        state := STATE9;
        maxDigits := maxDigits - 1;
    end else begin
        state := STATE3;
    end;
end; {Update 4x}


{
    Check for a Roman numeral representing at most 899, 89, or 8;
    state should have the value STATE8. maxDigits will be 3, 2, or 1
    depending on which of the values is being checked for.
    Proceed by looking for D, L, or V, depending on maxDigits.
    If it is found, the next thing to look for will be 399, 39, or 3;
    if not, the next thing to look for will be 499, 49, or 4.
}
procedure Update8x (var maxDigits: integer; var state: StateType;
    line: LineType; length: integer; var linePos: integer);
begin {Update 8x}
    if linePos > length then begin
        state := SUCCESS;
    end else if line[linePos] = FIVEDIGITS[maxDigits] then begin
        linePos := linePos + 1;
        state := STATE3;
    end else begin
        state := STATE4;
    end;
end; {Update 8x}


{
    Check for the end of the numeral.
    If there are more digits, the numeral is illegal;
    otherwise, a Roman numeral has been successfully recognized.
}
procedure Update0 (var state: StateType; length, linePos: integer);
begin {Update 0}
```

```
            if linePos = length + 1 then begin
                state := SUCCESS;
            end else begin
                state := ERROR;
            end;
        end; {Update 0}


        {Return true exactly when line contains a legal Roman numeral.}
        function IsRoman (line: LineType; length: integer): boolean;
        var
            state: StateType;
            maxDigits, linePos: integer;
        begin {Is Roman?}
            state := STATE3;
            maxDigits := 4;
            linePos := 1;
            while (state <> ERROR) and (state <> SUCCESS) do begin
                if DEBUGGING then begin
                    write('*** linePos = ', linePos : 1, ', ');
                    case state of
                        STATE3: write('state = 3, ');
                        STATE9: write('state = 9, ');
                        STATE4: write('state = 4, ');
                        STATE8: write('state = 8, ');
                    end;
                    write('maxDigits = ', maxDigits : 1, ', ');
                    WritelnLine(line, length, linePos);
                end;
                if maxDigits = 0 then begin
                    Update0(state, length, linePos);
                end else begin
                    case state of
                        STATE3: Update3x(maxDigits, state,
                                    line, length, linePos);
                        STATE9: Update9x(maxDigits, state,
                                    line, length, linePos);
                        STATE8: Update8x(maxDigits, state,
                                    line, length, linePos);
                        STATE4: Update4x(maxDigits, state,
                                    line, length, linePos);
                    end;
                end;
            end;
            IsRoman := state = SUCCESS;
        end; {Is Roman?}
```

CHAPTER 6

Space Text

(190)

XCIII.

Printing. | *Typographia.*

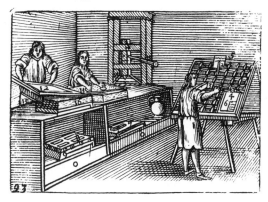

The Printer **hath** Copper Letters **in a great number put into** Boxes. 5.	*Typographus* habet *aneos Typos,* magno numero, diſtributos per *Loculamenta.* 5.
The Compoſitor 1. **taketh them out one by one, and** (**according to** the Copy, **which he hath faſtened before him in a** Viſorum 2.) **compoſeth words**	*Typotheta* 1. eximit illos ſingulatim, & componit (ſecundùm *Exemplar,* quod *Retinaculo* **2.** ſibi præfixum habet) verba **in**

The programmer taketh spaces one by one and placeth them between words much like compositors of yore.

Computers now make desktop publishing possible. Publishing software allows users to display text in much the same way as it is displayed in books. This case study describes the development of a procedure that could be inserted into a word-processing program to display text flush with the right and left margins.

Problem Statement

Write and test a procedure named SpaceText that will "space out" a line of text to a specified line length. (The procedure might be used by a word-processing program to right-align lines of output.) SpaceText will have the following header:

```
procedure SpaceText (var line: StringType; var length: integer;
    desiredLength: integer; var status: StatusType);
```

The parameters for SpaceText are as follows:

- line is an array of characters, representing a line of text.
- length is the length of the line represented.
- desiredLength is the *desired* length of the line.
- status is a variable in which the result of the spacing-out process is recorded.

Assume that StringType has been defined in the program that will contain SpaceText as an array of at least desiredLength characters.

SpaceText should insert blanks evenly between words in the line, starting at the left, so that the line is exactly the desired length and there are no blanks at either end. SpaceText should also adjust length accordingly. A "word" is a sequence of nonblank characters that either starts at the beginning of the line or is preceded by a blank, and either ends at the end of the line or is followed by a blank. Blank spaces already occurring between words should be preserved. It may be necessary to add one more blank between some pairs of words than between others.

SpaceText will not be able to insert blanks between words as specified under the following conditions:

- The line starts or ends with a blank.
- The length of the line is already longer than desiredLength.
- The line contains no words.
- The line contains only one word.

In these cases, line and length should be left unchanged, and one of the following values should be returned in status:

- ENDBLANK, when the line starts or ends with a blank
- TOOLONG, when desiredLength is less than length
- EMPTYLINE, when length = 0
- ONEWORD, when only one word appears on the line

When none of these situations occurs, the value OK should be assigned to status. If more than one of the situations occur, any of the specified values should be assigned to status. Assume that the identifiers ENDBLANK, TOOLONG, EMPTYLINE, ONEWORD, and OK have been defined as values of type StatusType in the program that will contain SpaceText.

Suppose, for an example, that the desired line length is 10 characters. Some sample lines and the results SpaceText would return are given below. (The numbers indicate the length of the line.)

line on entry to SpaceText	length on entry to SpaceText	line on return from SpaceText	status on return from SpaceText
`1234567890`		`1234567890`	
`now is the`	10	`now`	OK
`a b c`	5	`a    b    c`	OK
`a   b c`	7	`a     b  c`	OK
`a. b; ?*`	8	`a.  b;  7*`	OK
`  xyzabcdefgh`	12	`  xyzabcdefgh`	ENDBLANK or TOOLONG or ONEWORD
`5+6=9.`	6	`5+6=9.`	ONEWORD
`now is `	7	`now is `	ENDBLANK
`now is the time`	15	`now is the time`	TOOLONG

Other than using the types StringType and StatusType and the constants ENDBLANK, TOOLONG, EMPTYLINE, ONEWORD, and OK, SpaceText and the procedures it calls should be independent of the remainder of the program.

Analysis 6.1 Show how SpaceText handles input with several blanks between words.

Analysis 6.2 According to the definition of "word," how many words appear in the line

```
That's no gentleman--that's my coauthor.
```

Analysis 6.3 When should SpaceText add a different number of blanks between some pairs of words than between others?

Analysis 6.4 Prove that the four exceptional situations described in the problem statement cover all the cases where it is not possible to insert blanks between words to fill the line to the desired length.

Analysis 6.5 Give examples of all situations in which more than one of the exceptional situations occur (examples of situations in which there are more than one possible value to return in status).

Analysis 6.6 Why is desiredLength a value parameter while the others are var parameters?

Reflection 6.7 What are the advantages of making SpaceText independent of the rest of the program?

Application 6.8 Explain how SpaceText might be used in a word processor.

📖 *Testing* 6.9 Does your text editor provide a way to fill lines so that they have a given length? If so, does it always fill from left to right? What does it do in the four exceptional situations? Experiment to find out.

Preparation

Solutions in this case study require understanding of loops, arrays, and data types (but not records).

Initial Approach

What is the problem asking for? The problem statement says to write and test a *procedure* called SpaceText that inserts blanks between words in a line of text. This procedure is to be pretty much independent of the remainder of the program that contains it.

Stop & Predict ➤ *Will* SpaceText *contain any* read *or* readln *statements? Why or why not?*

What this means is that SpaceText will not have any **side effects** other than those specified—that is, it will store a value in the status parameter and perhaps will change the values in the line and length parameters. It won't change or even use any global variables. It won't do any input or output, because that might interfere with whatever the calling program is doing. In particular, it won't read the values for the parameters; these are supplied by the calling program when SpaceText is called, and reading more values for the parameters would overwrite those they already contain!

How will SpaceText be tested?

For SpaceText to be tested, however, it clearly must be contained in a complete program. We will have to write it, as well as SpaceText itself. The test program is not part of the solution to the problem, but it is necessary to show that the procedure works correctly.

We've done the same kind of activity in earlier case studies. There, we applied the strategy of incremental development to test procedures and functions a few at a time. This typically involved writing a **driver program** to read values, send them to the procedure, and then print out the result it returned. The difference is that we knew in earlier case studies what the remainder of the program looked like; here, we're not allowed to make any assumptions about the calling program.

Why would someone design a procedure without a program to accompany it?

This kind of programming happens often in team projects. Someone decides how to split up the solution to a problem; members of the team then design and develop pieces of the solution and put them all together afterward. If the pieces are sufficiently well specified, then the program should work perfectly.

A programmer may also wish to create a **library** of subprograms to use in future solutions. The contents of the library could be subprograms that perform common actions or computations.

Stop & Help ➤

How could SpaceText *be used in a program to align the left and right margins of text in paragraphs?*

Why should the procedure be independent of the calling program?

In either situation, the advantages of designing the procedure to minimize its dependence on the calling program are clear. When programming in a team, one should make the tasks of the other team members as easy as possible. The more their code has to set up when calling a procedure, the more chances there are for errors. When preparing a procedure for a library, one should make it **general**, that is, usable in a variety of programs. The more dependent a subprogram is on the calling program, the less general it will be, and the fewer opportunities one will have to use it without modifying it.

It's good to make subprograms as independent of their caller as possible, even in code we write for ourselves, not intended for a library. Such **modular** code, able to be plugged into a program like an amplifier or tape deck module into a stereo system, will be useful in future programs. Moreover, it's more understandable; one can always look to the subprogram parameters to see what effect the subprogram has on the calling program, rather than having to look through the entire program listing for uses of global variables.

What will the program to test SpaceText do?

Back to the design of SpaceText. It won't be difficult to create a program to test SpaceText. In addition, if SpaceText needs incremental development, it would be nice to have a program for testing the increments already created. We can design test data for SpaceText using the black-box approach, without even knowing what the code is. Finally, inventing a test program will give us a sense of accomplishment about finishing part of the problem. Thus, we decide to start by designing a test program and test data.

The test program should read values for SpaceText's arguments, call SpaceText, then print the results as in earlier case studies. Including "input, process, output" in a loop will make it easier to test SpaceText on a variety of data.

Stop & Help ➤ *Describe the template needed to create an "input, process, output" loop.*

The calling program needs to supply four things to SpaceText: a line, a length, a desired length, and a status variable. The line is just a character array; its contents and length can be read using the ReadLine procedure from the *Is It Legal?* programs. The desired length is an integer no greater than the maximum number of characters in the line; the ReadInInteger procedure from *Is It Legal?* or a simpler procedure ReadDesired can be used to get this value. Here is the code:

```
while true do begin
    ReadLine(line, length);
    ReadDesired(desiredLength);
    SpaceText(line, length, desiredLength, status);
    print line, length, and status;
end;
```

How are the variable
types defined?

All the variables must of course be declared. The problem statement says that line is of type StringType, an array of characters. For the purposes of testing, we can choose the size for the array. We code this as a Pascal constant, and declare the array as follows:

```
const
    MAXSTRLEN = 30;   {large enough for testing}

type
    StringType = array [1..MAXSTRLEN] of char;

var
    line: StringType;
```

Similar declarations appeared in the programs for *Roman Calculator Construction* and *Is It Legal?*

The length and desiredLength variables will be declared as integers. But what about status? We aren't told much about it: only that it is of type StatusType, as are the constants ENDBLANK, TOOLONG, EMPTYLINE, ONEWORD, and OK. StatusType can be defined in several ways. Recall from *The Calendar Shop* and *Is It Legal?* that similar constants were defined as integers. We decide to do the same thing for the purposes of testing.

Stop & Consider ➤   *In what other ways can* StatusType *be defined?*

(Note that SpaceText is not allowed to rely on StatusType being the same as integer. The problem statement says that ENDBLANK and so on may be used, but it doesn't say how, implying that we may make no assumptions about how they are defined.) The complete set of definitions and declarations is then

```
const
    MAXSTRLEN = 30;   {large enough for testing}
    ENDBLANK = 1;
    TOOLONG = 2;
    EMPTYLINE = 3;
    ONEWORD = 4;
    OK = 5;

type
    StringType = array [1..MAXSTRLEN] of char;
    StatusType = integer;

var
    line: StringType;
    length, desiredLength: integer;
    status: StatusType;
```

How will the information be printed?

Our test program will print the line and its length after calling SpaceText. Printing the length is easy. Printing the line is an application of the "process every element of an array" template, where the "processing" is printing the element. We will be checking the output for correct spacing, so we should make this easier by including a line of column headings similar to those in the problem statement. Since the line and its length go together, we group these into a OutputLine procedure:

```
procedure OutputLine(line: StringType; length: integer);
var
    k: integer;
begin
    writeln('123456789012345678901234567890');
    for k := 1 to length do begin
        write(line[k]);
    end;
    writeln;
    writeln('length = ', length);
    writeln;  {extra blank line for nice spacing}
end;
```

The value of status must also be printed. This is best done in its own procedure. We would like to see words in the output rather than numbers, so a case statement is appropriate:

```
case status of
    OK: writeln('ok');
    ENDBLANK: writeln('line ends with a blank');
    TOOLONG: writeln('line is longer than desired');
    EMPTYLINE: writeln('line is empty');
```

```
        ONEWORD: writeln('line contains only one word');
end;
```

After a stub for the SpaceText procedure is added, the test program is complete. It appears in the Pascal Code section.

Stop & Predict ➤   *What errors are likely to be detected during testing?*

What data should be used to test the completed SpaceText procedure?

A complete specification includes a set of data. To complete the specification of the SpaceText procedure, we devise a set of test data, using the black-box approach. We repeat the approach used in earlier case studies of noticing numeric quantities associated with the problem. We choose data for which those quantities have their maximum legal values, their maximum legal values plus 1 and minus 1, their minimum legal values, and their minimum legal values plus and minus 1.

Stop & Predict ➤   *What numeric quantities are associated with this problem?*

As in the *Roman Calculator Construction* program, we must be concerned with varying lengths of lines. Thus an empty line, a line of one character, and a line as long as possible are good test data choices. The number of blanks to add is another numeric quantity, so we make sure to test lines to which no blanks are to be added, lines where one blank is added, and lines to which the maximum number of blanks are added. The number of words leads us to include lines with no words, one word, and the maximum number of words.

🔋 *Analysis*   6.10   Design test data in each of the categories just mentioned, and indicate the results that SpaceText should produce for each set of input.

Reflection   6.11   Almost all the procedures in the test program use line and length. It seems to be a waste of time to pass them as parameters to all the procedures. What advantages are there to passing line and length as parameters?

Reflection   6.12   What subprograms would you put into your personal subprogram library? Why?

🔳 🔋 *Modification*   6.13   We can build some simple test cases into the test program and save ourselves the effort of always having to type them. Modify the test program so that, before it enters the "input, process, output" loop, it calls SpaceText on an empty line and on lines that begin and end with blanks.

🔳 🔋 *Modification*   6.14   The output produced by the test program makes it somewhat difficult to tell if the line being printed contains trailing blanks. Devise a better output format that would make this situation easier to see quickly, and modify the program to produce output in your revised format.

Alternative Designs for SpaceText

How is SpaceText designed? With the test program as a secure base, we move on to the design of Space-Text. The problem statement says that "SpaceText should insert blanks evenly between words in the line, starting at the left, so that the line is exactly the desired length and there are no blanks at either end. SpaceText should also adjust length accordingly." We will need to figure out how many blanks to insert and how to insert them.

How many blanks need to be inserted? It is easy to compute the number of blanks to insert by subtracting length from desiredLength. We will call this quantity numToInsert.

Stop & Predict ➤ *What values of numToInsert require special treatment?*

If numToInsert is equal to 0, SpaceText should return line and length unchanged with status = OK. If numToInsert is less than 0, then the line is already longer than desired, so SpaceText should return line and length unchanged with status = TOOLONG.

As for doing the insertion of blanks, the problem statement suggests two possible decompositions. Both involve loops. One is to repeat some action once for each blank to insert:

```
for k := 1 to numToInsert do begin
    ⋮
end;
```

The other decomposition is to repeat some action once for each word in line, or perhaps for each gap between words. In pseudocode:

```
for each gap in line, do the following:
    insert the right number of blanks into the gap.
```

Which solution seems best? The blank-by-blank approach sounds simpler, the gap-by-gap approach more efficient—since in general there will be fewer gaps than blanks to insert—and perhaps more elegant. We'll explore both approaches, the simpler one first.

Reflection 6.15 Which approach seems better to you, the blank-by-blank approach or the gap-by-gap approach? Why?

Reflection 6.16 What are probable advantages of working on the simpler solution first? What are possible disadvantages?

Blank-by-Blank Approach

What action is to be repeated for each blank to be inserted?

The blank-by-blank approach, expressed in pseudocode, is as follows:

```
for k := 1 to numToInsert do begin
    insert the kth blank in the correct place in line;
end;
```

The "correct place in the line" will be somewhere between words. The insertion operation will require a position in the line at which to insert the blank; thus the loop body will have to include code to find the insertion position.

How is the insertion position found?

One idea for refining the loop body is the following: at each iteration, the position of the *next blank* in line is found and the new blank inserted there. In pseudocode:

```
for k := 1 to numToInsert do begin
    find the position of the next blank in line;
    insert the kth blank there;
end;
```

Stop & Predict ➤ *Will this work?*

The problem statement requires that "blank spaces already occurring between words should be preserved" and that "SpaceText should insert blanks evenly between words." This solution inserts too many blanks into a gap that already contains more than one blank. Thus it's not enough merely to find the next blank in the line; the program must instead look for the *next gap*, as in the following pseudocode:

```
for k := 1 to numToInsert do begin
    find the position of the next gap in line;
    insert the kth blank there;
end;
```

Stop & Help ➤ *Show how searching for the next blank and adding a blank there leads to incorrect results in the following line:*

```
        Hi.   How are you?  I'm fine.   See you around.
```

Table 6.1 illustrates how insertion that cycles through the gaps in the line would work. It starts with a line of 17 characters and produces a line 27 characters long.

A variable is needed to keep track of the insertion position; we'll call it currentPosition. To cycle through the gaps, we need to find the position of a blank in the next gap; we'll call that gapPosition. Adding these refinements leads to the following pseudocode.

```
initialize currentPosition;
for k := 1 to numToInsert do begin
    gapPosition := the position of the next gap in line;
```

```
123456789012345678901234567   desired line length of 27
now is   the time             actual line length of 17
now is   the time             first cycle: insert into the first gap
now is    the time             insert into the second gap
now is    the  time            insert into the third gap
now  is    the  time          second cycle
now  is     the  time
now  is     the   time
now   is     the   time        third cycle
now   is      the   time
now   is      the    time
now    is       the    time    fourth cycle
```

Table 6.1 *An example of blank-by-blank insertion*

```
    insert the kth blank at gapPosition;
        currentPosition := gapPosition;
end;
```

One may notice a similarity between this loop and the loop in the week-by-week version of *The Calendar Shop* program:

```
startOfWeek := 1 - dayForFirst;
for 1 := 1 to numberWeeks do begin
    PrintWeek(startOfWeek, numberDates);
    startOfWeek := startOfWeek + 7;
end;
```

Both loops involve a variable that's keeping track of a position. In the gap-finding loop, it's a position in line; in the week-printing loop, it's a position (date) in the month. In each case, the loop begins with processing that involves the position. The last statement in the loop updates the position.

Since the position of the next gap in line is just a single integer and finding it requires no changes to any other variable, a function to return the position is appropriate. A descriptive name for this function is NextGapPosition.

Stop & Predict ➤ *How should* currentPosition *be initialized?*

Stop & Predict ➤ *What should* NextGapPosition *return when the end of the line is reached?*

What parameters will NextGapPosition have? NextGapPosition obviously needs line as a parameter. In addition, NextGapPosition needs to know where to start looking for the next gap; currentPosition is as good a place as any. Finally, it needs to know how long line is in order to know when to cycle back to the beginning. All of these can be value parameters, as is conventional with functions. Thus the header for NextGapPosition is

```
function NextGapPosition(line: StringType;
    length, currentPosition: integer): integer;
```

and the assignment statement

```
gapPosition := NextGapPosition(line, length, currentPosition);
```

can be used in the loop.

Stop & Predict ➤

What are the steps in NextGapPosition?

How is a gap detected?

We now design NextGapPosition. One step in finding a gap is finding the position of a blank character. This is easy. It involves applying the "search an array" template introduced in *Is It Legal?* to line:

```
k := currentPosition;
blankFound := false;
while not blankFound do begin
    if k > length then begin
        action if k runs off the end of line;
    end else if line[k] = BLANK then begin
        blankFound := true;
    end else begin
        k := k + 1;
    end;
end;
```

Should k reach the end of the line, it should start over at the beginning; the statement

```
k := 1;
```

should replace the "action if k runs off the end of the line" above.

Finding a blank is not enough to detect a gap. A gap arises when a blank is preceded by a nonblank. Finding a nonblank—that is, skipping blanks—is done with the same template:

```
k := currentPosition;
nonblankFound := false;
while not nonblankFound do begin
    if k > length then begin
        k := 1;
    end else if line[k] <> BLANK then begin
        nonblankFound := true;
    end else begin
        k := k + 1;
    end;
end;
```

Stop & Predict ➤

How is a blank preceded by a nonblank detected?

What will the preconditions of NextGapPosition *be?*

We must now put this code together. Careful design of NextGapPosition requires, as in earlier case studies, that we consider its preconditions and postconditions.

In general, when NextGapPosition is called, currentPosition will contain the location of the first blank in the previous gap. Thus, NextGapPosition should skip past any other blanks in that gap, skip all the nonblank characters following the last blank, and find the first blank in the next gap. It should work to add the blank-finding code to the end of the blank-skipping code and match up the variables they use. Here's the code:

```
k := currentPosition;
nonblankFound := false;
while not nonblankFound do begin   {skip blanks}
    if k > length then begin
        k := 1;
    end else if line[k] <> BLANK then begin
        nonblankFound := true;
    end else begin
        k := k + 1;
    end;
end;
blankFound := false;
while not blankFound do begin   {find a blank}
    if k > length then begin
        k := 1;
    end else if line[k] = BLANK then begin
        blankFound := true;
    end else begin
        k := k + 1;
    end;
end;
```

At the end of the second loop, k should contain the position of the first blank in the next gap.

What conditions could cause problems?

With any loop, one should make sure it terminates. Suppose that line is all blank or contains no blanks. Either situation causes one of the two loops to continue infinitely. Thus NextGapPosition must not be called unless there are at least two words in line.

Stop & Predict ➤

What will prevent SpaceText *from calling* NextGapPosition *with only one word in the line?*

We have assumed that line[currentPosition] is blank when NextGapPosition is called. We have not yet determined an initial value for currentPosition, however. What if line[currentPosition] is not blank when NextGapPosition is first called? This turns out not to cause a problem. The blank-skipping loop exits right away, since there are no blanks to skip. Then the blank-finding loop finds the position of the next blank.

We draw two conclusions. First, currentPosition may be initialized to 1 before the blank-insertion loop. This makes sense because we wish to find the first gap starting from the beginning of the line. Second, NextGap-Position returns the position of the first blank in a gap if it is called with currentPosition anywhere either in the word before the gap or in the gap that precedes that word, as shown in the diagram below.

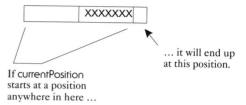

... it will end up at this position.

If currentPosition starts at a position anywhere in here ...

Stop & Consider ➤   *Why not initialize* currentPosition *to 0?*

How can the code be simplified?

The code just designed does more work than necessary. If there are at least two words in line when NextGapPosition is called, each loop will terminate in only one way when it finds a nonblank or a blank respectively. Thus the blankFound and nonblankFound variables can be eliminated. Furthermore, the declaration of currentPosition as a value parameter means that the function may change it without affecting its value in the calling program. The following code results.

```
function NextGapPosition (line: StringType; length: integer;
            currentPosition : integer): integer;
begin
    while line [currentPosition] = BLANK do begin
        currentPosition := currentPosition + 1;
        if currentPosition > length then begin
            currentPosition := 1;
        end;
    end;
    while line [currentPosition] <> BLANK do begin
        currentPosition := currentPosition + 1;
        if currentPosition > length then begin
            currentPosition := 1;
        end;
    end;
    NextGapPosition := currentPosition;
end;
```

How is a blank inserted?

Inserting a blank is a three-step process similar to the process of compression that we used in replacing prefixes in *Is It Legal?* First, space for the blank needs to be created by moving all the characters after the insertion point over one space. Then the blank can be inserted in the space. Finally, the length of the line is updated. A descriptive name for this procedure is InsertOneBlank. An example, in which a blank is inserted into position 4, is illustrated as follows:

Shifting subsequent elements over one position:

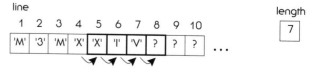

Storing the blank:

line   length

1	2	3	4	5	6	7	8	9	10
'M'	'3'	'M'		'X'	'X'	'I'	'V'	?	?	...

length: 7

Contents of line and length after insertion:

line   length

1	2	3	4	5	6	7	8	9	10
'M'	'3'	'X'		'X'	'I'	'V'	'V'	?	?	...

length: 8

Stop & Predict ➤ *Characters after the insertion point can be shifted over from left to right or from right to left. Does it matter?*

What are the parameters of InsertOneBlank?

InsertOneBlank has three parameters: line, length, and position. (We use position rather than gapPosition or currentPosition because this is a general insertion procedure that can be used in a variety of insertion applications.) Since line is expanded by the procedure, it must be a var parameter; length must be updated to account for the newly added character, and so it must also be a var parameter.

What is the pseudocode for InsertOneBlank?

InsertOneBlank involves another application of the "process every element of an array" template, where the "processing" is copying an element to the position immediately following it. As with compression in *Is It Legal?* the template is applied only to those elements at and following the insertion position. A careless programmer might fall into the trap of applying the template as follows:

```
for k:= position+1 to length do begin
    line[k] := line[k-1];
end;
```

Stop & Predict ➤ *What's wrong with this code?*

This code has a serious flaw. The copying must proceed in the opposite order. Here's the code for the complete procedure.

```
procedure InsertOneBlank(var line: StringType; var length: integer;
    position: integer);
var
    k: integer;
begin
    for k := length downto position+1 do begin
        line[k] := line[k-1];
    end;
    line[position] := BLANK;
    length := length + 1;
end;
```

Stop & Predict ➤ *This procedure still has a bug. Identify it.*

What is the decomposition for the blank-by-blank solution?

The decomposition arrived at for the blank-by-blank solution is summarized in the outline below.

Insert blanks one blank at a time:
    For each blank to insert, do the following:
        Find the position of the next gap:
            Find the next nonblank on the line.
            Find the next blank on the line, moving from the end
              to the beginning if necessary.
        Insert a blank there:
            Move characters over to make room for it.
            Store the blank.
            Increase the line's length by 1.

What does SpaceText look like?

We now have all the pieces for the blank-by-blank version of SpaceText. It calls NextGapPosition and InsertOneBlank until all the blanks are inserted. We have not, however, yet dealt with the various exceptional cases mentioned in the problem statement: an empty line, a line that starts or ends with a blank, a line that's already longer than desired, or a line with only one word.

How are the exceptional cases handled?

The exceptional cases should be checked before NextGapPosition is called, since one of the preconditions to NextGapPosition is that line contains at least two words. The problem statement allows flexibility in the order in which the checks are made. Each exceptional case is handled by assigning the corresponding return value to status. This leads to the following code:

```
if length = 0 then begin
    status := EMPTYLINE;
end else if (line[1] = BLANK) or (line[length] = BLANK) then begin
    status := ENDBLANK;
end else if desiredLength < length then begin
    status := TOOLONG;
end else if line contains no blanks then begin
    status := ONEWORD;
end else begin
    space out the words using the blank-by-blank code;
end;
```

Stop & Help ➤ *Can the checks for the various exceptional cases be made in any order? Explain why or why not.*

All we need is a boolean function that returns true if line contains a blank to complete this section. (We call it ContainsBlank.) The complete collection of subprograms is in the Pascal Code section.

Stop & Help ➤ *Write the boolean function.*

Stop & Consider ➤ *Why did we create a function ContainsBlank rather than a function ContainsNo-Blank?*

How is the code tested?

Recall that we have already used the black-box approach to design a set of test data. It included the following categories of lines:

- an empty line
- a line containing one character
- a line containing MAXSTRLEN characters
- a line longer than desired
- a line exactly as long as desired
- a line where one blank is to be added
- a line where the maximum number of blanks is to be added
- a line with no words
- a line with one word
- a line with the maximum number of words
- a line that starts with a blank
- a line that ends with a blank
- a line that starts *and* ends with a blank

Now that the code is written, we can use the glass-box approach to augment the set of test lines. The loops in NextGapPosition suggest lines that contain words and gaps of one character, two characters, and the maximum number of characters. The cycling behavior should be exercised as well, so a line that requires a second pass of insertions should also be part of the test data.

Stop & Help ➤   *Devise a set of test lines for the code just designed, and test the code.*

What bugs are encountered?

The coding and testing process reveals some bugs in this code. Blanks are inserted in incorrect places, even at the end of the line. SpaceText is too simple to contain that bug. InsertOneBlank seems to be inserting correctly, but in the wrong places. That narrows the bug to NextGapPosition, where we notice that the code says if currentPosition > MAXSTRLEN instead of if currentPosition > length.

Another flaw is that the last character of the line is not getting printed. We check OutputLine, but we had made sure it worked before. Apparently, the length OutputLine receives is incorrect. InsertOneBlank is the only routine that affects the length, so we check it to find (after some confusion) that the for loop is going from length downto position+1 rather than length+1 downto position+1.

Stop & Predict ➤   *What would be symptoms of off-by-one errors in* NextGapPosition?

How can more evidence be found that a set of test lines is comprehensive?

The bugs we encountered and the large number of categories of test data we devised suggest that this procedure is highly susceptible to off-by-one errors. One technique for showing that a set of test data is likely to expose such an error is called **mutation testing**. It involves *introducing* common bugs into the program, then checking that at least one of the test lines causes the bug to be displayed. One might, for instance, remove a + 1 or replace it by a − 1 or a + 2. One might interchange the order of two statements, replace a > by < or >=, or vice-versa. Things we then should look for are errors in handling the ends of the line, of a word, or of a gap.

Stop & Help ➤ *Generate a set of "mutations" of the code just designed, and check that at least one of the test lines you've devised provides evidence of each mutation.*

◀

Application 6.17 Write the code for an insertion function that inserts a blank next to *each blank* in line rather than in each gap. (This was referred to in the commentary as the solution of a "careless programmer.")

Analysis 6.18 Give an example of a line with multiple blanks between words for which the careless programmer's approach works correctly.

Analysis 6.19 The stated precondition for NextGapPosition, that line contains at least two words, is stronger than necessary to avoid an infinite loop. What is the weakest possible requirement for line that ensures that NextGapPosition will return some value?

Analysis 6.20 Can either of the while statements in NextGapPosition be replaced by a repeat statement without adding an accompanying if statement? Why or why not?

Modification 6.21 Rewrite SpaceText to use only one position variable rather than two.

Reflection 6.22 Why is it best to make the two while loops in NextGapPosition as similar as possible?

Testing 6.23 What test lines will provide the best evidence that the NextGapPosition will find the *first* gap correctly? Briefly explain.

Debugging 6.24 What would happen if SpaceText did not test for the case of a line with initial blanks? How would such a line be treated?

Modification 6.25 The blank-finding loop in the first version of NextGapPosition used the double-negative expression not nonblankFound. Recode this loop so that it is easier to understand.

Gap-by-Gap Decomposition

What about adding blanks to each gap only once?

Rather than cycling, it must be possible to figure out how many blanks to add to each gap. The program would then go through the line only once, inserting the right number of blanks between each pair of words. This can be called the "gap-by-gap" solution. The example below illustrates this approach, again extending a line of length 17 to the desired length of 27.

```
12345678901234567890123 4567
```

```
now is   the time
```

```
now     is   the time                    insert four blanks into the first gap
```

```
now     is       the time                insert three blanks into the second gap
```

```
now     is       the      time           insert three blanks into the third gap
```

The gap-by-gap decomposition will put the correct number of blanks in each gap rather than inserting a single blank in successive gaps until all the blanks are assigned.

To insert the right number of blanks we need to know how many gaps there are, find each gap, and insert the blanks. In pseudocode:

```
count the gaps in the line;
for k := 1 to numberGaps, do the following:
    find the kth gap;
    insert the correct number of blanks there;
```

Finding the kth gap can probably be done as in the blank-by-blank solution. The hard parts seems to be to counting the gaps and figuring out how many blanks to insert in each gap.

Stop & Predict ➤   *What parts of the blank-by-blank decomposition can be recycled for the gap-by-gap decomposition?*

How can the gaps be counted?   We devise a function for returning the number of gaps and call it Gap-Count. One idea for counting the gaps is to call NextGapPosition, counting gaps until the end of the line is reached.

Stop & Help ➤   *Why use a function for* GapCount *rather than a procedure?*

Stop & Predict ➤   *Can* NextGapPosition *be used unchanged to count the gaps in the line? Explain why or why not.*

This idea has several flaws, however. Repeated calls to NextGapPosition will return the positions of all the gaps, but NextGapPosition was designed to "wrap around" the line and return the first gap after returning the last gap. Furthermore, NextGapPosition isn't designed to work if there is only one word in line—but how do we know this before we count the gaps?

These problems can be solved by using a modified version of NextGap-Position. A better idea, however, is to return to the definition of gap on which NextGapPosition was based: a gap is signaled by a nonblank immediately preceding a blank. We can apply the "process every element of an array" template straightforwardly to scan line for occurrences of the non-blank-blank pair:

```
function GapCount(line: StringType; length: integer): integer;
var
    numGaps, k: integer;
begin
    numGaps := 0;
    for k := 1 to length-1 do begin
        if (line[k] <> BLANK) and (line[k+1] = BLANK) then begin
            numGaps := numGaps + 1;
        end;
    end;
    GapCount := numGaps;
end;
```

Stop & Help ➤   *What does* GapCount *return for a line containing no gaps? How about an empty line, a line for which* length *contains 0?*

Stop & Help ➤   *What are the preconditions for* GapCount?

What is the "correct number of blanks" to insert at each gap?

The next step is to figure out how many blanks to insert in each gap. Again, a table of values will help:

Number of blanks	Number of gaps	Distribution of gaps
5	2	3, 2
5	3	2, 2, 1
5	4	2, 1, 1, 1
4	3	2, 1, 1

"Even distribution" of blanks into gaps suggests the use of the div function to get the number of blanks to add to each gap. The mod function will give the number of remaining gaps, so we add these values to the table.

Number of blanks	Number of gaps	Distribution of blanks	# blanks div # gaps	# blanks mod # gaps
5	2	3, 2	2	1
5	3	2, 2, 1	1	2
5	4	2, 1, 1, 1	1	1
4	3	2, 1, 1	1	1

The table shows that the number of gaps with an extra blank is just the number of blanks mod the number of gaps. This makes sense, since it's the remainder when an identical number of blanks have been added to each gap.

Stop & Help ➤   *Suppose* (numToInsert div # *gaps*) + 1 *blanks were inserted into each gap. How many gaps would have an extra blank?*

How does blank insertion work?

Pseudocode for computing the number of blanks to insert according to the above discussion is the following:

```
for k := 1 to numGaps, do the following:
    find the kth gap;
    insert (numToInsert div numGaps) blanks;
    if k <= numToInsert mod numGaps then
        insert one more blank;
```

The blank insertion can be done with a loop around InsertOneBlank. Finding the kth gap involves maintaining a position variable as in the blank-by-blank version and finding the *next* gap each time through the loop.

What does the gap-by-gap version of SpaceText look like?

Putting these procedures together and checking for special cases as in the blank-by-blank version yields the gap-by-gap version of SpaceText in the Pascal Code section.

Stop & Help ➤ *Devise cases and test the gap-by-gap version of SpaceText. Use all the cases previously tested, plus additional test lines as just described.*

How is the code tested?

The glass-box approach suggests testing GapCount with a line that has a gap as early in the line as possible and as late in the line as possible. Test data previously devised are also suitable here. We also look for things that can go wrong. For instance, the code uses div and mod, which do division and shouldn't divide by zero. We must make sure that division by zero never happens.

Stop & Help ➤ *How is the possibility of dividing by zero avoided?*

◀

📖 💾 *Modification* 6.26 Modify InsertOneBlank from the blank-by-blank solution to take an extra argument, the number of blanks to insert. Name the new procedure InsertBlanks, and modify SpaceText to call it to insert blanks.

📖 💾 *Modification* 6.27 If the line is guaranteed to contain at least one gap, NextGapPosition can be used to count gaps as follows: it is called once to find the starting position of the first gap, then called repeatedly until it returns that starting position. Code a version of GapCount that uses this approach.

📖 💾 *Debugging* 6.28 Insert a bug into the gap-by-gap version of SpaceText, and get a fellow programmer to find the bug. Which bugs are hardest to find?

📖 💾 *Analysis* 6.29 The gap-by-gap version was alleged to be more efficient than the blank-by-blank version, since in general there will be fewer gaps than blanks to insert. Choose a number of test lines and count (or modify the procedure to count) the number of assignment statements that fill or copy array elements in each version of SpaceText. Does the gap-by-gap version do fewer assignments? Explain.

Improving the Program

What parts of SpaceText could be improved?

Both versions of SpaceText designed so far do a lot of shifting of characters, pushing characters one space to the right at each insertion. One may check this by analyzing the code by hand or by **instrumenting** it, that is, adding code that measures how many operations are executed by incrementing a variable each time a statement is executed. (Some Pascal environments allow these execution counts to be produced automatically.) All this shifting could take a lot of time, perhaps as many pushes per insertion as there are characters in line. A revision to the gap-by-gap version can eliminate this inefficiency.

What is an efficient way to insert the blanks?

Since insertions always happen from left to right in the gap-by-gap solution, once a gap is filled, that part of the line will remain unchanged. Thus, if SpaceText copies the contents of line into another array while it searches for gaps, it can add blanks to the new array instead of inserting them into line. No shifting is necessary with this approach. The diagrams below illustrate the two processes.

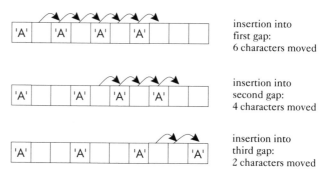

Insertion in place: 12 characters moved

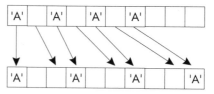

Insertion via copying into a second array
7 characters copied

What are ways to code the more efficient algorithm?

One way to implement this algorithm would be to design a complex loop that copies as it searches for a gap. An approach that reuses more of the code already designed separates the process of finding the next gap from the process of copying. An outline for a revision using this approach is given below, with revisions in italics.

Insert blanks using a second array called newLine:

> Count the gaps in line.
>
> Determine how many blanks to insert.
>
> *Initialize* newLine *along with position variables for* line *and* newLine.
>
> For each gap, do the following:
>
>> Find the position of the next gap in line.
>>
>> Copy characters into newLine from the old position in line to the gap position in line.
>>
>> Add the correct number of blanks to newLine.
>>
>> Update the position variables for line and newLine.
>
> Copy the last word from line to newLine.
>
> *Copy* newLine *back to* line.

The code for finding the next gap can be used unchanged in this solution.

What code occurs more than once in this approach?

This approach requires a lot of copying from one array to another. This suggests that we design a general copying procedure that copies a given sequence of characters from one array to another. We'll call this procedure CopySequence.

Stop & Help ➤ *What will be the parameters of* CopySequence?

How is CopySequence coded?

Two of CopySequence's parameters will be the source line (*from which* characters are copied) and the destination line (*to which* characters are copied). CopySequence will also need to know where in the source to start copying and where to finish, and where in the destination to start copying. The procedure heading for CopySequence follows; anticipating the usefulness of a copying procedure with any array, we give the parameters general rather than specific names.

```
procedure CopySequence(source: StringType;
    sourceStart, sourceEnd: integer;
    var destination: StringType; destStart: integer);
```

Stop & Help ➤ *Why is the starting position in the destination not the same as the starting position in the source?*

To design CopySequence, we once again apply the template "process every element of an array." The relevant elements are those between positions sourceStart and sourceEnd; the "processing" done is copying the element into destination. One extra bit of work to do for each element copied is to increment the position in destination. Here's the code:

```
for k := sourceStart to sourceEnd do begin
    destination[destStart] := source[k];
    destStart := destStart + 1;
end;
```

We note that making destStart a var parameter removes the need to update it in the SpaceText code. We do this, simultaneously renaming destStart to destPosition.

How are blanks added to the new line?

Blanks are always added to the end of newLine in this approach. Thus we design a procedure AddBlanksToEnd, whose parameters will be the line, a position at which to add blanks, and the number of blanks to add. The position will be a var parameter so that it will be updated when the procedure returns. Here's the code.

```
procedure AddBlanksToEnd(var line: StringType;
    var position: integer; numBlanks: integer);
var
    k: integer;
begin
    for k := 1 to numBlanks do begin
        line[position] := BLANK;
        position := position + 1;
    end;
end;
```

Stop & Help ➤ *What are the preconditions and postconditions of* AddBlanksToEnd?

How are calls to these procedures combined?

Putting it all together requires attention to the preconditions and postconditions of the various routines. Here's the code:

```
currentPosition := 1;
newLinePosition := 1;
numToInsert := desiredLength - length;
numGaps := GapCount(line, length);
numPerGap := numToInsert div numGaps;
numExtras := numToInsert mod numGaps;
for k := 1 to numGaps do begin
    gapPosition := NextGapPosition(line, length, currentPosition);
    CopySequence(line, currentPosition, gapPosition,
        newLine, newLinePosition);
    if k <= numExtras then begin
        AddBlanksToEnd(newLine, newLinePosition, numPerGap+1);
    end else begin
        AddBlanksToEnd(newLine, newLinePosition, numPerGap);
    end;
    currentPosition := gapPosition;
end;
CopySequence(line, currentPosition, length, newLine, newLinePosition);
```

The final program in the Pascal Code section contains the result. The test data devised for the earlier versions should suffice to test this one.

◀

▣ ▤ *Debugging* 6.30 Suppose an almost correct version of the program just designed prints the line exactly as entered, no matter how long. What simple thing was probably omitted?

🖳 🖫 *Analysis*   6.31 Choose a number of test lines and count (or modify the procedure to count) the number of assignment statements that fill or copy array elements in the revised version of SpaceText. Does the revised version do fewer assignments? Explain.

🖳 🖫 *Modification*   6.32 Modify the program just designed to use only one array (the argument to SpaceText), and to insert blanks into it from right to left rather than from left to right.

Application   6.33 Why might efficiency matter for this procedure?

Outline of Design and Development Questions

These questions summarize the main points of the commentary.

Initial Approach
What is the problem asking for?
    How will SpaceText be tested?
    Why would someone design a procedure without a program to accompany it?
    Why should the procedure be independent of the calling program?
What will the program to test SpaceText do?
    How are the variable types defined?
    How will the information be printed?
What data should be used to test the completed SpaceText procedure?

Alternative Designs for SpaceText
How is SpaceText designed?
How many blanks need to be inserted?
Which solution seems best?

Blank-by-Blank Approach
What action is to be repeated for each blank to be inserted?
How is the insertion position found?
    What parameters will NextGapPosition have?
    What are the steps in NextGapPosition?
    How is a blank preceded by a nonblank detected?
    What conditions could cause problems?
How can the code be simplified?
How is a blank inserted?
    What are the parameters of InsertOneBlank?
    What is the pseudocode for InsertOneBlank?

What is the decomposition for the blank-by-blank solution?
What does SpaceText look like?
>How are the exceptional cases handled?
How is the code tested?
>What bugs are encountered?
>How can more evidence be found that a set of test lines
is comprehensive?

Gap-by-Gap Decomposition
What about adding blanks to each gap only once?
How can the gaps be counted?
What is the "correct number of blanks" to insert at each gap?
How does blank insertion work?
What does the gap-by-gap version of SpaceText look like?
How is the code tested?

Improving the program
What parts of SpaceText could be improved?
What is an efficient way to insert the blanks?
What are ways to code the more efficient algorithm?
What code occurs more than once in this approach?
How is CopySequence coded?
How are blanks added to the new line?
How are calls to these procedures combined?

Programmers' Summary

This case study considers the problem of adding blanks between words in
a line of text to fill it out to a specified length. Three solutions are described. One is organized around a blank-by-blank loop that adds a single
blank at a time to successive gaps between words. The second is organized around a loop that makes one pass through the line, inserting the
correct number of blanks into each gap. Finally, a version of the gap-by-
gap solution is considered in which a *copy* of the line was used to avoid the
inefficiency of in-place insertion of blanks.

The problem statement specifies that a *procedure* called SpaceText be designed and developed. The program in which the procedure will be included is unspecified. This requirement is nothing new; procedures have
been tested in isolation in every case study so far.

Apart from using predefined types for strings and status values and predefined constants for status values, the procedure is also required to be *independent* of the calling program. This is a new requirement, illustrating
new dimensions of the Recycling and Divide and Conquer principles.

The goal of the problem is not to build an entire structure, but to build a *component*, a building block that can be used in a variety of programs. The more *modular*—independent of its surroundings—such a component is, the easier it is to use, both in a personal library of code for templates, and for team members working on a large program.

The problem statement introduces the use of a status variable, a more flexible and general way to gather and report on exceptional conditions that arise during processing. In our test program, we implement the status variable as an integer. Each status message is associated with a value for the integer. To ease implementation, following the Literacy principle, we give each condition a name such as ARRAYTOOLONG.

The line of text is represented in an array. Arrays in earlier case studies were used in relatively static ways. For example, the only dynamic change to an array in *Roman Calculator Construction* was to substitute single Roman digits for prefix pairs. Here, the whole point is to add new elements to the array. The use of box diagrams as in *Is It Legal?*, with arrows to show the direction of copying, provides a good alternative representation of the process (applying the Multiple Representations principle).

One array template is recycled directly: "search a one-dimensional array." Another, "process every element of an array," is specialized to (a) copy an array segment, (b) process elements while accumulating or updating a separate piece of information, and (c) shift elements of an array to make room for an insertion. These template specializations seem likely to occur in future applications.

The blank-by-blank approach illustrates how templates can be recycled to achieve a relatively short and uncomplicated program. This preliminary solution is used as a basis for a more efficient solution. Sometimes a quest for efficiency leads to code that's more complicated than necessary. However, when we add the auxiliary line array, we reject the complicated decomposition of copying while searching for a gap in favor of one that splits the searching and copying operations and therefore applies templates in a more straightforward way.

Analysis is important in the design. The two loops in NextGapPosition that skip blanks and search for the next blank are coordinated by matching the postcondition of one with the precondition of the other. The conditions under which these loops would fail to terminate determine the precondition of NextGapPosition and therefore dictate the order of exceptional-case testing in the main SpaceText routine.

Analysis also reveals that the blank-by-blank program does a lot of character shifting. (This analysis may be done by hand, by *instrumenting* the code with variables that count how many times certain sections are executed, or by taking advantage of features of the programming environment that provide counts of the number of times each statement in a program is executed.) The gap-by-gap design, in combination with the use of an auxiliary array, eliminates the need for shifting, at the cost of having to recopy the expanded line back into the original array.

Integer arithmetic with mod and div shows up yet again, this time to compute how many blanks should be inserted in each gap.

The test program for SpaceText is designed before the procedure (partly as a confidence builder). It includes output that makes clear the column positions within the line, to make it easier to notice errors. Much of the *test data* are designed beforehand as well, using the black-box approach to complete the problem specification. As in previous case studies, we notice numeric quantities associated with the problem and choose test data that bring these quantities to their extreme values. Because there are a lot of quantities, the procedure is somewhat difficult to test.

One suggested way of providing more confidence in the test data is *mutation testing*, in which bugs are intentionally introduced into the procedure to make sure that they are exposed during testing. (We do this after fixing a couple of unintentionally introduced bugs.) There is ample opportunity to associate bugs—typically off-by-one errors—with their symptoms, as suggested in the Fingerprint principle.

Making Sense of *Space Text*

Modification 6.34 Instead of characterizing a gap as a nonblank followed by a blank, one may instead consider a gap to arise from a blank followed by a nonblank. Rewrite each version of SpaceText to base the location of a gap on this new definition.

Analysis 6.35 What happens in each version of SpaceText if the check for a line ending with a blank is omitted?

Modification 6.36 Modify each version of SpaceText to take an extra boolean parameter that specifies whether the insertion of blanks should proceed left to right or right to left, and to insert blanks appropriately. In which version of SpaceText is this modification made most easily?

Modification 6.37 Modify each version of SpaceText to use a data structure consisting of two arrays, one containing the words in the line, the other containing the number of blanks that follow each word in the line. The new SpaceByGaps will change the number of blanks after each word so that the total line length is as desired. An illustration of the new data structure appears on the next page.

```
Hi.  How are you?  I'm fine.  See you around.
```

Word	Number of blanks that follow it
Hi.	2
How	1
are	1
you?	2
I'm	1
fine.	2
See	1
you	1
around.	0

Testing 6.38 To test and debug the modification described in question 6.37, you will need to change the ReadLine and OutputLine procedures as well as the procedures that insert blanks. Suppose you were going to change and test one routine at a time, in order to be as sure as possible that bugs in one routine don't affect the behavior of another. In what order should you make the changes to ReadLine, OutputLine, and the insertion routines, and how would you test them?

Modification 6.39 In modern typesetting systems, characters have different widths. The letter "w," for instance, is wider than the letter "i." The width of each character is expressed in number of *pixels* (picture elements); "w" might be 11 pixels wide and "i" only 3.

Suppose we have defined an array charTable (standing for "character table") of the following type,

```
type CharTabType = array [char] of integer;
```

and included a routine ReadCharTable that fills each element of the array with the width in pixels of each character. Now we wish to use the table of widths to fill a line so that its width in pixels is a particular length. Modify each version of SpaceText to do this. Assume that a blank is one pixel wide.

Analysis 6.40 Once the modification of question 6.39 has been made, how do the relative efficiencies of the blank-by-blank version and the gap-by-gap version compare?

Reflection 6.41 Which of the three versions is easiest for you to understand? Which contains code that will be easiest for you to reuse? Which do you prefer? Explain.

Linking to Previous Case Studies

🖳 💾 *Modification*   6.42   Modify the subprograms in *Is It Legal?* to return a status value rather than a boolean value. If there is an error in the argument, the status value should indicate what's wrong.

🖳 💾 *Modification*   6.43   Modify the week-by-week version of *The Calendar Shop* to implement a three-step process: fill an array with the values 1, 2, ..., up to the number of days in the month being printed; insert zeroes at the start of the array to represent the blank spaces at the beginning of the month; print the array, seven values to a line, substituting blanks for zeroes.

PASCAL CODE **PASCAL CODE**

Test Program

```pascal
program adjust (input, output);

const
    MAXSTRLEN = 30;
    ENDBLANK = 1;
    TOOLONG = 2;
    EMPTYLINE = 3;
    ONEWORD = 4;
    OK = 5;
    BLANK = ' ';

type
    StringType = array[1..MAXSTRLEN] of char;
    StatusType = integer;

var
    line: StringType;
    length, desiredLength: integer;
    status: StatusType;

{
    Read the desired length.
}
procedure ReadDesired (var n: integer);
begin {Read Desired}
    write('How long do you want the line to be? ');
    readln(n);
end; {Read Desired}

{
    Read a line, discarding characters that don't fit in a string.
```

```
}
procedure ReadLine (var line: StringType; var length: integer);
var
    k: integer;
    ch: char;
begin {Read Line}
    length := 0;
    for k := 1 to MAXSTRLEN do begin
        line[k] := BLANK;
    end;
    while not eoln do begin
        read(ch);
        length := length + 1;
        if length <= MAXSTRLEN then begin
            line[length] := ch;
        end;
    end;
    readln;
end; {Read Line}

{
    Insert blanks between words in the line as described in the
    problem statement.
}
procedure SpaceText (var line: StringType; length, desiredLength: integer;
    var status: StatusType);
begin {Space Text}
    status := OK;
end; {Space Text}

{
    Print the line so that its length can easily be determined.
}
procedure OutputLine (line: StringType; length: integer);
var
    k: integer;
begin {Output Line}
    writeln('12345678901234567890123457890');
    for k := 1 to length do begin
        write(line[k]);
    end;
    writeln;
    writeln('length = ', length : 1);
    writeln;   {extra blank line for nice spacing}
end; {Output Line}

{
    Print an explanation of the status.
}
procedure WritelnStatus (status: StatusType);
begin {Writeln Status}
    case status of
        OK: writeln('ok');
        ENDBLANK: writeln('line ends with a blank');
        TOOLONG: writeln('line is longer than desired');
        EMPTYLINE: writeln('line is empty');
```

```pascal
            ONEWORD: writeln('line contains only one word');
        end;
end; {Writeln Status}


begin {main program}
    while true do begin
        ReadLine(line, length);
        ReadDesired(desiredLength);
        SpaceText(line, length, desiredLength, status);
        WritelnStatus(status);
        OutputLine(line, length);
    end;
end.
```

Blank-by-Blank Solution

```pascal
{
    Return the position of the next gap (space between words) in line,
    starting the search at position currentPosition. If searching reaches
    the end of the line, restart it at the beginning of the line.
    Precondition: line must contain at least one blank.
}
function NextGapPosition (line: StringType;
    length, currentPosition: integer): integer;
begin {Next Gap Position}
    while line[currentPosition] = BLANK do begin
        currentPosition := currentPosition + 1;
        if currentPosition > length then begin
            currentPosition := 1;
        end;
    end;
    while line[currentPosition] <> BLANK do begin
        currentPosition := currentPosition + 1;
        if currentPosition > length then begin
            currentPosition := 1;
        end;
    end;
    NextGapPosition := currentPosition;
end; {Next Gap Position}


{
    Insert a single blank into line at the given position.
    The line length increases by one.
}
procedure InsertOneBlank (var line: StringType; var length: integer;
    position: integer);
var
    k: integer;
begin {Insert One Blank}
    for k := length + 1 downto position + 1 do begin
        line[k] := line[k - 1];
    end;
    line[position] := BLANK;
    length := length + 1;
```

```
end; {Insert One Blank}

{
    Return true exactly when line contains a blank character.
}
function ContainsBlank (line: StringType; length: integer): boolean;
var
    k: integer;
begin {Contains Blank?}
    ContainsBlank := false;
    for k := 1 to length do begin
        if line[k] = BLANK then begin
            ContainsBlank := true;
        end;
    end;
end; {Contains Blank?}

{
    Insert blanks between words in the line as described in the problem
    statement.
}
procedure SpaceText (var line: StringType;
    var length: integer; desiredLength: integer; var status: StatusType);
var
    numToInsert, currentPosition, gapPosition, k: integer;
begin {Space Text}
    if length = 0 then begin
        status := EMPTYLINE;
    end else if (line[1] = BLANK) or (line[length] = BLANK) then begin
        status := ENDBLANK;
    end else if desiredLength < length then begin
        status := TOOLONG;
    end else if not ContainsBlank(line, length) then begin
        status := ONEWORD;
    end else begin
        numToInsert := desiredLength - length;
        currentPosition := 1;
        for k := 1 to numToInsert do begin
            gapPosition := NextGapPosition(line, length, currentPosition);
            InsertOneBlank(line, length, gapPosition);
            currentPosition := gapPosition;
        end;
        status := OK;
    end;
end; {Space Text}
```

Gap-by-Gap Solution

This code uses some of the procedures from the blank-by-blank solution.

```
{
    Return the number of gaps in line.
    (This should be the number of words minus 1.)
}
```

```
function GapCount (line: StringType; length: integer): integer;
var
    numGaps, k: integer;
begin {Gap Count}
    numGaps := 0;
    for k := 1 to length - 1 do begin
        if (line[k] <> BLANK) and (line[k + 1] = BLANK) then begin
            numGaps := numGaps + 1;
        end;
    end;
    GapCount := numGaps;
end;


{
    Insert blanks between words in the line as described in the problem
    statement.
}
procedure SpaceText (var line: StringType;
    var length: integer; desiredLength: integer; var status: StatusType);
var
    numToInsert, currentPosition, numGaps, k, j: integer;
begin {Space Text}
    if length = 0 then ...
        {check for exceptional situations as in previous solution}
    end else begin
        numToInsert := desiredLength - length;
        currentPosition := 1;
        numGaps := GapCount(line, length);
        for k := 1 to numGaps do begin
            currentPosition := NextGapPosition(line,length,
                currentPosition);
            for j := 1 to numToInsert div numGaps do begin
                InsertOneBlank(line, length, currentPosition);
            end;
            if k <= numToInsert mod numGaps then begin
                InsertOneBlank(line, length, currentPosition);
            end;
        end;
        status := OK;
    end;
end; {Space Text}
```

Revised Gap-by-Gap Solution

```
{
    Copy characters from positions sourceStart through sourceEnd of source
    to destination starting at position destPosition. Update destPosition
    to be one past the position in destination of the last character
    copied.
}
procedure CopySequence (source: StringType;
    sourceStart, sourceEnd: integer;
    var destination: StringType; var destPosition: integer);
var
```

```
        k: integer;
begin {Copy Sequence}
    for k := sourceStart to sourceEnd do begin
        destination[destPosition] := source[k];
        destPosition := destPosition + 1;
    end;
end; {Copy Sequence}


{
    Add numBlanks blank characters to line starting at the given position.
}
procedure AddBlanksToEnd (var line: StringType; var position: integer;
    numBlanks: integer);
var
    k: integer;
begin {Add Blanks to End}
    for k := 1 to numBlanks do begin
        line[position] := BLANK;
        position := position + 1;
    end;
end; {Add Blanks to End}


{
    Insert blanks between words in the line as described in the problem
    statement.
}
procedure SpaceText (var line: StringType; var length: integer;
    desiredLength: integer; var status: StatusType);
var
    currentPosition, newLinePosition, k: integer;
    newLine: StringType;
    gapPosition, numToInsert, numGaps, numPerGap, numExtras: integer;
begin {Space Text}
    if length = 0 then ...
        {check for exceptional cases as in previous solutions}
    end else begin
        currentPosition := 1;
        newLinePosition := 1;
        numToInsert := desiredLength - length;
        numGaps := GapCount(line, length);
        numPerGap := numToInsert div numGaps;
        numExtras := numToInsert mod numGaps;
        for k := 1 to numGaps do begin
            gapPosition := NextGapPosition(line, length,
                    currentPosition);
            CopySequence(line, currentPosition, gapPosition,
                newLine, newLinePosition);
            if k <= numExtras then begin
                AddBlanksToEnd(newLine, newLinePosition, numPerGap + 1);
            end else begin
                AddBlanksToEnd(newLine, newLinePosition, numPerGap);
            end;
            currentPosition := gapPosition + 1;
        end;
        CopySequence(line, currentPosition, length,
            newLine, newLinePosition);
```

```
                line := newLine;
                length := desiredLength;
                status := OK;
           end;
     end; {Space Text}
```

CHAPTER 7

You Are What You Eat

Eating fresh fruits and vegetables keeps fat and calories low. Use this program to chart your progress.

The current enthusiasm for choosing a healthy diet motivates people to keep track of the calories, fat, and cholesterol they consume. Suppose you were asked to design a program to help. This case study describes how a programmer might respond.

Problem Statement

Our friend Terry is just learning about computers and comes to us with a request. It sounds straightforward so we agree to help. Here is our conversation.

TERRY: Can you write a program for my new home computer to help me keep track of my diet? My computer is the same brand as yours.

MIKE AND MARCIA: What should the program do?

TERRY: Well, I want it to keep track of the fat and calories in the food I eat, figure out daily averages, and stuff like that. I've been using pencil and paper, but I lose track.

MIKE AND MARCIA: So you would type in fat and calorie numbers and the program would keep track of these and compute averages?

TERRY: Right.

MIKE AND MARCIA: How many days should be averaged?

TERRY: Could the program print the average over the last thirty days? I know that sometimes I overeat, or give in to the temptation for a dish of ice cream. I'm trying to keep fat and calories low overall, though.

MIKE AND MARCIA: A running thirty-day average would be easy to compute. We could even have it graph your last thirty days of fat and calories if you want.

TERRY: Great!

MIKE AND MARCIA: We're still a bit confused, though. When you run the program, what do you expect to give it as input?

TERRY: Well, now I write down the fat and calories for everything I eat. I want to give the program all those numbers each day.

MIKE AND MARCIA: So the program should total them all up to get your daily total for fat and calories.

TERRY: It can do that, right?

MIKE AND MARCIA: Yes, that will be easy. You'll run the program every day?

TERRY: Right.

MIKE AND MARCIA: And, you want the average and the graph printed every day. Let's see, for a graph it would help to know the maximum number of fat and calories to expect. What have the values been like?

TERRY: I've never eaten more than 6000 calories in a day. I think the fat has been as high as 400 grams, but I'm working on lowering that.

MIKE AND MARCIA: We can display the graph on the screen. Is your screen just like ours?

TERRY: They look the same.

MIKE AND MARCIA: Do you have a disk drive on your computer? The program will need to keep a permanent file on your disk.

TERRY: Yes, it has a hard disk. Will that do?

MIKE AND MARCIA: Yes. Give us a few days and we'll come up with something you can try out.

TERRY: Great!

Analysis 7.1 Why do we need to know about screen size?

Analysis 7.2 Why do we need to know the maximum amounts of fat and calories for the graph?

Reflection 7.3 What special needs will an inexperienced computer user have?

Analysis 7.4 Sketch an interaction between Terry and the program.

Reflection 7.5 What additional information from Terry might be useful for designing the program?

Analysis 7.6 What sophisticated features might an experienced computer user desire of a program that keeps track of nutrition information?

Reflection 7.7 Why have we agreed to write a program instead of telling Terry to use a commercial product?

Preparation

The reader is expected to be familiar with arrays and records; this case study introduces the reset and rewrite procedures and the eof function used with text files.

Planning the Program

How can this program meet the needs of the user?

Successful programs not only compute information desired by the user but also allow the user to communicate "intuitively" with the computer. Because Terry has limited computer experience, the program should be crashproof, its error messages should make sense to a novice, and there should be ways to get help. Most important, the interface should be "intuitive" in the sense that it should anticipate Terry's view of the problem.

Will the needs of the user change?

Because Terry is inexperienced, he may not anticipate all the ways a program can help him. He did not, for instance, think of having a graph of his nutrition information. It is likely that more features will be added to the program as Terry tests it. Thus, we need to design a program that is easy to modify.

Stop & Consider ➤ *What modifications might Terry ask for when he sees the program?*

Stop & Predict ➤ *List the main steps of the program before proceeding. Check yours against those indicated.*

What are the main steps in the program?

The discussion with Terry suggests five main steps for the program.

- Input—read lines containing fat and calorie figures from Terry.

- Compute daily total—add up the values to get a total for the day.

- Compute and output average—access the values for the last 29 days, compute the average of these values combined with the value for the current day, and print the average.

- Output graph—print a graph displaying the daily total for the current day and the previous 29 days.

- Update accumulated data—add the current day's data to the collection of data.

Stop & Predict ➤ *Why is the data for the past 29 days differentiated from the data for the current day?*

What parts of this program can be solved by recyling solutions to other problems?

The program will prompt Terry for input. It should be possible to recycle input and error-checking procedures developed in *Is It Legal?* Computing the average sounds like a place for the "process every element" template. Printing a graph might share similarities with printing block letters or printing calendar months.

If an array for storing the collection of nutrition data is involved, then templates used earlier for array manipulation may be applicable here.

| What data structures are needed? | The collection of fat and calorie data must be stored external to the program so it can be accessed each time the program is run. That means that a file must be used; we'll call it historyFile. We also need to manipulate the data internally to compute the average and print the graph. We call this internal structure recentHistory. |

Stop & Predict ➤   *Why not just use the external data structure for both storage and computation?*

Access to data in a file is much slower than access to data in an array. Thus it is typical to read data from a file into **internal variables**—those corresponding to memory locations, like simple variables, arrays, or records—do whatever computations are necessary using those variables, and then write the results back to the file. Another reason for using an internal structure is that file operations are limited to reading and writing *in sequence*. To compute the average and print the graph we will need to access elements nonsequentially.

Which should be refined first, the data structures or the algorithms?

At this point, we could design the main program, the procedures for getting input from Terry, and so on. In earlier case studies, deciding what to do next was more a matter of taste; one might prefer to tackle hard things first, or easy things. In this situation, however, where the program is likely to change with feedback from Terry, we try not to make decisions that will cost a lot of time later when the program must be modified.

For this program the goal is clear—keeping track of fat and calories—but the specific details may change. In general, the data structures in a program are most sensitive to changes in the details of problem specifications. If Terry needed merely to know the maximum and minimum fat and calorie intake over the last month, we could use two simple variables as internal storage. But for this problem, we will need a more complicated structure. Terry's future needs may complicate the situation still more. Thus it is important to design the program in such a way that changes, particularly to the program's data structures, will have minimal impact.

The internal history structure and the external file seem to be important to the rest of the program as well, since every processing step uses one or the other of them. Thus we will consider their design first and produce code that isolates as much as possible the effects of using a different representation for each one.

How are data types designed?

What we're really designing here is the **data type**. The data structure is a variable of that type. The design involves specifying the operations that will be applied to a variable of each type and then selecting an implementation.

What operations are applied to historyFile?

The program will apply two operations to historyFile. First, the program will read at least the previous 29 days of fat and calorie data from the file. Second, the program will add the current day's data to the file.

How should historyFile be implemented?	A text file offers a straightforward implementation for historyFile. Each line can contain a given day's fat and calorie data (two numbers).
	Terry asked us to keep track of thirty days worth of data. We decide, however, to store *all* the fat and calorie data in the file, just in case Terry decides to chart long-term trends. It is fairly easy to keep track of extra data and impossible to reconstruct data that has been deleted.
Stop & Consider ➤	*What is a disadvantage of storing all the fat and calorie data?*
How should the entries in historyFile be ordered?	Storing the most recent 29 days' worth of data *together* in the file will make it easier to access. A straightforward approach is to organize the data in historyFile by date. Either the file will *start* with the most recent data or it will *end* with the most recent data. Inserting the first 29 entries into recentHistory will then consist of reading either the first 29 lines in the file or the last 29 lines in the file; output of the current day's entry will require rewriting the file with a new first line or with a new last line.
	We postpone deciding whether the entries should be ordered most recent first or least recent first until the operations on recentHistory are defined; we consider these next.
Stop & Help ➤	*Suppose the entries were stored by amount of calories consumed. What information would have to be stored with each entry to allow access to the last 29 days' data?*
What will be the operations on recentHistory?	The program will fill the recentHistory structure with 29 days' data, add the current day's data, use the data to compute the average and generate the graph, and update historyFile with the current data.
	All the operations involve accessing the data by day:

- Initializing 29 days from historyFile means reading the most recent data into recentHistory.

- Adding the current day's data means storing the data for the current day into recentHistory.

- Computing the average means summing the values for each day and dividing by the number of days.

- Generating the graph means determining the line or column for the graph that corresponds to the data value for each day, and producing appropriate output.

- Updating the history file means either writing the whole collection of data or at least the current day's data into historyFile.

How will the data be represented internally?	The program will manipulate 30 days' data. This suggests one or more arrays of thirty elements. Each day's data consists of a fat quantity and a cal-

orie quantity, and perhaps the date as well. Given a day, we will want to access both the fat and calorie figures.

Stop & Predict ➤ *Which provides a better way to store the recent history: a two-dimensional array, an array of records, or two separate arrays?*

An array of records is most appropriate for this purpose. Other programming languages may require two separate arrays to store the fat and the calories, and we could also do that in Pascal. However, *grouping* the fat and calories for a given day in a Pascal record makes clear their association, and reduces the likelihood of bugs in which the indexes for fat and calories are "off-by-one."

How should the date be represented?

The date could be a part of the record. This seems unnecessary, however. If the data is ordered in the array by date, the date will not be needed to create the graph. In an array indexed from 0 to 29, the kth element would store the information for the day that's k days before the current day. The operations on recentHistory can easily be implemented with such an array.

Stop & Predict ➤ *Why might Terry want to know the day or date associated with a given entry?*

On further consideration, we wonder if Terry might want to know more about data for particular dates, for instance to compare weekday data and weekend data. We decide to start a list of things to ask Terry.

?
Questions for Terry
- Should any dates be specially indicated in the history file?

Stop & Predict ➤ *How would the data type for recentHistory be declared in Pascal?*

The type for recentHistory may be defined as shown below. Just in case Terry later decides that he wants graphs over a different history interval, we define a constant called HISTORYSIZE for the size of the array.

```
const
    HISTORYSIZE = 29;

type
    EntryType = record
        fat, calories: integer;
    end;
    HistoryType = array[0..HISTORYSIZE] of EntryType;

var
    recentHistory: HistoryType;
```

How should data be ordered in historyFile?

We postponed deciding how to order entries in historyFile until the operations for recenthistory were defined. Two operations involve both historyFile and recenthistory: initializing recenthistory and updating historyFile.

How should values be input from historyFile?

Suppose that entries were stored most recent first. Then recentHistory would be initialized by reading and storing the first 29 entries from historyFile. Now suppose that the entries in historyFile were stored most recent last. Then the last 29 entries are to be stored in recentHistory. Reading the first 29 entries in a file into an array is easy. Reading the last 29 entries is harder. (How can the program detect when it's 29 entries from the end?)

Stop & Help ➤   *Design pseudocode that initializes* recentHistory *by reading the last 29 entries in a file into elements 1 through 29 of an array.*

How is historyFile updated?   Updating historyFile means essentially inserting the new day's data into the file, using only sequential reading from and writing to the file. This is like inserting an element into an array, while only accessing the array elements sequentially. We can recycle the two-array approach used in *Space Text*.

Suppose that the entries are stored most recent first in historyFile, and the first 29 elements have been read into recentHistory. The new entry, recentHistory[0], is to be inserted at the beginning of the file. A Pascal file cannot be read from and written to simultaneously; in order to write to the file, the rewrite procedure must be used, but it empties the file. Thus the insertion must take place as follows:

- The entire contents of historyFile (some of which is already in recentHistory) is copied to a temporary file.

- A rewrite operation is performed on historyFile.

- The new element is written to the beginning of historyFile.

- The contents of the temporary file are copied back to historyFile.

The last two steps are similar to the insertion approach used in *Space Text*. If the entries are stored most recent last, the updating is very similar. We still need to copy historyFile to a temporary file since the rewrite procedure empties the file.

Stop & Predict ➤   *Which is better, storing data most recent first or storing data most recent last?*

The input step is straightforward if historyFile entries are ordered most recent first, complicated if they are ordered most recent last. Updating of historyFile seems to be equally difficult with each option. Thus we choose to order the entries in historyFile from most recent to least recent.

What do we have so far?   We now have two data types defined, one for the history file and one for the recent history. We summarize the operations for each type:

Operations on the recent history

- Find the average figure for fat or calorie consumption.

- Print a graph of fat or calorie consumption.

- Add the current day's data to the recent history.

Operations on both the recent history and the history file

- Read the most recent 29 days' data from the history file into the recent history.

- Write the most recent 30 days' data from the recent history to the history file.

Our goal is to design the program so that it is easy to modify. Therefore we will represent each of these operations by a subprogram so that they are localized, group these subprograms together in the program so that they will be easy to find, and write the remainder of the program so that access to the history file or the recent history always involves calling one of these subprograms.

Stop & Help ➤   *Explain how these steps for organizing the program make future modification of the program easier.*

Analysis   7.8   Why is input and output to the external data structure separated from Terry's input and print output?

Analysis   7.9   What changes in the specifications would require changes to the data structures?

Reflection   7.10   Why is recentHistory a better name for the internal data structure than monthData or some other name indicating that it contains thirty days of information?

Analysis   7.11   Why not have an array into which *all* the data from the history file is read, rather than just the recent data?

Solving the Problem

What is the top-level decomposition of the solution?

Linking these newly designed data types to the main steps of the program results in new steps as follows:

Input and process information from Terry: Read individual fat and calorie figures from Terry and add them up. Store the totals into a new entry. Add the new entry to recentHistory as its most recent element.

Input from file: Initialize the remaining values for recentHistory from historyFile.

Output to Terry: Compute an average and generate a graph from the entries in recentHistory.

Output to the file: Write a revised version of historyFile.

Stop & Help ➤ *Compare these input-process-output steps to the main steps identified at the beginning of the design process.*

This leads to the following code for the main program:

```
ReadEntry (entry);
Initialize (historyFile, entry, recentHistory);
PrintAverages (recentHistory)
PrintGraph (recentHistory);
Update (historyFile, recentHistory);
```

Stop & Consider ➤ *Why not code the first statement in the above code as* ReadEntry(recentHistory[0])*?*

Stop & Consider ➤ *Does it matter which procedures are designed next?*

How should the program ask for input?

We start with the first step, input from Terry. As usual the program will print a prompt, then read some input.

Stop & Predict ➤ *Should we ask Terry for both fat and calorie amounts at once?*

Since a confused user might type the values in the wrong order or insert punctuation between them, it is better to ask for each input separately. We decide to prompt and read values for fat and calories separately.

Stop & Predict ➤ *How can the prompts meet the needs of an inexperienced user?*

We should also make sure that there is no confusion about the meaning of the input value. For calories, that's not a problem. Fat is usually specified in grams, but not always. The prompt for fat amount should ask for the number of grams.

A survey of a number of food labels suggests that fat and calorie values should be integers rather than fractions. Not having to worry about values with decimal points will make our programming task easier. We add this to the list of things to check with Terry, however.

?

Questions for Terry
- Should any dates be specially indicated in the history file?
- Is it OK to use integer values for fat?

How does the program detect that all the data are entered?

How will Terry tell the program that he is finished entering data? One way is to ask Terry how much input he has. Since computers are better at counting than people, a better approach is to provide a **sentinel value** that signals no more data.

To make the sentinel intuitive to Terry we consider several alternatives. A number is bad because it requires Terry to translate the concept of being finished into a number, and unnecessary because the program will have to read values as characters rather than integers anyway to be bulletproof.

To make the interface intuitive, Terry should indicate when he is finished entering data by typing a word, like "done." Such a sentinel is also unlikely to be typed by accident.

Stop & Help ➤   *How can we be sure that Terry remembers the sentinel value?*

We could remind Terry of the sentinel value every time a prompt is given, but this seems excessive. We decide to ask Terry to advise us.

?   Questions for Terry
- Should any dates be specially indicated in the history file?
- Is it OK to use integer values for fat?
- Can you remember "done," or should this be in the prompt?

What is the pseudocode for the input step?

This yields the following pseudocode steps in the solution:

initialize totalCalories and totalFat to 0;
repeat the following until done:
      prompt Terry for a fat amount (expressed in grams);
      read and error-check the input, continuing to prompt
         and reread until an integer or the word "done" is typed;
      if not done, then
         prompt Terry for a calorie amount;
         read and error-check the input, continuing to prompt
            and reread until an integer is typed;
         add the values to totalCalories and totalFat;

Stop & Predict ➤   *Devise a plan for breaking this pseudocode into manageable procedures. What code can be recycled from previous case studies?*

How are the fat and calorie values input?

To code each prompt, read, and error-check loop, we can recycle the ReadInteger code from *Is It Legal?* This code may be simplified by storing the line and its length together in a record:

```
type
    LineType = record
        length: integer;
        chars: array [1..MAXLINELEN] of char;
    end;
```

Using a record means that all the procedures called from ReadInteger now have only one parameter, a variable of type LineType, rather than having separate parameters for the length and the input array. Where each procedure formerly referred to length, it now refers to line.length; where it referred to line or line[k], it now refers to line.chars or line.chars[k]. With these modifications, we generate two copies of ReadInteger, one called ReadFat that includes an additional check for the word "done," and the other called ReadCalories.

Stop & Help ➤   *Write the code for* ReadFat *and* ReadCalories.

An application of the "input and process until done" template produces code that calls ReadFat and ReadCalories:

```
procedure ReadEntry (var entry: EntryType);
var
    fat, calories: integer;
    done: boolean;
begin
    entry.fat := 0;
    entry.calories := 0;
    repeat
        ReadFat (fat, done);
        if not done then begin
            ReadCalories (calories);
            entry.fat := entry.fat + fat;
            entry.calories := entry.calories + calories;
        end;
    until done;
end;
```

How is the initialization step coded?

We move on to code the Initialize procedure. To initialize recentHistory we need some kind of a loop. Since there are 29 elements to be read, a for loop is an obvious choice.

```
for k := 1 to HISTORYSIZE do begin
    readln (historyFile, recentHistory[k].fat,
        recentHistory[k].calories);
end;
```

Stop & Predict ➤   *Why is a* for *loop inappropriate for initializing* recentHistory?

A for loop won't work if historyFile does not contain 29 entries. When Terry first runs the program, there will be no history. (This problem will also show up when the data are graphed.) The problem can be fixed either by complicating the input loop to handle a premature end of file or by ensuring that historyFile does contain 29 lines by starting it out that way. Taking the conservative approach, we choose the former option. The following code is an application of the "fill an array" template:

```
procedure Initialize (var historyFile: text; entry: EntryType;
    var recentHistory: HistoryType);
var
    numEntries, k: integer;
    done: boolean;
begin
    done := false;
    numEntries := 0;
    recentHistory[0] := entry;
    while not done do begin
        if eof then begin
            done := true;
        end else if numEntries = HISTORYSIZE then begin
            done := true;
        end else begin
            numEntries := numEntries + 1;
```

COMMENTARY **COMMENTARY**

```
                    readln (historyFile, recentHistory[numEntries].fat,
                        recentHistory[numEntries].calories);
            end;
        end;
        for k := numEntries+1 to HISTORYSIZE do begin
            recentHistory[k].fat := 0;
            recentHistory[k].calories := 0;
        end;
    end;
```

Stop & Help ➤   *Why is it necessary to have the* for *loop at the end of* Initialize?

Stop & Help ➤   *Why is coding a more complicated input loop a more "conservative approach"*
than ensuring that historyFile *always contains at least 29 values?*

Stop & Predict ➤   *Must the values read from* historyFile *be error-checked? Why or why not?*

The code will probably crash if there are format errors in historyFile. A primary consideration in the program design is the avoidance of crashes. However, there is no reason to believe that Terry will touch the file; it is accessed and updated only by the program. Thus, if any errors are present in the file, the program has a bug and shouldn't be available to Terry anyway. We add to our list for Terry a note to remind him not to alter the file.

? Questions for Terry
- Should any dates be specially indicated in the history file?
- Is it OK to use integer values for fat?
- Can you remember "done," or should this be in the prompt?
- Can we rely on you not to touch historyFile?

How are averages computed? Computing the average fat and calorie consumption is straightforward: it is just an application of the "process every element of an array" template. The representation we have chosen for the recent history requires separate subprograms for averaging the fat and averaging the calories, since a field name of a record can't be passed as a parameter to a single averaging subprogram. We'll code two functions, and call them FatAverage and CalorieAverage.

Stop & Help ➤   *Write the code for* FatAverage *and* CalorieAverage.

How is the history file updated? We postpone PrintGraph briefly, since the Update procedure has already essentially been designed. It implements a five-step process that uses a temporary file named tempFile:

- Rewrite tempFile, thereby emptying it.

- Write the 30 elements of recentHistory to tempFile, one element per line.

- Copy the rest of historyFile to tempFile.

- Reset tempFile in order to read from it starting at the beginning, and re-write historyFile, thereby emptying it.

- Copy the contents of tempFile to historyFile.

Stop & Help ➤   *What are* Update's *preconditions?*

Stop & Consider ➤   *Explain the function of* rewrite *and* reset *in Pascal. What makes these terms confusing?*

Writing the code is straightforward. The rewrite and reset steps translate directly to Pascal. The "process every element in an array" template is applied to write the elements of recentHistory. To copy the rest of historyFile, we note that the "input and process until done" template works just as well for files as it does for input from the terminal. The procedure appears below.

```
procedure Update (var historyFile: text; recentHistory: HistoryType);
var
    dayNum: integer;
    fat, calories: integer;
    tempFile: text;
begin
    rewrite (tempFile);
    for dayNum := 0 to HISTORYSIZE do begin
        writeln (tempFile, recentHistory[dayNum].fat,
            recentHistory[dayNum].calories);
    end;
    while not eof (historyFile) do begin
        readln (historyFile, fat, calories);
        writeln (tempFile, fat, calories);
    end;
    reset (tempFile);
    rewrite (historyFile);
    while not eof (historyFile) do begin
        readln (tempFile, fat, calories);
        writeln (historyFile, fat, calories);
    end;
end;
```

Stop & Help ➤   *Test the code designed so far, since it can be run and checked without the averaging and graphing procedures.*

What should the graph look like?   To determine the decomposition for the graph step we need to figure out how the graph will look. We decide on two graphs, one for fat and one for calories. We already determined that the axes will be time and either fat or calories.

Several choices must be made:

- Which quantity is to be measured on the vertical (up-down) axis and which on the horizontal (left-right) axis?

- In which direction should the numbers on each axis go?

- How should a given value on the graph be displayed? (For instance, should it appear as a single point or as a bar?)

Probably high fat/calorie values should appear at the right or at the top of the graph. Displaying each day's calorie total as a point seems reasonable. We try some example graphs to settle the other questions.

```
calories
10000 |
 9000 |
 8000 |
 7000 |
 6000 |
 5000 |
 4000 |
 3000 |
 2000 |
 1000 |
    0 +------------------------------------------------------------
        0 0 0 0 0 0 0 0 0 0 1 1 1 1 1 1 1 1 1 1 2 2 2 2 2 2 2 2 2 2 days
        0 1 2 3 4 5 6 7 8 9 0 1 2 3 4 5 6 7 8 9 0 1 2 3 4 5 6 7 8 9  ago
```
Calories on vertical axis, time on horizontal axis from most recent to least recent

```
calories
10000 |
 9000 |
 8000 |
 7000 |
 6000 |
 5000 |
 4000 |
 3000 |
 2000 |
 1000 |
    0 +------------------------------------------------------------
        2 2 2 2 2 2 2 2 2 2 1 1 1 1 1 1 1 1 1 1 0 0 0 0 0 0 0 0 0 0 days
        9 8 7 6 5 4 3 2 1 0 9 8 7 6 5 4 3 2 1 0 9 8 7 6 5 4 3 2 1 0  ago
```
Calories on vertical axis, time on horizontal axis from least recent to most recent

```
days ago
  0 |
  1 |
  2 |
  3 |
  4 |

  ⋮

 25 |
 26 |
 27 |
 28 |
 29 |
    +---------------------------------------------
     0  1000  2000  3000  4000  ... 10000 calories
```
Time on vertical axis with most recent at top, calories on horizontal axis

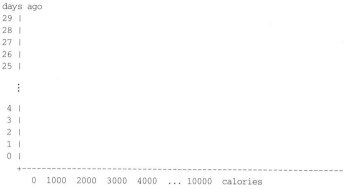

```
days ago
29 |
28 |
27 |
26 |
25 |
    ⋮
 4 |
 3 |
 2 |
 1 |
 0 |
   +---------------------------------------------------------------
    0  1000  2000  3000  4000  ... 10000  calories
```

Time on vertical axis with most recent on bottom, calories on horizontal axis

Which is best?

Looking at these graphs, we imagine that Terry will want to compare his fat and calorie consumption over a given range of days. Since the graphs will appear one above the other, comparison will be easiest if the time is on the horizontal axis. Furthermore, to reduce clutter, we decide to print every 5th day on the horizontal axis.

We add this decision to the list of things we want to check with Terry.

? Questions for Terry
- Should any dates be specially indicated in the history file?
- Is it OK to use integer values for fat?
- Can you remember "done," or should this be in the prompt?
- Can we rely on you not to touch historyFile?
- Does the proposed graph look OK?

What should the intervals for calorie consumption be?

Ten intervals for calorie consumption look about right, but we keep in mind that this may change after Terry has some experience with the program.

How is the task of displaying the graph decomposed?

As were letters in the *Banners With CLASS* program and months in *The Calendar Shop* program, the graph will be plotted line by line.

Stop & Predict ➤

Describe the steps in the decomposition. Then check your ideas against the list below.

Here is a reasonable approach:

Print the word "calories," followed by a carriage return.
For each calorie interval from the maximum down to 0, print the interval title, a vertical bar, and the X's in appropriate columns, followed by a carriage return.
Print the horizontal axis, followed by a carriage return.
Print the labels for the horizontal axis: one line of digits and blanks followed by a carriage return, then the centered phrase "days ago" and another carriage return.

Here is a graph that might result.

```
calories
5401-6000 |
4801-5400 |
4201-4800 |
3601-4200 |   X                                          X
3001-3600 | X           X X          X X          X              X X
2401-3000 |   X              X          X X
1801-2400 |        X        X                          X X   X X
1201-1800 |     X X   X        X X X        X X X         X
 601-1200 |
   0- 600 |
          +--------------------------------------------------------
          0      5      10     15     20     25
                          days ago
```

Printing a single word is straightforward. Printing a line of hyphens is almost as easy. We now consider the other two steps.

How is the step of printing the data in the graph decomposed?

Printing the data in the graph consists of printing ten lines. We define a constant called MAXGRAPHLINES to make it easier to change the number of lines if Terry requests it. The data-printing step is then a for loop:

```
for lineNum := 1 to MAXGRAPHLINES do begin
    print the interval title, a vertical bar, and X's in the appropriate columns;
    writeln;
end;
```

How is the interval that corresponds to each line determined?

Printing a line of the graph involves first determining the interval for that line. There are ten lines, so each interval represents one-tenth of the available range. This is similar to printing weeks in *The Calendar Shop*. Since there are two values for each interval it makes sense to maintain two variables to hold the endpoint values, and to update these variables each time through the loop. We refine our loop as follows:

```
Initialize leftValue and rightValue.
for lineNum := 1 to MAXGRAPHLINES do begin
    write (leftValue:4, '-', rightValue:5, ' |');
    print X's in the appropriate columns;
    writeln;
    rightValue := leftValue;
    reduce leftValue;
end;
```

Terry indicated that he consumed at most 400 grams of fat and 6000 calories per day. We will use these as the maximum values for the graph but define them as Pascal constants so that they can be easily changed later if necessary. We continue refining the pseudocode:

```
rightValue := MAXCALORIES;
leftValue := rightValue - MAXCALORIES div MAXGRAPHLINES + 1;
for lineNum := 1 to MAXGRAPHLINES do begin
    write (leftValue:4, '-', rightValue:5, ' |');
    print X's in the appropriate columns;
```

```
        writeln;
        rightValue := leftValue - 1;
        leftValue := leftValue - MAXCALORIES div MAXGRAPHLINES;
end;
```

How are the X's on each line produced?

All that remains is to print the X's; actually this means printing a line containing X's and blanks. If X's were to appear for each of the last 30 days, the loop would be

```
for dayNum := 0 to HISTORYSIZE begin
    write ('X ');
end;
writeln;
```

X's should not appear that often, however. An X should be printed when the corresponding day's calorie total falls within the given interval. This is a straightforward refinement:

```
for dayNum := 0 to HISTORYSIZE do begin
    if (recentHistory[dayNum].calories >= leftValue)
      and (recentHistory[dayNum].calories <= rightValue) then begin
        write ('X ');
    end else begin
        write ('  ');
    end;
end;
writeln;
```

Here we have another application of the "process every element of an array" template.

How is the horizontal axis label produced?

The label for the time axis comprises two lines. On the first line, it displays values between 29 and 0 that are divisible by 5. On the second line, some blanks are printed, then the words "days ago."

A loop to print the first line on the time axis is similar to code used in the day-by-day solution for *The Calendar Shop*. It's an application of a template for processing in cycles:

```
for dayNum := 0 to HISTORYSIZE to begin
    if dayNum mod 5 = 0 then begin
        write (dayNum:2);
    end else begin
        write ('  ');
    end;
end;
```

The last line is just a writeln of the string "days ago," with the field width determined by experimentation.

The program is now ready for feedback from Terry. It will be easy to find the procedures that he wants modified, and most changes can be localized rather than distributed across the program. The code for the entire program appears in the Pascal Code section. It's relatively large; the call diagram appears below.

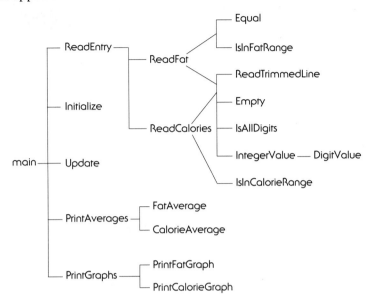

Analysis 7.12 Indicate on the call diagram the routines that receive input from Terry. Do the same for the routines that access the history file and the routines that manipulate the recent history.

Modification 7.13 Modify the graph-printing procedures to use the constant BLANK along with a field width whenever blanks are to be printed.

Reflection 7.14 Why would it be preferable to use the constant BLANK instead of an explicitly specified string constant?

Modification 7.15 Modify the program to use a history file whose lines are arranged least recent to most recent.

Testing the Program

How is the program tested and debugged?

Since the program is so large, there are many alternatives for a sequence in which to test and debug the code. The program structure isn't complicated—it's merely a variant of the "input, process, output" template—so there is no need to test the main program using stubs for subprograms. Instead, we will develop the program bottom-up, starting from the bottom of the call tree.

What parts of the program are tested first?

We choose first to test the routines that read from Terry. Almost all of them have already been tested in developing the *Is It Legal?* program. However, lines may be lost while copying, or a typographical error may be introduced while modifying the code.

Stop & Help ➤ *Write a main program to test the* ReadEntry *procedure and the subprograms it calls.*

How might the testing process be made easier?

A technique to relieve the pain of testing a program is to set up a *file* to contain data normally typed by the user. This requires an extra declaration, a call to reset, plus modification of all uses of read, readln, and eoln. The latter all appear in the ReadTrimmedLine procedure, so they could be changed there. In order to get test input from a file, one might then use a DEBUGGING switch—we've done this in earlier case studies—and change each read statement in ReadTrimmedLine as follows:

```
if DEBUGGING then begin
    code that reads from a file;
end else begin
    code that reads from the terminal;
end;
```

An idea that requires copying less code is to have all the calls to read, readln, and eoln use a file argument that is passed into ReadTrimmedLine. When ReadTrimmedLine is called using input as argument, test input is read from the terminal. For ease and clarity of coding, we set up *all* the Read... procedures to take a file argument, then have the if DEBUGGING ... code appear in the main program:

```
if DEBUGGING then begin
    reset (testFile);
    ReadEntry (testFile, entry);
end else begin
    ReadEntry (input, entry);
end;
```

How is the file input code tested?

Next to be tested is the code to read from the history file. Test files will have differing numbers of lines: 0, 1, 28, 29, 30. As noted before, we assume that lines in historyFile are correctly formatted, so there is no need to try error cases.

Stop & Help ➤ *Write a main program to test the* Initialize *procedure.*

There are two options for the next development step: we can test either the averaging/graphing code or the file updating code. It doesn't make much difference which we do, except that graphing is harder and could be put off for that reason.

How is the file updating code tested?

The file updating code can be tested with the same sample files as the file input code. We can, of course, check the file after each test to see if its contents are correct, but it will be easier to include debugging output that prints a copy of everything written to the file on the screen as well.

How is the graphing code tested?

Last comes the graph printing procedures. Test data here should be chosen to ensure that data values fall into the correct graphing interval. Thus data values at or within 1 of interval boundaries are appropriate.

Debugging 7.16 Introduce a bug into the program, and get a fellow programmer to find it. Which bugs are easiest to locate? Which are most difficult?

Debugging 7.17 Create "mutations" of your program to provide evidence that you've devised a comprehensive set of test data.

Outline of Design and Development Questions

These questions summarize the main points of the commentary.

Planning the Program
How can this program meet the needs of the user?
  Will the needs of the user change?
What are the main steps in the program?
What parts of this program can be solved by recyling solutions to other problems?
What data structures are needed?
Which should be refined first, the data structures or the algorithms?
How are data types designed?
What operations are applied to historyFile?
  How should historyFile be implemented?
  How should the entries in historyFile be ordered?
What will be the operations on recentHistory?
  How will the data be represented internally?
  How should the date be represented?
How should data be ordered in historyFile?
  How should values be input from historyFile?
  How is historyFile updated?
What do we have so far?

Solving the Problem
What is the top-level decomposition of the solution?
How should the program ask for input?

How does the program detect that all the data are entered?

What is the pseudocode for the input step?

How are the fat and calorie values input?

How is the initialization step coded?

How are averages computed?

How is the history file updated?

What should the graph look like?

Which graph is best?

What should the intervals for calorie consumption be?

How is the task of displaying the graph decomposed?

How is the step of printing the data in the graph decomposed?

How is the interval that corresponds to each line determined?

How are the X's on each line produced?

How is the horizontal axis label produced?

Testing the program

How is the program tested and debugged?

What parts of the program are tested first?

How might the testing process be made easier?

How is the file input code tested?

How is the file updating code tested?

How is the graphing code tested?

Programmers' Summary

In this case study a program is designed for a client. Typically clients specify the goal of the program but not the details. For this problem the goal is to keep track of daily intake of calories and fat; the details include such questions as (a) Is it acceptable to represent fat as an integer? and (b) Is it necessary to restate the sentinel value every time a value is added? To resolve such details programmers usually develop a prototype version of the program and get feedback from the client. One challenge is to design the program so that feedback can be easily incorporated.

This problem is further complicated because the user has little computer experience. Inexperienced users typically do not understand computer jargon, are not able to recover from program errors, and may make input errors without realizing it.

This program and any foreseeable variant is organized around the "input, process, output" template. Feedback is most likely to result in change to the *data structures*. Thus the data structures are isolated from the action of the program to make changes easy to implement.

Accesses to each potentially modifiable data structure are localized in one place. Ideally, changing a detail of the specification should require modifications in only one part of the program. One example of this type of data isolation occurred in previous case studies when Pascal constants were used to represent values that were constant when the program was designed but could change in the future. Coding array dimensions, loop bounds, and so on in terms of Pascal constants rather than actual numeric values means that a single change to the constant definition propagates to the whole program.

For more complex data, we design *types* of data—the values stored and the operations performed on them. The goal is to *localize* and *minimize* the amount of code to be modified if the data type must be represented differently. The operations for each data type are then coded in subprograms. All direct manipulation of the data storage is done by these subprograms. The other parts of the program interact with the data only through these subprograms. If the storage of the values must change, only these routines need to be changed.

Designing for inexperienced clients requires that the user interface be extremely helpful and easy to understand. The input routines from *Is It Legal?* can check for any illegal values. Once an illegal value is detected, good error messages are needed so that the user can improve the input. Some errors, such as using the wrong units for an input value, cannot be detected. In these cases we elaborate the prompts to remind the user of the information expected (such as that fat is to be entered in grams). Communicating the output to the user can also be confusing. We consider several possibilities for each output graph, choosing one with minimal clutter in which fat and calorie trends over time can easily be compared.

In this case study, we extend the Persecution Complex principle to the interaction between the designer and the client. To make it easier to get feedback later, we keep a list of the decisions we made for the client. These mostly concern the user interface; one decision, however, would require a different history file representation if made differently.

To store the collection of fat/calorie values, we choose between files and arrays. A file is necessary to preserve the values between program runs. File access, however, is inefficient and clumsy, since Standard Pascal allows only sequential reads from and writes to a file, and it prohibits simultaneous read and write access to a file. We decide to read part of the file into an array indexed by an integer value representing a number of days prior to the current day. This allows much more convenient access for computation. Applying the Literacy Principle, we choose to pair fat and calorie values for a given day in a record. (We also use a record to pair the input line with its length, which shortens the parameter lists for the various input routines.)

Almost the entire design consists of recycled code from earlier case studies. Routines from *Is It Legal?* for reading an integer value need only minor modification. Reading all the data for the current day is a simple application of the "input and process until done" template. Routines for file handling are patterned on those in the *Space Text* program for inserting into an array using an auxiliary array. To average fat and calorie values, we accumulate the sum over array elements. To graph them, we code a line-by-line loop similar to that found in the week-by-week version of *The Calendar Shop* program and we code a "process every array element" loop within to print a given line in the graph.

Since the program structure is straightforward, it makes more sense to develop from the bottom of the call tree to the top rather than top-down. Output to a file is invisible while a program is run, so we make sure to copy file output to the terminal if requested by a DEBUGGING switch. Testing is simplified by using a file of input rather than typing in values for each test.

◀ Making Sense of *You Are What You Eat*

Testing 7.18 Some Pascal environments allow reset and rewrite to take a string variable containing the name of a file as a second argument. Is this feature provided in your Pascal environment? If so, explain the difference between the file variable historyFile and a file name that might be given as the second argument to reset or rewrite.

Reflection 7.19 Explain how the feature described in question 7.18 would make it easier to test the program.

Modification 7.20 If your Pascal environment provides the feature described in question 7.18, modify the program to request a file name from the user from which to read history data. Incorporate as much error checking and help for the user as possible.

Analysis 7.21 Terry may forget to collect data about the food he eats on a given day. How should the program be modified to handle the case of a missing day of data?

Modification 7.22 Modify the program to use a history file whose first line contains a single integer that says how many days of data the file contains.

Modification 7.23 Change the EntryType definition to be a two-element array instead of a two-field record, define two constants called FAT and CALORIES, and update the rest of the program accordingly. Then combine the FatAverage and CalorieAverage functions into a single function with an extra parameter. The new function would be called with an argument of FAT to compute the fat average and an argument of CALORIES to compute the calorie average.

🖫 *Analysis* 7.24 Can PrintFatGraph and PrintCaloriesGraph be combined using the technique described in question 7.23? Why or why not?

🖫 *Analysis* 7.25 Describe what parts of the program would need to be changed if Terry wanted to print graphs for the last 60 days instead of the last 30 days.

🖳 🖫 *Modification* 7.26 Suppose Terry decides that he wants each entry in the graph to represent the average fat and calories he consumed for two days. Modify the program so that it displays 30 data points on the graph, each data point representing the average fat or calories for two days.

🖳 🖫 *Modification* 7.27 Terry is concerned about the percent of calories he consumes that come from fat. He says it is reasonable to assume that one gram of fat has about 10 calories. Write a procedure that will print a graph of the percent of calories that come from fat for the last 30 days. Reuse templates as much as possible.

🖳 🖫 *Debugging* 7.28 Terry notices that the graph for calories seems to give values that are consistently higher than he expects from looking at the average calorie consumption. Describe two types of errors that could result in this pattern.

🖳 🖫 *Debugging* 7.29 After using the program for 15 days, Terry calls to say that he is consuming fewer and fewer calories but the average is increasing every day. What kind of error could cause this pattern of results?

🖳 🖫 *Modification* 7.30 Write a procedure to print a graph of the average calories consumed by each day in the month. The most recent day will display the average for the past 30 days. The previous day will display the average for the 29 days leading up to it, and so on.

◢ Linking to Previous Case Studies

🖳 🖫 *Modification* 7.31 Modify the program to read the current date from Terry, then annotate the output with actual dates instead of the number of days ago. Recycle code from *The Calendar Shop* program.

🖫 *Analysis* 7.32 Describe how the *Check That Number!* program could be modified to check values with any number of digits. Use techniques from *You Are What You Eat*.

🖫 *Reflection* 7.33 Compare the use of Pascal constants in other case studies to the methods for isolating data in this program. How are both helpful when programs need modification?

🖫 *Analysis* 7.34 How might a user of the *Space Text* procedure want it to be modified? Describe two possible modifications and discuss why they are easy or difficult to implement.

Program to Be Tested

```pascal
program nutrition (input, output, historyFile, testFile);

const
    HISTORYSIZE = 29;
    DONESTR = 'done      ';  {needs MAXLINELEN characters}
    BLANK = ' ';
    MAXLINELEN = 10;
    MAXGRAPHLINES = 10;
    MAXFAT = 400;
    MAXCALORIES = 6000;
    DEBUGGING = true;

type
    EntryType = record
        fat, calories: integer;
    end;
    HistoryType = array[0..HISTORYSIZE] of EntryType;
    StringType = packed array[1..MAXLINELEN] of char;
    LineType = record
        length: integer;
        chars: StringType;
    end;

var
    historyFile, testFile: text;
    entry: EntryType;
    recentHistory: HistoryType;

{
    Read a line from inFile, without its leading blanks.
}
procedure ReadTrimmedLine (var inFile: text; var line: LineType);
var
    done: boolean;
    ch: char;
begin {Read Trimmed Line}
    done := false;
    ch := BLANK;
    line.length := 0;
    while not done do begin  {skip blanks}
        if eoln(inFile) then begin
            done := true;
```

```
            end else begin
                read(inFile, ch);
                if ch <> BLANK then begin
                    done := true;
                end;
            end;
        end;
        if ch <> BLANK then begin
            line.length := 1;
            line.chars[1] := ch;
            while not eoln(inFile) do begin
                read(inFile, ch);
                if line.length < MAXLINELEN then begin
                    line.length := line.length + 1;
                    line.chars[line.length] := ch;
                end;
            end;
        end;
    end;
    readln(inFile);
end; {Read Trimmed Line}

{
    Return true exactly when the line is empty (contains no characters).
}
function Empty (line: LineType): boolean;
begin {Empty}
    Empty := line.length = 0;
end; {Empty}

{
    Return true exactly when line contains the same characters as s.
}
function Equal (line: LineType; s: StringType): boolean;
var
    k: integer;
begin {Equal?}
    Equal := true;
    for k := 1 to line.length do begin
        if line.chars[k] <> s[k] then begin
            Equal := false;
        end;
    end;
    for k := line.length + 1 to MAXLINELEN do begin
        if s[k] <> BLANK then begin
            Equal := false;
        end;
    end;
end; {Equal?}

{
    Return true exactly when line consists entirely of digits.
}
function IsAllDigits (line: LineType): boolean;
var
    k: integer;
begin {Is All Digits?}
```

```
        IsAllDigits := true;
        for k := 1 to line.length do begin
            if not (line.chars[k] in ['0'..'9']) then begin
                IsAllDigits := false;
            end;
        end;
end; {Is All Digits?}


{
    Return the integer value of the given digit.
    Precondition: ch is one of '0', '1', ..., '9'.
}
function DigitValue (ch: char): integer;
begin {Digit Value}
    DigitValue := ord(ch) - ord('0');
end; {Digit Value}


{
    Return the integer value of the numeral stored in line.
    Precondition: All characters in line are digits.
}
function IntegerValue (line: LineType): integer;
var
    k, value: integer;
begin {Integer Value}
    value := 0;
    for k := 1 to line.length do begin
        value := value * 10 + DigitValue(line.chars[k]);
    end;
    IntegerValue := value;
end; {Integer Value}


{
    Return true exactly when the given fat figure is reasonable.
}
function IsInFatRange (fat: integer): boolean;
begin {Is In Fat Range?}
    IsInFatRange := (fat >= 0) and (fat <= MAXFAT);
end; {Is In Fat Range?}


{
    Return true exactly when the given calories figure is reasonable.
}
function IsInCaloriesRange (calories: integer): boolean;
begin {Is In Calories Range?}
    IsInCaloriesRange := (calories >= 0) and (calories <= MAXCALORIES);
end; {Is In Calories Range?}


{
    Read a value for fat consumption from inFile, and keep prompting until
    a legal value is provided. Return a true value for done if a line
    containing the string 'done' is provided.
}
procedure ReadFat (var inFile: text; var fat: integer; var done: boolean);
var
    error: boolean;
```

```
            line: LineType;
begin {Read Fat}
    done := false;
    repeat
        error := false;
        writeln('How much fat? Please type a whole number of grams, ');
        writeln('or type the word "done"--without the quotes--',
            'if you''re finished.');
        ReadTrimmedLine(input, line);
        if Empty(line) then begin
            error := true;
        end else if Equal(line, DONESTR) then begin
            done := true;
        end else if not IsAllDigits(line) then begin
            error := true;
        end else begin
            fat := IntegerValue(line);
            if not IsInFatRange(fat) then begin
                error := true;
            end;
        end;
        if error then begin
            writeln('You must provide an integer number of grams,',
                ' no more than', MAXFAT);
        end;
    until done or not error;
end; {Read Fat}

{
    Read a value for fat consumption from inFile, and keep prompting until
    a legal value is provided.
}
procedure ReadCalories (var inFile: text; var calories: integer);
var
    error: boolean;
    line: LineType;
begin {Read Calories}
    repeat
        error := false;
        writeln('How many calories? Please type a whole number.');
        ReadTrimmedLine(inFile, line);
        if Empty(line) then begin
            error := true;
        end else if not IsAllDigits(line) then begin
            error := true;
        end else begin
            calories := IntegerValue(line);
            if not IsInCaloriesRange(calories) then begin
                error := true;
            end;
        end;
        if error then begin
            writeln('You must provide an integer number of calories,',
                ' no more than', MAXCALORIES);
        end;
    until not error;
```

```
end; {Read Calories}

{
    Read an entry consisting of a value for fat consumption and a value
    for calories consumption from inFile.
}
procedure ReadEntry (var inFile: text; var entry: EntryType);
var
    fat, calories: integer;
    done: boolean;
begin {Read Entry}
    entry.fat := 0;
    entry.calories := 0;
    repeat
        ReadFat(inFile, fat, done);
        if not done then begin
            ReadCalories(inFile, calories);
            entry.fat := entry.fat + fat;
            entry.calories := entry.calories + calories;
        end;
    until done;
end; {Read Entry}

{
    Fill recentHistory[0] with the given entry, and fill
    recentHistory[1..HISTORYSIZE] with the most recent HISTORYSIZE entries
    from historyFile. If there are fewer than HISTORYSIZE entries in
    historyFile, the remainder are assumed to contain fat and calorie
    values of 0.
}
procedure Initialize (var historyFile: text; entry: EntryType;
    var recentHistory: HistoryType);
var
    numEntries, k: integer;
    done: boolean;
begin {Initialize}
    done := false;
    reset(historyFile, 'historyFile');
    numEntries := 0;
    recentHistory[0] := entry;
    while not done do begin
        if eof(historyFile) then begin
            done := true;
        end else if numEntries = HISTORYSIZE then begin
            done := true;
        end else begin
            numEntries := numEntries + 1;
            readln(historyFile, recentHistory[numEntries].fat,
                recentHistory[numEntries].calories);
        end;
    end;
    for k := numEntries + 1 to HISTORYSIZE do begin
        recentHistory[k].fat := 0;
        recentHistory[k].calories := 0;
    end;
end; {Initialize}
```

```
{
    Return the average fat consumption of entries in recentHistory.
}
function FatAverage (recentHistory: HistoryType): real;
var
    sum, dayNum: integer;
begin {Fat Average}
    sum := 0;
    for dayNum := 0 to HISTORYSIZE do begin
        sum := sum + recentHistory[dayNum].fat;
    end;
    FatAverage := sum / HISTORYSIZE;
end; {Fat Average}


{
    Return the average calorie consumption of entries in recentHistory.
}
function CalorieAverage (recentHistory: HistoryType): real;
var
    dayNum: integer;
    sum: real;
begin {Calorie Average}
    sum := 0;
    for dayNum := 0 to HISTORYSIZE do begin
        sum := sum + recentHistory[dayNum].calories;
    end;
    CalorieAverage := sum / HISTORYSIZE;
end; {Calorie Average}


{
    Print the average fat and calorie consumption.
}
procedure PrintAverages (recentHistory: HistoryType);
begin {Print Averages}
    writeln('Over the last ', HISTORYSIZE + 1 : 1, ' days,');
    writeln('the average fat consumption has been ',
        FatAverage(recentHistory) : 6 : 2, ' grams, and');
    writeln('the average calorie consumption has been ',
        CalorieAverage(recentHistory) : 6 : 2, ' calories.');
    writeln;
end; {Print Averages}


{
    Print the graph of fat consumption.
}
procedure PrintFatGraph (recentHistory: HistoryType);
var
    leftValue, rightValue, dayNum, lineNum: integer;
begin {Print Fat Graph}
    writeln('Fat intake in grams:');
    rightValue := MAXFAT;
    leftValue := rightValue - MAXFAT div MAXGRAPHLINES + 1;
    for lineNum := 1 to MAXGRAPHLINES do begin
        write(leftValue : 4, '-', rightValue : 5, ' |');
        for dayNum := 0 to HISTORYSIZE do begin
```

```pascal
            if (recentHistory[dayNum].fat >= leftValue)
              and (recentHistory[dayNum].fat <= rightValue) then begin
                write('X' : 2);
            end else begin
                write(BLANK : 2);
            end;
        end;
        writeln;
        rightValue := leftValue - 1;
        leftValue := leftValue - MAXFAT div MAXGRAPHLINES;
    end;
    write(BLANK : 11, '+');
    for dayNum := 0 to HISTORYSIZE do begin
        write('--');
    end;
    writeln;
    write(BLANK : 12);
    for dayNum := 0 to HISTORYSIZE do begin
        if dayNum mod 5 = 0 then begin
            write(dayNum : 2);
        end else begin
            write(BLANK : 2);
        end;
    end;
    writeln;
    writeln(BLANK : 35, 'days ago');
end; {Print Fat Graph}

{
    Print the graph of calorie consumption.
}
procedure PrintCalorieGraph (recentHistory: HistoryType);
var
    leftValue, rightValue, dayNum, lineNum: integer;
begin {Print Calorie Graph}
    writeln('Calorie intake:');
    rightValue := MAXCALORIES;
    leftValue := rightValue - MAXCALORIES div MAXGRAPHLINES + 1;
    for lineNum := 1 to MAXGRAPHLINES do begin
        write(leftValue : 4, '-', rightValue : 5, ' |');
        for dayNum := 0 to HISTORYSIZE do begin
            if (recentHistory[dayNum].calories>=leftValue)
              and (recentHistory[dayNum].calories<=rightValue) then begin
                write('X' : 2);
            end else begin
                write(BLANK : 2);
            end;
        end;
        writeln;
        rightValue := leftValue - 1;
        leftValue := leftValue - MAXCALORIES div MAXGRAPHLINES;
    end;
    write(BLANK : 11, '+');
    for dayNum := 0 to HISTORYSIZE do begin
        write('--');
    end;
```

```
            writeln;
            write(BLANK : 12);
            for dayNum := 0 to HISTORYSIZE do begin
                if dayNum mod 5 = 0 then begin
                    write(dayNum : 2);
                end else begin
                    write(BLANK : 2);
                end;
            end;
            writeln;
            writeln(BLANK : 35, 'days ago');
end; {Print Calorie Graph}


{
    Print the fat and calorie consumption graphs.
}
procedure PrintGraphs (recentHistory: HistoryType);
begin {Print Graphs}
    PrintFatGraph(recentHistory);
    writeln;
    writeln;
    PrintCalorieGraph(recentHistory);
end; {Print Graphs}


{
    Write the updated contents of recentHistory to the history file.
}
procedure Update (var historyFile: text; recentHistory: HistoryType);
var
    dayNum: integer;
    fat, calories: integer;
    tempFile: text;
begin {Update}
    rewrite(tempFile);
    for dayNum := 0 to HISTORYSIZE do begin
        writeln(tempFile, recentHistory[dayNum].fat,
            recentHistory[dayNum].calories);
    end;
    while not eof(historyFile) do begin
        readln(historyFile, fat, calories);
        writeln(tempFile, fat, calories);
        if DEBUGGING then begin
            writeln('*** to temp file: ', fat, calories);
        end;
    end;
    reset(tempFile);
    rewrite(historyFile);
    while not eof(tempFile) do begin
        readln(tempFile, fat, calories);
        writeln(historyFile, fat, calories);
        if DEBUGGING then begin
            writeln('*** to history file: ', fat, calories);
        end;
    end;
end; {Update}
```

```
begin {main program}
    if DEBUGGING then begin
        reset (testFile);
        ReadEntry(testFile, entry);
    end else begin
        ReadEntry(input, entry);
    end;
    Initialize(historyFile, entry, recentHistory);
    PrintAverages(recentHistory);
    PrintGraphs(recentHistory);
    Update(historyFile, recentHistory);
end.
```

You Forgot What You Ate

Drawing by Cheney; © 1989 The New Yorker, Inc.

The user of the *You Are What You Eat* program has more trouble recalling what he ate than anticipated. He also wonders if the computer can keep track of the fat and calories in each thing he eats so that he only has to enter it once. This case study describes how a programmer might respond to problems encountered by users. What does "user-friendly" really mean?

Problem Statement

We encounter Terry a few days after giving him the *You Are What You Eat* program.

MIKE AND MARCIA: How's the program working out?

TERRY: It's OK, but ... (pause)

MIKE AND MARCIA: We wouldn't mind trying to improve the program a bit, if you have some things to suggest.

TERRY: Well, I always have to look up the amounts of fat and calories each food I eat has. Can you make the program do that instead?

MIKE AND MARCIA: That would be possible. You would want to enter the food and how many servings of it you had, right? Then the program would report how much fat and how many calories you had eaten?

TERRY: Right.

MIKE AND MARCIA: All the information for each food would be stored in a disk file. There will be a lot of it. Do you have room on your disk?

TERRY: I think so.

MIKE AND MARCIA: Are you having any other problems with the program?

TERRY: It would be nice to be able to print a copy of the graph the program produces.

MIKE AND MARCIA: That's possible too. You can get printed versions of text files on your computer, right? What else?

TERRY: On Friday, after running the program, I remembered something else I ate. Then I was gone all day on Saturday, and I was too tired to run the program when I got home. When I ran the program on Sunday I put in Sunday's foods before Saturday's, so they were out of order. To fix the problem, I edited the history file with my text editor even though you told me not to. I made a mistake, so when I ran the program it crashed. I knew it was my fault so I fixed the file, but I was worried that I had messed up something somehow.

MIKE AND MARCIA: Calm down, it's OK, no harm done. Suppose we write a program that will let you change what's in the file. It can give you a chance to correct any mistakes you make and add stuff you forget.

TERRY: That would be great!

MIKE AND MARCIA: OK, give us another day or two.

Analysis	8.1	What additional questions might the programmers have asked Terry in order to clarify the planned modifications?
Analysis	8.2	What additional features might help the user of the program?
Analysis	8.3	What should the program do about foods that are not found in the food information file?
Analysis	8.4	Sketch an interaction between Terry and the revised program.
Reflection	8.5	What are the drawbacks to this process of trial and refinement of the program?
Reflection	8.6	What kinds of programs benefit from the process of trial and refinement used to develop this program?

Preparation

Solutions in this case study use files of records, along with arrays. This case study introduces the use of enumerated types, along with the pred and succ functions.

Planning the Modifications

What new features
were requested?

Terry requested three new features to make the program more useful:

- Rather than requiring the user to enter fat and calories for each food eaten, the program should ask for the name of the food and the number of servings eaten, and look up the food in a file. From the information stored in the file, the program should compute the fat and calorie amounts for the food.

- Rather than just showing the graphs of fat and calories use on the screen, the program should also create a file that can be printed.

- Rather than assuming that the input from the history file is correctly organized, the program should allow the user to correct errors and insert data into the history file.

Stop & Help ➤ *Why didn't Terry ask for these features in the first place?*

To determine how to add these features to the program, we review the program structure, expressed in the call diagram below.

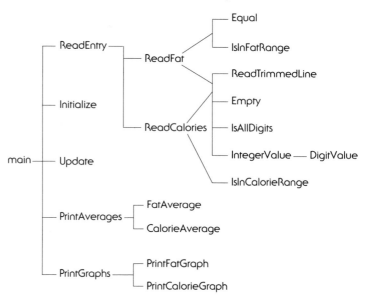

Stop & Predict ➤ *What parts of these changes require only recycling prior solutions?*

What changes will produce a file containing the graphs?

Printing the graphs to a file involves just recycling the solution for printing to the screen. The PrintGraph procedure is the obvious place to add code. The change involves adding a rewrite statement to initialize the file, and duplicating each write and writeln statement to write to the file as well as to the screen. A good name for the file is graphFile. A new question for Terry is whether he has a file by this name. Once the files are created, Terry can print them using whatever procedure he normally uses to print text files.

? Questions for Terry
- Do you (or will you ever) have a file named graphFile?

Stop & Help ➤ *Why do we need to ask Terry if he has a file named* graphFile?

Stop & Help ➤ *How do you get printed versions of text files created by programs on your computer system?*

What changes will implement the new input format?

The main change to the input is entering a food name and serving size rather than entering fat and calories. The code in *You Are What You Eat* can be almost completely recycled.

The input procedures all have names starting with "read." ReadEntry calls ReadFat and ReadCalories to get values for fat and calories for a food; each of those procedures calls ReadTrimmedLine to read a line from the user.

The program should still read lines from the user, so ReadTrimmedLine should work for the new input. ReadTrimmedLine can be used in the revised program to read a line containing "ice cream" or "broccoli." Read-Food and ReadServings are obvious replacements for ReadFat and ReadCalories.

After reading a food name, the program should search the food information file to determine the values to return to ReadEntry. We'll assume that the food information file is called foodInfo; this name must be checked with Terry.

Stop & Predict ➤ *What details are being postponed here?*

Stop & Help ➤ *What changes to the error-checking procedures are needed?*

What changes will allow the user to add forgotten data and correct errors?

To change or correct data, Terry needs to be able to edit the history file. Currently the program allows the user only to add the current day's data to the history file. Providing an editing feature means providing a way to add data for other dates to the file and to select data already in the file in order to update it. Updates will have to be reflected in the graphs produced by the program. The current program accesses only the most recent 30 days' data, but Terry might decide to change data gathered much earlier. This feature changes the way Terry will interact with the program and requires more than recycling the prior solution.

Stop & Predict ➤ *Should the file editing function be added to the existing program or addressed in a new program?*

How might the modifications be incorporated?

We consider the alternatives of adding the editing feature to the current program or creating a new program to edit the history file. Either approach has advantages. Having a separate program—and thereby creating a *system* of programs—results in two smaller programs rather than one big program. It requires (at least in Standard Pascal) that copies of common code occur in each program. If, for instance, the format of the history file were changed, the new format would have to be implemented in two places rather than one.

It's not clear which option is better for Terry. He might not be able to predict whether it would be easier to use two programs or one program; he would probably want to know more about how the programs would work.

We will create a separate program, which we'll call the history file editor, to update the history file. Creating two programs helps to communicate that each program performs a separate function and is, therefore, more intuitive for the user. The *You Are What You Eat* program will continue to handle the *normal* situation in which the current day's data is collected and the history displayed in graphs. The history file editor will be available for the *exceptional* situation of changing previously entered data.

We can postpone the implementation of the history file editor until we finish updating *You Are What You Eat*. However, providing the editing facility may have implications for *You Are What You Eat*, so we keep the editing program in mind while making the modifications.

Stop & Help ➤ *What criteria would Terry use to decide about one or two programs? How are these different from the criteria used by a programmer?*

Stop & Consider ➤ *Compare the approach we're about to take with the approach of having a single program do* all *the data collection and updating, and another program produce the graphs and statistics.*

How will the history file editor work? The history file editor will repeatedly read and execute commands from the user. The commands will be such things as "list history entries," "change this entry," and "add an entry."

How will the history file format change? Terry seems to think of entries by date. To make the interface intuitive, the entries should be identified by date. For example, the "change" command should be "change the entry for a given date."

In designing *You Are What You Eat* we decided not to store the date because it was redundant with the sequence of entries. Now there is a need for the date because an entry might be missing or incomplete. Thus, to implement the file editor we need to add the date to each file entry. This means changing *You Are What You Eat* to include the date with each entry.

How will the date for the current entry be determined? Figuring out the date for the file entry about to be added can be done in several ways.

- The *You Are What You Eat* program can figure it out from the information stored in the history file.

- The program can ask the user.

- Some Pascal environments provide a procedure to retrieve the current date from the operating system. (Of course, this could cause problems if the data being input is not for the current date.)

Terry intends to record information for every day. Thus the most intuitive approach is to verify that the information to be recorded is for the "next" day. The program should determine the date from the history file by computing the day after the date of the most recent file entry. The program should either print the date or ask the user to verify the date. We add this choice to the list we have for Terry.

Stop & Help ➤   *Why is this a question that Terry can answer while choosing between one and two programs was not?*

?

Questions for Terry
- Do you (or will you ever) have a file named graphFile?
- Do you (or will you ever) have a file named foodInfo?
- Is it OK for the program to display the date it will store for the current entry and have you verify it?

What modifications are needed to go with the new file format?

In designing *You Are What You Eat* we isolated references to the data structures so that it would be easy to update them without making major changes in the program. The Initialize procedure reads from historyFile, and the Update procedure writes to the file. These are the two main places where changes are needed.

Stop & Predict ➤   *What other parts of the program are likely to need changes to accommodate the updated file format?*

What changes to *You Are What You Eat* are to be made?

Planned changes to *You Are What You Eat* are summarized as follows:

- ReadEntry will be rewritten to read from the user the name and number of servings of a food and to look up the corresponding fat and calorie amounts in foodInfo, the file of food information. Procedures ReadFat and ReadCalories will be replaced by procedures ReadFood and Read-Servings.

- PrintGraph will be revised to print the graphs to a file as well as to the terminal screen.

- Initialize will be modified to include a date as part of each file entry read from historyFile, to define a date for the current day's file entry, and to inform the user of the date.

- Update will be modified to include a date as part of each file entry written to tempFile and historyFile.

- A date will be included in EntryType.

Stop & Predict ➤   *How do these changes influence the decomposition of* You Are What You Eat?

Stop & Predict ➤   *Which changes are minor and which are major?*

What comes first? A beneficial aspect of the way we designed the program is that the rewritten version of ReadEntry can be tested and debugged independent of the other revisions. The same holds for the change to PrintGraph. We will thus make these revisions before implementing the date-handling code, which seems to require more changes to the program.

Analysis 8.7 Suppose that instead of locating a data file on fat and calories Terry wanted to store the information he entered and add new information only for new foods. How would this change the way the program was updated?

Reflection 8.8 How might the need for the date in the history file have been anticipated in the first version of *You Are What You Eat?*

Implementing Changes to *You Are What You Eat*

How is PrintGraph changed? We start with the easiest change, updating PrintGraph. The only change needed is to add a rewrite statement and to duplicate all the write and writeln statements as follows.

```
write ( ... );
```

is duplicated as

```
write ( ... );
write (graphFile, ... );
```

and

```
writeln ( ... );
```

is duplicated as

```
writeln ( ... );
writeln (graphFile, ... );
```

Stop & Help ➤ *Test the code using the test data designed in* You Are What You Eat.

How is ReadEntry rewritten? The old version of ReadEntry called ReadFat and ReadCalories to read fat and calorie values from the user. It makes sense to retain this structure by calling ReadFood first, then ReadServings. At some point the specified food name must be looked up in foodInfo and associated with fat and calorie figures. These would then be accumulated in the same way as in the original program. Here is a pseudocode design:

```
entry.fat := 0;
entry.calories := 0;
repeat
```

```
ReadFood (inFile, food, done);
if not done then begin
    ReadServings (inFile, numServings);
    entry.fat := entry.fat + numServings * fat from food;
    entry.calories := entry.calories + numServings * calories from food;
end;
until done;
```

In which procedure should the food be looked up?

Lookup of the food name entered by the user then must occur in ReadEntry, ReadFood, or ReadServings.

Stop & Predict ➤ *Which procedure should contain the lookup code?*

ReadServings would be a poor choice. The number of servings is not related to the kind of food. ReadEntry is a possibility; immediately prior to the call to ReadServings, we might insert code to search the food file.

The best choice, however, is ReadFood. Recall that ReadFat and ReadCalories were designed to return *legal values* for fat and calories to ReadEntry in the original program. Thus ReadFood should similarly return a legal food to ReadEntry. A food that isn't in the food file is illegal.

Stop & Help ➤ *What kinds of errors should be detected for the food name?*

What is the format of the food information file?

As long as ReadFood is looking up the food name, it might as well return the entire entry from foodInfo. Thus foodInfo should be structured to make this easy. The food name, something about a serving size, and the corresponding fat and calorie values should be stored together in foodInfo so that once the name is found, all the other information for the food will be immediately available. One way to represent foodInfo would then be as lines of text, each containing information for one food, for instance:

```
broccoli, raw; 1 spear; 40; 0
```

The semicolons are separators for the various pieces of food information. The problem with this format is extracting the components from the line of text.

A better approach is to impose more structure on the file by making it a *file of records*. Reading a record would involve reading each of the components. Though such a file could not be printed or edited with a text editor, that's fine; the user need not meddle with the file except through this program. The file can be defined as follows:

```
type
    StringType = array [1..MAXSTRLEN] of char;
    FoodEntryType = record
        foodName: StringType;
        servingDescr: StringType;
        fat, calories: integer;
    end;
    FoodInfoType = file of FoodEntryType;
```

How is a file of records created?

A program is needed to create a file of records—a text editor cannot do it. The program is straightforward, however. All that is needed is a loop containing some input statements and a statement that writes the input values to the file.

How is the error checking coded?

The input and error-checking code that uses this file would then be patterned on code in ReadFat as follows. It uses a Search procedure that returns either a food entry or an indication that none was found in foodInfo.

```
done := false;
repeat
    error := false;
    writeln('Please type either a food name');
    writeln('or type the word "done"--without the quotes--');
    writeln('if you''re finished.');
    ReadTrimmedLine (line);
    if Empty (line) then begin
        error := true;
    end else if Equal (line, DONESTR) then begin
        done := true;
    end else begin
        Search (line, foodEntry, found);
        if not found then begin
            error := true;
        end;
    end;
    if error then begin
        writeln('That food is not in the dictionary of foods.');
    end;
until done or not error;
```

On exit from the loop, either the user has typed "done," and therefore done is true, or the user has typed a recognized food name, foodEntry contains the information for that food, and done and error are both false.

Stop & Help ➤ *Is the prompt sufficient to tell the user that input like "slice of cake" is probably inappropriate? Why or why not?*

How is the file search coded?

The Search procedure searches the foodInfo file for an entry matching the given name. It is similar to linear search in an array:

```
procedure Search (line: LineType;
    var foodEntry: FoodEntryType; var found: boolean);
begin
    reset (foodInfo);
    found := false;
    while not eof and not found do begin
        read (foodInfo, foodEntry);
        found := Equal (line, foodEntry.foodName);
    end;
end;
```

How are the fat and calorie amounts coded?

The number of servings is read in the same way, using ReadTrimmedLine, IsAllDigits, and IntegerValue, as were the fat and calorie amounts in the original program. For a good user interface, the prompting message should indicate what a serving is, so the program should write the servingDescr field in foodEntry. Once converted to an integer, the input value should be checked for reasonableness: it should be at least 1 and probably less than 100 or so. Here's the code.

```
repeat
    error := false;
    write ('How many servings? (One serving = ',
            foodEntry.servingDescr, ') ');
    ReadTrimmedLine (line);
    if Empty (line) then begin
        error := true;
    end else if not IsAllDigits (line) then begin
        error := true;
    end else begin
        numServings := IntegerValue(line);
        if not IsInServingRange (numServings) then begin
            error := true;
        end;
    end;
    if error then begin
        writeln ('You must provide an integer number of servings.')
    end;
until not error;
```

Back in ReadEntry, the number of servings should be multiplied by foodEntry.fat to compute a fat amount and by foodEntry.calories to compute a calorie amount. Both amounts should be accumulated until the user is finished entering input.

How is the code tested? The revised Read... routines appear in the Pascal Code section. We test them as follows. First we write a program to create foodInfo; a file containing four elements should be sufficient to check boundary cases. Then we write a main program that repeatedly calls ReadEntry and prints the resulting fat and calorie figures. The only really new code is Search, so it must be tested most carefully; we make sure to check for foods at the start, at the end, and somewhere in the middle of foodInfo.

Stop & Help ➤ *Write the program to create* foodInfo.

Stop & Help ➤ *Write the main program to test* ReadEntry.

What modifications are necessary to keep track of dates? Including dates in the history file requires more widespread change to the program than was true for the other updates.

A date consists of a month, a day, and a year. A good structure for storing a date is a Pascal record with three fields. In Pascal, we may then make the following definitions:

```
type
    MonthType = (JANUARY, FEBRUARY, MARCH, APRIL, MAY, JUNE,
```

```
                    JULY, AUGUST, SEPTEMBER, OCTOBER, NOVEMBER, DECEMBER);
        DayType = 1..31;
        YearType = 1990..2100;
        DateType = récord
            month: MonthType;
            day: DayType;
            year: YearType;
        end;
        EntryType = record
            date: DateType;
            fat, calories: integer;
        end;
        HistoryType = array [0..HISTORYSIZE] of EntryType;
```

For clarity, we use subranges to represent days and years. We also use Pascal's enumerated type facility to represent months. In *The Calendar Shop*, integer constants were used for this purpose. The main difference here is that an enumerated type can be defined somewhat more concisely.

Stop & Predict ➤   *What are the advantages of making the history file a file of records?*

In the first version of the program, the history file was of type text. It makes sense to have it be a file of records like the food information file, since it will always be read and updated under control of one of the programs we write. Thus, one more definition:

```
        HistoryFileType = file of EntryType;
```

Stop & Help ➤   *Write a program to create a version of* historyFile *to use for testing the updated program.*

We will have to get together with Terry to copy the fat and calorie data collected so far to a file in the new format.

How will Initialize and Update be modified to handle the new file format?

In *You Are What You Eat*, we considered and rejected the option of initializing the file to contain at least 30 entries, then using a for loop in Initialize. This allowed for the possibility that a desperate user would edit the history file and remove some of the lines. Since editing a file of records is impossible, we return to the simpler code:

```
for dayNum := 1 to HISTORYSIZE do begin
    readln (historyFile, recentHistory[dayNum].fat,
    recentHistory[dayNum].calories);
end;
```

Three revisions are necessary. The historyFile parameter is now of type HistoryFileType. The read procedure must be used instead of readln, since input is no longer coming from a text file. Instead of reading the fat and calorie components separately, the code reads each record from the file in its entirety. Here is the rewritten code:

```
reset(historyFile);
for dayNum := 1 to HISTORYSIZE do begin
```

```
        read(historyFile, recentHistory[dayNum]);
end;
```

The Update procedure is revised in similar ways: historyFile is defined as a HistoryFileType, and read and write statements taking a file and a record argument are used instead of readln and writeln.

Stop & Help ➤   *Modify* Update *as just described.*

How is the date of the current entry computed?

Next the current date must be determined, by computing the successor of the date in recentHistory[1], and then printed. A procedure to find the date, which uses code from *The Calendar Shop*, is the following:

```
procedure FindSuccessor (current: DateType; var next: DateType);
begin
    if current.day < NumberOfDaysIn (current.month) then begin
        next.month := current.month;
        next.day := current.day + 1;
        next.year := current.year;
    end else if current.month < DECEMBER then begin
        next.month := succ (current.month);
        next.day := 1;
        next.year := current.year;
    end else begin
        next.month := JANUARY;
        next.day := 1;
        next.year := current.year + 1;
    end;
end;
```

The succ function is used to determine the successor of the enumerated type value.

What changes to the top-level decomposition are necessary?

A remaining question is where to put the code that determines the current date and stores it in a file entry. The original decomposition was

```
ReadEntry (entry);
Initialize (historyFile, entry, recentHistory);
PrintAverages (recentHistory)
PrintGraph (recentHistory);
Update (historyFile, recentHistory);
```

However, we would like to inform Terry of the current date *before* he starts entering data. That suggests that the first two procedure calls be reversed:

```
Initialize (historyFile, entry, recentHistory);
ReadEntry (entry);
```

The entry to be read, however, is recentHistory[0], which suggests the following code:

```
Initialize (historyFile, recentHistory);
ReadEntry (recentHistory[0], recentHistory[1].date);
```

In this decomposition, Initialize would fill elements 1 through 30 of recentHistory, and ReadEntry would be given an entry to fill and a date to print and store into that entry.

Stop & Predict ➤ *What do you think of this decomposition?*

The problem with this code is that it increases the number of places in the program that access recentHistory directly. Our design all along has aimed to minimize and localize such accesses. In the original program, neither the main program nor ReadEntry needed to know exactly how recentHistory was represented, and we would like to maintain that localization.

Stop & Predict ➤ *How should the code be organized to limit direct accesses to* recentHistory?

The solution is to call ReadEntry from *inside* Initialize. The code below would immediately follow the for loop:

```
FindSuccessor(recentHistory[1].date, today);
write('The food data you are about to enter is assumed to be for ');
WritelnDate(today);
write('Quit this program and run the history file editor');
writeln(' if this is incorrect.');
ReadEntry(input, today, recentHistory[0]);
```

ReadEntry must still be modified to take an extra argument, the date to be stored in the entry.

Designing a procedure WritelnDate to print the date is straightforward. It, together with the other code just designed, appears in the Pascal Code section. The call diagram appears in Figure 8.1; subprograms that were revised or added are boxed.

How is the code tested? The initializing and updating code is tested as in *You Are What You Eat.* Other tests should exercise all parts of the FindSuccessor procedure; thus we should provide test files whose most recent entry occurs in the middle of a month, at the end of a month, and at the end of the year.

The complete program is over 500 lines long. A single DEBUGGING true-or-false switch isn't enough; it would generate either no output or too much. What we'd like is a *selective* debugging facility that could be used to generate debugging output only for a particular section of code.

One way to do this is to define the DEBUGGING constant as an integer interpreted as an indicator of which code is being debugged. A value of 1 might mean that the history file operations are being debugged, 2 might mean the date code, and so on. We would define constants to give names to these values and then include code like

```
if DEBUGGING = HISTORYFILEOPS then ...
```

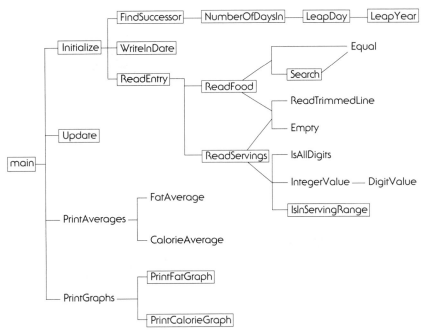

Figure 8.1 *Call diagram for the revised* You Are What You Eat *program*

A problem with this approach is that DEBUGGING can take on only one value at a time. We have used the debugging switch not only to produce extra output, but also to cause input to be read from a test file rather than the terminal. It is likely that we'd want both to happen simultaneously during some test runs.

For this program, we choose a simpler approach, that of having more than one debugging constant. The ones used in the Pascal Code section are listed below.

Constant	Use
FILEINPUT	true if test data should be read from a file, false if it should be read from the terminal
DEBUGHISTORY	true if we're debugging operations for reading from and writing to the history file
DEBUGFOOD	true if we're debugging operations for searching the food file
DEBUGDATES	true if we're debugging code for manipulating dates

💾 *Testing*   8.9   Make a table of tests needed for the program and indicate the values that would be tested.

📀 💾 *Modification*   8.10 Modify the program to print both the day (e.g. Sunday or Monday) and the date of the next entry.

📀 💾 *Modification*   8.11 Modify the program to ask the user to verify the next date and to enter a different date if necessary.

📀 💾 *Modification*   8.12 Add a procedure called FoodMatch to this code that searches foodInfo for the first five letters of a food name and asks the user if the correct record has been located.

📀 💾 *Modification*   8.13 Modify the program to accept and process fractional serving sizes.

High-Level Design of the History Editor

What commands will be provided in the history file editor?

To edit the history file Terry needs to add, change, and delete information. Changing is really no more than deleting and adding, so to keep things simple we include only the add and delete commands:

add date
> Add an entry for the given date. The program will request two integer values, one for fat and one for calories. It is an error if there is already an entry with the given date in historyFile.

delete date
> Delete the entry for the given date. The program will print a message giving the date deleted and the values for calories and fat. It is an error if there is no entry with the given date in historyFile.

Stop & Predict ➤   *What other commands might users want?*

Terry will also wish to check to be sure an entry is accurate. Commands that allow segments of the history file to be displayed will help here:

list
> Print all entries in historyFile.

list date
> Print the entry for the given date; print an error message if there is no entry in historyFile for the date.

list start-date end-date
> Print all entries in historyFile with dates between those specified; print an error message if no entries are in the specified range.

We figure the user may forget the commands so we provide help with a help command:

help
> Print a list of legal commands.

Finally, a quit command allows the user to signal that the editing is complete:

quit

   Exit the program.

We make a note to ask Terry if this is a reasonable set of commands.

? Questions for Terry
- Do you (or will you ever) have a file named graphFile?
- Do you (or will you ever) have a file named foodInfo?
- Is it OK for the program to display the date it will store for the current entry and have you verify it?
- Are the commands we've designed—add, delete, list, help, and quit—sufficient for your purposes?

Stop & Predict ➤ *How should users enter dates into the program?*

The format of a date will be the usual month/day/year. We need to make clear to Terry whether a legal year should be 91 or 1991. For now, we'll assume the latter.

Stop & Consider ➤ *Which do you prefer, two-digit years or four-digit years? Why?*

How is the history file editor organized? We will organize the program as an instance of the "input and process until done" template, where the input step will read a command from the user and the process step will execute the command. In pseudocode, the main program will appear as follows:

initialize;
repeat
     get a command;
     execute the command;
until no more commands;
finish up;

This kind of program is common enough to have a name: **command interpreter.** ("Interpreting" a command means executing it.)

How are the history entries represented? As we did in *You Are What You Eat*, we delay considering the procedural decomposition any further until we decide how to represent the collection of history entries in the program.

Stop & Predict ➤ *What are the options for representing the history entries?*

Currently, the history entries are stored in a disk file. One option is to retain this implementation and represent the collection internally as a Pascal file. Another option is to use an array. It is possible—even likely—that the representation we choose will have to be changed in some future version of the program. Designing first around the *abstraction* of the collection of entries, then choosing an implementation, will make changing the implementation much easier.

How do we create an
abstract view?

To get a comprehensive idea of the representation we need, we build "views" of the collection of history entries and the actions that will be performed on them. Views are perspectives on the actions of the program on the data objects. Generally, the least detailed view is the view the user has of the editor commands acting on the entries. The programmer's view of the actions of the program on the data is likely to be more detailed and more precise than the users. In this case the programmer views a *sequenced* collection of entries that can be searched, traversed, and added to, whose size can be determined, and each of which has a date, a calorie entry, and a fat entry that can be modified. A third view is the programmer's detailed view where the particulars of the Pascal constructs are considered.

In the abstract view, we are concerned with a *sequence* of history entries, ordered by date, most recent first. The commands can be translated into the following abstract operations:

- Initialize the sequence.

- Find the position in the sequence of the entry with a given date or the position in the sequence where an entry with that date would go.

- Insert a new entry at a given position in the sequence.

- Delete the entry at a given position in the sequence.

- Print all entries in the sequence.

- Print all entries between two given dates in the sequence.

The operations are complete, yet simultaneously they provide the flexibility of implementing the sequence either as a file or as an array.

Stop & Help ➤

Explain why a file or an array would work with these operations.

What operations have
we left out?

Operations for comparing dates will also be necessary. We'll postpone thinking about them for now.

How are the commands and
abstract operations related?

For each of the commands, here is its action in terms of the abstract operations:

add date

Find the position of an entry with the given date. If an entry with that date already exists, signal error; otherwise construct a new entry and insert it at that position.

delete date

Find the position of an entry with the given date. If an entry with that date does not exist, signal error; otherwise delete the entry.

list
> Print the information in all entries.

list date
> Find the position of an entry with the given date. If an entry with that date does not already exist, signal error; otherwise print the information in the entry.

list start-date end-date
> Find the position of an entry whose date is the same as or preceding end-date. Then print the information in all entries between end-date and start-date.

Is a file or an array best? For this program, we choose to implement the collection as a Pascal file. First, the size of the collection is unknown, so we cannot easily define an array that will accommodate all the data. Perhaps Terry will collect years of data. Second, all we want to do is put together a prototype program quickly, and a file will work fine for this purpose. Terry will then use it, and we will decide what needs to be improved based on his feedback.

We focus now on coding the six abstract operations—initialize, find the position of an entry, insert a new entry at a given position, delete the entry at a given position, print all entries, and print a given range of entries—using Pascal files.

Modification 8.14 Suppose Terry found that he frequently needed to exchange the information for one date with the information for another date. Describe commands that might be added to make this easy, and explain how they would be implemented in terms of the abstract operations already designed.

Analysis 8.15 A user might find it easier to understand a list command with only one variation rather than three. Explain how one can produce the output of the zero-argument and one-argument variations of the list command by using the two-argument list command.

Reflection 8.16 Would it be better to have just one variation of the list command or three as we have proposed? Explain.

Analysis 8.17 Describe the advantages of using an array rather than a file for the collection of fat and calories.

Implementing the Abstract Operations

How is the "find" operation coded? All of the intended commands will use the "find" operation, so we'll work on that first. The "find" operation will take as parameters the file and the date whose entry is to be located. Moreover, it must return an indication of whether or not the entry is found, and the position at which it is found. Thus the procedure header will be

```
procedure Find (var history: SequenceType; date: DateType;
        var found: boolean; var position: PositionType);
```

The history file is passed as a *var* parameter, both because Pascal does not allow files to be passed by value and because, should the history be stored in an array, passing it by value would result in the inefficiency of copying the array.

Stop & Predict ➤   *What is the position of an entry in a file?*

The meaning of a position is obvious with an array; its meaning for a file is much less clear, so we postpone this problem for now.

How is a file searched?   Since elements of files are accessed sequentially, the "find" operation requires a linear search. The code for searching a file is similar to code for searching an array, so we can adapt the searching template from *Is It Legal?* and *Space Text*. Recall that the entries in the file are stored most recent first; thus finding the position where an entry with the given date would go means finding the first entry in the file with a date that's the same as or earlier than the given date.

```
reset (history);
foundAtOrBefore := false;
while not foundAtOrBefore and not eof (history) do begin
    read (history, entry);
    if entry's date is at or before the given date then begin
        foundAtOrBefore := true;
    end;
end;
```

At the end of this loop, there are three possibilities: foundAtOrBefore is false, so Find should return failure; foundAtOrBefore is true but the entry date is earlier than the given date, so Find should return failure; or found-AtOrBefore is true and the entry date is identical to the given date, so Find should return success. Thus the following code must be added:

```
if foundAtOrBefore then begin
    set found to true if date and entry.date are the same, and to false otherwise;
end else begin
    found := false;
end;
```

What happens when an entry is found?   When an entry is found, it may be deleted, or an entry may be added resulting in a change to the file. Either requires the file to be copied; only the list command requires finding an entry without modifying the file. Thus, it seems efficient to build the copying into the operation of finding an entry:

```
reset (history);
rewrite (temp)
foundAtOrBefore := false;
while not foundAtOrBefore and not eof (history) do begin
    read (history, entry);
    if AtOrBefore (entry.date, date) then begin
        foundAtOrBefore := true;
    end else begin
        write (temp, entry);
    end;
end;
if foundAtOrBefore then begin
    set found to true if date and entry.date are the same, and to false otherwise;
end else begin
    found := false;
end;
```

The history entry whose date is at or before the given date will not have been written to the temporary file when Find returns.

The temp file will need to be used by other file operations, and thus it should be a parameter. This seems undesirable, since if the sequence of history entries were to be represented as an array instead of a file, it would be inappropriate to have such a parameter. An intriguing thought is to use the temp file as the position parameter. We'll try that. Thus temp replaces position in the parameter list, and PositionType, the type of a "position" in the sequence, will be defined to be file of EntryType, just like Sequence-Type.

How is the "insert" operation coded?

The "insert" operation will assume that a "find" has just been done. Its parameters will be the history, the entry to be inserted, and the place to put it:

```
procedure Insert (var history: SequenceType; entry: EntryType;
        temp: PositionType);
```

Insertion into the history means writing it to the temporary file, copying the rest of the file to the temporary file, then copying the whole file back to the original. (We did this in *You Are What You Eat*.) The "delete" operation will need to perform a similar operation, so we put the copying and copying back code into a separate procedure:

```
write (temp, entry);
CopyThenCopyBack (history, temp);
```

Copying is easy:

```
procedure CopyThenCopyBack (var original: SequenceType;
        temp: PositionType);
var
    entry: EntryType;
begin
    while not eof (original) do begin
        read (original, entry);
```

```
            write (temp, entry);
        end;
        reset (temp);
        rewrite (original);
        while not eof (temp) do begin
            read (temp, entry);
            write (original, entry);
        end;
    end;
```

How is the "delete" operation coded?

Delete is similar to Insert. It also assumes that Find has just been called:

```
procedure Delete (var history: SequenceType;  var temp: PositionType);
begin
    CopyThenCopyBack (history, temp);
end;
```

How is the "print all entries" operation coded?

Printing all the history entries is another application of the "input and process until done" template:

```
procedure PrintAll (var history: SequenceType);
var
    entry: EntryType;
begin
    reset (history);
    while not eof (history) do begin
        read (history, entry);
        PrintEntry (entry);
    end;
end;
```

Stop & Predict ➤

What patterns can be recycled to create the procedure that prints the entries between two dates?

How is the "print all entries between two given dates" operation coded?

The "print all entries between two given dates" operation is done after finding an entry whose date is the same as or preceding the later of the two dates. (Recall that the entries are arranged most recent first in the file.) Subsequent entries are read and printed until an entry preceding the earlier of the two dates is encountered. The code is almost exactly the same as the code for the first version of Find:

```
procedure PrintUpTo (var history: HistoryType; date: DateType;
        position: PositionType);
begin
    done := false;
    while not done and not eof (history) do begin
        read (history, entry);
        PrintEntry (entry);
        if entry date is before the earlier date then begin
            done := true;
        end;
    end;
end;
```

Note that a position parameter is necessary to be consistent with the other procedures that follow a call to Find.

Stop & Help ➤   *Find the bug in the above code.*

How is the "initialize" operation coded?

Last is the "initialize" operation. Since every operation that reads through the file starting at the beginning does its own reset, no initialization is necessary. Thus the corresponding procedure is empty:

```
procedure Initialize (var history: HistoryType);
begin
end;
```

Stop & Predict ➤   *What sort of functions are best for comparing the dates?*

What about the code that manipulates dates?

Find and PrintUpTo both involve comparison of two dates. We will use two boolean functions: Precedes and SameDate. Recall that a date has three components, a year, a month, and a day. A date stored in date1 is earlier than a date stored in date2 if date1's year is earlier than date2's, if the years are the same and date1's month is earlier than date2's, or if the years and months are the same and date1's day is earlier than date2's. Two dates are the same if all their components are equal. Here's the code for the two functions:

```
function Precedes (date1, date2: DateType): boolean;
begin
    if date1.year < date2.year then begin
        Precedes := true;
    end else if date1.year > date2.year then begin
        Precedes := false;
    end else if date1.month < date2.month then begin
        Precedes := true;
    end else if date1.month > date2.month then begin
        Precedes := false;
    end else begin
        Precedes := date1.day < date2.day;
    end;
end;

function SameDate (date1, date2: DateType): boolean;
begin
    SameDate := (date1.year = date2.year)
        and (date1.month = date2.month)
        and (date1.day = date2.day);
end;
```

(Standard Pascal does not allow comparison of entire records.)

How can the code be tested?

The routines written so far can be combined with a driver program and tested. We do this now.

The first development step is to test the file printing routines. Once working, they provide a way to test the other code. The test data for the file handling code is similar to what would be used with an array: check the middle values along with the boundary values. Here, we are interested in values not in the file as well as those in the file, so we test PrintUpTo with the latest and earliest dates in the file as well as dates following the latest date and preceding the earliest date. A diagram representing these test cases appears below.

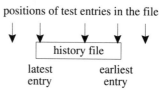

positions of test entries in the file

history file

latest entry   earliest entry

What bugs are encountered?

A bug arises from a mismatch between the program that created the file and the driver program used for testing. In the driver program, MonthType is declared as integer to simplify input of test values, while in the creation program MonthType is declared as an enumerated type. Most Pascal environments do no error checking at all for input from non-text files, assuming that they will be read in the same way they were written. Any source of inconsistency will cause errors. This may be regarded as a disadvantage of this representation.

Testing also reveals a bug in PrintUpTo; the symptom is that one too many entries are getting printed. The problem turns out to be that the first entry outside the requested range was printed before it was checked. We rearrange the code to put the call to PrintEntry inside an if statement, but then we get the comparison backward. One more test run reveals this bug and leads to the code in the Pascal Code section.

Find is next to be tested, since the other operations use it. Test values are similar to those used with PrintUpTo. Finally all the other operations are tested; again we focus mainly on boundary values.

While testing and analyzing the code just written, we realize that the decision to store the file in reverse order introduces an extra level of confusion. We have to worry not only about the search test being off by one entry, but also about the direction of the error. We resolve to be especially careful in checking for errors in operations that search the file, and to look for an opportunity to simplify the code in future revisions of the program.

Analysis   8.18 Should Find always search the entire file? Why or why not?

Modification 8.19 Modify the Initialize procedure to check that dates of file entries are ordered from most recent to least recent and to print a warning message if they are not.

🖥 💾 *Modification*   8.20   Modify the Initialize procedure to check that there are no duplicate dates in history entries and to print a warning message if there are entries with duplicate dates.

Reflection   8.21   List bugs that programmers should anticipate when writing routines that process files.

Designing and Developing the Remainder of the History Editor

What remains to be designed?   Now that the routines to manipulate the history data structure are designed and tested, we can proceed to the main program and the command scanner.

Recall that we decomposed the main program as follows:

```
initialize;
repeat
    get a command;
    execute the command;
until no more commands;
finish up;
```

Hidden in that decomposition are such details as reading characters from the input, isolating and translating commands and date arguments, and checking for errors.

What should the "get a command" step do?   Getting a command is an ambiguous step. How much work should the "get a command" step do? Here are two possibilities at opposite ends of the spectrum.

Get just the first word of the command: Read characters until the first word of the command is isolated, then check that word. Once the command word is recognized, subsequent input and processing is handled in the "execute the command" step.

Get a complete legal command: Read the complete command including its arguments, check it for errors, and translate it into an internal form. The "execute the command" step then performs only the appropriate history file operations.

Stop & Predict ➤   *What are some alternatives for the "get a command" step between these extremes?*

What worked before?   In *Is it Legal?* we used the "read one, process one" template for input and found it advantageous to read a whole line of input before processing. This suggests a third possibility, which also eliminates checks for end-of-line after the input step.

Get the line, process the command word: Read an entire line, then isolate the first word on the line and make sure it specifies a legal command. Subsequent isolation of arguments on the line is handled in the "execute the command" step.

This seems better than the "get just the command word" alternative.

How do we select an alternative?

The choice between "get the line, process the command word" and "get a complete legal command" consists mainly in deciding how much to analyze the commands in the "get a command" code. The goal is to make the code clear and to avoid unnecessary repetition.

The decision will depend on the *form* of the commands. Similar commands can be analyzed by the same code; commands that differ in form must be analyzed separately.

In addition, the code for command execution will be clearer if error checking is done when the command is read. Error checks in the command execution routines can obscure the processing performed by the routines. However, if error checks and command interpretation are similar, they are best combined in the command execution step.

The choice of how much processing to do in the "get a command" step arises in the design of any command interpreter. To decide for this program, we gather some more information about the commands.

Stop & Predict ➤ *What common command errors will need to be checked?*

What errors will the program check?

To determine where to put the error-checking routines, we make a list of the possible errors in the arguments to the various commands.

list   too many arguments (3 or more) are specified
one of the arguments isn't a date
there is no history entry with the given date
there is no history entry in the given range of dates

add   too many arguments (2 or more) are specified
too few arguments (0) are specified
the argument isn't a date
a history entry with the given date already exists

delete   too many arguments (2 or more) are specified
too few arguments (0) are specified
the argument isn't a date
no history entry with the given date exists

help   no errors are possible

quit   no errors are possible

What are the pros and cons of each decomposition?

Examining the possible errors does not completely clarify what the "get a command" step should do. The number of arguments varies with the command, arguing against error checking in the "get a command" step.

On the other hand, all the arguments are dates, so it makes sense to have a single routine to check that each date argument is legal.

The choice is between "get the line, process the command word" and "get a complete legal command." We decide to design both solutions and compare them.

Analysis 8.22 In this design the output requested by the user is deduced by examining the arguments to the list command. Instead, one might provide several different list commands such as listAll, listSome, and listOne. Explain the advantages and disadvantages of each approach.

Reflection 8.23 Given the nature of novice computer users, what kinds of help besides a list of legal commands might be added to the program? Justify each suggestion.

Analysis 8.24 Provide a pseudocode description of an interactive interface for this program that asks the user for a date only if the command requires date information. What are the advantages of this approach?

The "Get the Line, Process the Command Word" Design

What will GetCommand and ExecuteCommand do?

In the "get the line, process the command word" design, the GetCommand procedure will start by reading a line. It will then isolate the first word in the line, make sure it's a command, and return. Depending on the command, ExecuteCommand will call one of the specialized execution procedures ExecuteList, ExecuteInsert, ExecuteDelete, ExecuteHelp, or ExecuteQuit. Some of these will isolate the following word(s) on the line, convert them to dates, and apply the appropriate history file operations.

How will GetCommand and ExecuteCommand **communicate?**

GetCommand and ExecuteCommand both need to access the line containing the command. Thus the line will need to be either a parameter to both or a variable global to both. To make clear just what is getting communicated to what, we will make the line a parameter to both procedures.

ExecuteCommand will need to know the position in the line at which to start looking for arguments. This might also be passed as a parameter. Rather than store it separately from the line, however, we will combine it with the line in a record.

Stop & Help ➤ *Write a declaration for the record that will hold the line and the position.*

How will ExecuteCommand **work?**

ExecuteCommand conceptually is an application of the "select from alternatives" template. In earlier case studies we used a case statement to select alternatives. Pascal does not allow the use of strings as case selectors. One solution is to define an enumerated type with one element for each command, since members of an enumerated type can be used as case selectors. GetCommand can then translate the isolated command word into a member of that type before returning.

What are the headers for these procedures?

This solution leads to the following type definitions and procedure headers for GetCommand and ExecuteCommand:

```
type
    LineType = record
        chars: array [1..MAXLENGTH] of char;
        length: integer;
        position: integer;
    end;
    CommandType = (LISTCMD, ADDCMD, DELETECMD, HELPCMD, QUITCMD, UNKNOWN);

procedure GetCommand (var line: LineType; var command: CommandType);

procedure ExecuteCommand (var line: LineType; command: CommandType;
        var history: SequenceType; var status: StatusType);
```

What is a consistent design for the Get... procedures?

Note that there is a lot of "getting" going on: "getting" a line, "getting" a command, "getting" an argument, and so on. It makes sense to have the corresponding procedures be as similar as possible. Each should have a parameter of the type being "gotten."

Stop & Help ▶ *Create informative names for the parameters that each procedure "gets."*

What about illegal commands?

Suppose that there is an error in the user's command. Each "get" routine must have a way of indicating to its caller that there was nothing to get or that the thing being gotten was of the wrong type.

In *Is It Legal?* a parameter of type boolean was used to indicate an error. In this situation, there are two types of error the program should indicate:

- error because there is nothing left on the line or in the input
- error because there is something on the line or in the input, but it is of the wrong type

Stop & Predict ▶ *List the specific errors that the program might detect on the line.*

How should the errors be indicated?

To indicate the status of the processing of the line we provide an extra parameter to each of the Get... routines. We define an enumerated type whose members are status values. They represent errors detectable either in GetCommand or ExecuteCommand:

SUCCESS	The command could be completed successfully.
NOINPUT	GetLine found no line to return (it encountered end-of-file on input).
LINETOOLONG	GetLine found too many characters to read on the line.

NOWORD	GetWord found no further things on the line to read.
WORDTOOLONG	GetWord found a word longer than it had room for.
NOCOMMAND	GetCommand found a blank line.
BADCOMMAND	The first word on the line was not a legal command.
NODATE	The last thing on the line has been read.
TOOMANYDATES	Too many arguments were specified on the command line.
BADDATE	An argument isn't a correctly formatted date.
ALREADYTHERE	A request to add an entry duplicated an existing date.
NOTTHERE	A delete or list request specified a nonexistent entry.
EMPTYRANGE	A list request specified a range of dates that contained no history entries.

Here are revisions to the type definitions and procedure headers provided so far:

```
type
    StatusType = (SUCCESS, NOINPUT, LINETOOLONG, NOWORD, WORDTOOLONG,
        NOCOMMAND, BADCOMMAND, NODATE, TOOMANYDATES, BADDATE,
        ALREADYTHERE, NOTTHERE, EMPTYRANGE);

procedure GetCommand (var line: LineType; var command: CommandType;
        var status: StatusType);
```

How is GetCommand coded? The code for GetCommand is now straightforward.

```
procedure GetCommand (var line: LineType; var command: CommandType;
        var status: StatusType);
begin
    write('COMMAND? ');
    GetLine (line, status);
    if status = SUCCESS then begin
        GetCmdWord (line, command, status);
    end;
end;
```

The GetLine and GetCmdWord procedures are similar to procedures used in *Is It Legal?* and *Space Text*.

```
procedure GetLine (var line: LineType; var status: StatusType);
var
    ch: char;
begin
    status := SUCCESS;
    if eof then begin
        status := NOINPUT;
    end else begin
        line.length := 0;
        line.position := 1;
        while not eoln do begin
            read (ch);
            if line.length = MAXLINELEN then begin
```

```
                        status := LINETOOLONG;
                    end else begin
                        line.length := line.length + 1;
                        line.chars[line.length] := ch;
                    end;
                end;
                readln;
            end;
    end;

    procedure GetCmdWord (var line: LineType; var command: CommandType;
            var status: StatusType);
    var
        word: WordType;
    begin
        status := SUCCESS;
        command := UNKNOWN;
        GetWord (line, word, status);
        if status = NOWORD then begin
            status := NOCOMMAND;
        end else if word = LISTWORD then begin
            command := LISTCMD;
        end else if word = ADDWORD then begin
            command := ADDCMD;
        end else if word = DELETEWORD then begin
            command := DELETECMD;
        end else if word = HELPWORD then begin
            command := HELPCMD;
        end else if word = QUITWORD then begin
            command := QUITCMD;
        end else begin
            status := BADCOMMAND;
        end;
    end;
```

Stop & Help ➤ *Write the* GetWord *procedure. Its arguments are the line, a packed array of characters, and a status. It will return the next word from the line in the array and update the line position appropriately.*

How does the design of GetCommand affect the main program?

GetCommand returns either with status = SUCCESS and command containing a translated command or with status indicating some error and command = UNKNOWN. The next question is where to handle the latter case. If status does not equal SUCCESS, code to print an error message could be added to the end of GetCommand. Or the main program could contain this code. Or ExecuteCommand might be written to handle an unknown command as well as all the legal commands.

A complicating factor is that one non-SUCCESS value for status, namely NOINPUT, represents an alternative way to quit the program. Thus either the main program will have to examine the contents of status, or GetCommand will have to return a value of QUITCMD in this case.

Somewhat arbitrarily, we choose to complicate both GetCommand and the main program slightly by adding status checks to each. The revised code follows.

```
procedure GetCommand (var line: LineType; var command: CommandType;
        var status: StatusType);
begin
    write('COMMAND? ');
    GetLine(line, status);
    if status = NOINPUT then begin
        command := QUITCMD;
        status := SUCCESS;
    end else if status = SUCCESS then begin
        GetCmdWord(line, command, status);
    end;
end;

{*** main program ***}
begin
    Initialize(history);
    done := false;
    repeat
        GetCommand(line, command, status);
        if status = SUCCESS then begin
            ExecuteCommand(line, command, history, status);
        end;
        if status <> SUCCESS then begin
            PrintErrorMsg(status);
        end;
    until command = QUITCMD;
end.
```

The main program uses a PrintErrorMsg procedure to print an error message. It is useful to print all error messages in one place, just in case we wish in a future revision to change their format or keep track of which errors are most commonly made by users.

How is ExecuteCommand designed?

Given a legal command, ExecuteCommand merely needs to decide which command it is and then execute it. A straightforward decomposition is to have a different execution procedure for each command. Deciding which of the procedures to call can be done in a case statement:

```
case command of
    LISTCMD:   ExecuteList (line, history, status);
    ADDCMD:    ExecuteAdd (line, history, status);
    DELETECMD: ExecuteDelete (line, history, status);
    HELPCMD:   ExecuteHelp (line, history, status);
    QUITCMD:   ExecuteQuit (line, history, status);
end;
```

ExecuteHelp and ExecuteQuit don't really need any arguments, but we code them the same as the other execution procedures for consistency.

How is ExecuteList **designed?**

ExecuteList is the hardest of the execution procedures, since it may take 0, 1, or 2 arguments. Thus we attack it first. It reads dates from the command line, then performs the appropriate operation on the history file.

Reading the command arguments will be done using a GetDate procedure whose parameters are the line, a date to be returned, and a status. Date arguments will be counted and stored in an array of size 2. The process is very similar to that of reading a line, as shown in the table below.

Operation	Reading a line	Getting date arguments from the line
getting the next item	read(ch);	GetDate(tempDate);
check if done	if eoln then ...	if status <> SUCCESS then ...
check for overflow	if length = MAXLINELEN then ...	if numDates = 2 then ...
storing the date	line.chars[line.length] := ch;	dates[numDates] := tempDate;

The main difference is that eoln rather than read is called to see if there are no more characters, but GetDate is called to find that there are no more dates. Here's the code:

```
procedure ExecuteList (var line: LineType; var history: SequenceType;
        var status: StatusType);
var
    dates: array [1..2] of DateType;
    tempDate: DateType;
    numDates: integer;
    done, found: boolean;
    position: PositionType;
    entry: EntryType;
begin
    done := false;
    numDates := 0;
    while not done do begin
        GetDate (line, tempDate, status);
        if status <> SUCCESS then begin
            done := true;
        end else if numDates = 2 then begin
            status := TOOMANYDATES;
            done := true;
        end else begin
            numDates := numDates + 1;
            dates [numDates] := tempDate;
        end;
    end;
    if status = NODATE then begin
        status := SUCCESS;
        case numDates of
        0:  PrintAll(history);
```

```
1:   begin
         Find(history, dates[1], found, entry, position);
         if found then begin
             PrintEntry(entry);
         end else begin
             status := NOTTHERE;
         end;
     end;
2:   begin
         Find(history, dates[2], found, entry, position);
         if not (AtOrBefore(entry.date, dates[2])
            and AtOrBefore(dates[1], entry.date)) then begin
             status := EMPTYRANGE;
         end else begin
             PrintEntry(entry);
             PrintUpTo(history, dates[1]);
         end;
       end;
     end;
   end;
end;
```

How is ExecuteAdd coded?

ExecuteAdd will be easier to code, since the add command takes exactly one date argument. The argument will be retrieved from the line, the line will be checked to make sure no more dates have been provided, the code from the revised *You Are What You Eat* will be inserted to collect a day's data from the user, and then the appropriate history file operation will be applied. Here's the code:

```
procedure ExecuteAdd (var line: LineType; var status: StatusType);
var
    date, tempDate: DateType;
    entry: EntryType;
    found: boolean;  position: PositionType;
begin
    GetDate (line, date, status);
    if status = SUCCESS then begin
        GetDate (line, tempDate, status);
        if status = SUCCESS then begin
            status := TOOMANYDATES;
        end else if status = NODATE then begin
            status := SUCCESS;
        end;
    end;
    if status = SUCCESS then begin
        Find(history, date, found, entry, position);
        if found then begin
            status := ALREADYTHERE;
        end else begin
            entry.date := date;
            ReadEntry(entry);
            Insert(history, entry, position);
        end;
    end;
end;
```

How are the remaining Execute **routines coded?**

ExecuteDelete is even simpler than ExecuteInsert. The coding is straightforward.

Stop & Help ➤ *Code the* ExecuteDelete *procedure.*

ExecuteHelp merely prints a helpful message about all the commands. ExecuteQuit need do nothing, but perhaps a message saying something like "Exiting history file editor" would be reasonable.

How is the GetDate **procedure designed?**

All that's left is the GetDate procedure. Recall that the format of a date is month/day/year. GetDate must retrieve and analyze the components of the date from the line. For consistency with GetCmdWord, GetDate will first call GetWord to isolate the next argument from the line, and then work with the isolated word.

What are possible errors in a date?

To aid in decomposing GetDate, it will help to list all the possible errors that can appear in a nonempty date.

- It doesn't start with digits.
- It starts with digits that represent a value less than 1 or greater than 12.
- The digits aren't followed by a slash.
- The slash isn't followed by digits.
- The digits following the slash represent a value less than 1 or greater than the number of days in the month.
- The digits are followed by something other than a slash.
- The second slash isn't followed by digits.
- The remaining digits represent a value that isn't a legal year.
- A year is followed by anything other than the end of the word.

How is GetDate **decomposed?**

We could process the date word with a sequence of character accesses and tests, but this would be clumsy. Another option is to provide procedures to get an integer and a slash, analogous to the other Get... procedures. This leads to the following code:

```
GetInteger (word, int, status);
if status = NOINT then begin
    status := BADDATE;
end else if not (int in [1..12]) then begin
    status := BADDATE;
end else begin
    GetSlash (word, status);
    if status = NOSLASH then begin
        status := BADDATE;
    end else begin
        GetInteger (word, int, status);
        if status = NOINT then begin
            status := BADDATE;
        end else begin
            ⋮
```

Stop & Help ➤   *Complete the code just outlined.*

This is clumsy. Extra tests could reduce the nesting of the code as follows:

```
GetInteger (word, int, status);
if status = NOINT then begin
    status := BADDATE;
end else if not (int in [1..12]) then begin
    status := BADDATE;
end;
if status = SUCCESS then begin
    GetSlash (word, status);
    if status = NOSLASH then begin
        status := BADDATE;
    end;
end;
if status = SUCCESS then begin
       ⋮
```

Stop & Help ➤   *Complete the code above.*

This is still clumsy. Some sort of loop is preferable. We try a state-based approach similar to that used in *Is It Legal?* but it is too complicated. Sometimes a brute-force approach is best of all, despite its inelegance; this seems to be such a situation. The following code, in which checks of form (for example, that the month has 1 or 2 digits) precede checks for content (for example, that the month value is at most 12), results.

```
procedure GetDate (var line: LineType; var date: DateType;
        var status: StatusType);
var
    word: WordType;
    index: integer;
    month, day, year: integer;
begin
    GetWord(line, word, status);
    if status = NOWORD then begin
        status := NODATE;
    end;
    if status = SUCCESS then begin
        index := 1;
        GetOneOrTwoDigits(word, index, month, status);
    end;
    if status = SUCCESS then begin
        GetSeparator(word, index, status);
    end;
    if status = SUCCESS then begin
        GetOneOrTwoDigits(word, index, day, status);
    end;
    if status = SUCCESS then begin
        GetSeparator(word, index, status);
    end;
    if status = SUCCESS then begin
        GetFourDigits(word, index, year, status);
```

```
        end;
    if status = SUCCESS then begin
        CheckNoMore(word, index, status);
    end;
    if status = SUCCESS then begin
        if not LegalDate(month, day, year) then begin
            status := BADDATE;
        end else begin
            date.month := MonthEquiv(month);
            date.day := day;
            date.year := year;
        end;
    end;
end;
```

Each Get... procedure above checks for the specified characters, increments index if it finds them, and stores an error value in status if it does not. For example, here's the code for GetOneOrTwoDigits:

```
if IsDigit(word[index]) and not IsDigit(word[index + 1]) then begin
    n := DigitValue(word[index]);
    index := index + 1;
end else if IsDigit(word[index]) and IsDigit(word[index + 1]) then begin
    n := 10 * DigitValue(word[index]) + DigitValue(word[index + 1]);
    index := index + 2;
end else begin
    status := BADNUM;
end;
```

Not pretty, but it works. We also invent several new status values, and add corresponding error messages to PrintErrorMsg:

BADNUM   Either the month, the day, or the year is incorrectly formatted.

BADSEP   A slash (separator) was not found where expected.

EXTRAJUNK   There were nonblank characters after the year.

That completes the program.

Stop & Help ➤   *Produce the call diagram for the program just completed.*

How is all this code tested and debugged?   The file-manipulating routines were tested previously, so what remains are the procedures to get a date and execute commands. We test GetDate separately (together with subprograms IsDigit, DigitValue, GetWord, GetLine, WriteInDate, LeapYear, LeapDay, NumberOfDaysIn, and the procedures GetDate calls directly) with a program that repeatedly reads a date and prints it. With test data, we make sure that boundary dates at the start and end of months are handled correctly and that values with one too many or one too few digits are detected.

Finally, we test the remainder of the program. Unlike code in earlier case studies, this program does not include a DEBUGGING switch, since we feel that the list command provides as much information as necessary to detect bugs.

⏴

🖳 💾 *Application* 8.25 Add a command called Copy to the "get a line, process a command word" version that copies the fat and calorie information from the history file entry for one date as the fat and calorie information for another date. Change the program as little as possible.

💾 *Analysis* 8.26 Suppose a boolean function NoMoreWords had been written that returned true exactly where there were no more words on its line argument. In which routines should NoMoreWords be called?

🖳 💾 *Modification* 8.27 Write the NoMoreWords function, and modify the program to call it where appropriate.

Reflection 8.28 Compare the brute-force approach to the attempt at elegance in processing dates. What features of a date make the brute-force approach reasonable?

💾 *Testing* 8.29 Design a collection of test cases for GetDate. Describe why each is necessary and explain why this set of cases will adequately test the routine.

The "Get a Complete Legal Command" Design

What are the differences between the two designs?

Having implemented the "get a line, process the command word" version of this program, it is easy to convert the design to "get a complete legal command." The only real difference is that dates must be isolated and analyzed in the GetCommand procedure rather than in the ExecuteCommand procedure. There will be several changes in details, however.

Stop & Predict ➤ *What subprograms will need to be modified?*

How will the main program change?

First, the main program will change. ExecuteCommand will no longer need the line as an argument, since GetCommand will have completely processed the line. (It will still need a status argument, since there are still errors to detect after the command is read.) The command will now include the arguments as well as the command word; thus a new definition is provided for CommandType:

```
CmdWordType = (LISTCMD, ..., UNKNOWN); {the old CommandType}
CommandType = record
    cmdWord: CmdWordType;
    numArgs: integer;
    args: array [1..2] of DateType;
end;
```

Here's the rewritten main program:

```
Initialize(history);
done := false;
repeat
    GetCommand(line, command, status);
    if status = SUCCESS then begin
        ExecuteCommand(command, history, status);
    end;
    if status <> SUCCESS then begin
        PrintErrorMsg(status);
    end;
until command.cmdWord = QUITCMD;
```

**How will the Execute...
procedures change?**

These changes are propagated to the command-handling routines. Instead of taking a line as a first argument, they take a command. They no longer "get" the arguments themselves; each routine is cut roughly in half as a result. Here, for example, is ExecuteAdd:

```
procedure ExecuteAdd (var command: CommandType;
    var history: SequenceType;
    var status: StatusType);
var
    found: boolean;
    entry: EntryType;
    position: PositionType;
begin
    Find(history, command.args[1], found, entry, position);
    if found then begin
        status := ALREADYTHERE;
    end else begin
        entry.date := command.args[1];
        ReadEntry(entry);
        Insert(history, entry, position);
    end;
end;
```

None of the history file operations changes.

**How will the new
GetCommand be
organized?**

To design the new GetCommand, we repeat an approach taken in *Is It Legal?* that applies successively more stringent checks to the contents of the line. The checks follow.

- Has a nonempty line been entered?

- Does the line contain at least one word and at most three?

- Is the first word a command word, and is the number of words that remain consistent with that command?

- Do the remaining words represent dates?

The diagram below represents how these checks focus increasingly on the line contents.

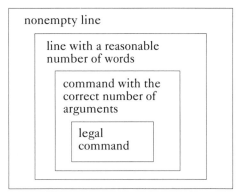

Assuming that each check is done in a separate procedure, we code Get-Command as shown below.

```
procedure GetCommand (var line: LineType; var command: CommandType;
        var status: StatusType);
var
    words: WordArrayType;
begin
    write('COMMAND? ');
    GetLine(line, status);
    if status = NOINPUT then begin
        command.cmdWord := QUITCMD;
        command.numArgs := 0;
        status := SUCCESS;
    end else begin
        if status = SUCCESS then begin
            GetWords(line, words, status);
        end;
        if status = SUCCESS then begin
            ConvertToCommand(words, command, status);
        end;
        if status = SUCCESS then begin
            ConvertToArgs(words, command, status);
        end;
    end;
end;
```

The type WordArrayType represents an array of the words on the command line. Patterning it on LineType, we supply the following definitions:

```
const
    MAXCMDLEN = 3;

type
    WordArrayType = record
        length: integer;
        words: array [1..MAXCMDLEN] of WordType;
    end;   {WordType was defined in the earlier version of the program.}
```

COMMENTARY **COMMENTARY**

How is the command
word analyzed?

GetLine is unchanged. GetWords is coded to resemble GetLine and the argument-reading code from the earlier version of the history editor. ConvertToCommand is patterned on GetCmdWord from the earlier version; it checks in addition that the number of arguments matches the command, as follows:

```
procedure ConvertToCommand (var words: WordArrayType;
        var command: CommandType; var status: StatusType);
begin
    status := SUCCESS;
    command.cmdWord := UNKNOWN;
    if words.length = 0 then begin
        status := NOCOMMAND;
    end else if words.words[1] = LISTWORD then begin
        command.cmdWord := LISTCMD;
        command.numArgs := words.length - 1;
    end else if words.words[1] = ADDWORD then begin
        command.cmdWord := ADDCMD;
        if words.length < 2 then begin
            status := NODATE;
        end else if words.length > 2 then begin
            status := TOOMANYDATES;
        end else begin
            command.numArgs := 1;
        end;
    end else if words.words[1] = DELETEWORD then begin
        command.cmdWord := DELETECMD;
        if words.length < 2 then begin
            status := NODATE;
        end else if words.length > 2 then begin
            status := TOOMANYDATES;
        end else begin
            command.numArgs := 1;
        end;
    end else if words.words[1] = HELPWORD then begin
        command.cmdWord := HELPCMD;
        command.numArgs := 0;
    end else if words.words[1] = QUITWORD then begin
        command.cmdWord := QUITCMD;
        command.numArgs := 0;
    end else begin
        status := BADCOMMAND;
    end;
end;
```

How are the arguments
analyzed?

ConvertToArgs converts the arguments to dates. It calls a procedure ConvertToDate once for each argument. ConvertToDate is essentially GetDate from the earlier version without the initial call to GetWord.

Which version is better?

The subprograms that are different in the two versions appear in the Pascal Code section. The "get a complete legal command" version is slightly longer than the "get a line, process the command word" version. It should, however, be much easier to add a command to the "get a complete legal command" version, provided that it sufficiently resembles the other commands.

Analysis 8.30 Describe a modification to the program that would be easier to make to the "get a line, process the command word" version than to the "get a complete legal command" version. Explain in general what kinds of changes would be easier to add to each version of the code.

Application 8.31 Create a boolean function called LegalDate that returns true if the correct number of legal dates were input and returns false otherwise. The function should call GetDate.

Modification 8.32 Modify the GetDate procedure to handle dates entered in the format 1-2-91 as well as in the format 1/2/91.

Testing, Reflection 8.33 Provide a set of test data for the "get a complete legal command" version. Which of the two versions is easier to test?

Reflection 8.34 Which of the two versions is easier for you to understand? Why?

Outline of Design and Development Questions

These questions summarize the main points of the commentary.

Planning the Modifications
What new features were requested?
What changes will produce a file containing the graphs?
What changes will implement the new input format?
What changes will allow the user to add forgotten data and correct errors?
How might the modifications be incorporated?
How will the history file editor work?
How will the history file format change?
How will the date for the current entry be determined?
What modifications are needed to go with the new file format?
What changes to *You Are What You Eat* are to be made?
What comes first?

Implementing Changes to *You Are What You Eat*
How is PrintGraph changed?
How is ReadEntry rewritten?

In which procedure should the food be looked up?
What is the format of the food information file?
How is a file of records created?
How is the error checking coded?
How is the file search coded?
How are the fat and calorie amounts coded?
How is the code tested?
What modifications are necessary to keep track of dates?
   How will Initialize and Update be modified to handle the new file
      format?
   How is the date of the current entry computed?
What changes to the top-level decomposition are necessary?
How is the code tested?

High-Level Design of the History Editor
What commands will be provided in the history file editor?
How is the history file editor organized?
How are the history entries represented?
How do we create an abstract view?
What operations have we left out?
How are the commands and abstract operations related?
Is a file or an array best?

Implementing the Abstract Operations
How is the "find" operation coded?
   How is a file searched?
   What happens when an entry is found?
How is the "insert" operation coded?
How is the "delete" operation coded?
How is the "print all entries" operation coded?
How is the "print all entries between two given dates" operation coded?
How is the "initialize" operation coded?
What about the code that manipulates dates?
How can the code be tested?
   What bugs are encountered?

Designing and Developing the Remainder of the History Editor
What remains to be designed?
What should the "get a command" step do?
What worked before?
How do we select an alternative?
What errors will the program check?
What are the pros and cons of each decomposition?

The "Get the Line, Process the Command Word" Design
What will GetCommand and ExecuteCommand do?
How will GetCommand and ExecuteCommand communicate?

How will ExecuteCommand work?

What are the headers for these procedures?

What is a consistent design for the Get... procedures?

> What about illegal commands?

> How should the errors be indicated?

How is GetCommand coded?

> How does the design of GetCommand affect the main program?

How is ExecuteCommand designed?

How is ExecuteList designed?

How is ExecuteAdd coded?

How are the remaining Execute routines coded?

How is the GetDate procedure designed?

> What are possible errors in a date?

> How is GetDate decomposed?

How is all this code tested and debugged?

The "Get a Complete Legal Command" Design

What are the differences between the two designs?

How will the main program change?

How will the Execute... procedures change?

How will the new GetCommand be organized?

How is the command word analyzed?

How are the arguments analyzed?

Which version is better?

Programmers' Summary

In this case study, we add three features to the *You Are What You Eat* program. One is to copy the fat and calorie graphs to a file, allowing the user to print them or refer to them later. Another is the use of a food information file to let the user enter food names and serving sizes rather than actual fat and calorie values. The third provides a way for the user to edit the history file.

We could add all the new features to the original program. We choose instead to invent a separate program to do the editing, hoping to provide a *system* of programs that is both easier for the user to understand and easier for us to manage.

Even as separate programs, they each contain several hundred lines of code, larger than any of the programs in earlier case studies. Yet implementing the changes to the *You Are What You Eat* program is straightforward, as is designing and developing the history file editor. Why? There are two main reasons.

First, each program can be decomposed into sections to handle input, processing, and output, along with another section for accessing and updating the history file. We isolate interaction with the user in the input section, access to the history file in history file section, and so on. As a result, it is clear where to make each modification to the original *You Are What You Eat* program. Each of the sections in both programs can be tested separately, reducing the probability of undetected bugs.

Second, almost all the code results from applying templates from previous case studies. Array searching and processing templates are adapted to search and process the history and food files. (These templates suggest good test data as well.) The "select from alternatives" template forms the backbone of the code to execute commands in the history file editor. Routines to read food names, servings, editor commands, and arguments are patterned on code from *Is It Legal?*, *Space Text*, and *You Are What You Eat*. Code to check dates for legality is copied from *The Calendar Shop*. This reliance on previously developed code makes the program both easier to design, since we are designing very little code from scratch, and easier to test and debug, since we have already tested the code or something very similar before.

We use multiple debugging switches in the new version of *You Are What You Eat* so that we can focus on the actions in a particular program section rather than wade through debugging output for all the sections. In the history file editor, we do not have any debugging switch, relying instead on the list commands already being built into the editor. (For this reason, the list command is the first command we test and debug.)

The decision made in *You Are What You Eat* to store file entries most recent first may have been unwise. It complicates the design of code to search the file and leads to at least one bug.

The main program for the history file editor is an application of the "input one, process one" template, commonly known as a **command interpreter**. It consists of a loop that first reads, then executes a command. In any command interpreter, there is the question of how much to do in each step. "Reading" a command might be as little as reading its characters into a string or as much as analyzing all the command's components for legality and translating them into an internal form. We design two versions of the code. In one, the "get a line, process the command word" version, the "read a command" step reads a line of input, then classifies the first word as a command; command execution routines isolate the command arguments from the line. In the other, the "get a complete legal command" version, the "read a command" step reads and analyzes the entire command. The choice between the two approaches depends on how similar commands are to one another—the more similar, the better the "get a complete legal command" version—and on what modifications are anticipated for the program.

Several decomposition questions are encountered. At what point should the food name be looked up in the food information file? At what point should the current date be determined? Where should errors be handled? These all are answered to maintain consistency with other parts of the program and to isolate references to program data structures in a small number of routines.

Pascal constructs introduced in this case study include enumerated types (for commands and error status indicators) and files of records. Members of an enumerated type are used in the same way as integer constants were in *The Calendar Shop* and *Is It Legal?* The advantage of an enumerated type is that it can be concisely defined; its disadvantage is that values of the type cannot be printed and can be manipulated only with the ord, pred, and succ functions. A file of records allows information to be input without being analyzed. This saves code and execution time. The disadvantages of a file of records are that it can be created only by a program, not by a text editor; its contents can be printed only by a program; and one must ensure that the file-creating program and the file-reading program are using identical definitions for the components of the file.

Making Sense of *You Forgot What You Ate*

Analysis 8.35 Describe the advantages of using an array rather than a file for the history entries. What routines would have been designed differently if an array had been used?

Reflection 8.36 Would a replace command have been more confusing than the add and delete commands? Why or why not?

Reflection 8.37 Would the design process have been just as easy if we had started with the "get a complete legal command" version of the program instead of the "get a line, process the command word" version? Why or why not?

Reflection 8.38 Suppose one of your friends volunteered to make the revisions to *You Are What You Eat*. What would you need to tell your friend about the program in order to orient him or her to the code and design most effectively?

Reflection 8.39 Suppose you were working with a programming partner on the revisions. How would you split the task most equitably? What coordination problems would you expect?

Debugging   8.40   Add mutations to the code, and get another programmer to find them. Where in the code are bugs most difficult to detect?

Debugging   8.41   It is possible for the history file editor in the Pascal Code section to leave fewer than thirty entries in the history file, and the revised *You Are What You Eat* program will crash as a result. Describe circumstances under which this will happen.

Reflection   8.42   The bug described in question 8.41 involved the interaction between two programs. How does testing and debugging the interaction between two programs differ from testing and debugging the interaction between two subprograms?

Modification   8.43   Fix the bug described in question 8.41. In which program should the fix be incorporated?

Modification   8.44   Modify the programs designed in *You Forgot What You Ate* so that all the user input of fat and calorie information is read in one program, and all the graphing is done in another. Compare this organization to the one we produced.

Application   8.45   Write a program to manipulate a library data base. Each entry in the data base contains information about a book: its title, its lending status, and the date it is to be returned. The program should accept commands that add a book to the data base, delete a book from the data base, signal that the book has been borrowed, signal that the book has been returned, and list all the books currently loaned out.

Linking to Previous Case Studies

Reflection   8.46   In both *You Are What You Eat* and in *You Forgot What You Ate*, we encountered a choice between using an array and using a file. Compare the circumstances in the two case studies. Which circumstances were similar and which were different?

Reflection   8.47   How does separating the design of abstract operations for a data type from the design of the code for those operations help isolate code that may later need to be modified?

Reflection   8.48   In what ways are the design of abstract operations for a data type similar to those of postponing details in *The Calendar Shop?*

Application   8.49   The programs in this case study use code from *The Calendar Shop* to manipulate dates. Describe some other applications in which code that manipulates dates would be useful, and indicate what other operations on dates would have to be implemented in the applications you describe.

Revisions to *You Are What You Eat*

```pascal
type
    MonthType = (JANUARY, FEBRUARY, MARCH, APRIL, MAY, JUNE,
        JULY, AUGUST, SEPTEMBER, OCTOBER, NOVEMBER, DECEMBER);
    DayType = 1..31;
    YearType = 1990..2100;
    DateType = record
        month: MonthType;
        day: DayType;
        year: YearType;
    end;
    EntryType = record
        date: DateType;
        fat, calories: integer;
    end;
    HistoryType = array[0..HISTORYSIZE] of EntryType;
    HistoryFileType = file of EntryType;
    StringType = packed array[1..MAXSTRLEN] of char;
    FoodEntryType = record
        foodName: StringType;
        servingDescr: StringType;
        fat, calories: integer;
    end;
    FoodInfoType = file of FoodEntryType;

var
    historyFile: HistoryFileType;
    foodInfo: FoodInfoType;
    testFile: text;
    entry: EntryType;
    recentHistory: HistoryType;


{
    Print the date, followed by a carriage return.
}
procedure WritelnDate (date: DateType);
begin {Writeln Date}
    case date.month of
        JANUARY:   write('January ');
        FEBRUARY:  write('February ');
        MARCH:     write('March ');
        APRIL:     write('April ');
        MAY:       write('May ');
        JUNE:      write('June ');
        JULY:      write('July ');
        AUGUST:    write('August ');
        SEPTEMBER: write('September ');
        OCTOBER:   write('October ');
        NOVEMBER:  write('November ');
        DECEMBER:  write('December ');
    end;
    writeln(date.day : 1, ', ', date.year : 4);
end; {Writeln Date}
```

```
{
    Return true exactly when year is a leap year.
}
function LeapYear (year: YearType): boolean;
begin {Leap Year?}
    LeapYear := (year div 400 = 0)
        or ((year div 4 = 0) and (year div 100 <> 0));
end; {Leap Year?}

{
    Return 1 when year is a leap year, 0 otherwise.
}
function LeapDay (year: YearType): integer;
begin {Leap Day}
    if LeapYear(year) then begin
        LeapDay := 1;
    end else begin
        LeapDay := 0;
    end;
end; {Leap Day}

{
    Return the number of days in the given month.
}
function NumberOfDaysIn (month: MonthType; year: YearType): DayType;
begin {Number Of Days In}
    case month of
        JANUARY, MARCH, MAY, JULY, AUGUST, OCTOBER, DECEMBER:
            NumberOfDaysIn := 31;
        FEBRUARY:
            NumberOfDaysIn := 28 + LeapDay(year);
        APRIL, JUNE, SEPTEMBER, NOVEMBER:
            NumberOfDaysIn := 30;
    end;
end; {Number Of Days In}

{
    Return in next the date after the date in current.
}
procedure FindSuccessor (current: DateType; var next: DateType);
begin {Find Successor}
    if current.day < NumberOfDaysIn(current.month, current.year)
      then begin
        next.month := current.month;
        next.day := current.day + 1;
        next.year := current.year;
    end else if current.month < DECEMBER then begin
        next.month := succ(current.month);
        next.day := 1;
        next.year := current.year;
    end else begin
        next.month := JANUARY;
        next.day := 1;
        next.year := current.year + 1;
    end;
```

```
        if DEBUGDATES then begin
            write ('*** the day after ');
            WritelnDate (current);
            write ('    is ');
            WritelnDate (next);
        end;
end; {Find Successor}


{
    Return true exactly when numServings constitutes a reasonable serving
    size.
}
function IsInServingRange (numServings: integer): boolean;
begin {Is In Serving Range?}
    IsInServingRange := (numServings >= 0)
        and (numServings <= MAXSERVINGS);
end; {Is In Serving Range?}


{
    line contains a food name. Search for it in foodInfo. If it's there,
    return true in found and return the corresponding food entry in
    foodEntry; otherwise return false in found.
}
procedure Search (line: LineType; var foodEntry: FoodEntryType;
    var found: boolean);
begin {Search}
    reset(foodInfo);
    found := false;
    while not eof(foodInfo) and not found do begin
        read(foodInfo, foodEntry);
        found := Equal(line, foodEntry.foodName);
        if DEBUGFOOD then begin
            writeln ('*** checking ', foodEntry.foodName);
        end;
    end;
end; {Search}


{
    Ask the user for a food name, and keep prompting until a legal food
    name is provided. The user may either supply a food name, in which case
    the corresponding entry from foodInfo is returned in foodEntry and
    false is returned in done, or the word "done", in which case true is
    returned in done.
}
procedure ReadFood (var inFile: text; var foodEntry: FoodEntryType;
    var done: boolean);
var
    error, found: boolean; line: LineType;
begin {Read Food}
    done := false;
    repeat
        error := false;
        writeln('Please type either a food name');
        writeln('or type the word "done"--without the quotes--',
            'if you''re finished.');
        ReadTrimmedLine(inFile, line);
```

```
                           if Empty(line) then begin
                               error := true;
                           end else if Equal(line, DONESTR) then begin
                               done := true;
                           end else begin
                               Search(line, foodEntry, found);
                               if not found then begin
                                   error := true;
                               end;
                           end;
                           if error then begin
                               writeln('That food is not in the dictionary of foods.');
                           end;
                    until done or not error;
                end; {Read Food}


                {
                    Ask the user for a number of servings, and keep prompting until a legal
                    number is provided. foodEntry contains information about the serving
                    units that is printed in the prompt. Return the number in numServings.
                }
                procedure ReadServings (var inFile: text; foodEntry: FoodEntryType;
                    var numServings: integer);
                var
                    error: boolean; line: LineType;
                begin {Read Servings}
                    repeat
                        error := false;
                        writeln('How many servings? One serving = ',
                            foodEntry.servingDescr);
                        ReadTrimmedLine(inFile, line);
                        if Empty(line) then begin
                            error := true;
                        end else if not IsAllDigits(line) then begin
                            error := true;
                        end else begin
                            numServings := IntegerValue(line);
                            if not IsInServingRange(numServings) then begin
                                error := true;
                            end;
                        end;
                        if error then begin
                            writeln('You must provide an integer number of servings, ',
                                'no more than', MAXSERVINGS);
                        end;
                    until not error;
                end; {Read Servings}


                {
                    Read today's food entry from the user, returning it in entry.
                }
                procedure ReadEntry (var inFile: text; today: DateType;
                    var entry: EntryType);
                var
                    numServings: integer; done: boolean; foodEntry: FoodEntryType;
                begin {Read Entry}
```

```
        entry.date := today;
        entry.fat := 0;
        entry.calories := 0;
        repeat
            ReadFood(inFile, foodEntry, done);
            if not done then begin
                ReadServings(inFile, foodEntry, numServings);
                entry.fat := entry.fat + numServings * foodEntry.fat;
                entry.calories := entry.calories
                    + numServings * foodEntry.calories;
                if DEBUGFOOD then begin
                    writeln ('*** accumulated fat = ', entry.fat:1,
                        '  accumulated calories = ', entry.calories:1);
                end;
            end;
        until done;
end; {Read Entry}


{
    Initialize recentHistory from this history file.
}
procedure Initialize (var historyFile: HistoryFileType;
    var recentHistory: HistoryType);
var
    testFile: text; numEntries, dayNum: integer;
    entry: EntryType; today: DateType;
begin {Initialize}
    numEntries := 0;
    reset(historyFile);
    for dayNum := 1 to HISTORYSIZE do begin
        read(historyFile, recentHistory[dayNum]);
        if DEBUGHISTORY then begin
            write ('*** from history: ');
            WritelnDate (recentHistory[dayNum].date);
            writeln ('    fat = ', recentHistory[dayNum].fat:1,
                '  calories = ', recentHistory[dayNum].calories:1);
        end;
    end;
    FindSuccessor(recentHistory[1].date, today);
    write('The food data you are about to enter is assumed to be for ');
    WritelnDate(today);
    writeln('Quit this program and run the history file editor ',
        'if this is incorrect.');
    if FILEINPUT then begin
        ReadEntry(testFile, today, recentHistory[0]);
    end else begin
        ReadEntry(input, today, recentHistory[0]);
    end;
end; {Initialize}


{
    Write the new recentHistory values to the history file.
}
procedure Update (var historyFile: HistoryFileType;
    recentHistory: HistoryType);
var
```

```
                    dayNum: integer; entry: EntryType; tempFile: HistoryFileType;
      begin {Update}
          rewrite(tempFile);
          for dayNum := 0 to HISTORYSIZE do begin
              write(tempFile, recentHistory[dayNum]);
          end;
          while not eof(historyFile) do begin
              read(historyFile, entry);
              write(tempFile, entry);
              if DEBUGHISTORY then begin
                  writeln('*** to temp file: ', entry.fat, entry.calories);
              end;
          end;
          reset(tempFile);
          rewrite(historyFile);
          while not eof(tempFile) do begin
              read(tempFile, entry);
              write(historyFile, entry);
              if DEBUGHISTORY then begin
                  writeln('*** to history file: ', entry.fat, entry.calories);
              end;
          end;
      end; {Update}

      begin
          reset(foodInfo);
          Initialize(historyFile, recentHistory);
          PrintAverages(recentHistory);
          PrintGraphs(recentHistory);
          Update(historyFile, recentHistory);
      end.
```

Implementation of the Abstract History File Operations

```
{
    Print the information in the given entry.
}
procedure PrintEntry (entry: EntryType);
begin {Print Entry}
    write('Date = ');
    WritelnDate(entry.date);
    writeln('Fat = ', entry.fat : 1, ', calories = ', entry.calories : 1);
end; {Print Entry}

{
    Read the information for a food entry.
}
procedure ReadEntry (var entry: EntryType);
{The code for ReadEntry appears in the previous section.}

{
    Copy remaining elements from original to temp, then copy all elements
```

```
        in temp back to original.
}
procedure CopyThenCopyBack (var original: SequenceType;
    var temp: PositionType);
var
    entry: EntryType;
begin {Copy Then Copy Back}
    while not eof(original) do begin
        read(original, entry);
        write(temp, entry);
    end;
    reset(temp);
    rewrite(original);
    while not eof(temp) do begin
        read(temp, entry);
        write(original, entry);
    end;
end; {Copy Then Copy Back}

{
    Search for an entry with the given date in history, while copying
    entries from history to temp. Read only as far as necessary in history.
    If an entry with the given date is found, return it in entry and return
    true in found; otherwise return false in found. temp will represent
    the position either of the entry found or the entry with the next
    earlier date if the search is unsuccessful.
}
procedure Find (var history: SequenceType; date: DateType;
    var found: boolean; var entry: EntryType; var temp: PositionType);
var
    foundAtOrBefore: boolean;
begin {Find}
    reset(history);
    rewrite(temp);
    foundAtOrBefore := false;
    while not foundAtOrBefore and not eof(history) do begin
        read(history, entry);
        if AtOrBefore(entry.date, date) then begin
            foundAtOrBefore := true;
        end else begin
            write(temp, entry);
        end;
    end;
    if foundAtOrBefore then begin
        found := Same(date, entry.date);
    end else begin
        found := false;
    end;
end; {Find}

{
    Insert the given entry at the given position (temp) in history.
}
procedure Insert (var history: SequenceType; entry: EntryType;
    var temp: PositionType);
begin {Insert}
```

```
            write(temp, entry);
            CopyThenCopyBack(history, temp);
    end; {Insert}


    {
        Delete the entry at the given position (temp) in history.
    }
    procedure Delete (var history: SequenceType; var temp: PositionType);
    begin {Delete}
        CopyThenCopyBack(history, temp);
    end; {Delete}


    {
        Print all entries in history.
    }
    procedure PrintAll (var history: SequenceType);
    var
        entry: EntryType;
    begin {Print All}
        reset(history);
        while not eof(history) do begin
            read(history, entry);
            PrintEntry(entry);
        end;
    end; {Print All}


    {
        Print all entries in history up to and including the given date.
    }
    procedure PrintUpTo (var history: SequenceType; date: DateType;
        var temp: PositionType);
    var
        done: boolean; entry: EntryType;
    begin {Print Up To}
        done := false;
        while not done and not eof(history) do begin
            read(history, entry);
            if AtOrBefore(date, entry.date) then begin
                PrintEntry(entry);
            end else begin
                done := true;
            end;
        end;
    end; {Print Up To}


    {
        Initialize history.
    }
    procedure Initialize (var history: SequenceType);
    begin {Initialize}
        reset(history);
    end; {Initialize}
```

The Rest of the History Editor

```pascal
program HistoryEditor (input, output, history);

const
    BLANK = ' ';
    DATESEPARATOR = '/';
    MAXLINELEN = 80;
    MAXWORDLEN = 20;
    LISTWORD    = 'list                ';
    ADDWORD     = 'add                 ';
    DELETEWORD  = 'delete              ';
    HELPWORD    = 'help                ';
    QUITWORD    = 'quit                ';
    BLANKWORD   = '                    ';

type
    LineType = record
        chars: array[1..MAXLINELEN] of char;
        length: integer;
        position: integer;
    end;
    WordType = packed array[1..MAXWORDLEN] of char;

    CommandType = (LISTCMD, ADDCMD, DELETECMD, HELPCMD, QUITCMD, UNKNOWN);
    StatusType = (SUCCESS, NOINPUT, LINETOOLONG, NOWORD, WORDTOOLONG,
        NOCOMMAND, BADCOMMAND, NODATE, TOOMANYDATES, BADNUM, BADSEP,
        EXTRAJUNK, BADDATE, ALREADYTHERE, NOTTHERE, EMPTYRANGE);

    MonthType = (JANUARY, FEBRUARY, MARCH, APRIL, MAY, JUNE,
        JULY, AUGUST, SEPTEMBER, OCTOBER, NOVEMBER, DECEMBER);
    DayType = 1..31;
    YearType = 1990..2100;
    DateType = record
        month: MonthType;
        day: DayType;
        year: YearType;
    end;
    EntryType = record
        date: DateType;
        fat, calories: integer;
    end;
    SequenceType = file of EntryType;
    PositionType = file of EntryType;

var
    history: SequenceType;
    done: boolean;
    line: LineType;
    command: CommandType;
    status: StatusType;

{*** error message printer ***}

procedure PrintErrorMsg (status: StatusType);
begin {Print Error Message}
```

```
            case status of
                SUCCESS:      writeln('*** INTERNAL ERROR IN PROGRAM ***');
                NOINPUT:      writeln('*** Input ran out unexpectedly. ***');
                LINETOOLONG: writeln('*** There is too much text ',
                    'on the command line. ***');
                NOWORD:       writeln('*** INTERNAL ERROR IN PROGRAM ***');
                WORDTOOLONG: writeln('*** A word on the command line ',
                    'is too long. ***');
                NOCOMMAND:   writeln('*** There is nothing ',
                    'on the command line. ***');
                BADCOMMAND:  writeln('*** The first word on the line ',
                    'is not a legal command. ***');
                NODATE:       writeln('*** INTERNAL ERROR IN PROGRAM ***');
                TOOMANYDATES: writeln('*** Too many dates were specified ',
                    'for this command. ***');
                BADNUM:       writeln('*** The month, day, or year ',
                    'is illegal. ***');
                BADSEP:       writeln('*** The month and day must ',
                    be separated by a slash, as must the day and year. ***');
                EXTRAJUNK:   writeln('*** Extra text appears ',
                    'after the year. ***');
                BADDATE:      writeln('*** The number of days in the month ',
                    'is incorrect. ***');
                ALREADYTHERE: writeln('*** There is already an entry ',
                    'for that date. ***');
                NOTTHERE:     writeln('*** There is no entry for that date. ***');
                EMPTYRANGE:  writeln('*** There are no entries between ',
                    'the two given dates. ***');
            end;
        end; {Print Error Message}

        {*** utility routines ***}

        {
            Return true exactly when ch is a digit.
        }
        function IsDigit (ch: char): boolean;
        begin {Is Digit?}
            IsDigit := ch in ['0'..'9'];
        end; {Is Digit?}

        {
            Return the numeric value of the given digit.
        }
        function DigitValue (ch: char): integer;
        begin {Digit Value}
            DigitValue := ord(ch) - ord('0');
        end; {Digit Value}

        {
            Get the next word from line and return it in word. Update the line
            position. Return the result of the word scanning in status: success,
            no words left in line, or too long a word.
        }
        procedure GetWord (var line: LineType; var word: WordType;
            var status: StatusType);
```

```
var
    done: boolean; length: integer;
begin {Get Word}
    status := SUCCESS;
    done := false;
    while not done do begin
        if line.position > line.length then begin
            status := NOWORD;
            done := true;
        end else if line.chars[line.position] <> BLANK then begin
            done := true;
        end else begin
            line.position := line.position + 1;
        end;
    end;
    if status = SUCCESS then begin
        done := false;
        word := BLANKWORD;
        length := 1;
        word[1] := line.chars[line.position];
        line.position := line.position + 1;
        while not done do begin
            if line.position > line.length then begin
                done := true;
            end else if line.chars[line.position] = BLANK then begin
                done := true;
            end else if length = MAXWORDLEN then begin
                status := WORDTOOLONG;
                done := true;
            end else begin
                length := length + 1;
                word[length] := line.chars[line.position];
                line.position := line.position + 1;
            end;
        end;
    end;
end; {Get Word}


{
    Read a line from the user. Possible values to return in status are
    success, no lines to read (user indicated end-of-file), or line too
    long to store.
}
procedure GetLine (var line: LineType; var status: StatusType);
var
    ch: char;
begin {Get Line}
    status := SUCCESS;
    if eof then begin
        status := NOINPUT;
    end else begin
        line.length := 0;
        line.position := 1;
        while not eoln do begin
            read(ch);
            if line.length = MAXLINELEN then begin
```

```
                                status := LINETOOLONG;
                        end else begin
                            line.length := line.length + 1;
                            line.chars[line.length] := ch;
                        end;
                end;
                readln;
        end;
end; {Get Line}

{*** date operations ***}

{
    Return true exactly when date1 precedes date2.
}
function Precedes (date1, date2: DateType): boolean;
begin {Precedes?}
    if date1.year < date2.year then begin
        Precedes := true;
    end else if date1.year > date2.year then begin
        Precedes := false;
    end else if date1.month < date2.month then begin
        Precedes := true;
    end else if date1.month > date2.month then begin
        Precedes := false;
    end else begin
        Precedes := date1.day < date2.day;
    end;
end; {Precedes?}

{
    Return true exactly when date1 and date2 are identical.
}
function Same (date1, date2: DateType): boolean;
begin {Same?}
    Same := (date1.month = date2.month) and (date1.day = date2.day)
        and (date1.year = date2.year);
end; {Same?}

{
    Return true when date1 comes at or before date2.
}
function AtOrBefore (date1, date2: DateType): boolean;
begin {At or Before?}
    AtOrBefore := Same(date1, date2) or Precedes(date1, date2);
end; {At or Before?}

{
    Return true exactly when year is a leap year.
}
function LeapYear (year: YearType): boolean;
begin {Leap Year?}
    LeapYear := (year mod 400 = 0)
        or ((year mod 4 = 0) and (year mod 100 <> 0));
end; {Leap Year?}
```

```
{
    Return 1 if year is a leap year, 0 otherwise.
}
function LeapDay (year: YearType): integer;
begin {Leap Day}
    if LeapYear(year) then begin
        LeapDay := 1;
    end else begin
        LeapDay := 0;
    end;
end; {Leap Day}


{
    Return the number of days in the given month in the given year.
}
function NumberOfDaysIn (month: integer; year: YearType): DayType;
begin {Number Of Days In}
    case month of
        1, 3, 5, 7, 8, 10, 12:
            NumberOfDaysIn := 31;
        2:
            NumberOfDaysIn := 28 + LeapDay(year);
        4, 6, 9, 11:
            NumberOfDaysIn := 30;
    end;
end; {Number Of Days In}


{
    Return the nth element of the MonthType enumerated type.
}
function MonthEquiv (n: integer): MonthType;
var
    k: integer; m: MonthType;
begin {Month Equivalent}
    m := JANUARY;
    for k := 1 to n - 1 do begin
        m := succ(m);
    end;
    MonthEquiv := m;
end; {Month Equivalent}


{
    Print a date followed by a carriage return.
}
procedure WritelnDate (date: DateType);
begin {Writeln Date}
    case date.month of
        JANUARY:   write('January ');
        FEBRUARY:  write('February ');
        MARCH:     write('March ');
        APRIL:     write('April ');
        MAY:       write('May ');
        JUNE:      write('June ');
        JULY:      write('July ');
        AUGUST:    write('August ');
        SEPTEMBER: write('September ');
```

```
                        OCTOBER:    write('October ');
                        NOVEMBER:   write('November ');
                        DECEMBER:   write('December ');
                    end;
                writeln(date.day : 1, ', ', date.year : 4);
            end; {Writeln Date}


            {
                Translate word to a one- or two-digit numeric value and return the
                result in n. Also increment the index position in word.
                If word doesn't contain one or two digits, indicate an error in status.
            }
            procedure GetOneOrTwoDigits (word: WordType; var index: integer;
                var n: integer; var status: StatusType);
            begin {Get One or Two Digits}
                if IsDigit(word[index]) and not IsDigit(word[index + 1]) then begin
                    n := DigitValue(word[index]);
                    index := index + 1;
                end else if IsDigit(word[index])
                  and IsDigit(word[index + 1]) then begin
                    n := 10 * DigitValue(word[index]) + DigitValue(word[index + 1]);
                    index := index + 2;
                end else begin
                    status := BADNUM;
                end;
            end; {Get One or Two Digits}


            {
                If the character in the given position in word (index) is a date
                separator, increment the position; otherwise indicate error in status.
            }
            procedure GetSeparator (word: WordType; var index: integer;
                var status: StatusType);
            begin {Get Separator}
                if word[index] = DATESEPARATOR then begin
                    index := index + 1;
                end else begin
                    status := BADSEP;
                end;
            end; {Get Separator}


            {
                Translate word to a four-digit numeric value and return the result in
                n. Also increment the index position in word.
                If word doesn't contain four digits, indicate an error in status.
            }
            procedure GetFourDigits (word: WordType; var index: integer;
                var n: integer; var status: StatusType);
            begin {Get Four Digits}
                if IsDigit(word[index]) and IsDigit(word[index+1])
                  and IsDigit(word[index+2]) and IsDigit(word[index+3]) then begin
                    n := 1000 * DigitValue(word[index])
                        + 100 * DigitValue(word[index + 1])
                        + 10 * DigitValue(word[index + 2])
                        + DigitValue(word[index + 3]);
                    index := index + 4;
```

```
        end else begin
            status := BADNUM;
        end;
end; {Get Four Digits}

{
    If there are unprocessed characters in word, indicate that in status.
}
procedure CheckNoMore (word: WordType; index: integer;
    var status: StatusType);
begin {Check No More}
    if word[index] <> BLANK then begin
        status := EXTRAJUNK;
    end;
end; {Check No More}

{
    Return true exactly when month, day, and year collectively represent
    a legal date.
}
function LegalDate (month, day, year: integer): boolean;
begin {Legal Date?}
    if not (month in [1..12]) then begin
        LegalDate := false;
    end else begin
        LegalDate := day in [1..NumberOfDaysIn(month, year)];
    end;
end; {Legal Date?}

{
    Get a legal date from line, and return it in date. If the next word in
    line does not represent a legal date, indicate the fact in status.
}
procedure GetDate (var line: LineType;
    var date: DateType; var status: StatusType);
var
    word: WordType; index: integer; month, day, year: integer;
begin {Get Date}
    GetWord(line, word, status);
    if status = NOWORD then begin
        status := NODATE;
    end;
    if status = SUCCESS then begin
        index := 1;
        GetOneOrTwoDigits(word, index, month, status);
    end;
    if status = SUCCESS then begin
        GetSeparator(word, index, status);
    end;
    if status = SUCCESS then begin
        GetOneOrTwoDigits(word, index, day, status);
    end;
    if status = SUCCESS then begin
        GetSeparator(word, index, status);
    end;
    if status = SUCCESS then begin
```

```
                GetFourDigits(word, index, year, status);
        end;
        if status = SUCCESS then begin
            CheckNoMore(word, index, status);
        end;
        if status = SUCCESS then begin
            if not LegalDate(month, day, year) then begin
                status := BADDATE;
            end else begin
                date.month := MonthEquiv(month);
                date.day := day;
                date.year := year;
            end;
        end;
end; {Get Date}


{*** operations on the history file are in the previous section ***}

{*** Command-scanning procedures ***}

{
    Get a command word from the line, and return it (translated to the
    corresponding CommandType member} in command. If the next word in line
    does not represent a legal command, indicate the fact in status.
}
procedure GetCmdWord (var line: LineType;
    var command: CommandType; var status: StatusType);
var
    word: WordType;
begin {Get Command Word}
    status := SUCCESS;
    command := UNKNOWN;
    GetWord(line, word, status);
    if status = NOWORD then begin
        status := NOCOMMAND;
    end else if word = LISTWORD then begin
        command := LISTCMD;
    end else if word = ADDWORD then begin
        command := ADDCMD;
    end else if word = DELETEWORD then begin
        command := DELETECMD;
    end else if word = HELPWORD then begin
        command := HELPCMD;
    end else if word = QUITWORD then begin
        command := QUITCMD;
    end else begin
        status := BADCOMMAND;
    end;
end; {Get Command Word}


{
    Prompt the user for a command, and return what is typed in command and
    the result of analyzing its first word in status.
}
procedure GetCommand (var line: LineType;
    var command: CommandType; var status: StatusType);
```

```
                    begin {Get a Command}
                        write('COMMAND? ');
                        GetLine(line, status);
                        if status = NOINPUT then begin
                            command := QUITCMD;
                            status := SUCCESS;
                        end else if status = SUCCESS then begin
                            GetCmdWord(line, command, status);
                        end;
                    end; {Get a Command}

                    {*** command interpreting procedures ***}

                    {
                        A list command has been given; analyze its arguments and, if it's
                        legal, execute it. A legal list command has one of the following forms:
                        To print the entire history:
                            list
                        To print the entry for a given date:
                            list date
                        To print all entries between two dates:
                            list date1 date2
                    }
                    procedure ExecuteList (var line: LineType;
                        var history: SequenceType; var status: StatusType);
                    var
                        dates: array[1..2] of DateType;
                        tempDate: DateType; numDates: integer;
                        done, found: boolean; position: PositionType; entry: EntryType;
                    begin {Execute List}
                        done := false;
                        numDates := 0;
                        while not done do begin
                            GetDate(line, tempDate, status);
                            if status <> SUCCESS then begin
                                done := true;
                            end else if numDates = 2 then begin
                                status := TOOMANYDATES;
                                done := true;
                            end else begin
                                numDates := numDates + 1;
                                dates[numDates] := tempDate;
                            end;
                        end;
                        if status = NODATE then begin
                            status := SUCCESS;
                            case numDates of
                                0:  PrintAll(history);
                                1:  begin
                                        Find(history, dates[1], found, entry, position);
                                        if found then begin
                                            PrintEntry(entry);
                                        end else begin
                                            status := NOTTHERE;
                                        end;
                                    end;
```

```
         2:  begin
                 Find(history, dates[1], found, entry, position);
                 if not (AtOrBefore(entry.date, dates[2])
                  and AtOrBefore(dates[1], entry.date)) then begin
                     status := EMPTYRANGE;
                 end else begin
                     PrintEntry(entry);
                     PrintUpTo(history, dates[1], position);
                 end;
             end;
         end;
     end;
end; {Execute List}

{
    An add command has been given; analyze its arguments and, if it's
    legal, execute it. The add command has the following format:
        add date
    The history must not contain an entry with the given date.
}
procedure ExecuteAdd (var line: LineType;
    var history: SequenceType; var status: StatusType);
var
    date, tempDate: DateType;
    entry: EntryType; found: boolean; position: PositionType;
begin {Execute Add}
    GetDate(line, date, status);
    if status = SUCCESS then begin
        GetDate(line, tempDate, status);
        if status = SUCCESS then begin
            status := TOOMANYDATES;
        end else if status = NODATE then begin
            status := SUCCESS;
        end;
    end;
    if status = SUCCESS then begin
        Find(history, date, found, entry, position);
        if found then begin
            status := ALREADYTHERE;
        end else begin
            entry.date := date;
            ReadEntry(entry);
            Insert(history, entry, position);
        end;
    end;
end; {Execute Add}

{
    A delete command has been given; analyze its arguments and, if it's
    legal, execute it. The delete command has the following format:
        delete date
    The history must contain an entry with the given date.
}
procedure ExecuteDelete (var line: LineType;
    var history: SequenceType; var status: StatusType);
var
```

```
            date, tempDate: DateType;
            entry: EntryType; found: boolean; position: PositionType;
        begin {Execute Delete}
            GetDate(line, date, status);
            if status = SUCCESS then begin
                GetDate(line, tempDate, status);
                if status = SUCCESS then begin
                    status := TOOMANYDATES;
                end else if status = NODATE then begin
                    status := SUCCESS;
                end;
            end;
            if status = SUCCESS then begin
                Find(history, date, found, entry, position);
                if not found then begin
                    status := NOTTHERE;
                end else begin
                    entry.date := date;
                    Delete(history, position);
                end;
            end;
        end; {Execute Delete}


        {
            Print helpful information.
        }
        procedure ExecuteHelp (var line: LineType;
            var history: SequenceType; var status: StatusType);
        begin {Execute Help}
            writeln('Command formats appear below. Where the notation <date>');
            writeln('appears, you''re supposed to supply a legal date, ');
            writeln('for instance, 9/24/1992.');
            writeln('To get this message:');
            writeln('  help');
            writeln('To leave the history editor:');
            writeln('  quit');
            writeln('To list the information for all history entries:');
            writeln('  list');
            writeln('To list the information for the entry for a given date:');
            writeln('  list <date>');
            writeln('To list the information for all entries between two dates:');
            writeln('  list <early date> <later date>');
            writeln('To add an entry for a given date:');
            writeln('  add <date>');
            writeln('To delete the entry for a given date:');
            writeln('  delete <date>');
            writeln;
        end; {Execute Help}


        {
            The user has typed a quit command.
        }
        procedure ExecuteQuit (var line: LineType;
            var history: SequenceType; var status: StatusType);
        begin {Execute Quit}
            writeln('Leaving the history editor.');
```

```
end; {Execute Quit}

{
    Execute the given command. Its remaining arguments are still on line.
}
procedure ExecuteCommand (var line: LineType; command: CommandType;
    var history: SequenceType; var status: StatusType);
begin {Execute Command}
    case command of
        LISTCMD:    ExecuteList(line, history, status);
        ADDCMD:     ExecuteAdd(line, history, status);
        DELETECMD:  ExecuteDelete(line, history, status);
        HELPCMD:    ExecuteHelp(line, history, status);
        QUITCMD:    ExecuteQuit(line, history, status);
    end;
end; {Execute Command}

{*** main program ***}
begin
    Initialize(history);
    done := false;
    repeat
        GetCommand(line, command, status);
        if status = SUCCESS then begin
            ExecuteCommand(line, command, history, status);
        end;
        if status <> SUCCESS then begin
            PrintErrorMsg(status);
        end;
    until command = QUITCMD;
end.
```

Revisions for the "Get a Complete Legal Command" Approach

```
const
    MAXCMDLEN = 3;

type
    WordArrayType = record
        length: integer;
        words: array[1..MAXCMDLEN] of WordType;
    end;

    StatusType = (SUCCESS, NOINPUT, LINETOOLONG, NOWORD, WORDTOOLONG,
        NOCOMMAND, BADCOMMAND, NODATE, TOOMANYDATES, BADNUM, BADSEP,
        EXTRAJUNK, BADDATE, ALREADYTHERE, NOTTHERE, EMPTYRANGE);

    CmdWordType = (LISTCMD, ADDCMD, DELETECMD, HELPCMD, QUITCMD, UNKNOWN);
    CommandType = record
        cmdWord: CmdWordType;
        numArgs: integer;
        args: array[1..2] of DateType;
```

CHAPTER 8: YOU FORGOT WHAT YOU ATE

```
    end;

{
    Get all the words on the line and return them in words. There can be
    no more than MAXCMDLEN words on the line; if more are provided,
    indicate error in status.
}
procedure GetWords (var line: LineType;
    var words: WordArrayType; var status: StatusType);
var
    done: boolean; word: WordType;
begin {Get Words}
    words.length := 0;
    done := false;
    while not done do begin
        GetWord(line, word, status);
        if status = NOWORD then begin
            status := SUCCESS;
            done := true;
        end else if words.length = MAXCMDLEN then begin
            status := TOOMANYDATES;
            done := true;
        end else begin
            words.length := words.length + 1;
            words.words[words.length] := word;
        end;
    end;
end; {Get Words}

{*** Command-scanning procedures ***}

{
    Convert the first word in words to a command. Return the result in
    command, and indicate success or any irregularities in status.
}
procedure ConvertToCommand (var words: WordArrayType;
    var command: CommandType; var status: StatusType);
var
    word: WordType;
begin {Convert to Command}
    status := SUCCESS;
    command.cmdWord := UNKNOWN;
    if words.length = 0 then begin
        status := NOCOMMAND;
    end else if words.words[1] = LISTWORD then begin
        command.cmdWord := LISTCMD;
        command.numArgs := words.length - 1;
    end else if words.words[1] = ADDWORD then begin
        command.cmdWord := ADDCMD;
        if words.length < 2 then begin
            status := NODATE;
        end else if words.length > 2 then begin
            status := TOOMANYDATES;
        end else begin
            command.numArgs := 1;
        end;
```

```
            end else if words.words[1] = DELETEWORD then begin
                command.cmdWord := DELETECMD;
                if words.length < 2 then begin
                    status := NODATE;
                end else if words.length > 2 then begin
                    status := TOOMANYDATES;
                end else begin
                    command.numArgs := 1;
                end;
            end else if words.words[1] = HELPWORD then begin
                command.cmdWord := HELPCMD;
                command.numArgs := 0;
            end else if words.words[1] = QUITWORD then begin
                command.cmdWord := QUITCMD;
                command.numArgs := 0;
            end else begin
                status := BADCOMMAND;
            end;
end; {Convert to Command}


{
    Convert remaining words in words to date arguments in command.
}
procedure ConvertToArgs (words: WordArrayType; var command: CommandType;
    var status: StatusType);
begin {Convert to Arguments}
    if command.numArgs > 0 then begin
        ConvertToDate(words.words[2], command.args[1], status);
    end;
    if (status = SUCCESS) and (command.numArgs > 1) then begin
        ConvertToDate(words.words[3], command.args[2], status);
    end;
end; {Convert to Arguments}


{
    Get a command from the user. If the user types an illegal command,
    indicate the fact in status.
}
procedure GetCommand (var line: LineType;
    var command: CommandType; var status: StatusType);
var
    words: WordArrayType;
begin {Get a Command}
    write('COMMAND? ');
    GetLine(line, status);
    if status = NOINPUT then begin
        command.cmdWord := QUITCMD;
        command.numArgs := 0;
        status := SUCCESS;
    end else begin
        if status = SUCCESS then begin
            GetWords(line, words, status);
        end;
        if status = SUCCESS then begin
            ConvertToCommand(words, command, status);
        end;
```

```
                    if status = SUCCESS then begin
                        ConvertToArgs(words, command, status);
                    end;
            end;
    end; {Get a Command}


{*** command interpreting procedures ***}


{
    Execute a legal list command.
}
procedure ExecuteList (command: CommandType;
    var history: SequenceType; var status: StatusType);
var
    found: boolean; entry: EntryType; position: PositionType;
begin {Execute List}
    case command.numArgs of
        0:  PrintAll(history);
        1:  begin
            Find(history, command.args[1], found, entry, position);
            if found then begin
                PrintEntry(entry);
            end else begin
                status := NOTTHERE;
            end;
        end;
        2:  begin
            Find(history, command.args[2], found, entry, position);
            if not (AtOrBefore(entry.date, command.args[2])
             and AtOrBefore(command.args[1], entry.date)) then begin
                status := EMPTYRANGE;
            end else begin
                PrintEntry(entry);
                PrintUpTo(history, command.args[1], position);
            end;
        end;
    end;
end; {Execute List}


{
    Execute a legal add command.
}
procedure ExecuteAdd (var command: CommandType;
    var history: SequenceType; var status: StatusType);
var
    found: boolean; entry: EntryType; position: PositionType;
begin {Execute Add}
    Find(history, command.args[1], found, entry, position);
    if found then begin
        status := ALREADYTHERE;
    end else begin
        entry.date := command.args[1];
        ReadEntry(entry);
        Insert(history, entry, position);
    end;
end; {Execute Add}
```

```
{
    Execute a legal delete command.
}
procedure ExecuteDelete (var command: CommandType;
    var history: SequenceType; var status: StatusType);
var
    found: boolean; entry: EntryType; position: PositionType;
begin {Execute Delete}
    Find(history, command.args[1], found, entry, position);
    if not found then begin
        status := NOTTHERE;
    end else begin
        entry.date := command.args[1];
        Delete(history, position);
    end;
end; {Execute Delete}


{
    Execute a legal command.
}
procedure ExecuteCommand (command: CommandType;
    var history: SequenceType; var status: StatusType);
begin {Execute a Command}
    case command.cmdWord of
        LISTCMD:    ExecuteList(command, history, status);
        ADDCMD:     ExecuteAdd(command, history, status);
        DELETECMD:  ExecuteDelete(command, history, status);
        HELPCMD:    ExecuteHelp(command, history, status);
        QUITCMD:    ExecuteQuit(command, history, status);
    end;
end; {Execute a Command}

{*** main program ***}
begin
    Initialize(history);
    done := false;
    repeat
        GetCommand(line, command, status);
        if status = SUCCESS then begin
            ExecuteCommand(command, history, status);
        end;
        if status <> SUCCESS then begin
            PrintErrorMsg(status);
        end;
    until command.cmdWord = QUITCMD;
end.
```

CHAPTER 9

Chess Challenges

Even a child can learn the moves, but chess challenges everyone.

Computer programs that play chess, solve chess puzzles, or create chess problems are widespread. There is even an annual contest pitting chess-playing programs against each other and against human experts. This case study addresses a simple problem related to chess.

Background

The game of chess is played on an 8-by-8 board. The most powerful chess piece is the queen. From a given position, a queen may move anywhere along the same row, column, or diagonal, provided only that it doesn't jump over pieces. The shaded squares in the figure below illustrate the possible queen moves.

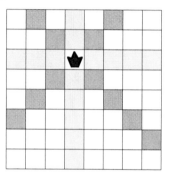

Two queens are said to attack each other if either can move to the position of the other—if they are in the same row, column, or diagonal, and no pieces lie between. The figure below shows examples of attacking and nonattacking queens.

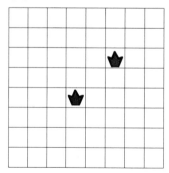

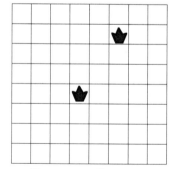

Two attacking queens   *Two nonattacking queens*

A puzzle problem dating from the 1700s is to place as many nonattacking queens on the chessboard as possible. In this case study, we will design part of the solution to this problem: code to *check* if any of a set of queens attack one another.

Problem Statement

Design a type to represent a chessboard on which each square either is empty or contains a queen. Also design and test subprograms with the following headers and descriptions.

```
procedure ReadBoard (var board: BoardType);
```

> ReadBoard asks the user to indicate which positions on the board contain queens. (ReadBoard may do this in any manner and need not check for invalid input.)

```
procedure PrintBoard (board: BoardType);
```

> PrintBoard prints the contents of the board as eight lines of eight characters each; the character 'Q' represents a square on the board that contains a queen, and the character '.' represents an empty board square.

```
function Safe (board: BoardType): boolean;
```

> Safe returns true exactly when the board contains a "safe" position, one in which no two queens on the board attack each other. Two queens attack each other exactly when they lie in the same row, column, or diagonal, and no pieces lie between them on the diagonal.

Each subprogram, except for its use of BoardType, should be independent of the remainder of the program.

Analysis 9.1 How many possibilities are there for two queens on the board to attack each other?

Analysis 9.2 How many diagonals are there on a chess board?

Application 9.3 How many queens can be placed on the chessboard so that none of them attacks one another?

Preparation

The reader should be familiar with records and arrays of records. The solutions in this case study also introduce the manipulation of two-dimensional arrays.

Understanding the Problem and Selecting an Implementation

How does this problem resemble problems in earlier case studies?

For this problem, we are to design a *type* along with three subprograms that use the type. This resembles the problem of *Space Text*, in which we were to design and test a single procedure that could be used in a variety of programs. As in the *Space Text* program, the *Chess Challenges* subprograms we write must be independent of the program that contains them to allow easy incorporation of the code into other chess programs.

Chess Challenges also resembles the first part of our solution to *You Are What You Eat*, in which we designed a type to contain history entries. We need not invent the operations to apply to the chessboard type; they are specified for us already, namely reading and printing a board and checking it for safe queen placement.

What else is required for a solution?

We will also need to write a driver program to test our code. This should be straightforward, since together the three subprograms fit nicely into an input-process-output test loop:

```
while true do begin
    ReadBoard(board);
    PrintBoard(board);
    if Safe(board) then begin
        writeln('Board is safe.');
    end else begin
        writeln('Two queens attack.');
    end;
end;
```

Stop & Predict ➤ *Should the program figure out which queens threaten each other?*

Note that the Safe function needs only to check *if* any queens threaten one another; it is not required to report *which* queens are doing the threatening.

What kind of data structure should be used, and how large should it be?

The representation of the board will probably involve some sort of array, since an array provides a good way to store a collection of similar objects (board squares or queens). To use an array, we must know how big to declare it. The problem statement does not say how many queens there will be. Presumably there will be more than one. There can be at most 64, the number of squares on the chessboard.

The chessboard resembles a two-dimensional array, so an 8-by-8 array is a possible choice for the BoardType data type. Each square of the chessboard would be one cell of the array. Since we need to store only whether or not each square contains a queen, the array elements could be of type boolean, and BoardType would be defined as follows:

```
type
    BoardType = array [1..8, 1..8] of boolean;
```

Stop & Predict ➤ *Why not use an array of one-dimensional arrays?*

We might also use an array of one-dimensional arrays, which would look like this:

```
type
    RowType = array [1..8] of boolean;
    DifferentBoardType = array [1..8] of RowType;
```

Which definition is better?

The two definitions are essentially equivalent in Pascal, so the way to choose between them is to see which one best communicates the use of the type. The definition of RowType says that a "row" is a meaningful object. The definition of DifferentBoardType says that a "board" is a collection of rows. These definitions would be appropriate if access to an individual cell always required selecting its row first. On a chessboard, however, rows aren't any more meaningful than columns. This symmetry is reflected in the original BoardType declaration.

Stop & Help ➤ *Write code that places a queen at a position identified by values in variables* rowLocation *and* columnLocation *for each choice for* BoardType *(a two-dimensional array and an array of arrays).*

Stop & Predict ➤ *What other representations might be used for the chessboard?*

Thus we choose to represent BoardType as an 8-by-8 array of booleans, where each cell containing true represents a square occupied by a queen and each cell containing false represents an empty square. We move on to design the three subprograms ReadBoard, Safe, and PrintBoard.

Stop & Predict ➤ *Which of the three subprograms is likely to be easiest to design, and which will be the most difficult?*

How is PrintBoard coded?

PrintBoard will be the easiest of the three subprograms to design. Printing a chessboard will be done line by line, as in the *Banners With CLASS* and *The Calendar Shop* programs:

```
for lineNum := 1 to 8 do begin
    print the lineNumth line of the chessboard;
end;
```

Each line of the output corresponds to a row of the board array. Even though we didn't define the row as a separate array type, we may still apply the "process every element of an array" template to print the row:

```
for column := 1 to 8 do begin
    if board[lineNum,column] then begin
        write('Q');
    end else begin
        write('.');
```

```
              end;
      end;
  writeln;
```

In what ways might board values be read from the user?

There are several ways to ask the user for input. We could ask the user about each square on the board, in an interaction like the following:

```
Is there a queen in square [1,1]?   no
Is there a queen in square [1,2]?   yes
Is there a queen in square [1,3]?   no
            ⋮
```

We could have the user type a diagram of the chessboard, eight lines of eight characters each, with one character representing a square containing a queen and another character representing a blank square. The input might then be as follows:

```
........
.....Q..
........
........
...Q....
........
........
........
```

Probably the easiest way for the user to type the data, however, is to provide just the row and column positions for each queen. A dialog to ask the user for the queen placement shown above might appear as follows:

```
Please type the row and column position for each queen.
Type 0 0 when done.
Queen row and column?   2   6
Queen row and column?   5   4
Queen row and column?   0   0
```

How will the input procedure work?

The ReadBoard procedure uses familiar templates to prompt the user for rows and columns. In each iteration, it reads a row and column and, if they are legal, sets the corresponding board entry to true. Here's the code:

```
for row := 1 to 8 do begin
    for column := 1 to 8 do begin
        board [row, column] := false;
    end;
end;

writeln ('Please type the row and column position for each queen.');
writeln ('Type 0 0 when done.');
write ('Queen row and column?  ');
readln (row, column);
while (row<>0) or (column<>0) do begin
    if (row in [1..8]) and (column in [1..8]) then begin
        board [row, column] := true;
    end else begin
        writeln ('Please type values between 1 and 8.');
```

```
      end;
      write ('Queen row and column?  ');
      readln (row, column);
   end;
```

Stop & Help ➤   *What templates are implemented in the* ReadBoard *procedure?*

What decompositions for the Safe function make sense?

Only the Safe function remains to be written. The Problem Background suggests two decompositions. It says: "Two queens are said to attack each other if either can move to the position of the other—if they are in the same row, column, or diagonal."

One approach is organized around queens; it will successively find each queen and see if it can move to the position of any other queen. We'll call this the *queen-by-queen* solution. Another approach checks whether any row, column, or diagonal, contains more than one queen. We'll call this the *line-by-line* solution.

What is the pseudocode for the queen-by-queen approach?

Translated into pseudocode, the queen-by-queen decomposition is

for each queen, do the following:
    check squares on the queen's row;
    if any contain another queen, return false;
    check squares on the queen's column;
    if any contain another queen, return false;
    check squares on the queen's diagonals;
    if any contain another queen, return false;
if no queen attacks another, return true;

Stop & Help ➤   *Why is this a better approach than comparing queens two at a time?*

What is the pseudocode for the line-by-line approach?

Pseudocode for the line-by-line solution is as follows:

for each row, do the following:
    if the row contains more than one queen, return false;
for each column, do the following:
    if the column contains more than one queen, return false;
for each diagonal, do the following:
    if the diagonal contains more than one queen, return false;
if no row, column, or diagonal has more than one queen, return true;

We will consider each decomposition in turn.

Analysis   9.4   Under what conditions might each of three ways described for reading a board from the user be appropriate?

Modification   9.5   Modify ReadBoard to ask the user about each square on the chessboard.

💾 💾 *Modification*   9.6   Modify ReadBoard to read a board configuration represented by eight lines of Q's and periods.

💾 *Modification*   9.7   Give Pascal type definitions that define BoardType as an 8-by-8 array of characters, with 'Q' representing a square with a queen and a blank representing an empty square.

💾 *Modification*   9.8   Give Pascal type definitions for a chessboard, each square of which may contain a queen, a king, a rook, a bishop, a knight, or a pawn.

💾 *Application*   9.9   Which of the following would probably be the better way to represent the seats in an auditorium?

```
RowType = array [1..NUMSEATS] of boolean;
AuditoriumType = array [1..NUMROWS] of RowType;
```

or

```
AuditoriumType = array[1..NUMSEATS, 1..NUMROWS] of boolean;
```

Briefly explain, by describing ways in which the auditorium data type might be used.

The Queen-by-Queen Solution

What are the main steps in the queen-by-queen solution?

The queen-by-queen solution involves searching the array board for queens and checking each queen to see if it attacks any other queen.

Stop & Predict ➤   *Does the program have to check every queen?*

How are queens located?

Queens are located by searching the array using the two-dimensional version of "process every element of an array":

```
for row := 1 to 8 do begin
    for column := 1 to 8 do begin
        process board[row, column];
    end;
end;
```

What should happen when a queen is located?

We can replace the "process" line in this template with code that checks if the cell contains a queen, then deals with the queen. We rename the row and column variables to be queenRow and queenCol to arrive at the following:

```
function Safe (board: BoardType): boolean;
var
    attacking: boolean;
    queenRow, queenCol: integer;
begin
    attacking := false;
    for queenRow := 1 to 8 do begin
        for queenCol := 1 to 8 do begin
```

```
                              if board [queenRow, queenCol] then begin
                                  check the squares in the queenRow-th row;
                                  if any contain another queen, set attacking to true;
                                  check the squares in the queenCol-th column;
                                  if any contain another queen, set attacking to true;
                                  check the squares appropriate diagonals;
                                  if any contain another queen, set attacking to true;
                              end;
                       end;
                end;
                Safe := not attacking;
       end;
```

Stop & Help ➤   *Why is* Safe *assigned the value* not attacking *at the end of the function?*

Stop & Predict ➤   *How many attacks will this code locate?*

How can attacking queens be found more efficiently?

This solution continues to search after two attacking queens have been located, since the for loops always check every row and column. A more efficient approach uses while loops with a boolean variable to indicate when an attacking queen is located. The pseudocode is as follows:

```
function Safe (board: BoardType): boolean;
var
      attacking: boolean;
      queenRow, queenCol: integer;
begin
      attacking := false;
      queenRow := 1;
      while not attacking and (queenRow <= 8) do begin
          queenCol := 1;
          while not attacking and (queenCol <= 8) do begin
              if board [queenRow, queenCol] then begin
                  check the squares in the queenRow-th row;
                  if any contain another queen, set attacking to true;
                  check the squares in the queenCol-th column;
                  if any contain another queen, set attacking to true;
                  check the squares appropriate diagonals;
                  if any contain another queen, set attacking to true;
              end;
              queenCol := queenCol+1;
          end;
          queenRow := queenRow+1;
      end;
      Safe := not attacking;
end;
```

Stop & Help ➤   *Which one-dimensional array template is extended to two-dimensional arrays in this pseudocode?*

How should the squares a queen can attack be checked?

To check for other queens in a given queen's row, column, and diagonals, one can either start at the queen's position and work forward and backward or start at the beginning of the row or column or diagonal and examine the whole thing, being careful to ignore the queen. The two ways are diagrammed below. We start with the first way. The second way resembles the line-by-line decomposition we plan to try next.

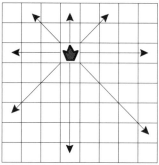

Starting at the queen's position

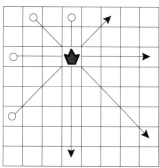

Starting at the beginning of the row, column, or diagonal

Stop & Predict ➤   *Which of the two ways for checking the squares a queen can move to will be easier to code?*

How are diagonals checked?   The diagonals are clearly the most difficult part of the program. To search a diagonal of the chessboard, we need a loop with two loop variables, the row index and the column index, that get updated *in parallel*. For example, to examine the ways the queen above can move "southeast," the array elements board [5,4], board [6,5], board [7,6], and board [8,7] must be checked.

Stop & Consider ➤   *Why not use two loops, one nested within the other?*

Stop & Help ➤   *Show how the row and column indexes change along "southeast" diagonals and "southwest" diagonals.*

Which is better, a for loop or a while loop?   Either a for loop or a while loop could be used to check the diagonals, since the number of squares to check can be computed from the queen's position. A for loop could be controlled by a variable that takes on values of (say) the row index, and whose body contains an update to a variable that takes on values of the column index. The for loop approach would highlight one of the index variables by selecting it as the loop variable.

However, since both the row and the column index variables are equally important and used in pretty much the same way, the highlighting of one of the variables obscures the purpose of the code. We prefer to use a while loop to show the equal importance of the row and column variables more clearly. In addition, the use of while makes clear (in the same way as in the Safe function) that it is not necessary to check the rest of the diagonal once a queen is located.

Stop & Predict ➤ *When should the program stop checking in the southeast direction? In the southwest direction?*

The code below checks the queen's southeast moves.

```
row := queenRow+1;
col := queenCol+1;
while not attacking and (row <= 8) and (col <= 8) do begin
    if board [row, col] then begin
        attacking := true;
    end else begin
        row := row+1;
        col := col+1;
    end;
end;
```

Stop & Help ➤ *Write code to check the queen's southwest moves.*

Stop & Predict ➤ *Are four diagonal-checking procedures needed?*

How can a single function be used to check all four diagonals?

Four procedures to do essentially the same thing seem like too much. Instead, we convert the separate procedures into a single procedure that takes the direction of search and the location of the queen as parameters.

Stop & Predict ➤ *Write the general procedure for checking all four diagonals before looking at the code in the Pascal Code section.*

How can rows and columns be checked?

We code the row and column searches as while loops, to be consistent with the diagonal searches. This results in the function listed in the Pascal Code section.

How can the code be tested?

Before testing this code, we note that the queen-by-queen solution looks for *pairs* of queens. Thus, simple tests of the program's correctness require boards that contain only *two* queens. Simple test data make it easier to zero in on bugs if they do turn up.

Testing the queen-by-queen solution involves anticipating all the usual problems with arrays.

Stop & Help ➤ *What cases test for the common array bugs?*

What boundary cases should be tested?

For our purposes, boundary cases are the first row and column and the eighth row and column. Other boundary cases involve the *relative* positions of the queens; we should test situations where the queens are adjacent, as well as situations where the queens are as far apart as possible.

What other cases are important?

Every possibility for queen placement should be tested. We should include boards in which two queens can attack each other as well as boards in which there are no attacking queens. It happens that we can test *all* the ways for two queens to attack each other:

- two queens in the same row
- two queens in the same column
- two queens in the same northeast/southwest diagonal
- two queens in the same northwest/southeast diagonal

Stop & Help ➤   *Devise a comprehensive set of test cases and test the program just designed.*

Analysis   9.10   What are the differences between the row searches and the diagonal searches? What are the similarities?

Analysis   9.11   Suppose that the board contains queens at positions [3,6] and [5,4]. How many board squares are examined by the just-designed Safe function to determine whether or not the two queens attack each other? (A board square at position [row, col] is "examined" when board[row, col] is evaluated.) If a board square is examined more than once, include it once in the count for each examination.

Analysis   9.12   How many board squares are examined in the Safe function for a board containing queens at positions [3,3] and [7,6]?

Modification   9.13   Modify the Safe function to count the number of board squares it examines and print the result before it returns.

Modification   9.14   Code the row and column searches as a single procedure that takes the row and column location of the queen and an indicator of what is being searched as parameters.

Modification   9.15   Write a single search function that has two integer parameters in place of the direction parameter. Both of the integers will have value 0, –1, or +1. One will be the amount to increment the row variable each time through the search loop; the other will be the amount to increment the col variable each time through the loop. Recode Safe to call the new function for row, column, and diagonal search.

Modification, Reflection   9.16   Recode the while loops in the Safe function to use a while not done, as in earlier case studies, instead of the and expression. Which version do you think is better and why?

Debugging   9.17   Consider the following code to check if other queens are on the same row as the queen at position [queenRow, queenCol].

```
for k := 1 to 8 do begin
    if board[queenRow, queenCol] then begin
        attacking := true;
    end;
end;
```

What is wrong with the code?

Testing   9.18   For what test cases will the above code *correctly* set attacking to true?

The Line-by-Line Solution

How is this solution different from the queen-by-queen solution?

The line-by-line solution checks each row, column, or diagonal to see if it contains more than one queen. The main difference is that the program keeps track of how many queens appear instead of just searching for a single queen.

Stop & Predict ➤

Which one-dimensional array template can be applied to searching rows in a two-dimensional array?

How are the rows searched for queens?

Searching rows for multiple queens involves counting the number of true entries in a row and then setting the boolean variable attacking to true if we find a row that contains more than one queen. The code looks like this:

```
numQueens := 0;
col := 1;
while not attacking and (col <= 8) do begin
    if board [row, col] then begin
        numQueens := numQueens+1;
    end else begin
        col := col+1;
    end;
    attacking := (numQueens > 1);
end;
```

Stop & Help ➤

Why is attacking *set to* (numQueens > 1)*?*

We code this as a function RowAttack, which returns a boolean value saying whether two queens attack each other along some row. A boolean function is better than a procedure since we need to know only *if* any two queens attack, not how many attacking queens are in the row.

Stop & Help ➤

Create a boolean function called ColumnAttack.

Stop & Help ➤

Express the row and column checks as calls to a single function.

How should the diagonals be checked?

Just as checking the diagonals was the hardest part of the queen-by-queen approach, it is the most difficult part of the line-by-line approach. Since the checking can start at the beginning of each diagonal rather than somewhere in the middle, we need consider only two directions (say, northeast and southeast). Figure 9.1 illustrates the process.

What is the pattern for searching diagonals?

Figure 9.1 suggests a natural subdivision for the diagonals as follows:

- Search the southeast diagonals that start in the first column.
- Search the southeast diagonals that start in the first row.
- Search the northeast diagonals that start in the first column.
- Search the northeast diagonals that start in the eighth row.

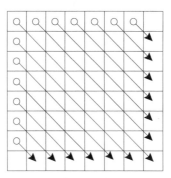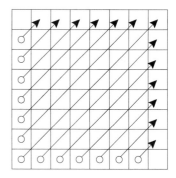

Figure 9.1 *Process for checking chess board diagonals*

The southeast diagonals that start in the first column are those starting in row 1, row 2, ..., up to row 7. They can be searched with the following loop:

```
row := 1;
while not attacking and (row<=7) do begin
    search the southeast diagonal starting at [row, 1];
    row := row + 1;
end;
```

Similarly, searching the southeast diagonals that start in the first row can be done as follows:

```
col := 1;
while not attacking and (col<=7) do begin
    search the southeast diagonal starting at [1, col];
    col := col + 1;
end;
```

Stop & Help ➤   *Write pseudocode for searching the northeast diagonals.*

Stop &Predict ➤   *How are these searches similar?*

How can these search routines be coded as a single subprogram?

The pseudocode for all the diagonal searches is quite similar. In fact, it is similar to the code for the searches of the rows and columns.

We compare the code for searching a row with the code for searching the southeast diagonals:

```
{Search a row.}
numQueens := 0;
col := 1;
attacking := false;
while not attacking and (col <= 8) do begin
    if board [row, col] then begin
        numQueens := numQueens+1;
    end;
    col := col+1;
```

```
        attacking := (numQueens > 1);
end;

{Search a southeast diagonal.}
numQueens := 0;
row := 1;
attacking := false;
while not attacking and (row <= 7) do begin
    if board [row, col] then begin
        numQueens := numQueens+1;
    end;
    row := row-1;
    col := col+1;
    attacking := (numQueens > 1);
end;
```

Stop & Help ➤   *How are these routines similar, and where are they different?*

There are four places where these routines vary: the initial row and column at which the search is to start and the amounts that row and col are incremented each time through the loop. Using these four values along with the board itself as parameters, we can write a single function that does all the searching:

```
function LineAttack (board: BoardType;
    rowStart, colStart: integer; rowChange, colChange: integer);
var
    row, col, numQueens: integer;
    attacking: boolean;
begin
    numQueens := 0;
    row := rowStart;
    col := colStart;
    attacking := false;
    while not attacking and (row in [1..8]) and (col in [1..8]) do begin
        if board [row, col] then begin
            numQueens := numQueens+1;
        end;
        row := row+rowChange;
        col := col+colChange;
        attacking := (numQueens > 1);
    end;
    LineAttack := attacking;
end;
```

How would LineAttack be called to search a row?

A row search could be done by the following code:

```
if LineAttack (board, row, 1, 1, 0) then …
```

Stop & Help ➤   *Call LineAttack to search a given column and to search all the diagonals.*

Putting it all together, we get the function in the Pascal Code section.

Stop & Help ➤   *Create test cases and test the program just designed.*

📁 *Testing* — 9.19 — What special test cases are needed for the line-by-line version that are not needed for the queen-by-queen solution?

Analysis — 9.20 — Describe the template for searching a two-dimensional array, using a verbal description, pseudocode, code, and an illustration.

💻 📁 *Application* — 9.21 — Create a program that takes as input the locations of queens and indicates on a chessboard the squares that are not threatened by any queen. The program should output rows of 8 characters where ones indicate threatened squares and zeroes indicate unthreatened squares.

💻 *Debugging* — 9.22 — Consider the following version of RowAttack.

```
while not attacking and (col <= 8) do begin
    if board[row, col] then begin
        numQueens := numQueens + 1;
        attacking := (numQueens > 1);
    end else begin
        col := col + 1;
    end;
end;
```

There's a bug in the code. Find and fix it.

💻 📁 *Analysis* — 9.23 — Describe all rows for which attacking has the *correct* value upon termination of the while loop in the version of RowAttack in question 9.22.

Reflection — 9.24 — Describe bugs that could arise when using two-dimensional arrays but that would probably not arise in applications using one-dimensional arrays.

💻 *Debugging* — 9.25 — Suppose a version of LineAttack never detected queens in the same column. Is the bug in LineAttack or in the code that calls LineAttack? How would you find out for sure?

💻 📁 *Analysis* — 9.26 — How many board squares are examined in the line-by-line version of the Safe function for a board containing queens at positions [3,6] and [5,4]? If a board square is examined more than once, include it once in the count for each examination.

💻 📁 *Analysis* — 9.27 — How many board squares are examined in the line-by-line version of the Safe function for a board containing queens at positions [3,3] and [7,6]?

💻 📁 *Modification* — 9.28 — Modify the line-by-line version of the Safe function to count the number of board squares it examines and print the result before it returns.

The Queen Position Representation

What aspects of the solution could be improved?

We considered the two-dimensional array representation of the chessboard because the board resembles a two-dimensional array in form. A problem with this representation, however, is that the Safe function wastes a lot of time examining squares that do not contain a queen.

More generally, the BoardType data type represents a *set* of queen positions, each indicated by a row index and a column index. Typically there are (at least) two ways to represent a set of elements. One is as a boolean array, with cells for all possible elements in the set. The two-dimensional boolean chessboard was an example. A second way to represent a set is to store its elements in a one-dimensional array. To represent a chessboard, the array would contain the queen positions: the first element would contain the position of the first queen, the second element would contain the position of the second queen, and so on.

Stop & Predict ➤ *Given the row and column positions of two queens, determine if they attack each other.*

How could the row and column indices be represented?

Each queen position has two components, a row index and a column index. This suggests the use of a record to store an individual queen position. We then represent the board as an array of 64 queen positions, along with the number of queens on the board, packaged in a record as follows:

```
type
    QueenPosType = record
        row, col: 1..8;
    end;
    BoardType = record
        queens: array [1..64] of QueenPosType;
        numQueens: integer;
    end;
```

The figure below displays this representation.

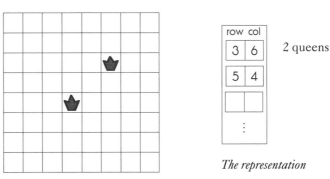

The chessboard

The representation

How do the row and column indices of two queens determine if the queens attack?

A solution using this representation would take advantage of the numerical relationships between the position indices of queens that attack each other. Certainly two queens attack if their row values are identical, or their column values are identical. Again we have a problem with the diagonals.

How can the diagonals be checked?

To find a computational way to check the diagonals we use the usual procedure of looking for a pattern in the diagonal locations.

Stop & Predict ➤ *What aspects of diagonals make it likely that a pattern exists?*

We inspect two sample diagonals, one southeast, the other northeast. These are pictured below.

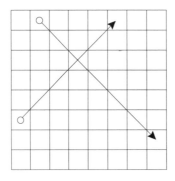

Positions on the northeast diagonal	Positions on the southeast diagonal
row 6, col 1	row 1, col 2
row 5, col 2	row 2, col 3
row 4, col 3	row 3, col 4
row 3, col 4	row 4, col 5
row 2, col 5	row 5, col 6
row 1, col 6	row 6, col 7
	row 7, col 8

What is the pattern?

Consider moving along the northeast diagonal. Whenever the row index goes down, the column index goes up by the same amount. That is, the *sum* of the row and column indexes stays the same. Looking at the figure above, the row and column indexes of any position on the given northeast diagonal add to 7.

Stop & Predict ➤ *What happens on the southeast diagonal?*

For the southeast diagonal, an increase in the row index corresponds to an *increase* in the column index, by the same amount. Therefore, the *difference* of the row and column indexes stays the same. On the southeast diagonal pictured above, the difference between the row and column indexes is always –1.

How can this information be used to detect an attack?

These observations provide a way to detect an attack along the diagonal. Suppose we have two queens, one at position [row1, column1], the other at position [row2, column2]. If the sum of row1 and column1 is the same as the sum of row2 and column2, the two queens are on the same northeast diagonal. If the difference of row1 and column1 is the same as the sum of row2 and column2, the two queens are on the same southeast diagonal.

Stop &Help ➤ *Write the code to compare the diagonal values of the two queens described above.*

What shortcuts can be used?

It seems clear that if more than eight queens are input at least two will be in the same row or column. Thus Safe can begin by checking if the number of queens is 8 or more, and return true if so.

How will the code work?

Given an array of queens each represented as a QueenPosType, we compare each pair of queens to see if they are on the same row, column, or diagonal. Pairs of elements in an array are processed by applying a variation of the template "process every element of an array"; the "processing" here is to consider all pairs that involve the given element. In order not to consider a given pair of queens twice, we pair each queen with all the queens that follow it in the array. To do that, however, we merely apply the template again to the *subarray* of queens that follow the given element. The figure below illustrates this process.

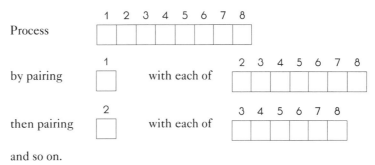

and so on.

Processing every distinct pair of array elements

Here is the code.

```
j := 1;
done := false;
while (j<=number of elements) and not done do begin
    k := j+1;
    while (k<=number of elements) and not done do begin
        see if the j-th and k-th elements of the array satisfies the condition,
        and if so, set done to true;
        k := k + 1;
    end;
    j := j + 1;
end;
```

What does the code look like?

We apply this template, providing a better name for "done," and substituting the code for the attack condition:

```
(queens[j].row = queens[k].row)
or (queens[j].col = queens[k].col)
or (queens[j].row + queens[j].col = queens[k].row + queens[k].col)
or (queens[j].row - queens[j].col = queens[k].row - queens[k].col)
```

This test is messy enough to warrant putting it into a function to hide its details. We'll call it Attack.

How is ReadBoard coded for this representation?

The ReadBoard procedure for this version is even easier to write than the ReadBoard procedure for the first representation, since the way we are storing the board corresponds exactly to the way we are requesting queen positions from the user. The code mainly consists of a loop around two statements, one that reads values for row and column, the other that sets the corresponding board entry to true.

How is PrintBoard coded for this representation?

PrintBoard, on the other hand, requires some thought. The line-by-line loop will still be appropriate, as will the column-by-column loop within it. Printing the character for each board position, however, requires determining whether or not a queen appears at that position.

Stop & Predict ➤ *How should the character to print at a given row and column position be determined?*

One way to find out if a queen is at a given position is to search for the row-column pair in the board array. This approach merely requires that we copy a search procedure from earlier programs.

Another way is to set up a "board image" array similar to the board representation used in the earlier versions of this program. The board image will be an 8-by-8 array of characters, each either '.' or 'Q'; once constructed, it can be printed using the "process every element of a two-dimensional array" template.

Constructing the array is straightforward. First comes an initialization step, in which all the array elements are set to '.'. Then we process every element of the board array, setting the corresponding board image element to 'Q'.

The Pascal Code section contains the complete set of revised subprograms and type definitions.

Stop & Help ➤ *Devise test data and check this version of the program. How is a comprehensive set of test data for this version different from test boards used for the other two versions?*

◀

🔲 🖫 *Analysis* 9.29 Does the order in which the queens are stored in the array affect the number of board squares examined in the Safe function? Why or why not?

🔲 🖫 *Analysis* 9.30 Does the order in which the queens are stored in the array affect the number of board squares examined in the PrintBoard function? Why or why not?

🔲 🖫 *Analysis* 9.31 How many board squares are examined in the version of the Safe function just designed for a board containing seven queens?

REVIEW

Σ ▣ ▤ *Analysis*   9.32   How many board squares are examined in the version of the Safe function just designed for a board containing N queens?

▣ ▤ *Modification*   9.33   Rewrite the PrintBoard procedure so that, instead of using a board image array, it searches the board array inside the printing loop to determine whether to print a '.' or a 'Q'. Which version do you prefer, and why?

Outline of Design and Development Questions

These questions summarize the main points of the commentary.

Understanding the Problem and Selecting an Implementation
How does this problem resemble problems in earlier case studies?

What else is required for a solution?

What kind of data structure should be used, and how large should it be?
> Which definition is better?

How is PrintBoard coded?

In what ways might board values be read from the user?
> How will the input procedure work?

What decompositions for the Safe function make sense?
> What is the pseudocode for the queen-by-queen approach?
> What is the pseudocode for the line-by-line approach?

The Queen-by-Queen Solution
What are the main steps in the queen-by-queen solution?
> How are queens located?
>> What should happen when a queen is located?
>>> How can attacking queens be found more efficiently?

How should the squares a queen can attack be checked?
> How are diagonals checked?
>> Which is better, a for loop or a while loop?
>> How can a single function be used to check all four diagonals?
> How can rows and columns be checked?

How can the code be tested?
> What boundary cases should be tested?
> What other cases are important?

The Line-by-Line Solution
How is this solution different from the queen-by-queen solution?

How are the rows searched for queens?

How should the diagonals be checked?

What is the pattern for searching diagonals?

How can these search routines be coded as a single subprogram?

How would LineAttack be called to search a row?

The Queen Position Representation

What aspects of the solution could be improved?

How could the row and column indices be represented?

How do the row and column indices of two queens determine
  if the queens attack?

How can the diagonals be checked?

What is the pattern?

How can this information be used to detect an attack?

What shortcuts can be used?

How will the code work?

What does the code look like?

How is ReadBoard coded for this representation?

How is PrintBoard coded for this representation?

Programmers' Summary

The problem in this case study is to design a data type to represent a chessboard containing queens and to implement three operations on the board: reading it, printing it, and checking if any of the queens are mutually attacking. The commentary contrasts two ways to represent *sets* of elements—in this case, sets of queens.

One approach is to indicate members of a set of elements with a boolean array, in which each possible element is represented by a *position* in the array. A value of true in an array cell means that the corresponding element is in the set, and a value of false means that the element is not in the set. A set of single-digit integers, for example, would be represented as a ten-element boolean array, and the set {3, 1, 4, 9} would be stored as follows:

0	1	2	3	4	5	6	7	8	9
false	true	false	true	true	false	false	false	false	true

Two of the solutions use an 8-by-8 boolean array of queen positions to represent the set of queens. The Pascal set data type is also stored internally in this way.

Another way to represent a set of elements is to store them in an array. The array would still be declared to have ten cells to allow for the largest possible set, but for smaller sets some of the array cells would be unused. Thus the set {3, 1, 4, 9} might be stored as

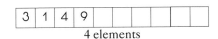

4 elements

or, to make certain set operations more efficient, as

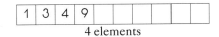

4 elements

where the set elements are stored in order. Another of our solutions uses this approach.

Code that uses the two-dimensional array representation of the board is designed using two-dimensional versions of templates previously used for one-dimensional arrays. Generally, two applications of the "process every array element" or "search an array" are involved, one to process or search the "array" of rows, the other to process or search the elements in the given row. Searching the board's diagonals is not so straightforward; it involves a *single* loop in which two index variables are updated in parallel.

Two solutions are described for the Safe function, which checks for attacking queens. One, the queen-by-queen solution, is organized around the queens on the board; it locates a queen and checks all the rows, columns, and diagonals that the queen threatens for other queens. Another, the line-by-line solution, searches each row, column, and diagonal for multiple queens. The line-by-line solution is less complicated, since entire "lines" (rows, columns, or diagonals) of a two-dimensional array can be processed more easily than partial lines. Straightforward coding produces separate search functions for the rows, the columns, and the diagonals. Further inspection, however, reveals that all these functions are performing essentially the same action; by adding two parameters that indicate the sequence in which board elements are to be examined, we can combine them all into one function.

The alternative board representation, the array of queen positions, leads to the simplest, shortest, and most efficient code for Safe. It avoids needlessly checking blank squares. It requires a bit of cleverness to devise, however, namely noticing the pattern of row and column indexes for each diagonal. Comparison of pairs of queens is done by applying the "process every element of an array" twice, once to select an element, the other to pair it with queens occurring subsequently in the array. Printing the board reuses the approach from the earlier versions by building and printing a two-dimensional board image array of characters.

Making Sense of *Chess Challenges*

Analysis 9.34 Compare the three solutions. The queen position solution is more efficient; why would efficiency matter? Which is more understandable? Which is easier to test and debug?

Modification 9.35 Write a routine that takes input from the 8-by-8 boolean array and converts it to the data structure used in the queen position solution.

Σ *Analysis* 9.36 Use algebra to compute the formulas for the diagonals and to show why the queen position solution works. Hint: The slopes of the diagonals are +1 and –1.

Application 9.37 Design a representation for a chessboard to be used in a program to play chess. It will contain pieces for two players. The queen is one of the pieces; others are the king, the rook, the bishop, the knight, and the pawn.

★ *Modification* 9.38 Modify each version of the code to use the data type designed in question 9.37. Check the board for pieces of one player that can attack pieces of the other. Here are some rules about chess pieces: A king attacks any piece in an adjacent square. A rook attacks a piece in the same row or column. A bishop attacks a piece on the same diagonal. A knight attacks a piece two squares in one row or column and one square in the perpendicular row or column. A pawn attacks a piece that's one square diagonally ahead of it.

Modification 9.39 Rewrite each version of the Safe function to return the positions of one of the pairs of attacking queens.

Analysis 9.40 What changes to the queen position solution would be necessary to stop checking as soon as two attacking queens were detected?

Analysis 9.41 Does an error occur in any of the programs if only one queen position is read in ReadBoard? Explain why or why not.

Reflection 9.42 Name the difficulties in extending templates for one-dimensional arrays to two-dimensional arrays.

Reflection 9.43 What did you learn from the queen-by-queen solution that made it easier to understand the queen position solution?

Application 9.44 The game of 5-in-a-row Tic-Tac-Toe is played by two players on a 19-by-19 board. The players take turns marking empty board squares, one player with an X, the other with an O. The first player to get five of his or her marks in a row, column, or diagonal wins. In a program to play 5-in-a-row Tic-Tac-Toe, is it better to store the board as a two-dimensional array of characters or as an array of positions of X's and O's? Explain.

Linking to Previous Case Studies

Analysis   9.45   Compare the use of for loops and while loops to search an array in *Space Text, You Are What You Eat, You Forgot What You Ate,* and *Chess Challenges.* When is it important to cut short the search by using a while loop, and what disadvantages arise as a result?

★ *Modification*   9.46   Modify the *Banners With CLASS* program to store letter patterns in a two-dimensional array. One advantage of doing this is that letters can be printed across the line as well as down the screen. What is a disadvantage?

Modification   9.47   Modify *The Calendar Shop* program to use a two-dimensional array to store the days of the month, then print it all at once.

Application   9.48   Why might one wish to store a calendar in a two-dimensional array?

Reflection   9.49   Compare the process used to print the fat and calorie graphs in *You Are What You Eat* with the process used to print the chess board in the queen position solution. What techniques are used in both?

Modification   9.50   Rewrite the graph-printing procedures in *You Are What You Eat* to construct and print a two-dimensional "graph-image" array.

Reflection   9.51   *Space Text, You Are What You Eat, You Forgot What You Ate,* and *Chess Challenges* all involve designing and implementing abstract operations for a given collection of information. What are the similarities and differences between the sets of operations designed in these case studies? What operations are likely to be needed for *any* abstract data type?

Queen-by-Queen Checking

```pascal
program chess (input, output);

const
     NW = 1;  NE = 2;  SE = 3;  SW = 4;
     DEBUGGING = true;

type
     BoardType = array[1..8, 1..8] of boolean;
     DirectionType = integer;
     StringType = packed array[1..35] of char;

var
```

```pascal
    board: BoardType;

{
    Read values for the board, coordinates for queen positions.
}
procedure ReadBoard (var board: BoardType);
var
    row, column: integer;
begin {Read Board}
    for row := 1 to 8 do begin
        for column := 1 to 8 do begin
            board[row, column] := false;
        end;
    end;
    writeln('Please type the row and column position for each queen.');
    writeln('Type 0 0 when done.');
    write('Queen row and column?  ');
    readln(row, column);
    while (row <> 0) or (column <> 0) do begin
        if (row in [1..8]) and (column in [1..8]) then begin
            board[row, column] := true;
        end else begin
            writeln('Please type values between 1 and 8.');
        end;
        write('Queen row and column?  ');
        readln(row, column);
    end;
end; {Read Board}

{
    Print the board, indicating a square that contains a queen by 'Q' and
    an empty square by '.'.
}
procedure PrintBoard (board: BoardType);
var
    lineNum, column: integer;
begin {Print Board}
    for lineNum := 1 to 8 do begin
        for column := 1 to 8 do begin
            if board[lineNum, column] then begin
                write('Q');
            end else begin
                write('.');
            end;
        end;
        writeln;
    end;
end; {Print Board}

procedure DebugPrint (msg: StringType; queenRow, queenCol: integer);
begin
    if DEBUGGING then begin
        writeln(msg, queenRow : 1, queenCol : 1);
    end;
end;
```

```
{
    Return true exactly when board contains another queen in the same row
    as [queenRow, queenCol].
}
function SafeRow (board: BoardType; queenRow, queenCol: integer): boolean;
var
    row, col: integer; attacking: boolean;
begin {Safe Row?}
    attacking := false;
    col := queenCol - 1;
    while (col >= 1) and not attacking do begin
        if board[queenRow, col] then begin
            attacking := true;
        end else begin
            col := col - 1;
        end;
    end;
    col := queenCol + 1;
    while (col <= 8) and not attacking do begin
        if board[queenRow, col] then begin
            attacking := true;
        end else begin
            col := col + 1;
        end;
    end;
    SafeRow := attacking;
end; {Safe Row?}


{
    Return true exactly when board contains another queen in the same
    column as [queenRow, queenCol].
}
function SafeCol (board: BoardType; queenRow, queenCol: integer): boolean;
var
    row, col: integer; attacking: boolean;
begin {Safe Column?}
    attacking := false;
    row := queenRow - 1;
    while (row >= 1) and not attacking do begin
        if board[row, queenCol] then begin
            attacking := true;
        end else begin
            row := row - 1;
        end;
    end;
    row := queenRow + 1;
    while (row <= 8) and not attacking do begin
        if board[row, queenCol] then begin
            attacking := true;
        end else begin
            row := row + 1;
        end;
    end;
    SafeCol := attacking;
end; {Safe Column?}
```

```
{
    Return true exactly when board contains another queen somewhere in the
    given direction from [queenRow, queenCol]. The direction will either
    be northwest (NW), northeast (NE), southwest (SW), or southeast (SE).
}
function SafeDiag (board: BoardType; queenRow, queenCol: integer;
    direction: DirectionType): boolean;
var
    row, col: integer; attacking: boolean;
begin {Safe Diagonal?}
    attacking := false;
    case direction of
        NE, NW: row := queenRow - 1;
        SE, SW: row := queenRow + 1;
    end;
    case direction of
        NW, SW: col := queenCol - 1;
        NE, SE: col := queenCol + 1;
    end;
    while not attacking and (row >= 1) and (row <= 8)
      and (col >= 1) and (col <= 8) do begin
        if board[row, col] then begin
            attacking := true;
        end else begin
            case direction of
                NE, NW: row := row - 1;
                SE, SW: row := row + 1;
            end;
            case direction of
                NW, SW: col := col - 1;
                NE, SE: col := col + 1;
            end;
        end;
    end;
    SafeDiag := attacking;
end; {Safe Diagonal?}

{
    Return true exactly when board contains two mutually attacking queens.
}
function Safe (board: BoardType): boolean;
var
    qRow, qCol: integer; attacking: boolean;
begin {Safe?}
    attacking := false;
    qRow := 1;
    while not attacking and (qRow <= 8) do begin
        qCol := 1;
        while not attacking and (qCol <= 8) do begin
            if board[qRow, qCol] then begin
                if SafeRow(board, qRow, qCol) then begin
                    attacking := true;
                    DebugPrint('queen on same row as ', qRow, qCol);
                end else if SafeCol(board, qRow, qCol) then begin
                    attacking := true;
                    DebugPrint('queen on same column as ', qRow, qCol);
```

```
                        end else if SafeDiag(board, qRow, qCol, NW) then begin
                            attacking := true;
                            DebugPrint('queen on same NW diagonal as ',
                              qRow, qCol);
                        end else if SafeDiag(board, qRow, qCol, NE) then begin
                            attacking := true;
                            DebugPrint('queen on same NE diagonal as ',
                                qRow, qCol);
                        end else if SafeDiag(board, qRow, qCol, SE) then begin
                            attacking := true;
                            DebugPrint('queen on same SE diagonal as ',
                                qRow, qCol);
                        end else if SafeDiag(board, qRow, qCol, SW) then begin
                            attacking := true;
                            DebugPrint('queen on same SW diagonal as ',
                                qRow, qCol);
                        end;
                    end;
                    qCol := qCol + 1;
                end;
                qRow := qRow + 1;
            end;
            Safe := not attacking;
        end; {Safe?}

    begin
        while true do begin
            ReadBoard(board);
            PrintBoard(board);
            if Safe(board) then begin
                writeln('Board is safe.');
            end else begin
                writeln('Two queens attack.');
            end;
        end;
    end.
```

Line-by-Line Checking

```
procedure DebugPrint (msg: StringType; n: integer);
begin
    if DEBUGGING then begin
        writeln(msg, n : 1);
    end;
end;

{
    Return true exactly when, starting at position [rowStart, colStart]
    and moving in the direction specified by rowChange and colChange, two
    or more queens are encountered on the board.
}
function LineAttack (board: BoardType; rowStart, colStart: integer;
    rowChange, colChange: integer): boolean;
var
```

```
            row, col, numQueens: integer;
begin {Line Attack?}
    numQueens := 0;
    row := rowStart;
    col := colStart;
    attacking := false;
    while not attacking and (row in [1..8]) and (col in [1..8]) do begin
        if board[row, col] then begin
            numQueens := numQueens + 1;
        end;
        row := row + rowChange;
        col := col + colChange;
        attacking := (numQueens > 1);
    end;
    LineAttack := attacking;
end; {Line Attack?}

{
    Return true exactly when board contains no mutually attacking queens.
}
function Safe (board: BoardType): boolean;
var
    row, col: integer; attacking: boolean;
begin {Safe?}
    row := 1;
    while not attacking and (row <= 8) do begin
        if LineAttack(board, row, 1, 0, +1) then begin
            attacking := true;
            DebugPrint('multiple queens found in row          ', row);
        end else if LineAttack(board, row, 1, +1, +1) then begin
            attacking := true;
            DebugPrint('multiple queens found going SE from row   ', row);
        end else if LineAttack(board, row, 1, -1, +1) then begin
            attacking := true;
            DebugPrint('multiple queens found going NE from row   ', row);
        end else begin
            row := row + 1;
        end;
    end;
    col := 1;
    while not attacking and (col <= 8) do begin
        if LineAttack(board, 1, col, +1, 0) then begin
            attacking := true;
            DebugPrint('multiple queens found in column          ', col);
        end else if LineAttack(board, 1, col, +1, +1) then begin
            attacking := true;
            DebugPrint('multiple queens going SE from column ', col);
        end else if LineAttack(board, 1, col, -1, +1) then begin
            attacking := true;
            DebugPrint('multiple queens going SW from column ', col);
        end else begin
            col := col + 1;
        end;
    end;
    Safe := not attacking;
end; {Safe?}
```

Queen Position Representation

```pascal
type
    QueenPosType = record
        row, col: integer;   {position of a queen}
    end;
    BoardType = record
        queens: array[1..64] of QueenPosType;
        numQueens: integer;
    end;
    StringType = packed array[1..43] of char;

var
    board: BoardType;

{
    Fill the board array with positions entered by the user.
}
procedure ReadBoard (var board: BoardType);
var
    queenPos: QueenPosType;
begin {Read Board}
    board.numQueens := 0;
    writeln('Please type the row and column position for each queen.');
    writeln('Type 0 0 when done.');
    write('Queen row and column?  ');
    readln(queenPos.row, queenPos.col);
    while (queenPos.row <> 0) or (queenPos.col <> 0) do begin
        if (queenPos.row in [1..8])
          and (queenPos.col in [1..8]) then begin
            board.numQueens := board.numQueens + 1;
            board.queens[board.numQueens] := queenPos;
        end else begin
            writeln('Please type values between 1 and 8.');
        end;
        write('Queen row and column?  ');
        readln(queenPos.row, queenPos.col);
    end;
end; {Read Board}

{
    Print the board.
}
procedure PrintBoard (board: BoardType);
var
    lineNum, column, k: integer;
    boardDisplay: array[1..8, 1..8] of char;
begin {Print Board}
    for lineNum := 1 to 8 do begin
        for column := 1 to 8 do begin
            boardDisplay[lineNum, column] := '.';
        end;
    end;
    for k := 1 to board.numQueens do begin
        boardDisplay[board.queens[k].row, board.queens[k].col] := 'Q';
    end;
```

```pascal
        for lineNum := 1 to 8 do begin
            for column := 1 to 8 do begin
                write(boardDisplay[lineNum, column]);
            end;
            writeln;
        end;
end;

procedure DebugPrint (q1, q2: QueenPosType);
begin
    if DEBUGGING then begin
        writeln('queens at positions [', q1.row : 1, ',', q1.col : 1,
            '] and [', q2.row : 1, ',', q2.col : 1, '] attack.');
    end;
end;

{
    Return true exactly when q1 and q2 represent positions on the same row,
    column, or diagonal of the chessboard.
}
function Attack (q1, q2: QueenPosType): boolean;
begin {Attack?}
    Attack := (q1.row = q2.row) or (q1.col = q2.col)
      or (q1.row + q1.col = q2.row + q2.col)
      or (q1.row - q1.col = q2.row - q2.col);
end; {Attack?}

{
    Return true exactly when board contains no mutually attacking queens.
}
function Safe (board: BoardType): boolean;
var
    j, k: integer;
    attacking: boolean;
begin {Safe?}
    j := 1;
    attacking := false;
    while (j <= board.numQueens) and not attacking do begin
        k := j + 1;
        while (k <= board.numQueens) and not attacking do begin
            attacking := Attack(board.queens[j], board.queens[k]);
            if attacking then begin
                DebugPrint(board.queens[j], board.queens[k]);
            end;
            k := k + 1;
        end;
        j := j + 1;
    end;
    Safe := not attacking;
end; {Safe?}
```

CHAPTER 10

The Shuffler's Dilemma

Is shuffling an art or a science? Check out this case study and see.

Anyone can shuffle cards by hand; getting a computer to do it takes talent. Should the computer imitate a human shuffler or behave like a machine? How can the results of a shuffle be evaluated? This case study describes programs implementing several different shuffling algorithms and compares the results.

Problem Statement

Write a procedure called Shuffle to rearrange a (simulated) deck of cards. Create a procedure that will rearrange the cards such that *any* ordering of the cards is equally probable. Shuffle will be used in programs that simulate the play of card games and that compare different shuffling algorithms.

The procedure will have the following header:

```
procedure Shuffle (var deck: DeckType);
```

It will assume the following definitions:

```
const
    DECKSIZE = 52;
type
    CardType = some type;
    DeckType = array [1..DECKSIZE] of CardType;
```

Shuffle will rearrange the contents of deck, returning its "cards" in a different order. Each element contained in deck when Shuffle is entered will also be somewhere in deck—possibly in a different position—when Shuffle returns. The procedure may make no assumptions about how CardType is defined, except to assume that assignments are possible between two CardType values.

Analysis	10.1	Suppose that a "deck" has only three cards. List all the ways the cards can be ordered.
Analysis	10.2	How many possible ways can N "cards" be arranged in a deck?
Ã *Analysis*	10.3	How many possible rearrangements of an N-card deck change the position of all N cards?
Application	10.4	Define a type that represents all the characteristics of an actual playing card used in a game such as gin rummy.

Preparation

The reader is expected to be familiar with arrays and records.

Understanding the Problem

What does "shuffling" a simulated deck mean?

This problem involves simulating an activity that is usually done by hand. It makes sense to pinpoint the similarities and differences between shuffling by hand and "shuffling" in a program. Shuffling a deck of actual cards means mixing them up. "Shuffling" a simulated deck means the same thing. Here's an example that uses a deck of four "cards," each being a letter.

Original deck contents

deck[1]	deck[2]	deck[3]	deck[4]
'A'	'B'	'C'	'D'

Possible result of "shuffling"

deck[1]	deck[2]	deck[3]	deck[4]
'C'	'B'	'D'	'A'

Another possible result of "shuffling"

deck[1]	deck[2]	deck[3]	deck[4]
'D'	'C'	'B'	'A'

Note that the result of shuffling need not move all the cards; the first shuffle above left card 'B' in the second position in the deck.

Stop & Consider ➤ *Might shuffling leave a deck unchanged? Why or why not?*

Stop & Help ➤ *How many possible ways can four cards be arranged in a deck?*

Stop & Help ➤ *How many possible rearrangements of a four-card deck change the position of all four cards?*

What is a successful shuffle?

The problem statement asks for a shuffle in which *any* of the possible rearrangements of the deck should be equally probable. Thus, the problem statement requires that the shuffling be "unpredictable." An example of a predictable shuffling routine would be one that *always* leaves the second card in the second position.

Stop & Help ➤ *Why might shuffling by hand yield predictable results?*

Why use the given declarations?

The problem statement requires that the procedure use specific declarations. These appear to be chosen so that the procedure will be **modular** and work with many different programs.

The use of the constant DECKSIZE to specify the size of the deck allows the size to be changed easily. Using a constant also makes it easier to test Shuffle on smaller problems. The same approach was used in *Space Text*.

The problem statement specifies that the Shuffle code must not depend on the characteristics of a CardType. Thus it should work as well if CardType were char (as in the above example) as if it were integer, or a more complicated type.

Analysis 10.5 How might the code of the Shuffle procedure depend on the characteristics of a CardType?

Application 10.6 Why might Shuffle be used for decks of size other than 52?

Reflection 10.7 What parts of hand shuffling would be difficult to simulate?

A "Perfect Shuffle"

How do people shuffle a deck of cards? One possible solution simulates how people shuffle cards. Most people split the deck in half and then interleave the cards, as shown in the diagram below.

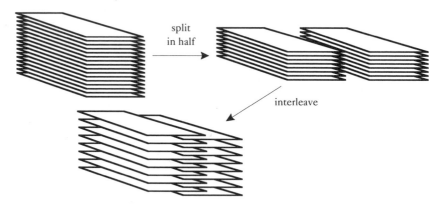

Applied to a deck of four cards (letters for the purposes of this example), this procedure works as follows:

What is a "perfect shuffle"? If the deck is split precisely in half, and the halves are precisely interleaved, the procedure is called a "perfect shuffle." We decide to implement a version of Shuffle using the perfect shuffle procedure first, on the assumption that this is close to the algorithm that many people use.

Stop & Predict ➤ *What are the limitations of the perfect shuffle solution?*

As in previous case studies, it helps to make a table of the desired rearrangement. The procedure illustrated above provides a table for shuffling a four-card deck. For a 52-card deck:

Position of card before shuffling	Position of card after shuffling
1	1
2	3
3	5
⋮	⋮
25	49
26	51
27	2
28	4
29	6
⋮	⋮
51	50
52	52

Stop & Help ➤ *Suppose the deck consists of the integers 1 through 52, arranged in increasing order. How are the integers ordered after a perfect shuffle?*

What implementation does the table suggest?

The table suggests a way to implement the shuffle. We can use two decks, the deck provided as a parameter and another deck—we'll call it shuffledDeck—used as a local variable. We can keep track of a position in each deck, oldPosition in deck and shuffledPosition in shuffledDeck. The shuffle then can consist of loops that copy deck[oldPosition] into shuffledDeck[shuffledPosition], then update oldPosition and shuffledPosition, in each iteration. The shuffle finishes by copying shuffledDeck back into deck.

Stop & Help ➤ *The code to copy* shuffledDeck *into* deck *is an example of a template used in previous case studies. Which template is it, and where was it used?*

For the first half of the deck, oldPosition starts at 1 and goes up by 1 at each step, and shuffledPosition starts at 1 and goes up by 2 at each step. The second half of the deck is handled similarly, except for different starting values. We will call this approach PerfectShuffle and implement it. Assuming for simplicity that the deck has an even number of cards, we arrive at the following code:

```
procedure PerfectShuffle (var deck: DeckType);
var
    oldPosition, shuffledPosition: integer;
begin
    oldPosition := 1;
    shuffledPosition := 1;
    while oldPosition <= DECKSIZE div 2 do begin
        shuffledDeck[shuffledPosition] := deck[oldPosition];
        oldPosition := oldPosition + 1;
        shuffledPosition := shuffledPosition + 2;
    end;
    shuffledPosition := 2;
    while oldPosition <= DECKSIZE do begin
        shuffledDeck[shuffledPosition] := deck[oldPosition];
        oldPosition := oldPosition + 1;
        shuffledPosition := shuffledPosition + 2;
    end;
    for oldPosition := 1 to DECKSIZE do begin
        deck[oldPosition] := shuffledDeck[oldPosition];
    end;
end;
```

Stop & Help ➤ | *Should* oldPosition *be reinitialized for the second loop in* PerfectShuffle*? Why or why not?*

Does the procedure satisfy the conditions of the problem statement? | The perfect shuffle procedure meets the problem specifications in that (a) it uses the given declarations, and (b) it makes no assumptions about Card-Type values other than that one CardType value can be assigned to a variable of type CardType.

Stop & Predict ➤ | *How effectively does* PerfectShuffle *shuffle the cards?*

How should PerfectShuffle be tested? | The PerfectShuffle procedure and a program to test it appear in the Pascal Code section. To test for predictability we print the result of repeated calls to PerfectShuffle. At each iteration the result of the previous shuffle is shuffled again. We hope that any patterns in the shuffling will show up in the resulting output.

Stop & Help ➤ | *Test* PerfectShuffle *using the program in the Pascal Code section with* DECKSIZE *set to 6.*

What is the result of the test? | The program produces a very predictable shuffle. Here is a table representing the shuffling process for a deck of four cards:

initial deck	'A'	'B'	'C'	'D'
first shuffle	'A'	'C'	'B'	'D'
second shuffle	'A'	'B'	'C'	'D'
third shuffle	'A'	'C'	'B'	'D'
fourth shuffle	'A'	'B'	'C'	'D'

Perhaps it works better with a bigger deck? Trying DECKSIZE = 8 results in equally disappointing behavior:

```
Deck:
 A  E  B  F  C  G  D  H

Deck:
 A  C  E  G  B  D  F  H

Deck:
 A  B  C  D  E  F  G  H

Deck:
 A  E  B  F  C  G  D  H

Deck:
 A  C  E  G  B  D  F  H

Deck:
 A  B  C  D  E  F  G  H
```

and so on.

We conclude that a perfect shuffle is too predictable to satisfy the problem specifications, so we go back to thinking up alternative solutions.

Modification, 10.8 Code the while loops in PerfectShuffle as for loops. Which version do
Reflection you prefer? Explain.

Reflection 10.9 Why does the use of shuffledDeck result in simpler code than would the use of only one deck variable?

Modification 10.10 Rewrite PerfectShuffle to use only one position variable. Compute the value of a card's position in the shuffled deck from the value of oldPosition, its value in the unshuffled deck.

Modification 10.11 Rather than compute the value of a card's position in the shuffled deck from the value of oldPosition as in question 10.10, one may instead compute the card's position in the unshuffled deck from shuffledPosition. Provide the missing expression for the loop below to rearrange the deck using a perfect shuffle. Hint: use mod and div.

```
for shuffledPosition := 1 to DECKSIZE do begin
    shuffledDeck[shuffledPosition]
        := deck [_____ ];
end;
```

Analysis 10.12 How many shuffles are needed for PerfectShuffle to return a 52-card deck to its original arrangement? (This is the basis of a magician's trick, in which the magician carefully shuffles the cards many times, apparently mixing them up thoroughly, yet is able to predict the order of cards in the deck.)

□ *Analysis*   10.13 Which statements in the program in the Pascal Code section depend on the characteristics of a CardType?

□ *Analysis*   10.14 If 52 were used throughout the code instead of the constant DECK-SIZE, how many changes would be necessary to test the program on a deck of size 4?

▣ □ *Debugging*   10.15 What would happen if the main program in the Pascal Code section reinitialized the deck inside the for loop?

▣ □ *Analysis*   10.16 What does PerfectShuffle do if DECKSIZE is odd?

▣ □ *Modification*   10.17 Fix PerfectShuffle to shuffle a deck containing an odd number of cards correctly.

Analysis   10.18 Suppose we interleaved the cards in a different order, as shown in the diagram below. Would this process yield a shuffle procedure that's better than PerfectShuffle?

Shuffling With a Random Number Generator

How can the shuffle procedure be made less predictable?

To get an unpredictable shuffle we need a **random number generator**. This is a function that, when called repeatedly, returns a sequence of numbers that appear random. (Since the numbers are produced by program code, they aren't really random; because of this, programmers sometimes call the function a "pseudorandom" number generator.) Almost all Pascal environments provide some sort of random number generator, either a function that returns a random integer or a function that returns a random real value between 0 and 1. In the remainder of the solution to this problem, we will assume that a function named RandomInt, which takes no arguments, is available that returns a random integer value.

Stop & Help ➤   *Find out which random number generator is available on your Pascal system.*

Stop & Help ➤   *Write a test program that calls the random number generator 100 times and prints the values it returns. Do they look "random"?*

Stop & Predict ➤   *How might the RandomInt function be used to shuffle the cards? List all your ideas.*

How can the RandomInt function be used in a card-shuffling procedure?

We can use RandomInt to simulate the choice of a random card from the deck. To determine how choice of a random card might be incorporated into a shuffling procedure, it helps to consider how this would work for hand shuffling. Some possibilities:

Shuffling by exchanging: A person might repeatedly choose two cards at random and exchange them.

Shuffling by selection: A person might randomly choose a card and add it to the shuffled deck until there are no more cards to be chosen.

Shuffling by insertion: A person might repeatedly take the top card in the deck and insert it next to a randomly chosen card.

We will pursue the first two of these approaches and leave the last for consideration in a study question.

📓 *Application*   10.19 Suppose that a Pascal system provides a function RandomReal that returns a random real value that's greater than 0 and at most 1. Implement RandomInt in terms of RandomReal.

📓 *Application*   10.20 Use RandomInt in a program to simulate repeated throws of two six-sided dice.

Analysis   10.21 RandomInt differs from other functions in one significant way. What is it?

Application   10.22 List other uses for a random number generator.

Reflection   10.23 Describe how prior case study solutions might be reused to implement these alternatives.

Shuffling by Random Exchanges

How can random exchanges of cards be done to shuffle the deck?

A descriptive name for the solution based on random exchanges is ExchangeShuffle. In pseudocode, the solution is as follows:

```
while not done do begin
    choose two random positions in deck;
    exchange the cards at those positions;
end;
```

The pseudocode doesn't specify a way to stop the loop. The body of the loop, however, isn't hard to design. Exchanging elements of an array is easy, and choosing two random positions in deck will involve calling RandomInt and using its result.

Stop & Predict ➤   *What will determine the ideal number of exchanges?*

How can a random position in the deck be found?

A random position in deck is merely a random integer between 1 and DECKSIZE, inclusive. RandomInt returns a random integer; abs(RandomInt) mod DECKSIZE returns a random integer between 0 and DECKSIZE−1, inclusive; thus (abs(RandomInt) mod DECKSIZE) + 1 returns the desired value. Since this expression will be used more than once (and will probably be useful in alternative solutions to the problem), we code it as a function:

```
function RandomDeckPos: integer;
begin
    RandomDeckPos := (abs(RandomInt) mod DECKSIZE) + 1;
end;
```

The pseudocode for ExchangeShuffle may then be refined to

```
while not done do begin
    pos1 := RandomDeckPos;
    pos2 := RandomDeckPos;
    exchange deck[pos1] with deck[pos2];
end;
```

Stop & Help ➤ *Explain why the call to* abs(RandomInt) mod DECKSIZE *will never return a value of* DECKSIZE.

How many exchanges are necessary to shuffle the deck adequately?

To determine how many exchanges are necessary, we try some possibilities. We examine as small a deck as necessary to give us the information we need; even a deck of size 4 gives a large number of possibilities, so we start with a deck of size 3. We create a diagram to determine all the possibilities (Figure 10.1).

Stop & Predict ➤ *Suppose two exchanges of cards are made—two randomly chosen cards are exchanged, and then two other randomly chosen cards are exchanged. Which pairs of exchanges return a "shuffled" deck identical to the original?*

Figure 10.1 indicates the possible deck orderings that result from one and two exchanges. There are nine possible ways to make the first exchange; for each of those, there are nine possible ways to make the second exchange. An exchange of, say, the first card with the second card is represented by "1↔2" in the figure, an exchange of the second card with the third card is represented by "2↔3," and so on. Potentially, RandomDeckPos might select the same card on two successive calls. The possibilities for this are "1↔1," "2↔2," and "3↔3." All three possibilities merely result in the corresponding card being "exchanged" with itself.

Figure 10.1 shows that the various rearrangements of the deck show up with the frequencies displayed in Table 10.2.

Stop & Help ➤ *List the 12 ways that the ordering* BAC *can be produced by two exchanges.*

Stop & Help ➤ *Verify the accuracy of Table 10.2.*

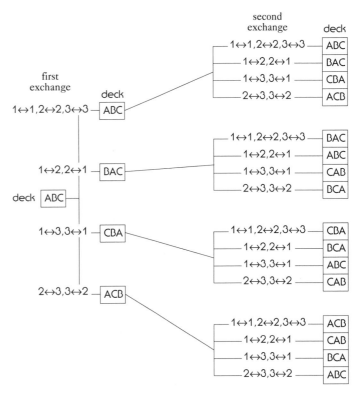

Figure 10.1 *Deck orderings that result from one exchange and two exchanges*

Arrangement	results from 1 exchange in	results from 2 exchanges in
ABC	3 ways	21 ways
ACB	2 ways	12 ways
BAC	2 ways	12 ways
BCA	0 ways	12 ways
CAB	0 ways	12 ways
CBA	2 ways	12 ways

Table 10.2 *Arrangement frequency*

Stop & Help ➤ Determine the frequency of the arrangements of the three-card deck that results from three exchanges.

Stop & Predict ➤ Are the shuffled versions of the deck equally probable?

Stop & Predict ➤ Does ExchangeShuffle meet the problem specifications?

It appears that some arrangements of cards (in particular, the original arrangement) occur much more frequently than others. We thus reject shuffling by exchanges.

Application 10.24 Write a program to verify the data in Figure 10.1.

Application 10.25 Write a program to produce the number of ways to arrive at each ordering of four cards using two exchanges.

Analysis 10.26 Is shuffling by exchanges any better if exchanges of a card with itself are prohibited? Explain.

Modification 10.27 Test your answer to question 10.26 by modifying the ExchangeShuffle procedure so that it keeps generating random positions until it finds two positions that are different. (This avoids exchanging a card with itself.)

Shuffling by Selection

How can random selection help shuffle the deck?

A descriptive name for a solution based on random selection of a card is SelectionShuffle. The approach is to choose a random card and add it to the shuffled deck until there are no more cards to be chosen. We note that the same card may be chosen twice. To avoid this problem we can keep track of the cards that have already been chosen and add a card to the shuffled deck only if it's not there already. In pseudocode:

```
set the number of cards already chosen to 0;
while number of cards already chosen < DECKSIZE do begin
    choose a random card;
    compare it with cards already chosen;
    if it doesn't match, then begin
        add it to the shuffled deck;
        add 1 to the number of cards already chosen;
    end;
end;
```

Stop & Predict ➤ *Which array templates are used to produce the code?*

We use the deck and shuffledDeck variables to refine the pseudocode into Pascal.

```
procedure SelectionShuffle (var deck: DeckType);
var
    k, numChosen: integer;
    shuffledDeck: DeckType;
begin
    numChosen := 0;
```

```
while numChosen < DECKSIZE do begin
    k := RandomDeckPos;
    if not Search (deck[k], shuffledDeck, numChosen) then begin
        numChosen := numChosen + 1;
        shuffledDeck[numChosen] := deck[k];
    end;
end;
end;
```

The loop body is similar to code used to fill an array. The Search function is a variation of code used in earlier case studies.

Stop & Help ➤ *Why not use a* for *loop in* SelectionShuffle *rather than a* while *loop?*

How well does this procedure work? The code for SelectionShuffle and the subprograms it calls appears in the Pascal Code section. The same main program used to test PerfectShuffle can be used with SelectionShuffle. As before, we test it on decks of size 4 and size 52. It seems to work fine.

Stop & Help ➤ *Test* SelectionShuffle *on your system. Compare the time it takes to shuffle a deck of 52 cards to the time* PerfectShuffle *takes.*

What flaws does SelectionShuffle have? One unsettling aspect of SelectionShuffle is that the while loop is not absolutely guaranteed to terminate.

Stop & Help ➤ *Explain why the* while *loop could take a long time to terminate.*

Admittedly the loop is unlikely to go on forever. Finishing up the shuffle of a deck of 52 cards, though, will require quite a few calls to RandomDeck-Pos to choose the cards that have not yet been included in the shuffle.

Stop & Help ➤ *Suppose the loop of* SelectionShuffle *has progressed to the point where* numChosen *is equal to* DECKSIZE−1. *Assuming that* RandomDeckPos *is equally likely to return any of the possible deck positions, what is the probability that one more execution of the loop body will finish the shuffle?*

How can SelectionShuffle be improved? The algorithm of SelectionShuffle does not accurately reflect what a person using the selection approach would do. A person would pick a random card, add it to a pile, pick a random card *from those that remain*, add it to the pile, and so on. Thus the first random card would be chosen from a deck of DECKSIZE cards, the next from a deck of DECKSIZE−1 cards, the third from a deck of DECKSIZE−2 cards, and so on. A descriptive name for this solution is EfficientSelectionShuffle. In pseudocode:

```
set the number of cards already chosen to 0;
while number of cards already chosen < DECKSIZE do begin
    choose a random card from those that remain in deck;
    add it to the shuffled deck;
    remove it from deck;
end;
```

Stop & Help ➤ *Are any changes to* SelectionShuffle *needed to add cards to the shuffled deck in* EfficientSelectionShuffle?

How can the deck be adjusted when cards are removed? We need to reduce the cards in deck when a card is removed so that choosing a random card from those that remain can be done efficiently. We could modify RandomDeckPos to return a card from a deck with a variable number of cards. The size of the deck can be supplied as a parameter. Thus the modified RandomDeckPos will be called with an argument of first DECKSIZE, then DECKSIZE−1, and so on.

Removing a card from the deck to make a smaller deck requires filling the place where the card is removed. One option is to shift all cards that follow it back one place in the deck as was done to compress a Roman numeral in *Is It Legal?* However, this involves much more work than is necessary. There is no need to preserve the order of the cards that remain. (We're shuffling them, after all!) We can fill the gap that results from removing a card merely by moving the last card in the deck to replace it.

Stop & Consider ➤ *How is this related to the* ExchangeShuffle *solution?*

These refinements result in the following code for EfficientSelectionShuffle. The program appears in the Pascal Code section.

```
for shuffledPos := 1 to DECKSIZE do begin
    k := RandomDeckPos (DECKSIZE-shuffledPos+1);
    shuffledDeck[shuffledPos] := deck[k];
    deck[k] := deck[DECKSIZE-shuffledPos+1];
end;
```

EfficientSelectionShuffle satisfies the constraints on use of CardType. It seems to shuffle the cards well, though there may be patterns in the shuffling that we don't notice. For a small deck of cards, EfficientSelectionShuffle does not seem much faster than SelectionShuffle, but efficiency increases when there are many cards. This version seems to meet all the requirements of the problem and is renamed Shuffle to conform to the conditions of the problem statement.

Modification 10.28 Instead of using a search routine to determine if a card has already been included in the shuffled deck, use a Pascal set positionsChosen to contain the positions already chosen, and replace the if test in SelectionShuffle by the code

```
if not (k in positionsChosen) then begin ...
```

Analysis 10.29 SelectionShuffle as written does not satisfy the specifications in the problem statement. Why not?

Testing 10.30 Add code to SelectionShuffle to count the number of times Random-DeckPos is called for any particular shuffle. Are you surprised by the result? Explain.

Testing 10.31 Run the program for EfficientSelectionShuffle. Is it noticeably faster than the program for SelectionShuffle for shuffling a 52-card deck? How about a 104-card deck?

Analysis 10.32 Why can a for loop be used in EfficientSelectionShuffle but was not appropriate for SelectionShuffle?

Analysis 10.33 After copying deck[DECKSIZE–shuffledPos+1] into deck[k], the code for EfficientSelectionShuffle doesn't store anything into deck[DECK-SIZE–shuffledPos+1]. Should it? Why or why not?

Outline of Design and Development Questions

These questions summarize the main points of the commentary.

Understanding the Problem
What does "shuffling" a simulated deck mean?
What is a successful shuffle?
Why use the given declarations?

A "Perfect Shuffle"
How do people shuffle a deck of cards?
What is a "perfect shuffle"?
What implementation does the table suggest?
Does the procedure satisfy the conditions of the problem statement?
 How should PerfectShuffle be tested?
 What is the result of the test?

Shuffling With a Random Number Generator
How can the shuffle procedure be made less predictable?
How can the RandomInt function be used in a card-shuffling procedure?

Shuffling by Random Exchanges
How can random exchanges of cards be done to shuffle the deck?
How can a random position in the deck be found?
How many exchanges are necessary to shuffle the deck adequately?

Shuffling by Selection
How can random selection help shuffle the deck?

How well does this procedure work?

What flaws does SelectionShuffle have?

How can SelectionShuffle be improved?

How can the deck be adjusted when cards are removed?

Programmers' Summary

This case study considers the problem of shuffling a computerized deck of cards. The shuffling procedure developed as a solution works with an array of any kind of "card," and thus should be a useful tool for a variety of applications.

Three alternative approaches are considered: a "perfect shuffle," based on interleaving the cards; repeated exchanges of randomly chosen cards; and repeated selection of randomly chosen cards. The latter two approaches use a random number generator, a function provided in Pascal environments to produce a sequence of random-looking values. The random selection approach is most successful at producing all possible card orderings with equal probability.

Different kinds of analysis are applied to the various methods. We implement the perfect shuffle and try it on small decks, noting that repeated shuffles lead quickly to the original arrangement! We analyze the random exchange method by hand and find that one arrangement (the original) consistently pops up more often than the others. After coding a version of selection shuffling, we analyze the code and find a way to improve its efficiency.

There are several uses of the Recycling principle, as array templates are applied to fill, copy, and search the deck array. The Multiple Representations principle suggests the use of a table to keep track of card rearrangement in the perfect shuffle and the use of a tree diagram to keep track of the possibilities for rearrangement via random exchanges.

Making Sense of *The Shuffler's Dilemma*

📖 *Application*   10.34 Sorting an array (putting its elements in order) may be viewed as "unshuffling" the array. Devise sorting algorithms based on each of the approaches discussed for sorting.

📖 *Application*   10.35 Design a shuffling procedure based on insertion, in which the top card of the deck is inserted next to a randomly chosen card.

Reflection 10.36 Which shuffling approach most closely resembles the "52-pickup" technique, where a deck of cards is flung into the air and then collected off the floor?

🔲 💾 *Modification* 10.37 Modify all the Shuffle procedures to use a deck represented as a record in which the number of cards is stored along with the cards themselves.

🔲 💾 *Modification* 10.38 Modify EfficientSelectionShuffle to use only the deck array and not the shuffledDeck array to do the shuffling. Thus only elements of deck will be exchanged to do the shuffling.

🔲 *Application* 10.39 Write a program to play Clock Solitaire. The player deals the cards face down into thirteen piles of four cards each and turns over the top card of the thirteenth pile. The player then puts the turned-over card face up under the pile corresponding to its rank—ace goes to the first pile, 2 to the second, and so on—and turns over the top card of that pile. The game is won if all other cards get turned over before the fourth king.

Analysis 10.40 Compare the code in EfficientSelectionShuffle to Pascal code that fills one array with the elements of another in reverse order. What are the similarities? What are the differences?

Reflection 10.41 Explain why considering several alternatives helps programmers come up with a better solution than considering just one.

Reflection 10.42 Analysis of small cases by hand allowed us to reject the approach of shuffling by exchanges. In what situations have you written an incorrect program that could have been avoided had you analyzed the situation by hand before coding?

Reflection 10.43 Why was it a good idea to start with PerfectShuffle even though this approach did not meet all the specifications of the problem?

Analysis 10.44 Give advice to a card player who asks if it matters how many times the cards are shuffled when the shuffling is done by hand. Would the same arguments apply to a selection shuffle?

Reflection 10.45 In what ways does the use of a random number generator make a program more difficult to test? How did we compensate for this in *The Shuffler's Dilemma?*

★ 🔲 💾 *Application* 10.46 Write a procedure that, given two integer arguments numCards and numExchanges, prints the number of times each arrangement of a deck of numCards cards results from numExchanges exchanges. Your procedure could be used to generate the data in Table 10.2. Hint: Use recursion.

Linking to Previous Case Studies

Analysis 10.47 In *Space Text*, an extra array was necessary to avoid the inefficiency of multiple insertions of blanks. Question 10.38 suggests that it is not necessary to use two arrays to shuffle a deck efficiently. Compare the two situations, and explain why efficient insertion into an array cannot be done without an extra array.

Modification 10.48 Modify the main program of *Banners With CLASS* to draw five random letters from P, A, S, C, and L. Each letter should have an equal chance of being chosen for the banner.

Modification 10.49 Modify the driver program of *Space Text* to generate a line containing a random number of randomly chosen words.

Application 10.50 Write a program that creates a history file for the *You Are What You Eat* program, using randomly chosen values for fat and calories.

Application 10.51 Describe two different ways to generate a random Roman numeral.

Reflection 10.52 Would randomly chosen test data have provided convincing evidence of the correctness of any of the programs in earlier case studies? In general, what kinds of programs would be best tested using random data?

Application 10.53 Describe two different ways to generate a random date in 1992.

Application 10.54 Write a program, modeled on the *Banners With CLASS* program, in which each of the letters A through Z corresponds to a particular randomly generated pattern stored in a two-dimensional array. The banner produced by the program would then be a combination of these patterns, a kind of computer art.

Reflection 10.55 List all variants of the "fill an array" template encountered so far in the case studies.

PerfectShuffle With Test Program

```
program testShuffle (output);
const
    DECKSIZE = 4;
    NUMSHUFFLES = 20;

type
    CardType = integer;
```

```
            DeckType = array [1..DECKSIZE] of CardType;

var
    deck: DeckType;
    k: integer;

{
    Shuffle the deck as described in the commentary.
}
procedure PerfectShuffle (var deck: DeckType);
var
    oldPosition, shuffledPosition: integer;
    shuffledDeck: DeckType;
begin {Perfect Shuffle}
    oldPosition := 1;
    shuffledPosition := 1;
    while oldPosition <= DECKSIZE div 2 do begin
        shuffledDeck[shuffledPosition] := deck[oldPosition];
        oldPosition := oldPosition + 1;
        shuffledPosition := shuffledPosition + 2;
    end;
    shuffledPosition := 2;
    while oldPosition <= DECKSIZE do begin
        shuffledDeck[shuffledPosition] := deck[oldPosition];
        oldPosition := oldPosition + 1;
        shuffledPosition := shuffledPosition + 2;
    end;
    for oldPosition := 1 to DECKSIZE do begin
        deck[oldPosition] := shuffledDeck[oldPosition];
    end;
end; {Perfect Shuffle}

{
    Initialize the deck with 52 easily-identifiable elements for the
    purposes of testing.
}
procedure Initialize (var deck: DeckType);
var
    k: integer;
begin {Initialize}
    for k := 1 to DECKSIZE do begin
        deck[k] := k;
    end;
end; {Initialize}

{
    Print the deck (this procedure is for test purposes only).
}
procedure Print (deck: DeckType);
var
    k: integer;
begin {Print}
    writeln ('Deck:');
    for k := 1 to DECKSIZE do begin
        write (deck[k]:3);
    end;
    writeln;
```

```
end; {Print}

begin
    Initialize (deck);
    for k := 1 to NUMSHUFFLES do begin
        PerfectShuffle (deck);
        Print (deck);
    end;
end.
```

SelectionShuffle and Accompanying Subprograms

```
{
    Return true exactly when card is equal to one of the first deckSize
    elements of deck.
}
function Search (card: CardType;
                var deck: DeckType; deckSize: integer): boolean;
var
    k: integer;
begin {Search}
    if deckSize = 0 then begin
        Search := false;
    end else begin
        k := 1;
        while (k < deckSize) and (card <> deck[k]) do begin
            k := k + 1;
        end;
        Search := card = deck[k];
    end;
end; {Search}

{
    Return a randomly chosen deck position (a number between 1 and
    DECKSIZE, inclusive.
}
function RandomDeckPos: integer;
begin {Random Deck Position}
    RandomDeckPos := (abs(RandomInt) mod DECKSIZE) + 1;
end; {Random Deck Position}

{
    Shuffle the deck by selection as described in the commentary.
}
procedure SelectionShuffle (var deck: DeckType);
var
    k, numChosen: integer;
    shuffledDeck: DeckType;
begin
    numChosen := 0;
    while numChosen < DECKSIZE do begin
        k := RandomDeckPos;
```

```
                   if not Search(deck[k], shuffledDeck, numChosen) then begin
                       numChosen := numChosen + 1;
                       shuffledDeck[numChosen] := deck[k];
                   end;
               end;
               for k := 1 to DECKSIZE do begin
                   deck[k] := shuffledDeck[k];
               end;
           end;
```

EfficientSelectionShuffle and the Modified RandomDeckPos

```
{
    Return a randomly chosen position in a segment of the deck (a random
    integer between 1 and n, inclusive).
}
function RandomDeckPos (n: integer): integer;
begin {Random Deck Position}
    RandomDeckPos := (abs(RandomInt) mod n) + 1;
end; {Random Deck Position}

procedure EfficientSelectionShuffle (var deck: DeckType);
var
    k, shuffledPos: integer;
    shuffledDeck: DeckType;
begin {Efficient Selection Shuffle}
    for shuffledPos := 1 to DECKSIZE do begin
        k := RandomDeckPos (DECKSIZE-shuffledPos+1);
        shuffledDeck[shuffledPos] := deck[k];
        deck[k] := deck[DECKSIZE-shuffledPos+1];
    end;
    for k := 1 to DECKSIZE do begin
        deck[k] := shuffledDeck[k];
    end;
end; {Efficient Selection Shuffle}
```

CHAPTER 11

Roman Calculator
Repair

Day and Night. © 1938 M.C. Escher/Cordon Art-Baarn-Holland.

How do you know that a program works? Julius Caesar Enterprises has constructed a program they claim will convert Roman numerals to their decimal equivalents. See if it works, fix it if it fails, and submit a bill for consultant services.

Problem Statement

A programmer brings you the first program in the Pascal Code section and claims that it is a solution to the problem described in *Roman Calculator Construction*. The programmer also shows you the program's output for a number of test cases:

```
Roman numeral?  I
1
Roman numeral?  IX
9
Roman numeral?  X
10
Roman numeral?  XI
11
Roman numeral?  XII
12
Roman numeral?  XIV
14
Roman numeral?  XL
40
Roman numeral?  XLIX
49
Roman numeral?  CMXCVII
997
Roman numeral?  MCMXCIX
1999
```

Determine whether the program solves the problem. If it solves the problem, provide a complete set of test data. If it does not solve the problem point out the program's bugs to the programmer so she can fix them.

Analysis 11.1 Review the rules for Roman numbers given in *Roman Calculator Construction*. Show that the new program performs correctly for all the test cases in the problem statement.

Testing 11.2 Suppose another student in the class said, "Of course the program works: it gives the correct answers for lots of test cases. I am happy when my program works for one case." Explain why you agree or disagree.

Testing 11.3   Are the test cases in the problem statement sufficient to determine whether the program performs correctly? Why or why not

Preparation

This case study introduces the use of recursion. No previous introduction to recursion is necessary.

Understanding the Program

How does one start to evaluate this program?

One way to try to get more information about the program is to run it, trying more test cases to see what answers they produce. Quite a few test cases have already been tried, and any new ones we would devise at this point would be mere "stabs in the dark." In order to get a better idea of how to test the program, we examine its code. Testing by itself can never completely show that a program works, so we must examine the code to convince ourselves of its correctness.

We focus on the program's flow of control. To understand the flow of control, we read the program from back to front, as we did in *The Calendar Shop*.

Stop & Help ➤   *What other aspects of the program might be interesting to examine besides its flow of control?*

What does the main program do?

The main program looks like a typical "driver" program. It loops forever, apparently reading a Roman numeral, somehow converting it to a decimal, and printing it out. We guess that ReadInRoman does both the reading and the conversion (since there is nothing else in the main program that can do this), and that it reads one Roman numeral per line (just like readln). We check the output supplied by the programmer to verify our hunch.

Stop & Help ➤   *Compare this main program to the one in* Roman Calculator Construction.

What does ReadInRoman do?

Moving to ReadInRoman, we note that it has a var parameter, valToReturn, in which it is probably returning a value. It prints a prompt, then waits for input (the eoln check does this). If an empty line is typed, the value to return is 0. Otherwise, ReadInRoman calls ReadRoman. We conclude that ReadRoman will fill valToReturn with the decimal value of the Roman numeral typed by the user.

Stop & Help ➤   *Compare* ReadInRoman *to the input code in* Roman Calculator Construction.

What does ReadRoman do?   Next we look at ReadRoman. It reads a character into romanDigit, a variable declared locally. It stores the character's decimal equivalent—computed by Translation—into romanInt. It then checks to see if all the characters in the line have been read. This is the base case of a recursive procedure. If all the characters in the line have been read—if eoln is true—it assigns romanDigit's decimal equivalent to valToReturn and returns. Otherwise, it calls itself and tests the returned value. This is a recursive routine.

Things are getting complicated!

Stop & Predict ➤   *How do programmers figure out what recursive procedures do?*

Can we trace this routine?   It often makes sense to "play computer" and trace the action of complicated procedures to understand them, so we try that with ReadRoman. Playing computer on a recursive procedure, however, involves a lot of bookkeeping.

What is special about tracing recursive subprograms?   To execute a recursive routine, the program must keep track of where to return. It must also save values of local variables and value parameters and restore those values when it returns. This is all much easier to do by computer than by hand.

Stop & Predict ➤   *What values are best for tracing recursive solutions?*

We trace recursive routines with the simplest arguments that will give us useful information. By "useful information," we mean information that results in being able to *predict* how the procedure will behave without having to consult the code.

In a recursive routine, though, this involves predicting what the routine will do *while trying to understand it*, since a recursive routine calls itself. A good way to trace recursive procedures is to start with a small case and then try a slightly larger case that involves the case already tested. We do this until we notice the pattern of the computation and are able to predict the result of the recursion without looking up the results of previous tests.

What values should be used to trace ReadRoman?   We plan to trace a series of progressively more complex cases to understand ReadRoman.

- First, we'll try a bunch of small examples—the base cases of the recursion—where we can keep track of the results.

- Second, we'll try some slightly larger examples. For the recursive call we plan to look up the result in the small examples we already tried.

- Third, we'll keep trying larger and larger examples, always building on the simpler ones, until it is clear how ReadRoman works.

Stop & Help ➤	*Explain why these steps are necessary to figure out whether the program works for large examples.*
How does ReadRoman work on one-digit Roman numerals?	The smallest cases are one-digit Roman numerals. We start with X and follow the steps:

First we read X into romanDigit.
Then we find the decimal value of X by calling Translation, and we store the result—10—into romanInt.
We've reached the end of the line, so we copy romanInt's value into val-ToReturn and return.

What does the trace reveal?	The value returned and printed is correct. We note that the processing for any single-digit Roman numeral is identical except for the value returned by Translation. Translation looks correct, so we conclude that ReadRoman will work correctly for any single-digit Roman numeral. We note also that the programmer's test data included two single-digit numerals, and the results were correct.
Stop & Help ➤	*Trace the action for V.*
How does ReadRoman work on two-digit Roman numerals?	Now we try a Roman numeral with two digits. We choose XI. Playing computer, we proceed as follows:

We read X into romanDigit.
We find the decimal value of X by calling Translation, and we store the result—10—into romanInt.
We're not at the end of the line yet, so we call ReadRoman recursively.
    We read I into a new copy of romanDigit.
    We store the decimal value of I, 1, into a new copy of romanInt.
    We are at the end of the line, so we copy 1 into valToReturn and return.
Back in the first ReadRoman, we compare its romanInt value, 10, with the value in valToReturn, 1.
romanInt's value is larger, so we add 10 to valToReturn and return.

As the test output confirms, valToReturn now correctly contains 11.

Stop & Help ➤	*Trace VI, another two-digit Roman numeral.*
How does formatting help with tracing a recursive routine?	Note the indenting of the trace at each recursive call. Indenting the trace in this way helps us keep track of where to return from the recursive call.
What other aspects of the program can be tested with two-digit Roman numerals?	The first two-digit number involved addition. Now we try a test case that involves subtraction, IX:

We read I into romanDigit.
We store 1, the decimal value of I, into romanInt.
We're not at the end of the line yet, so we call ReadRoman recursively.
    We read X into a new copy of romanDigit.

We store the decimal value of X, 10, into a new copy of romanInt.

We are at the end of the line, so we copy 10 into valToReturn and return.

Back in the first ReadRoman, we compare its romanInt value, 1, with the value in valToReturn, 10.

romanInt's value is smaller, so we subtract 1 from valToReturn and return.

As expected from the test output, valToReturn now contains 9, the correct value. The differences between IX, XI, and other two-digit Roman numerals again occur only in Translation, so we conclude that ReadRoman works for two-digit Roman numerals.

Stop & Help ➤   *Trace the action for IV to be sure it works.*

How does ReadRoman **work on three-digit Roman numerals?**

To make sure we have a good idea of the action in ReadRoman, we trace it on a three-digit Roman numeral. Again we choose a value that has already been tested so that we can check our work against the data the programmer has provided. XIV seems as if it would be a good test case, since it involves both addition and subtraction of intermediate values. The value we expect is 14. Here's the trace.

We read X into romanDigit.

We store its decimal value, 10, into romanInt.

We're not at the end of the line yet, so we call ReadRoman recursively.

> We read I into a new copy of romanDigit.
>
> We store its decimal value, 1, into a new copy of romanInt.
>
> We are still not at the end of the line, so we call ReadRoman recursively.
>
> > We read V into a third copy of romanDigit.
> >
> > We store 5 into a third copy of romanInt.
> >
> > We are at the end of the line, so we copy 5 into valToReturn and return.
>
> Back in the second ReadRoman, we compare its romanInt value, 1, with the value in valToReturn, 5.
>
> romanInt's value is smaller, so we subtract it from valToReturn (leaving 4) and return.

Back in the first ReadRoman, we compare its romanInt value, 10, with the value in valToReturn, 4.

romanInt's value is larger, so we add 10 to valToReturn and return.

As we expected, valToReturn now contains 14.

Stop & Help ➤   *Trace* ReadRoman *on another three-digit value.*

What does tracing ReadRoman **reveal?**

We now have a good idea of how ReadRoman works. It collects the Roman digits as it proceeds through the recursion. Once it has collected them all (and reached the end of the input line), it accumulates the decimal translation by adding or subtracting the various digit values.

What template does
ReadRoman use?

The action of ReadRoman resembles an example commonly used in text-books to introduce recursion, that of printing an input line backward:

```
procedure WriteBackward;
var
    ch: char;
begin
    if not eoln then begin
        read (ch);
        WriteBackward;
        write (ch);
    end;
end;
```

The example above is the simplest form of recursion that's not a **tail recursion**, that is, that involves some processing after returning from the recursive call. The trace pattern of WriteBackward is

```
read
    read
        read

            ⋮

        write
    write
write
```

ReadRoman is more complicated. Its trace pattern is

```
read
    read
        read

            ⋮

        compute
    compute
compute
```

as the analysis revealed.

Stop & Predict ➤

Suppose there were no more characters in the input line when ReadRoman *was called. What would happen?*

Can ReadRoman ever run off the
end of the input line?

Another difference between WriteBackward and ReadRoman is that WriteBackward checks for end of line before it reads a character, and ReadRoman does not. Can this cause a problem?

To find out, we assume that ReadRoman is somehow entered with no more characters to read in the input line, that is, with eoln true. Now we work backward to see how ReadRoman could have been called in such a state. There are two calls to ReadRoman, one in ReadRoman itself (the recursive call) and the other in ReadInRoman. Examining these two calls, we find that both are preceded by a call to eoln. These are executed only where eoln returns false. Thus ReadRoman cannot be called at the end of the line.

∎

Analysis 11.4 What would happen if an illegal Roman digit were entered as input to ReadRoman?

Modification 11.5 Modify the first version of the program so that it detects an illegal Roman digit. If an illegal digit is detected the program should print a message and exit.

Analysis 11.6 Explain why ReadRoman is not a tail-recursive program.

Reflection 11.7 Suppose a classmate said, "Why are we solving this problem again? We already have a solution." Explain why you agree or disagree.

Modification 11.8 Add output statements to the program to enable it to produce trace output automatically.

Reflection 11.9 Describe how tracing a recursive program helps one understand how it works.

Reflection 11.10 Describe what information is provided by tracing a recursive program that is not provided merely by running it on sample data.

Testing the Program

We consider doing more analysis of the program by hand or running additional test cases. Looking over the test cases supplied by the programmer, we decide to run the program to try a few of our own.

Stop & Predict ➤ *What other test cases should be tried?*

What additional tests are needed? *Roman Calculator Construction* and *Is It Legal?* identify criteria for choosing test data. These include single Roman digits, combinations of Roman digits without prefixes, and data containing one or more prefixes, in particular, a case that starts with a prefix. The test cases provided by the programmer include most of these, but there are a few holes.

Additonal tests yield the following (annotated) output:

```
Roman numeral?  C              trying another simple case
100

Roman numeral?  CLX            more simple cases
160

Roman numeral?  CLXX           double digit
170
```

```
Roman numeral?   CXL           prefix without a following digit
140
Roman numeral?   CXLI          prefix with a following digit
141
Roman numeral?   CLXXI         interior double digit
151
```

A wrong answer! Let's look for some more.

```
Roman numeral?   XXI           what part of CLXXI caused the problem?
1
```

Another wrong answer! Let's try a value with a triple digit.

```
Roman numeral?   III           simplest triple digit value
1
```

When do double digits fail? XXI caused an error, but XII didn't. Let's try some more.

```
Roman numeral?   X             just making sure
10
Roman numeral?   XX            double digit alone
10
Roman numeral?   XXI           double digit preceding a digit; wrong answer!
1
Roman numeral?   XXX           another triple digit; another wrong answer!
10
```

We're onto something here. The problem may involve interior sequences of Roman digits. Let's go back to ReadRoman and test III by hand.

We read I into romanDigit.
We store 1 into romanInt.
We're not at the end of the line yet, so we call ReadRoman recursively.
    We read I into a new copy of romanDigit.
    We store 1 into a new copy of romanInt.
    We're not at the end of the line yet; we call ReadRoman recursively.
        We read I into a new copy of romanDigit and store 1 into a new copy of romanInt.
        We are at the end of the line, so we copy 1 into valToReturn and return.
    Back in the second ReadRoman, we compare its romanInt value, 1, with the value in valToReturn, 1.
    romanInt's value is the same (not smaller), so we add 1 to valToReturn and return.
valToReturn now contains 2.
Back in the first ReadRoman, we compare its romanInt value, 1, with the value in valToReturn.
romanInt's value is smaller, so we subtract 1 from valToReturn and return.

Aha! valToReturn contains 1, not 3.

Stop & Predict ➤   *Describe the problem.*

What went wrong?   The last subtraction should have been an addition; that is, romanInt should have been added to valToReturn rather than subtracted from it. Checking the code to find the reason for the subtraction, we find that the comparison was incorrect. Instead of comparing the current digit's value with the following digit's value, the program compared it with the *accumulated value* returned for the rest of the input.

How can the bug be fixed?   The program really needs two pieces of information from the recursive call, not just one. The first is the accumulated value of the Roman numeral; that's what ReadRoman is currently passing back. The other is the digit immediately to the right of the digit currently being examined (or perhaps its value—either would work), in order to make the correct comparison to decide whether to add or subtract the current digit from the total.

Analysis   11.11 Prepare a written description of the bug for the person who wrote this version of ReadRoman. Include at least three examples.

Analysis   11.12 Explain why programmers generate a set of test cases in advance of writing the code.

🖫 *Analysis*   11.13 If your Pascal environment includes a debugger that allows you to interrupt a program at a designated point, describe good places at which this program could be interrupted to help debug it.

Reflection, Analysis   11.14 Explain why the accumulation bug probably got into the code.

🖳 🖫 *Modification*   11.15 Modify the current version of ReadRoman so that it detects illegal sequences of the same Roman digit such as VV, XXXX, etc. The program should print a message and ask for another Roman numeral to convert if an illegal sequence is detected.

A Possible Fix

The programmer responds to the bug description, suggesting a fix with the rewritten routines that appear in the Pascal Code section.

Stop & Predict ➤   *Examine this code. Keep a list of the questions you have and the problems you note.*

What are the differences between the new version and the previous version?   First we examine the differences between this and the original version. ReadRoman has an extra parameter, lastRoman, of type char. Addition of this parameter is the only change to ReadInRoman. The value of lastRoman is set when eoln is true following the read, and it is passed as a parameter in the recursive call to ReadRoman. The comparison between romanInt and valToReturn is replaced by a comparison between romanInt and Translation(lastRoman).

Do the differences address the bug found in the first version?

It appears that lastRoman holds the digit immediately to the right of the digit currently being examined. If so, the programmer has fixed the problem found in the previous version.

Does the program handle all previously tested cases?

We run all the previously tested cases and find that the program handles them correctly. The annotated output:

```
Roman numeral? CLXXI          buggy cases from version 1;
171
Roman numeral? XXI
21
Roman numeral? III
3
Roman numeral? XXX
30
Roman numeral? X             simple case
10
Roman numeral? XVI           simple addition
16
Roman numeral? XVII          double digit at the end of the numeral
17
Roman numeral? XVIII         triple digit at the end of the numeral
18
Roman numeral? XIV           prefix with nothing following it
14
Roman numeral? CXL           another one
140
Roman numeral? XC            an even easier one
90
Roman numeral? CLXXXI        interior triple digit
181
Roman numeral? CCCXXX        two triple digits
330
Roman numeral? CCCXXXVI      two interior triple digits, no prefix
336
Roman numeral? CCCXXXIV      two interior triple digits with a prefix
334
Roman numeral? CCCXXXVIII    three triple digits
338
```

Stop & Predict ➤ *What tests are still needed?*

How should the revised code be analyzed?

Since the revision to the program is the addition of the lastRoman parameter, it makes sense to analyze how the new parameter works.

We assume, because of its name, that lastRoman is the Roman digit immediately to the right of the digit currently being examined. When lastRoman is the last digit in the line and the eoln test succeeds, it gets passed back. That is correct. So far, so good. Also, romanInt gets compared to the translated value of lastRoman. This is the test missing from the previous version of the program.

One thing appears a bit odd. We note that lastRoman is not set when the program is *not* at the end of the line.

Stop & Consider ➤   *Compare your examination of this program with that of the experts. What are the differences?*

What does a trace reveal?   We now trace the new ReadRoman, focusing in particular on lastRoman. We use a Roman numeral that was handled incorrectly before: LXXX.

Stop & Predict ➤   *Is LXXX a good choice for tracing? Why or why not?*

We read L into romanDigit and store 50 into romanInt.
We're not at the end of the line yet, so we call ReadRoman recursively.
    We read X into a new copy of romanDigit and store 10 into a new copy of romanInt.
    We're not at the end of the line yet, so we call ReadRoman recursively.
        We read X into a new copy of romanDigit and store 10 into a new copy of romanInt.
        We're not at the end of the line yet, so we call ReadRoman recursively.
            We read X into a new copy of romanDigit and store 10 into a new copy of romanInt.
            We are at the end of the line, so we store X into lastRoman and 10 into valToReturn and return.
        Back in the third ReadRoman, we compare its romanInt value, 10, with the decimal value for lastRoman, 10.
        romanInt's value is the same (that is, not smaller), so we add 10 to valToReturn (giving 20) and return.
    Back in the second ReadRoman, we compare its romanInt value, 10, with the decimal value for lastRoman, 10.
    romanInt's value is the same (that is, not smaller), so we add 10 to valToReturn (giving 30) and return.
Back in the first ReadRoman, we compare its romanInt value, 50, with the decimal value for lastRoman, 10.
romanInt's value is larger, so we add 50 to valToReturn and return.

What does the trace of ReadRoman reveal?   For LXXX, the new ReadRoman computed the correct decimal value. The X, the last Roman digit, got passed back in lastRoman *all the way* to the beginning of the recursion. This leads us to wonder about prefixes that don't involve the last Roman digit.

Stop & Predict ➤   *Devise test cases with prefixes applied to some Roman digit other than the last one.*

What are the test results?   The tests reveal a problem:

```
Roman numeral?  CXL              one prefix
140

Roman numeral?  CXLIV            two prefixes; wrong answer!
164

Roman numeral?  XLIV             simpler version; also wrong!
64
```

What happens with a trace of XLIV?

We trace ReadRoman on XLIV.

We read X into romanDigit and store 10 into romanInt.
We're not at the end of the line yet, so we call ReadRoman recursively.
> We read L into a new copy of romanDigit and store 50 into a new copy of romanInt.
> We're not at the end of the line yet, so we call ReadRoman recursively.
>> We read I into a new copy of romanDigit and store 1 into a new copy of romanInt.
>> We're not at the end of the line yet, so we call ReadRoman recursively.
>>> We read V into a new copy of romanDigit and store 5 into a new copy of romanInt.
>>> We are at the end of the line, so we store V into lastRoman and 5 into valToReturn and return.
>> Back in the third ReadRoman, we compare its romanInt value, 1, with the decimal value for lastRoman, 5.
>> romanInt's value is smaller, so we subtract 1 from valToReturn (giving 4) and return. So far, so good.
> Back in the second ReadRoman, we compare its romanInt value, 50, with the decimal value for lastRoman, 5.
> romanInt's value is greater, so we add 50 to valToReturn (giving 54) and return.

Back in the first ReadRoman, we compare its romanInt value, 10, with the decimal value for lastRoman, 5.
romanInt's value is larger, so we add 10 to valToReturn and return.

What does the trace reveal?   The last step of the trace displays a bug: romanInt should have been compared with 50 (the decimal value for L), not 5. It appears that for any Roman numeral whose digits have the pattern

low1 high1 low2 high2

the program ends up comparing low1 with high2 rather than with high1.

COMMENTARY | **COMMENTARY**

What fix is needed? We were correct in asking why lastRoman was not set in all cases. Now we know that lastRoman needs to be updated in the code executed when eoln is false. The fix appears in boldface in this rewritten version of ReadRoman:

```
procedure ReadRoman (var valToReturn: integer; var lastRoman: char);
var
    romanDigit: char;
    romanInt: integer;
begin
    read (romanDigit);
    romanInt := Translation (romanDigit);
    if eoln then begin
        lastRoman := romanDigit;
        valToReturn := romanInt;
    end else begin
        ReadRoman (valToReturn, lastRoman);
        if romanInt < Translation (lastRoman) then begin
            valToReturn := valToReturn - romanInt;
        end else begin
            valToReturn := valToReturn + romanInt;
        end;
        lastRoman := romanDigit;
    end;
end;
```

Testing 11.16 What shorter Roman numeral would have demonstrated the bug in ReadRoman? Explain why.

Testing 11.17 Test the revised version of ReadRoman with all the test cases devised so far. Show your results. Why is it necessary to retest the program with cases that worked in the past?

Modification 11.18 Add output statements to the program to enable it to produce trace output automatically.

Testing 11.19 Summarize the categories of test cases used to test ReadRoman. Explain why the case that revealed the bug was missing.

Debugging 11.20 Create a complete list of categories of test cases for ReadRoman. Give examples of each. Explain why the list is complete.

Reflection 11.21 Even with this complete list of test cases, could the program still have an undetected bug? Why or why not?

Analysis 11.22 If your Pascal environment includes a debugger that allows you to interrupt a program at a designated point, describe good places at which this program could be interrupted to help debug it.

Analysis 11.23 What are the preconditions for the corrected version of ReadRoman?

Outline of Design and Development Questions

These questions summarize the main points of the commentary.

Understanding the Program

How does one start to evaluate this program?

What does the main program do?

What does ReadInRoman do?

What does ReadRoman do?

    Can we trace this routine?

    What is special about tracing recursive subprograms?

    What values should be used to trace ReadRoman?

    How does ReadRoman work on one-digit Roman numerals?

        What does the trace reveal?

    How does ReadRoman work on two-digit Roman numerals?

    How does formatting help with tracing a recursive routine?

    What other aspects of the program can be tested with two-digit Roman numerals?

    How does ReadRoman work on three-digit Roman numerals?

    What does tracing ReadRoman reveal?

    What template does ReadRoman use?

    Can ReadRoman ever run off the end of the input line?

Testing the Program

What additional tests are needed?

What went wrong?

How can the bug be fixed?

A Possible Fix

What are the differences between the new version and the previous version?

    Do the differences address the bug found in the first version?

    Does the program handle all previously tested cases?

How should the revised code be analyzed?

    What does a trace reveal?

    What does the trace of ReadRoman reveal?

    What are the test results?

    What happens with a trace of XLIV?

    What does the trace reveal?

What fix is needed?

Programmers' Summary

This case study discusses the analysis and testing of two solutions to the *Roman Calculator Construction* problem. Each solution includes a recursive procedure ReadRoman that reads Roman digits as it proceeds down the recursion, and that builds up the corresponding decimal value as it returns. The commentary illustrates several of the programming principles.

Analysis of the first program follows the Divide and Conquer principle. As in *The Calendar Shop*, the program is analyzed by moving from the "big picture" to the details. In contrast, when analyzing the second solution to the problem, this principle suggests focusing on the revisions rather than completely reanalyzing the program.

The Divide and Conquer principle also prescribes an approach to testing. Following this principle, the program is first tested with small cases. When these are successful, testing builds on the results to test with larger and more complex cases that reduce to the smaller cases during program execution. This approach is especially important when analyzing recursive procedures, since the goal is to notice the pattern of the computation and to be able to predict the result of the recursion without looking up the results of previous tests.

In tracing a recursion on paper, we follow the Multiple Representation principle by indenting the information for each recursive call. This representation, which resembles an outline, displays the structure of the recursion.

The Fingerprint, Literacy, and Recycling principles guide inspection of the code. Incorrect handling of end-of-line is a common source of errors, so we look for that in particular. Following the Literacy principle, we make sure that each variable name indicates its purpose correctly. We also look for familiar templates in the code. Errors often result from deviations from these patterns, or from code written without applying templates.

The ReadRoman procedure is based on the "read forward, process backward" pattern of processing. This template is illustrated in many introductory textbooks via the example of reading a line and printing it backward. It is an example of a more general recursive pattern:

```
if base case then
    return values immediately
otherwise
    set things up for the recursive call;
    make the recursive call;
    use the results of the recursive call to construct values to return.
```

Bugs in both programs result from misapplication of this pattern. In the first program, the recursive call does not return enough information to construct a return value properly. In the revision, the recursive case returns two values and the base case (mistakenly) only one.

The bugs in these programs could have been detected if the Persecution Complex principle had been applied properly. The exercises guide the user of the case study to generate a complete set of test cases and to reflect on why it is important to test programs rigorously.

 # Making Sense of *Roman Calculator Repair*

Debugging **11.24** A version of the translation program converts XVI to 21 and XI to 11. What seems to be wrong with the program? List additional test cases and explain why they would help detect the problem.

Debugging **11.25** Which parts of the translation program should be inspected to locate the bug described in the previous question? Explain why.

★ *Modification* **11.26** Modify the translation program so that it prints the value of the Roman numeral in words. For example, V should be printed as "five"; C should be printed as "one hundred".

Debugging **11.27** Introduce a bug into the translation program such that some Roman numerals are translated correctly and others are translated incorrectly. Also construct as convincing a set of test data as you can that contains only values for which the program produces correct results. How many of your fellow programmers can you fool?

Debugging **11.28** What extra opportunities for mutations does a recursive subprogram present, compared to a nonrecursive subprogram?

Application **11.29** Use the "read forward, process backward" template in a program that reads a string of text, replaces any sequences of the same letters with a single letter, and prints it out backward. For example, rooommaaann becomes namor; nnaaammooor becomes roman.

Testing **11.30** Test the revised version of ReadRoman with some illegal Roman numerals. Explain what happens.

Modification **11.31** Modify the translation program so that it detects all illegal Roman numerals and translates legal Roman numerals.

Application **11.32** Modern young Romans are having difficulty learning to interpret Roman numbers. Use the correct version of ReadRoman in a program that asks the user for a Roman numeral, asks for its decimal equivalent, and prints a message saying whether or not the translation was done correctly.

Application 11.33 Use the "read forward, process backward" template in a program that tests the contents of a string to see if it is a palindrome. A palindrome is a string that has the same sequence whether the characters are interpreted forward or backward. For example, "deed," "mom," and "94549" are palindromes.

Linking to Previous Case Studies

Analysis 11.34 Compare the recursive version of Roman numeral translation to the nonrecursive versions in *Roman Calculator Construction*. What are the advantages of a recursive solution?

Application 11.35 Describe how the "read forward, process backward" template could be used to solve the *Space Text* problem. Which solution do you prefer? Explain.

Application 11.36 Describe how the "read forward, process backward" template could be used to shuffle cards. When would this solution be advantageous?

Application 11.37 Implement a recursive version of the linear search algorithm.

Application 11.38 Implement a recursive version of the rule-confirmation approach to checking for Roman numerals.

Program to Solve the *Roman Calculator Construction* Problem

Note that the program has an input routine for testing and that it assumes that the input data will be legal.

```pascal
program RecursiveRoman (input, output);

var
    k: integer;

function Translation (romanDigit: char): integer;
begin
    case romanDigit of
    I:  Translation := 1;
    V:  Translation := 5;
    X:  Translation := 10;
```

```
        L:   Translation := 50;
        C:   Translation := 100;
        D:   Translation := 500;
        M:   Translation := 1000;
        end;
    end;

procedure ReadRoman (var valToReturn: integer);
var
    romanDigit: char;
    romanInt: integer;
begin
    read (romanDigit);
    romanInt := Translation (romanDigit);
    if eoln then begin
        valToReturn := romanInt;
    end else begin
        ReadRoman (valToReturn);
        if romanInt < valToReturn then begin
            valToReturn := valToReturn - romanInt;
        end else begin
            valToReturn := valToReturn + romanInt;
        end;
    end;
end;

procedure ReadlnRoman (var valToReturn: integer);
begin
    write ('Roman numeral?  ');
    if eoln then begin
        valToReturn := 0;
    end else begin
        ReadRoman (valToReturn);
    end;
    readln;
end;

begin
    while true do begin
        ReadlnRoman (k);
        writeln (k);
    end;
end.
```

An Attempt to Fix the Buggy Version

```
procedure ReadRoman (var valToReturn: integer; var lastRoman: char);
var
    romanDigit: char;
    romanInt: integer;
begin
    read (romanDigit);
    romanInt := Translation (romanDigit);
    if eoln then begin
```

```
            lastRoman := romanDigit;
            valToReturn := romanInt;
        end else begin
            ReadRoman (valToReturn, lastRoman);
            if romanInt < Translation (lastRoman) then begin
                valToReturn := valToReturn - romanInt;
            end else begin
                valToReturn := valToReturn + romanInt;
            end;
        end;
    end;
end;

procedure ReadlnRoman (var valToReturn: integer);
var
    lastRoman: char;
begin
    write ('Roman numeral?  ');
    if eoln then begin
        valToReturn := 0;
    end else begin
        ReadRoman (valToReturn, lastRoman);
    end;
    readln;
end;
```

CHAPTER 12

The Eating Club

We used these machines to sort cards when we were students. These machines eat cards. They prefer cards low in fat and calories.

Whole groups of people want to keep track of what they eat and to compare progress. This case study describes extensions to the *You Are What You Eat* and *You Forgot What You Ate* programs to handle a complex food list, multiple users, and several reporting formats. The program should be able to sort foods and entries and do it quickly.

Problem Statement

Terry calls us a couple of weeks after we give him the *You Forgot What You Ate* programs. Here is the conversation:

TERRY: A group of my friends and I have been comparing our progress in controlling our diets. I showed the program to them and they want to use it too. Is that OK?

MIKE AND MARCIA: Probably. What were the reactions of your friends?

TERRY: Well, they were excited. For example, my friend Erin has been looking for a program like this. She has lots of computer experience. She did say that the program is a bit slow. Is that what you mean?

MIKE AND MARCIA: We aren't surprised. Our goal was to put the program together quickly. We could make it more efficient.

TERRY: Well, that would make Erin happy.

MIKE AND MARCIA: Were there other comments?

TERRY: Well, several of us have been competing to see who can bring down their calories and fat intake the most. We'd like to compare our graphs. It would be easier if the graphs were all on the same scale. Is that possible?

MIKE AND MARCIA: That would be straightforward. We'd need to know what scales make sense. Are there different scales for men and women, for example?

TERRY: Maybe the program could just ask us for the maximum and minimum values for the graphs? See, I'm getting the idea of this user interface stuff!

MIKE AND MARCIA: Sounds good. Any other comments?

TERRY: One of my friends is from India. She eats some foods that aren't on the food list. Is there a way to add foods to the list?

MIKE AND MARCIA: That would be possible. What did you have in mind? Would each person have an individual food list or do you want to add the foods that everyone eats to a general list?

TERRY: We'd like to have a general list. Sometimes my friend invites all of us over for dinner so we all need these foods on our lists.

MIKE AND MARCIA: We will work on that. We'll get back to you in a few days.

TERRY: Thanks.

Analysis   12.1   What else should we have asked Terry?

Analysis   12.2   In what other ways might the program be customized or improved? Explain.

Reflection   12.3   How would you look for parts of a program that you could rewrite to be more efficient?

Reflection   12.4   We were somewhat reluctant to distribute our program to a large number of people before we worked on improving its efficiency. Suppose you had quickly put together a program for a friend. What aspects of the program would you have to fix before you would distribute it to a wider audience? Explain.

Analysis   12.5   It appears that Terry's friends will each use *separate* copies of the program and its associated data files. What arrangements should they make to ensure that they have the most up-to-date version of the food file?

Analysis   12.6   If Terry and his friends were intending to use the *same* copy of the program, how would the revisions he requested be different?

Analysis   12.7   Suppose that Terry and one of his friends have the same name for two different foods. For instance, the milk and flavoring combination that people in Massachusetts call a milk shake is a different nutritional story from the milk, flavoring, and ice cream combination that other people in the United States call a milk shake. (People in Massachusetts call the ice cream version a frappe!) How should this problem be handled?

Preparation

The reader should be familiar with files, arrays, and records, as well as the use of recursion.

Improvements to *You Forgot What You Ate*

What changes are desired?

The program would be more useful for Terry and his friends with three main changes. First, it needs to be more efficient. We knew the program wasn't too efficient, but we wanted to get it to work first. Now that the users are excited about it, it makes sense to improve its efficiency.

Second, the program needs to make it easier for users to compare progress. Terry did not mention this before so this is a new specification. We are happy to see that Terry is getting more sophisticated; he even suggested the option of asking the user for the maximum and minimum values for each graph.

Stop & Predict ➤ *What if the users forget the graph values they agreed on?*

We wonder if users will remember what values they all want to use. It would be better to supply some built-in **default** options if the user has no particular values in mind.

Third, the users need to be able to update the food list. We are immediately reminded of the history file editing program. We should be able to use the same approach for updates to the food file.

How are the graphing routines changed?

Fixing the graphs seems easiest, so we do that first. Two steps must be added to the graph printing procedures: one that asks the user for the maximum and minimum values over which the graph will be plotted, and one that computes reasonable values to use if the user doesn't have any specific ones picked out. The actual maximum and minimum data values are the obvious "reasonable" values; after some reflection, we decide to round them up (for the maximum) or down (for the minimum) to the next multiple of 100 to make the graph look nicer.

How are good default graph bounds computed?

Computing the maximum and minimum array values is straightforward. Rounding up or down is somewhat tricky. To compute the next lower multiple of 100, we replace the last two digits with zeroes as follows:

```
nextLower100 := (value div 100) * 100;
```

To compute the next higher multiple of 100, we add 1 to the hundreds place and replace the last two digits with zeroes, unless they are already zero.

```
if value mod 100 = 0 then begin
    nextHigher100 := value;
end else begin
    nextHigher100 := ((value div 100) + 1) * 100;
end;
```

Reading the values from the user can be done in PrintFatGraph and PrintCalorieGraph as follows. First, each can compute the default maximum and minimum values as just described. Then, each can call a ReadInteger procedure with the default value as an argument. If the user types an integer, it's returned; if the user types a blank line—merely hits "return" on the keyboard—the default value is returned and used in the graph.

How is the code tested?

All this code can be added to the program and tested immediately. We can create test files with the history file editor; thorough tests will ensure that both outcomes of the if statement above are exercised.

How can programs be made to run more quickly?

We can speed up a program by identifying and replacing slow operations. For instance, file operations are slow; it typically takes a thousand times longer to read an integer from a disk file than to copy an integer value into a variable. Thus code that reads information from a file into a large array and works on it there will be more efficient than code that reads through the file several times to perform its operations.

Stop & Help ➤ *Roughly how long does it take to read an integer from a disk file on your computer?*

Of course, we can also speed up a program if we reduce the number of operations it has to perform. For instance, the single statement

```
write('A':24);
```

will probably be executed more quickly than the equivalent segment

```
for k := 1 to 23 do begin
    write(BLANK);
end;
write('A');
```

Another example appears in the Equal function in the *You Are What You Eat* program:

```
Equal := true;
for k := 1 to line.length do begin
    if line.chars[k] <> s[k] then begin
        Equal := false;
    end;
end;
```

This could be recoded as a while loop, so that the loop would terminate as soon as a nonmatching character was found:

```
k := 1;
if line.length = 0 then begin
    Equal := true;
end else begin
    while (k < line.length) and (line.chars[k] = s[k]) do begin
        k := k + 1;
    end;
    Equal := line.chars[k] = s[k];
end;
```

Suppose that both line and s are 10 characters long, and the first characters of line and s don't match. Then the first loop would perform 11 comparisons of k with line.length (hidden in the operation of the for loop), 11 increments of k, and 10 comparisons of characters in line with characters in s. The second loop would perform 1 comparison of k with line.length, 1 increment of k, and 2 comparisons of line.chars[1] with s[1].

Stop & Predict ➤   *How many operations are likely to be saved by these revisions to the code?*

What good does rewriting code details do?

Rewriting code details will probably not make much difference in the speed of the program, however. In *You Are What You Eat*, the Equal function is called once for each fat value read, to check for the done sentinel. Eliminating 20 comparisons and 10 increments, each of which probably takes less than a microsecond, saves 30 microseconds—not a savings that Erin would appreciate.

Furthermore, the rewritten code is more complicated and likely to have errors. *Programmer efficiency* is important too.

Thus we target our attention on parts of the program where rewriting code is likely to make a big difference. In the programs for *You Forgot What You Ate*, this means examining areas where large numbers of operations are performed for each user input. Assuming that the data collection program is run much more often than the history editor, we focus on it.

Where in the program will optimizing prove most beneficial?

It will help to review the program's call diagram:

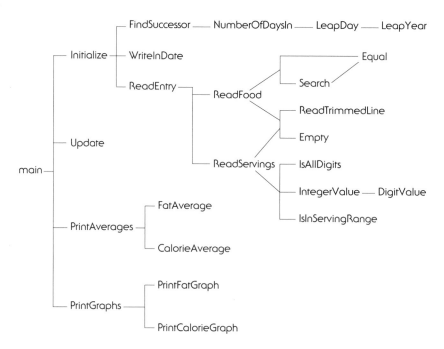

Initialize, Update, PrintAverages, and PrintGraphs are each called exactly once from the main program. FatAverage and CalorieAverage are called just once from PrintAverages, and PrintFatGraph and PrintCalorieGraph are called just once from PrintGraphs. FindSuccessor, WriteInDate, and ReadEntry are called once from Initialize. ReadFood and ReadServings are called once for each entry read from the user.

Equal is called once for each entry, as it was in *You Are What You Eat.* In the revised version in *You Forgot What You Ate,* however, it is also called once for each comparison between the input food and the entries in the food information file. The food file contains entries for roughly 800 foods. Here is a chance to reduce the program running time, since any improvement will be multiplied several hundred times.

We can rewrite Equal, as described above, so that it stops comparing when encountering a character mismatch in its two arguments. This should save some time, since almost all the comparisons will be between strings that differ.

Stop & Help ➤   *Test the program with* Equal *rewritten as described above. Do you notice any difference in the running time?*

Another source of inefficiency is that Search searches the food file for every user entry. It would be better, as mentioned earlier, to read the file once into an array and then search the array instead of the file. The size of the food file can be established in advance, so the bounds of the array will be known. We add an InitFoodInfo procedure to the program, call it from Initialize, and modify Search accordingly. (Changes to parameter lists of other subprograms are also necessary. This could have been avoided by better planning during the initial design of the program.)

Stop & Help ➤   *Test the program with the changes just described. Do you notice any difference in the running time?*

The actual search of the food information is also a good place to increase efficiency. What do humans do to make searches efficient? Consider large directories of entries that people use, like phone books. A person looking up a phone number doesn't search linearly through the phone book, but instead goes to the approximate section of the name list and examines only a few pages.

How can the search for a food name be sped up?

The key to the efficient phone book search is that the names are *alphabetically ordered*. Ordering a list of entries can result in efficient program search as well. Though a program may not be able to go directly to the approximate location of a name as humans do with phone books, a systematic approach called **binary search** can be applied that's almost as effective.

Stop & Consider ➤ *How do humans play the game of "guess my number" efficiently? In this game the guesser can ask questions with yes or no answers, such as "Is the number greater than 100?"*

How does the binary search algorithm work?

The binary search algorithm is used to search for an item in an array of elements. The elements of the array must be ordered so that one can tell when one item is less or greater than another. The algorithm continuously reduces the *range* of elements in which the item can be found. This range is identified by two indices into the array, low (the smallest position at which the item can occur) and high (the largest position at which the item can occur). Thus if low contains 5 and high contains 27, the item being sought can be in positions 5 through 27 of the array but cannot be in positions 1 through 4 or in a position later than 27.

Just as in a number guessing game, the most efficient way to search a range of values is to eliminate half of them with each query. Thus the binary search algorithm repeats the following process.

Find the middle element in the range low ... high.
Compare the item being sought with the middle element.
If it's equal, indicate a successful search, and return the position of the middle element.
If the item is less than the middle element, then it can't be in any of the positions from the middle to the end; thus the high end of the range is moved down to one prior to the middle position.
If the item is greater than the middle element, it can only be in the top half of the range; thus the low end of the range is moved up to one following the middle position.

The process terminates when the item is found or when the range shrinks to nothing, that is, when high is less than low. Figure 12.1 shows how the algorithm proceeds to locate element 350 in an array of 800 elements.

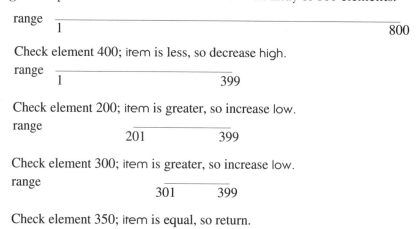

range
1   800

Check element 400; item is less, so decrease high.
range
1   399

Check element 200; item is greater, so increase low.
range
        201   399

Check element 300; item is greater, so increase low.
range
        301   399

Check element 350; item is equal, so return.

Figure 12.1 *Search for element 350 out of 800 using binary search*

Finding the 350th element using a linear search algorithm would have required 349 unsuccessful comparisons; with binary search, it required only four. Since the range of elements to examine is cut in half at each iteration, the largest possible number of comparisons is the number of times one can cut the range in half and still have some left. The mathematical expression for the amount one can cut a range of N elements in half is $\log_2 N$ (the base 2 logarithm of N). For an array of 800 elements, at most 10 comparisons are needed to find any element.

This algorithm can be implemented with a loop or with recursion. The two implementations, one using a loop and the other recursive, appear below.

```
{version using a loop}

procedure Search (line: LineType; var foodInfo: FoodInfoType;
        var foodEntry: FoodEntryType; var found: boolean);
var
    low, high, middle: integer;
begin
    low := 1;
    high := FOODINFOSIZE;
    found := false;
    while not found and (high >= low) do begin
        middle := (low + high) div 2;
        if Equal (line, foodInfo[middle].foodName) then begin
            found := true;
            foodEntry := foodInfo[middle];
        end else if LessThan (line, foodInfo[middle].foodName) then begin
            high := middle - 1;
        end else begin
            low := middle + 1;
        end;
    end;
end;


{recursive version}

procedure SearchHelper (line: LineType; var foodInfo: FoodInfoType;
        var foodEntry: FoodEntryType; var found: boolean;
        low, high: integer);
var
    middle: integer;
begin
    if high < low then begin
        found := false;
    end else begin
        middle := (low + high) div 2;
        if Equal (line, foodInfo[middle].foodName) then begin
            found := true;
            foodEntry := foodInfo[middle];
        end else if LessThan (line, foodInfo[middle].foodName) then begin
            SearchHelper (line, foodInfo, foodEntry, found,
                low, middle-1);
        end else begin
```

```
                        SearchHelper (line, foodInfo, foodEntry, found,
                            middle+1, high);
              end;
          end;
    end;

    procedure RecursiveSearch (line: LineType; var foodInfo: FoodInfoType;
            var foodEntry: FoodEntryType; var found: boolean);
    begin
        SearchHelper (line, foodInfo, foodEntry, found, 1, FOODINFOSIZE);
    end;
```

Both versions use a LessThan function that does not currently exist. The code can be patterned on that of Equal, however.

Stop & Consider ➤   *Which of these solutions is easier to understand?*

How can this algorithm be applied to the food information?

Binary search requires an ordered array. Since food names are to be looked up, the names in the array should be in alphabetical order. The file we provided Terry isn't in order, so we have to **sort** its entries.

We might be tempted to sort the food file every time the program is run, since we plan to allow users to add foods. This would be needless work, however; the code that adds food information can be written to put it in the correct place in the file, maintaining an ordered food file just as the history editor currently maintains an ordered history file. Thus the file needs to be sorted only once, so we'll write a separate program to do that.

How should the food information file be sorted?

There are many ways to sort, and entire books have been written on the subject. We might look up a sorting procedure in one of the books. Alternatively, we can design our own, based on ideas from earlier case studies. *The Shuffler's Dilemma* discussed three approaches to "disordering" cards by shuffling them: selection, exchange, and insertion. All three approaches also form the basis of sorting procedures.

Sorting by selection: Repeatedly choose the smallest value left in the array, remove it from the unsorted array, and add it to the end of the sorted array until no more elements remain in the unsorted array.

Sorting by insertion: Repeatedly take the next value in the unsorted array and insert it in its proper position in the sorted array.

Sorting by exchanging: Repeatedly choose two array elements and exchange them if they are out of order.

We'll consider the first two of these approaches here (leaving the third for consideration in study questions).

How does selection sorting work?

A procedure called SelectionSort may be represented by the following pseudocode:

```
procedure SelectionSort (var unsorted: ArrayType; var sorted: ArrayType);
var
    k: integer;
begin
    for k := 1 to the number of array elements do begin
        find the smallest value remaining in unsorted, remove it, and store it in sorted[k];
    end;
end;
```

The code framework is similar to EfficientSelectionShuffle. It uses the "process every element in an array" template. The difference between this code and EfficientSelectionShuffle is that the elements are processed in a different order.

Finding the smallest value remaining in unsorted will be easier if all the elements of unsorted are stored together. If we ensure that removal of an element compresses the array so that no "holes" are left, we can apply the template for processing all elements of an array:

```
smallestPos := 1;
for j := 2 to the number of elements currently in unsorted do begin
    if unsorted[j] < unsorted[smallestPos] then begin
        smallestPos := j;
    end;
end;
```

Copying the value thus found to sorted is easy:

```
sorted[k] := unsorted[smallestPos];
```

To remove it, we could shift all entries that follow it back one place in the array as was done to compress a Roman numeral in *Is It Legal?* We encountered the same situation in *The Shuffler's Dilemma* and instead filled the gap by moving the last card in the deck to replace it. (Again, we don't care about the order of values in unsorted, since we're sorting them.) This technique requires that we keep track of the number of elements currently in unsorted, and leads to the following code:

```
procedure SelectionSort (var unsorted: ArrayType; var sorted: ArrayType);
var
    k, j, unsortedSize: integer;
begin
    unsortedSize := the number of array elements;
    for k := 1 to the number of array elements do begin
        smallestPos := 1;
        for j := 2 to unsortedSize do begin
            if unsorted[j] < unsorted[smallestPos] then begin
                smallestPos := j;
            end;
        end;
        sorted[k] := unsorted[smallestPos];
        unsorted[smallestPos] := unsorted[unsortedSize];
        unsortedSize := unsortedSize - 1;
    end;
end;
```

How does insertion
sorting work?

A procedure called InsertionSort may be defined with the same arguments used for SelectionSort, namely an unsorted array and a sorted array. In pseudocode, the algorithm is as follows:

```
for k := 1 to the number of array elements do begin
    find the position in sorted where unsorted[k] should go;
    insert it there;
end;
```

In SelectionSort, we maintained a variable called unsortedSize that contained the current length of the unsorted array. Here, we might think it useful to maintain a variable to store the current length of the sorted array. We already have such a variable, however—the loop variable k is keeping track of this. (It's actually 1 larger than the quantity we want.) That allows the following refinement:

```
for k := 1 to the number of array elements do begin
    find the position in the k–1 elements of sorted where unsorted[k] should go;
    insert it there;
end;
```

Finding the position in sorted where unsorted[k] should go is just a search. We just finished a procedure to do an efficient binary search, so it makes sense to try to reuse the code.

How is the position for
insertion determined?

Two small modifications must be made to the iterative Search procedure, namely the addition of the number of elements in the array as a parameter and the use of this parameter in place of the constant FOODLISTSIZE. (The recursive version would not need this modification; to use it, we would just call SearchHelper directly.) Another problem arises, however, when we observe that Search had not previously intended the position argument to make sense in case the search was unsuccessful. Some analysis is necessary to figure out what to return.

Stop & Help ➤ *In the first call to* Search *in the insertion sort loop, the size of the array being searched is 0. Does this cause any problems?*

We start by analyzing a small situation, an array of two elements. We'll assume for simplicity that it's an array of integers containing, say, 2 and 4. There are three cases: the item should be inserted before the first element, between the two elements, or after the last element. Examples are 1, 3, and 5. Let's trace the behavior on each.

Search for 1:
    Set low to 1, high to 2, and middle to 1.
    The item 1 is less than the middle element, so set high to 0, causing the search loop to terminate.

Search for 3:
    Set low to 1, high to 2, and middle to 1.

The item 3 is greater than the middle element, so set low to 2 and middle to 2.

The item 3 is less than the middle element, so set high to 1, causing the search loop to terminate.

Search for 5:

Set low to 1, high to 2, and middle to 1.

The item 5 is greater than the middle element, so set low to 2 and middle to 2.

The item 5 is greater than the middle element, so set low to 3, causing the search loop to terminate.

At the end of the search loop, we have the following values:

item	low	middle	high	Correct insertion position
1	1	1	0	1
3	2	2	1	2
5	3	2	2	3

It appears that in case of an unsuccessful search, the value of low is the position value to return. (One can prove this mathematically.)

Code to insert the value into sorted once we know the position can be copied from the *Space Text* program. The code in the Pascal Code section results.

How is the code tested?
The new code may be tested in several ways. The safest approach is first to write driver programs to test them separately, then to install them individually into the *You Forgot What You Ate* code and test them there.

Testing 12.8 Consider the following variant of the binary search code.

```
while not found and (high >= low) do begin
    middle := (low+high) div 2;
    if Equal (line, foodList[middle].foodName) then begin
        found := true;
        foodEntry := foodList[middle];
    end else if LessThan (line, foodList[middle].foodName)
      then begin
        high := middle ;
    end else begin
        low := middle;
    end;
end;
```

Does it work correctly? If so, explain why. If not, provide an array and an item for which the code works incorrectly.

🖳 🖫 *Analysis* 12.9 Which improvement makes the biggest difference in running time—changing files to arrays, rewriting Equal, or incorporating binary search?

🖳 *Testing* 12.10 Suppose that you decide to incorporate the improvements into the program rather than test them separately first. In which order should they be added?

Analysis 12.11 For what values in a 63-element array containing the integers 1 through 63 does binary search make the most comparisons?

$\sum$ *Analysis* 12.12 What is the maximum number of comparisons made by SelectionSort to sort an array of N elements? What is the minimum number of comparisons it can make?

Analysis 12.13 How many comparisons does InsertionSort make to sort an array that contains the five elements 3, 1, 7, 4, 2 into increasing order?

Reflection 12.14 Explain why the recursive version of the binary search routine may be said to be more "elegant" than the iterative version. State criteria that could define elegance and say why the recursive version meets the criteria.

Improving the History File Editor and Adding a Food File Editor

How should the history file editor be improved?

In the same way an array was used to store the food file information internally, we can also use an array to store the history information while the user works with it. The Initialize procedure can fill the array, and either the main program or the ExecuteQuit procedure can write the information back to the file. We specifically planned for different history representations in the design of the history editor, so the change should be straightforward to implement.

Using an array to represent the history should address two defects of the editor. First, it will allow a user to undo errors. Before the history entries are written back to the file, the user can be asked to verify that the changes made in that editing session should be made permanent. Second, the new representation will speed up editing operations by eliminating the need to go back to the file on the disk.

There are two problems with using arrays. One is that, since all editing operations will be done in memory rather than on the disk file, a program crash will cause all the editing in the session to be lost. The other is inherent in the use of arrays—potentially the user will provide more data than the array has room to store. We make sure to point out these problems to

Terry, and we include messages that warn the user when he or she is approaching the program's storage limits.

What will change in the program?

An examination of the program reveals that little in the program must change and that almost all changes will be limited to the nine subprograms in the history file operations section. First, a type must be defined for internal storage of the history entries; we redefine SequenceType to be an array of EntryType rather than a file. (If this internal structure is to be named history, the history file variable must be renamed. We'll call it historyFile.)

Initialize must be expanded to fill the internal history file from the external file and to warn the user about too much data. A subprogram must be added to write the array entries back to the file, after checking with the user. We'll call this subprogram Terminate and call it in ExecuteQuit in order to be able to continue reading commands if the user doesn't want to update the file.

Changes to Find, Insert, Delete, PrintAll, and PrintUpTo use code we've used already in other case studies. Find can use the binary search code we designed earlier. All we need is functions LessThan and Equal that compare two dates; the program already includes functions AtOrBefore and Same that will suffice for this purpose. We must remember that history entries are stored in *reverse* order; this has already been a source of bugs. Insert and Delete apply templates for inserting and deleting array elements that were introduced in *Space Text* and *Is It Legal?* Insert must in addition include a check that the history structure is not too full. PrintAll and PrintUpTo are virtually identical to each other.

The process of converting the program to use an array is straightforward since the design in *You Forgot What You Ate* anticipated that the history data structures would change. Anticipation of using an array even included passing a position variable as a parameter to data structure access routines. The changes are easier to make than those made to the food file structure, where such changes were not anticipated.

How will the food file editor be designed?

The food file editor will be almost exactly the same as the history file editor. It will allow the same operations: add or delete a food, list foods, help, and quit. Only the details of food input will be different.

Neither program appears in the Pascal Code section. They are left for the reader to complete in study questions.

Modification 12.15 Complete the revisions to the history file editor.

Application 12.16 Which subprograms in the history file editor will not be needed in the food file editor?

⊟ Application   12.17 Which subprograms in the history file editor will need to be modified for inclusion in the food file editor?

⊟ Application   12.18 Which subprograms in the history file editor can be used in the food file editor?

⊠ ⊟ Application   12.19 Implement the food file editor.

⊠ ⊟ Modification   12.20 Implement an undo command with which the user can undo the most recent add, delete, or undo command.

⊠ ⊟ Modification   12.21 Implement a history command that displays the add and delete commands executed in the current editing session on numbered lines, for example as follows:

```
[1] add 9/13/1991
[2] add 9/14/1991
[3] delete 9/15/1991
```

⊠ ⊟ Modification   12.22 Implement an undo command that works together with the history facility from question 12.21. The undo command will take a single argument, the number of the add or delete command to undo. For example, given the example history in question 12.21, the command undo 3 would undo the delete 9/15/1991 command and restore the entry for 9/15/1991 to the history file. The undone command will then be removed from the list displayed by later history commands.

Outline of Design and Development Questions

These questions summarize the main points of the commentary.

Improvements to *You Forgot What You Ate*
What changes are desired?
How are the graphing routines changed?
    How are good default graph bounds computed?
    How is the code tested?
How can programs be made to run more quickly?
    What good does rewriting code details do?
    Where in the program will optimizing prove most beneficial?
    How can the search for a food name be sped up?
        How does the binary search algorithm work?
        How can this algorithm be applied to the food information?

How should the food information file be sorted?
How does selection sorting work?
How does insertion sorting work?
    How is the position for insertion determined?
How is the code tested?

Improving the History File Editor and Adding a Food File Editor
How should the history file editor be improved?
What will change in the program?
How will the food file editor be designed?

Programmers' Summary

This case study discusses three improvements to the collection of programs designed in *You Forgot What You Ate:*

- modification of the code to execute more efficiently

- redesign of the graphs to allow uniform comparison of results from multiple users

- addition of a food file editor

All the modifications are best organized by referring to the program call diagram. The graph redesign is easiest. It consists mainly of applying the "process every element of an array" template to compute the maximum and minimum values for fat and calories; these are used to determine the range of values over which the graph will be plotted, should the user decide not to specify them himself or herself.

In general, there are three ways to make code more efficient. One is to replace references to external files by in-memory processing using arrays, since the time required to read an element from a file is typically 1000 times the amount of time to access an element in an array. Another is to find code that is executed many times and rewrite it more concisely. A third is to replace an inefficient algorithm by an efficient algorithm.

Here, binary search replaces linear search. The binary search algorithm is used with an array whose elements are in order; it is "dividing and conquering" in a different setting. It works by repeatedly dividing the array in half and narrowing the search to one of the halves. The commentary presents both an iterative implementation and a recursive implementation, and it notes the particular importance of testing the code on the end elements of the array.

Before binary search can be used, the array must be sorted. Approaches described in *The Shuffler's Dilemma* to randomize array elements may also be applied to put them in order. The commentary describes sorting by selection and sorting by insertion (the latter also uses the binary search code); other approaches are considered in exercises.

The same approaches are used to improve the efficiency of the history file editor. These modifications are easier since we planned for them in the original design.

Finally, the commentary touches briefly on the design of an editor for the food file. A substantial amount of code from the history file editor can merely be copied for this application.

 ## Making Sense of *The Eating Club*

Analysis, Reflection

12.23 Suppose that you are working with a partner to revise the *You Forgot What You Ate* programs. How would you divide the revisions between you and your partner so that the two of you have roughly equal tasks to perform?

Application

12.24 Write a procedure called Quicksort that implements the **Quicksort** algorithm. It makes use of the divide-and-conquer strategy of binary search as follows. As in binary search, the arguments to Quicksort specify the range of elements within an array that are to be sorted. An element is chosen from the range as a "divider element"—there are several ways to do this, such as choosing the first element or a random element—and the remaining elements in the range are arranged so that all elements less than the divider element precede it and all elements greater than the divider follow it. The diagram below illustrates the result of this process.

elements smaller   divider   elements larger
than the divider   than the divider

Then the elements smaller than the divider are Quicksorted recursively, as are the elements larger than the divider. As in binary search, the base case of the recursion is a range that consists of 0 elements.

Testing

12.25 Run experiments with the Quicksort procedure you wrote for question 12.24 to see how it compares in efficiency to SelectionSort and InsertionSort.

Analysis, Reflection

12.26 How many values should there be in a list before it seems reasonable to implement an efficient search? Explain how such a decision might be made.

Reflection 12.27 Explain how adding an efficient search will help the programmer debug the program and how it will interfere with debugging of the program.

📟 *Application* 12.28 A modification of binary search called **interpolation search** more closely simulates what people do to look up a number in a phone book. It assumes that one can determine the approximate position of an entry in the array by doing some computation; for instance, one might guess that a name starting with S, the 19th letter, would be around 19/26 of the way through the array. Implement a search function based on this approach.

Analysis 12.29 Would the interpolation approach described in question 12.28 be more appropriate for the history file or the food file? Explain.

📟 💾 *Testing* 12.30 Add mutations to the programs designed in this case study, and get a fellow programmer to find them. What bugs are easiest to localize, and what bugs are most difficult? What aspects of the program make it easier or more difficult to find its bugs?

Modification 12.31 Describe a format for the history file that would allow the program to keep track of data for more than one person in the same file.

📟 *Application* 12.32 Write a set of programs to keep track of a checking account. Your programs should allow the user to enter a check (checks are normally written in numerical order), to enter a deposit, to void a check, and to mark that the check has been cashed and returned. The user should also be able to determine the balance in his or her account, and to generate a monthly summary of expenses and deposits.

◾ Linking to Previous Case Studies

💾 *Reflection* 12.33 Suppose we had planned from the start to add an efficient search to the *You Are What You Eat* program. How would the earlier programs have been different?

💾 *Reflection* 12.34 If you had been writing the programs for Erin, an experienced programmer, instead of for Terry, how would the earlier programs have been different?

💾 *Reflection* 12.35 Which templates for manipulating arrays have counterparts in templates for files, and which do not? Explain.

💾 *Analysis* 12.36 Suppose that the argument to the graph-printing procedures were an array of arrays, each element of which represents a separate person's fat and calorie consumption. For example, Terry's fat and calorie data might be the first element of the array, Erin's the second, and so forth. Each person's fat consumption is to be plotted on the *same* graph, using a different symbol; the same should be done for the calorie consumption. Would it be easier to use a line-by-line approach to generate the graph, or the graph-image approach mentioned in question 9.50?

🖫 🖫 *Modification* 12.37 Implement the graph-printing procedure described in question 12.36.

🖫 *Reflection* 12.38 Suppose you didn't have the time to make the modifications suggested by Terry, and a programmer friend of yours volunteered to do so. How would you explain the *You Forgot What You Ate* programs to your friend to provide him or her with sufficient background to make the revisions?

Further Revisions to the *You Are What You Eat* Program

```pascal
type
    FoodInfoType = record
        numFoods: integer;
        foods: array[1..FOODTABLESIZE] of FoodEntryType;
    end;
    FoodInfoFileType = file of FoodEntryType;

{
    Return true exactly when the characters in line match those in s.
}
function Equal (line: LineType; s: StringType): boolean;
var
    k: integer; match: boolean;
begin
    k := 1;
    match := true;
    if line.length > 0 then begin {see if nonblank characters in s match}
        while (k < line.length) and (line.chars[k] = s[k]) do begin
            k := k + 1;
        end;
        match := line.chars[k] = s[k];
    end;
    k := line.length + 1;
    while match and (k <= MAXSTRLEN) do begin
        if s[k] <> BLANK then begin
            match := false;
        end else begin
            k := k + 1;
```

```
                    end;
                end;
            Equal := match;
        end;

        {
            Return true exactly when the characters in line represent a word that
            alphabetically precedes the word represented by the characters in s.
        }
        function LessThan (line: LineType; s: StringType): boolean;
        var
            k: integer; match: boolean;
        begin
            k := 1;
            match := true;
            if line.length > 0 then begin {see if nonblank characters in s match}
                while (k < line.length) and (line.chars[k] = s[k]) do begin
                    k := k + 1;
                end;
                match := line.chars[k] = s[k];
            end;
            {   Possible reasons for loop termination:
                1. line ran out (match is true);
                2. some character in line doesn't match some character in s
                    (match is false).}
            if not match then begin
                LessThan := line.chars[k] < s[k];
            end else begin
                k := line.length + 1;
                while match and (k <= MAXSTRLEN) do begin
                    if s[k] <> BLANK then begin
                        match := false;
                    end else begin
                        k := k + 1;
                    end;
                end;
                LessThan := not match;
            end;
        end;

        {
            Search for an entry in elements low through high of foodInfo whose name
            matches the name in line. If the search is successful, return the entry
            in foodEntry and return true in found. If the search is unsuccessful,
            return false in found.
        }
        procedure SearchHelper (line: LineType; var foodInfo: FoodInfoType;
            var foodEntry: FoodEntryType; var found: boolean; low, high: integer);
        var
            middle: integer;
        begin
            if high < low then begin
                found := false;
            end else begin
                middle := (low + high) div 2;
                if Equal(line, foodInfo.foods[middle].foodName) then begin
```

```
                            found := true;
                            foodEntry := foodInfo.foods[middle];
                        end else if LessThan(line, foodInfo.foods[middle].foodName)
                          then begin
                            SearchHelper(line, foodInfo, foodEntry, found,low, middle-1);
                        end else begin
                            SearchHelper(line, foodInfo, foodEntry,found,middle+1, high);
                        end;
                end;
        end;


        {
            Search for an entry in foodInfo whose name matches the name in line.
            If the search is successful, return the entry in foodEntry and return
            true in found. If the search is unsuccessful, return false in found.
        }
        procedure Search (line: LineType; var foodInfo: FoodInfoType;
            var foodEntry: FoodEntryType; var found: boolean);
        begin
            SearchHelper(line, foodInfo, foodEntry, found, 1, foodInfo.numFoods);
        end;


        {
            Fill recentHistory from the history file, and foodInfo from the food
            information file.
        }
        procedure Initialize (var historyFile: HistoryFileType;
            var recentHistory: HistoryType; var foodInfo: FoodInfoType);
        var
            numEntries, dayNum: integer; entry: EntryType; today: DateType;
        begin
            reset(foodInfoFile);
            foodInfo.numFoods := 0;
            while not eof(foodInfoFile) do begin
                foodInfo.numFoods := foodInfo.numFoods + 1;
                read(foodInfoFile, foodInfo.foods[foodInfo.numFoods]);
            end;
            reset(historyFile);
            numEntries := 0;
            for dayNum := 1 to HISTORYSIZE do begin
                if not eof(historyFile) then begin
                    read(historyFile, recentHistory[dayNum]);
                end;
            end;
            FindSuccessor(recentHistory[1].date, today);
            write('The food data you are about to enter is assumed to be for ');
            WritelnDate(today);
            writeln('Quit this program and run the history file editor ',
                'if this is incorrect.');
            if DEBUGGING then begin
                reset(testFile);
                ReadEntry(testFile, foodInfo, today, recentHistory[0]);
            end else begin
                ReadEntry(input, foodInfo, today, recentHistory[0]);
            end;
        end;
```

Glossary

actual parameter Value or variable passed to a subprogram. Also called **argument**.

algorithm Solution outline that can be straightforwardly translated into a Pascal program. (See **pseudocode**.)

argument **Actual parameter**.

arithmetic expression Combination of arithmetic operators and integer or real variables, constants, or function calls that evaluates to an integer or real result.

base case Ending condition for a recursive process, involving an argument value for which the recursion can return a result without a recursive call.

binary search Efficient way to locate an element in an array whose elements are **sorted**. The binary search algorithm involves a **loop** or **recursion** in which the range of elements in which the item can be found is repeatedly reduced by half.

black-box testing Testing method that regards the program as a "black box" whose interior—the program code—is invisible. Black-box test data are derived only from the problem specification. (See **typical values**; **extreme values**; **boundary values**; **illegal values**; **glass-box testing**.)

boolean expression Combination of comparisons, the operators and, or, and not, and boolean variables, constants, or function calls that evaluates to either true or false. Also called **condition**.

bottom-up Describes an activity that proceeds from the bottom to the top. In reference to a **call diagram** for a program, bottom-up means from the lowest-level subprograms—those at the bottom of the call diagram—to the highest-level subprograms.

boundary values Values at or near the boundaries, or ends, of a given range. Also called **extreme values**. (See also **typical values**; **illegal values**; **testing**; **black-box testing**.)

bug Aspect of a program that causes it to perform incorrectly. Bugs can be straightforward syntax errors or subtle errors that are detected only when special conditions arise, such as when a variable has the value of zero.

bulk processing	Technique of storing all values before performing action on them. In this approach, all values are input and then all values are processed. (See also **one-by-one processing**.)
call diagram	Diagram indicating which subprograms in a program call which others. The names of subprograms appear as nodes in the diagram; a line (sometimes with an arrowhead to show direction) leads from one node to another when the subprogram represented by the first node calls the subprogram represented by the second.
command interpreter	Program that repeatedly reads a command from the user and performs a set of actions associated with the command. For example, *You Forgot What You Ate* describes a command interpreter that performs such actions as adding and deleting entries in a file.
condition	See **boolean expression**.
contents	Value that a **variable** contains.
data type	Describes the set of values that a variable may contain and the operations that may be performed on those values. Data types supplied in Pascal are integer, boolean, real, and char (character). Pascal also allows the definition of structured data types—arrays, records, files, and sets—for which the programmer must supply operations.
data structure	Instance of a structured **data type**. A data type is an abstract concept; a data structure refers to actual memory locations in a program.
declaration	Code used to define a **variable**.
decomposition	Activity of breaking down a problem into easier subproblems. (See **design**; **top-down**; **stepwise refinement**; **divide and conquer**.)
default	Value used or action performed when a value or action is not specified by the programmer or user. For example, Pascal environments assume default values for options for translating and executing Pascal programs.
definite iteration	Performance of a series of steps a specified number of times; usually done in Pascal with a for statement. (See also **indefinite iteration**.)
development	**Testing** and **debugging**. (See also **incremental development**.)
divide and conquer	Describes the approach of "dividing" a problem into (presumably easier) subproblems and solving the subproblems in order to "conquer" the problem. The Divide and Conquer principle applies to several aspects of design and development.
driver program	**Main program** used to test one or more subprograms in isolation. (See also **stub**; **incremental development**.)
element	Component value of a **data structure** or a structured **data type**. For example, each value in an array is an element of the array.

external variable	Variable of type file. (See **internal variable**.)
extreme values	Values at the end of a given range. Also referred to as **boundary values**. (See also **typical values**; **illegal values**; **testing**; **black-box testing**.)
field of a record	One of the components of a record.
function body	Statements between the first begin and the last end in a function.
function call	Expression that invokes a function, supplying its **arguments**. (See also **actual parameters**.)
general	Usable in a variety of programs.
glass-box testing	**Testing** method that regards the program as a "glass box" whose interior—the program code—can be seen. One purpose of glass-box testing is to ensure that all statements in a program are tested. Glass-box test data are also designed by examining the loop structure of a program and choosing values that maximize or minimize the number of times the loops are executed. (See **typical values**; **extreme values**; **boundary values**; **illegal values**; **mutation testing**.)
global	Describes, in reference to a subprogram, an identifier whose definition occurs outside the subprogram. (See **local**.)
illegal values	Input to a program that does not fit the program specifications. For example, if a program expects an integer value, a real value would be illegal.
immediate input	Feature of a Pascal environment where a value typed by the user is read and sent to the program before the user types a carriage return.
incremental development	Process of coding a small part of a program, then testing and debugging it before adding another part.
indefinite iteration	Performance of a series of steps until some condition is met; typically implemented in Pascal with a while or repeat statement. (See also **definite iteration**.)
index range	Span of values that an array index may take on. In array declarations the maximum and minimum index values are the limits of the range.
input-output behavior	Association of the action or value returned by a given code segment with the values it is supplied by the user or in parameters. The input-output behavior of a program can be inferred from the problem specification.
instrumenting	Adding code to a program to measure how many operations or statements are executed each time the program is run.
intermediate results	Values computed by a program in the course of solving a problem.
internal variable	Variable of type other than file. Such a variable will correspond to one or more locations in main computer memory. (See **external variable**.)

interpolation search	Elaboration on binary search in which statistical data is used to determine the next search location and the amount to reduce the search range.
invariant condition	Condition that is true at a particular point (usually the beginning or end) of every iteration of a **loop**.
local	Describes, in reference to a subprogram, an identifier whose definition occurs inside the subprogram. (See **global**.)
logical error	Error in a program's "logic," or execution sequence.
loop	Repeated segment of code; so called from the diagram that results from drawing an arrow from each statement in the loop to the statement that is executed immediately following it.
loop body	Set of statements executed during each iteration of a loop.
loop variable	Variable specified in a for statement; a new value is provided for the variable in each iteration of the for loop body.
main program	Part of a program where execution begins.
maximum number of times	Most executions possible for a **loop**.
minimum number of times	Fewest number of times a **loop** can be executed.
modifiability	Feature of a program that makes it easy for programmers to extend or change its behavior.
modular	Describes code that can be added to a program to perform a set of actions without **side effects**.
mutation testing	Way to evaluate a set of test data. When slight changes—"mutations," representing common **bugs**—are introduced into a program, test data should cause the bugs to be displayed.
multiple representations	Alternative ways to communicate the same information. In programming, common representations are code, **pseudocode**, verbal descriptions, and illustrations. To communicate generality, the action of programming **templates** is communicated using multiple representations.
named constant	Identifier defined with the Pascal const facility.
one-by-one processing	Technique of reading and processing one value, then reading and processing another value, and so on. (See **bulk processing**.)
open for input	Refers to a file from which values may be read.
open for output	Refers to a file to which values may be written. In Standard Pascal, a file may not be simultaneously open for input and open for output.
parallelism	Similarity among actions.
postcondition	Condition that must be true immediately after a code segment.

precondition	Condition that must be true immediately before a code sequence in order for the code to work properly.
procedure body	Statements between the first begin and the last end in a procedure.
procedure call	Statement that invokes a procedure, supplying its **arguments**. (See also **actual parameters**.)
prompt	Message from a program that requests input from the user.
pseudocode	Representation of the action of a program in a form that is closer to Pascal than to natural language but more abstract than actual code. In general pseudocode describes each main step in the action on a separate line, using natural language statements for complex actions. In the case studies, the general action of a template typically is first expressed abstractly in pseudocode and then translated into Pascal code.
Quicksort	Efficient algorithm for sorting elements of a list. It partitions the elements into "small values" and "large values," recursively sorts both sets of values, and concatenates the results.
random number generator	Function that when called repeatedly returns a sequence of numbers that appear random.
recursion	Action of a subprogram whose execution results in a call to itself.
recursive case	Condition under which a recursive subprogram calls itself.
refine	Add details to one or more steps in an algorithm.
rule confirmation	Method of error checking in which the process used to construct a given value is repeated. (If the process is successful, the value is legal.)
rule violation	Method of error checking in which various criteria for illegality are applied to a given value.
sentinel value	Value that signals something, usually that no more data are available to be read or processed.
side effect	Change by a subprogram to a variable in the calling program. In general, functions should not have side effects, and procedure side effects should change only the procedure's parameters. Side effects reduce a subprogram's **modularity**.
sort	Organize a list of elements from largest to smallest or smallest to largest.
state	Values of variables and conditions at a particular point in a program; more generally, any situation in a computation.
state diagram	Pictorial representation of all the possible **states** in a computation and **transitions** between them. Nodes in the diagram represent states; lines drawn between nodes represent transitions.

stepwise refinement	Writing an outline of a program and then expanding each step of the outline in turn.
string	One-dimensional array of characters.
stub	Procedure that accomplishes only part of its intended purpose.
subprogram	Procedure or a function.
subprogram library	Collection of subprograms that perform commonly used actions or computations.
symptom-bug association	Linkage between incorrect behavior of a computer program and the **bug** that caused the error. For example, the symptom that calendars for every month start on the same day might be associated with incorrect code for updating the start date.
tail recursion	Recursive process that merely returns after making a recursive call.
template	Reusable abstraction of programming knowledge. A template describes an action such as "input, process, output." It also includes specifics about how the action fits into a plan, likely implementation problems, **bugs** associated with the action, and test data that help detect the bugs.
termination condition	Condition that causes a loop to terminate. (See also **postcondition**.)
test	Run a program with some input and examine the output to see if the program functions properly.
top-down	Describes an activity that proceeds from the top to the bottom. A top-down design proceeds from the least detailed to the most detailed part of the program. This approach is generally preferred because it makes it easy to keep track of the structure of the program and how its parts fit together.
transition	Path between two **states**.
type	Same as **data type**; also, the Pascal construct by which types are defined.
typical value	Value to be expected in the course of program execution, or a value that's not exceptional in any way. (See **extreme** and **boundary value**.)
understandability	Feature of a program that makes it easy for someone other than the program's original author to make sense of it.
value parameter	**Formal parameter** of a **subprogram** that represents a **local** variable whose initial value is that of the corresponding **argument** of the subprogram call. A change to the value parameter has no effect on its argument.
variable	Identifier for a location in memory.
variable parameter	Parameter that renames the corresponding **argument** in the **subprogram** call. The argument must itself be a variable.

Templates introduced or elaborated	Pascal constructs required	Pascal constructs introduced
Prompt, then read	program heading	comment
Input, process, output	variable declaration	integer, real, char types
	writeln procedure	begin and end
	readln procedure	arithmetic operators
		comparison operators
		assignment statement
		write procedure
		read procedure
		ord and chr functions
		if statement

TEMPLATES TEMPLATES

Prompt, Then Read

Description and purpose

This template is used to request and read from the user a value for one or more variables. The action is to print an informative message (a prompt), then call a procedure to do the input. The printing is usually done with write, so that the user will type the value on the same line as the prompt. The reading is usually done with readln or with some other procedure that reads an entire line at a time.

Pseudocode

print a message asking for a given value;
read the value;

Code examples

```
{prompt}
write ('Please type a four-digit identification number: ');
{read}
readln (idNumber);

write ('Please type a four-digit identification number: ');
readln (d1, d2, d3, d4);
```

In *Check That Number!* the "prompt, then read" template is used to ask for and read the identification number to check.

In *Banners With CLASS*, the "prompt, then read" template is used to ask for and read the size of the letters on the banners.

In *Is It Legal?* the "prompt, then read" template is elaborated to include prompting, reading, and checking to be sure the input value is valid.

In *You Are What You Eat*, the "prompt, then read" template is used to get values for calories and fat. The prompt is made more informative by specifying the units (grams) for the fat input.

Subsequent case studies use the "prompt, then read" template for reading test data in driver programs.

Input, Process, Output

Description and purpose
This template is used to read some values, process the values, and print results. This template describes **bulk processing** in that all values are input and stored, all are processed, then output is produced.

Pseudocode
```
{bulk processing}
input all the values;
process the values;
output the results of the processing;
```

Code example
```
{input a number}
write ('Please type a four-digit identification number:   ');
readln (idNumber);
{process the number}
checkDigit := idNumber div 10;
digit1 := idNumber div 1000;
digit2 := (idNumber div 100) mod 10;
digit3 := (idNumber div 10) mod 10;
remainderDigit := (digit1+digit2+digit3) mod 7;
{output a message}
if remainderDigit = checkDigit then begin
    writeln ('The number is valid. Ready to make copies.');
end else begin
    writeln ('*** The number is not valid for this copier.');
end;
```

Use in case studies
This template or its variant, "input and process until done", (p. 405) is used in every case study.

In the first two *Check That Number!* programs, the "input, process, output" template is used to input an identification number, determine if it is valid, and output a message. In the third *Check That Number!* program, the digits of the identification number are read individually, all at once, and processed.

Roman Calculator Construction introduces the use of an array to store the input before bulk processing.

In *Is It Legal?* the template is elaborated in that the input step includes a check that the values read are legal.

In *You Are What You Eat*, history entries are read from a file before processing.

PASCAL PASCAL

Descriptions of Pascal constructs include words in this type face, which means that a term or expression in the category described is to be filled in. For example, the description

```
if Comparison then begin
    StatementSequence;
end;
```

means that a comparison should replace the word "Comparison" and a sequence of statements should replace the word "StatementSequence."

Program Heading

Format
```
program ProgramName (input, output);
```

Code example
```
program verifyId (input, output);
```

Purpose   The program heading indicates the name of the program, which must start with a letter and consist entirely of letters and digits. The terms "input" and "output" mean that the program will be requesting input from and printing output to the terminal. Some Pascal environments do not require "input" and "output" to be specified. See also file (p. 427).

Variable Declaration

Format
```
var
     NameList: Type;
     NameList: Type;

       .
       .
       .
```

```
var
    idNumber: integer;
    digit1, digit2, digit3, checkDigit: integer;

var
    d1, d2, d3, d4: char;
    digit1, digit2, digit3, checkDigit: integer;
    remainderDigit: integer;
```

Purpose **Variables** are where information is stored in programs. A variable has a name, which must start with a letter and consist entirely of letters and digits, a **type**, which describes the information the variable will contain, and exactly one value, the **contents** of the variable. Each variable name must appear in a **declaration**, in which the variable's type is specified.

idNumber

A variables is often drawn as a box, for example: ☐

See also integer (p. 392), real (p. 393), char (p. 393), assignment statement (p. 394), readln (p. 395), read (p. 396), boolean (p. 407), type (p. 413), array (p. 414), record (p. 426), file (p. 427), enumerated type (p. 430).

Comment

Format   {AnInformativeComment}

Code example
```
var
    idNumber: integer;   {the identification number read from the user}
```

Purpose Comments are any information enclosed between a left brace { and a right brace }. They are listed with the program but ignored by the Pascal compiler. A programmer typically accompanies variable and subprogram declarations and complicated code segments with comments. They can help the programmer remember the function of each part of a program, the meaning of a variable, or the rationale for a particular approach. Comments can also help those reading programs written by others to understand the program and to modify the program.

integer Type

Purpose A variable, if declared as type integer, may contain only an integer (whole number) value. The value may be either positive, negative, or zero. The constant maxint is predefined in Pascal as the largest positive integer representable on the computer.

real Type

Purpose   A variable, if declared as type real, may contain any numeric value. A constant real value must be specified with a decimal point and with at least one digit on each side of the decimal point. Thus 0.53 and 7.0 are legal real constants, but .53 and 7. are not. In nonscientific programming, the most common use for a real variable is to store an average.

char Type

Purpose   A variable, if declared as type char, may contain only a single character (essentially one of the letters, digits, punctuation marks, or special characters that the user can type at the keyboard). A constant of type char consists of a single character surrounded by single quotation marks, for example, 'A' or '2'.

begin and end

Format
```
begin
    StatementSequence;
end
```

Code example
```
begin
    write ('Please type a four-digit identification number:  ');
    readln (idNumber);
    checkDigit := idNumber div 10;
end;
```

Purpose   Begin and end are used to group statements. The grouped statements are separated by semicolons. Each program has a **main program** that starts with begin and ends with end followed by a period. Within the main program or within its subprograms, begin followed by a sequence of statements followed by end may appear anywhere a single statement may appear. See also if (p. 397), for (p. 404), procedure (p. 402), function (p. 408), while (p. 415).

Arithmetic Operators

Code examples
```
digit1 + digit2
letterSize - barHeight
3 * barHeight
sum / HISTORYSIZE
idPart div 10
idPart mod 10
```

Purpose   The arithmetic operators +, –, *, /, div, and mod are used to form **arithmetic expressions**. The div operator returns the integer quotient of its two operands; for example, the value of 7 div 3 is 2. The mod operand returns the integer remainder when its first operand is divided by its second; for example, the value of 7 mod 3 is 1. The operands for div and mod must both be of type integer. Operands for the other operators may be either integer or real. The result returned by +, –, and * is of type real unless both operands are of type integer; the result returned by / is always of type real.

To ensure that operations are performed in the intended order, use parentheses to isolate expressions.

Comparison Operators

Code examples
```
remainder = checkDigit
debug <> 0
year > 0
c >= '0'
k < length
date <= monthLength
```

Purpose   Expressions with numeric values may be compared using = (is equal to), > (is greater than), < (is less than), <> (is not equal to), >= (is greater than or equal, or is at least), and <= (is less than or equal to, or is at most). Expressions with character values may also be compared using these operators. (Characters may not be compared with numbers.) A comparison forms a **boolean expression** or **condition** that may be used with if, while, or repeat. See also if (p. 397), boolean (p. 407), boolean operators (p. 410), repeat (p. 409), while (p. 415).

Assignment Statement

Format   VariableName := ExpressionOfTheCorrectType;

Code example
```
checkDigit := idNumber div 10;
```

Purpose   The assignment statement is indicated by the := symbol; it assigns the result of evaluating the given expression to the named variable. Since a variable can contain only one value at a time, the original contents of the variable is lost. The types of the named variable and the expression must match, except in the single situation where the variable is of type real and the expression is of type integer.

The assignment statement provides one way to initialize a variable.

See also variable (p. 391), readln (p. 395), read (p. 396).

writeln Procedure

Format

```
writeln (ExpressionList);
writeln;
```

Code examples

```
writeln ('*** The number is not valid for this copier.');
writeln ('DEBUG: First value of idPart is ', idPart);
```

Purpose

The writeln procedure prints the values of expressions in the expression list. (The expressions are separated by commas.) If an expression is a sequence of characters surrounded by single quote marks (a string), the characters are printed without the quote marks. If an expression is the name of a variable, its value is printed. A more complicated expression is evaluated before printing. Finally, a carriage return is printed, so that the next thing printed will start a new line. If writeln is used without an expression list in parentheses, it merely prints a carriage return. See also write (p. 395), file (p. 427), rewrite (p. 429).

readln Procedure

Format

```
readln (VariableList);
```

Code examples

```
readln (idNumber);
readln (d1, d2, d3, d4);
```

Purpose

The readln procedure reads values from the current line into the specified variables. It then advances to the next line. If the user types fewer values on the line than there are variables in the list, readln will read the remaining values from the next line. If the user types more values on the line than there are variables in the list, the extra values are ignored.

Readln provides one way to initialize a variable. It is used when input typed at the terminal may be assumed to be error-free, for instance, in test programs.

See also read (p. 396), eoln (p. 416), file (p. 427), reset (p. 428), eof (p. 429).

write Procedure

Format

```
write (ExpressionList);
```

Code examples

```
write ('Please type a four-digit identification number: ');
write ('thank you');
```

Purpose

The write procedure acts exactly the same as the writeln procedure, except that it does not print a carriage return after printing the values of the given expressions. It is used mainly to print prompting messages, or to print part of a line in expectation that the rest of the line will be printed later in the program. See also writeln (p. 395), file (p. 427), rewrite (p. 429).

read Procedure

Format — `read (VariableList);`

Code example — `read (letter);`

Purpose — Like readln, the read procedure reads values from the current line into the specified variables. Unlike readln, it does not then advance to the next line. Thus it is used when the rest of the values on the line will be read later in the program.

The errors that potentially arise from losing track of where on the line values are coming from make it generally a bad idea to use read for anything but character input.

See also readln (p. 395), file (p. 427), reset (p. 428), eof (p. 429).

ord Function

Format — `ord (CharacterExpression);`

Code example — `digit1 := ord(d1) - ord('0');`

Purpose — Characters on any computer occur in a particular sequence, just like numbers. The ord function returns an integer value, the position in the sequence of the given character. The position is typically not useful on its own. More interesting is the *difference* between positions; for instance, the difference between a digit's position and the position of the digit '0' is the numeric value of the digit. Thus ord is used almost entirely for two purposes: to convert character digits to integer values and (with chr) to convert lower-case letters to upper case and vice versa. See also char (p. 393), chr (p. 396).

chr Function

Format — `chr (IntegerExpression);`

Code example — `UpperCase := chr (ord('A') + ord(lowerCaseLetter) - ord('a'));`

Purpose — Given an integer value representing the position of a character in the computer's character sequence, chr returns that character at that position. It is used almost entirely (with ord) to convert lower-case letters to upper case and vice versa. See also char (p. 393), ord (p. 396).

if Statement

Format

```
if Condition then begin
    StatementSequence;
end else begin
    StatementSequence;
end;

if Condition then begin
    StatementSequence;
end;
```

Code example

```
if remainderDigit = checkDigit then begin
    writeln ('The number is valid. Ready to make copies.');
end else begin
    writeln ('*** The number is not valid for this copy machine.');
end;

if debug <> 0 then begin
    writeln ('DEBUG: First value of idPart is ', idPart);
end;
```

Purpose

The if statement allows statements to be executed or not, according to the truth of the given condition. Here is how it works. The condition following the if is evaluated. If the condition is true then the statements following the then are executed; otherwise the statements following the else are executed. It is possible to omit the else, in which case the statements following the then are executed if the condition is true and not executed if the condition is false. See also comparison operators (p. 394), case (p. 403), boolean (p. 407), repeat (p. 409), while (p. 415).

Templates introduced or elaborated	Pascal constructs required	Pascal constructs introduced
Input one, process one	for statement	const definition
Do something a specified number of times		procedure declaration and use
Select from alternatives		value parameter
		case statement

TEMPLATES **TEMPLATES**

Input One, Process One

Description and purpose

This template is used to read a value, then process it, doing this over and over within a loop. Thus the sequence of operations performed is read, process, read, process, and so on. This template describes **one-by-one processing** in that a value is input and then processed before the next value is input. It is used when we are unable or unwilling to read all the input values before doing any processing.

This template generalizes the process step by including output as part of the processing. Thus, "processing" in this template refers to either processing without output or processing with output.

Contrast this template with the "input, process, output" template (p. 390). "Input, process, output" features bulk processing, where all values are read and stored in some way, then all the values are processed, and finally all the results are output.

Pseudocode

repeat the following steps:
  read a value;
  process it;

Pseudocode examples

do the following six times:
  read a letter;
  print the block version of the letter;

repeat the following:
    read a Roman digit;
    add the decimal value of the Roman digit into the sum;
until the end of the line is encountered;

Code example

```
write ('Type six letters, chosen from PASCL: ');
for letterNum := 1 to 6 do begin
    read (letter);
    case letter of
        'P': DrawP (letterSize);
        'A': DrawA (letterSize);
        'S': DrawS (letterSize);
        'C': DrawC (letterSize);
        'L': DrawL (letterSize);
    end;
end;
```

Use in case studies

One-by-one processing of input values is introduced in *Banners With CLASS*. Letters are entered and processed one at a time until the banner is completed. Processing involves computing the size of each part of the letter and printing the parts.

The "input one, process one" template is applied in *The Calendar Shop* to read a reasonable year value from the user. The framework program contains a loop that reads a year, then processes it by checking that it's legal. This pattern is elaborated in *Is It Legal?* by applying more complicated tests to the input.

The first version of the *Roman Calculator Construction* program reads and processes the digits of the Roman numeral one by one.

Subsequent case studies use this template in driver programs for the purposes of testing. The history file editor in *You Forgot What You Ate* and *The Eating Club* incorporate an example of this template called a **command interpreter**, in which commands are repeatedly read and processed.

Do Something a Specified Number of Times

Description and purpose

This template is used to perform some action a specified number of times. In general, a for loop is the easiest way to code this action.

As other templates are learned, alternatives will be possible. For example, performing an action a specified number of times can also be implemented as a special case of a template that performs an action until some condition is met.

Pseudocode

do the following a given number of times:
    perform some action;

Pseudocode examples

do the following six times:

read a letter;
draw the letter in block form;

do the following, width times:
print an asterisk;

Code examples

```
for colNum := 1 to width do begin
    write ('*');
end;

for weekNum := 1 to numWeeks do begin
    PrintWeek (startOfWeek, monthLength);
    startOfWeek := startOfWeek + 7;
end;
```

Use in case studies

This template is used over and over again in *Banners With CLASS* to draw each part of each letter that appears on the banner. In *The Calendar Shop*, the template is used to print each version of the calendar. Versions of the *Space Text* procedure apply the template to perform an action for each blank to insert, or for each gap between words in the line.

Select From Alternatives

Description and purpose

This template is used to choose from alternative actions based on a given value. In Pascal the case statement is most commonly used to select from alternatives. An if statement is used instead when the value used for selection is a structured value or when the alternatives are associated with ranges of values. In an advanced variation of this template, the selection values are members of an enumerated type.

Pseudocode examples

if the letter is P, draw a block P;
if the letter is A, draw a block A;
if the letter is S, draw a block S;
if the letter is C, draw a block C;
if the letter is L, draw a block L;

if the month is January, March, May, July, August, or October, return 31;
if the month is April, June, September, or November, return 30;
if the month is February, return 28 or 29;

Code examples

```
case letter of
    'P': DrawP(letterSize);
    'A': DrawA(letterSize);
    'S': DrawS(letterSize);
    'C': DrawC(letterSize);
    'L': DrawL(letterSize);
end;

case month of
    JAN, MAR, MAY, JUL, AUG, OCT, DEC:
        NumberOfDaysIn := 31;
```

```
      FEB:
          NumberOfDaysIn := 28 + LeapDay(year);
      APR, JUN, SEP, NOV:
          NumberOfDaysIn := 30;
  end;
```

Use in case studies The "select from alternatives" template is used in *Banners With CLASS* to select from procedures that draw the letters P, A, S, C, L. It is used in *The Calendar Shop* to select the proper number of days and to print the proper heading for a given month.

In *Roman Calculator Construction*, the "select from alternatives" template is used to select the value associated with a given Roman numeral.

An advanced variation of the template appears in *You Are What You Eat*, where each command (stored in a string) is first translated to a member of an enumerated type before the appropriate command-execution procedure is called.

PASCAL **PASCAL**

const Definition

Format
```
const
    Name = ConstantValue;
    AnotherName = AnotherConstantValue;
        .
        .
        .
```

Code examples
```
const
    BLANK = '';

const
    JAN = 1;  FEB = 2;  MAR = 3;  APR = 4;  MAY = 5;  JUN = 6;
    JUL = 7;  AUG = 8;  SEP = 9;  OCT = 10; NOV = 11; DEC = 12;
```

Purpose The const definition associates a specific value with an identifier to create a **named constant**. The value associated with the name cannot be changed within the program or subprogram in which the constant is defined.

Named constants can make a program much easier to read, since English words are used in the program instead of less meaningful numbers. Thus, the names of the months are declared as constants in *The Calendar Shop*.

By convention, names of constants in the case study programs are written in all capital letters. See also enumerated type (p. 430).

Procedure Declaration and Use

Format
```
procedure ProcedureName;
{definitions and variable declarations may appear here}
begin
    StatementSequence;
end;

procedure ProcedureName (ParameterList);
{definitions and variable declarations may appear here}
begin
    StatementSequence;
end;
```

Code example
```
procedure DrawL (letterSize: integer);
var
    barHeight, legHeight, legWidth: integer;
begin
    barHeight := letterSize div 4;
    legHeight := letterSize - barHeight;
    legWidth := barHeight;
    DrawBar(legHeight, legWidth);
    DrawBar(barHeight, letterSize);
end;
```

Purpose
The procedure is in essence a miniprogram. It isolates some action—the **procedure body**, a sequence of statements—and allows the user to reuse the action readily by calling the procedure as often as necessary. Procedures are helpful for naming the action of a sequence of statements and communicating the organization of a program.

Pascal has many built-in procedures; examples are writeln and readln.

Procedures are usually written with **formal parameters**, which provide generality by acting as place holders within the procedure. When a procedure is **called**, **actual parameters** or **arguments** are provided and substituted for the place holders one by one, in order.

Variables declared within a procedure (following the procedure heading) are **local** to the procedure. The statements in a procedure body may also use names declared or defined **globally**, that is, outside the procedure. Global variables are usually not used in a procedure so that the procedure will be more self-contained and easier to understand; however, named constants and types are often defined only in the main program and used in its subprograms.

See also value parameter (p. 403), function (p. 408), var parameter (p. 415).

Value Parameter

Format
```
procedure ProcedureName (ValueParameterList : Type) ;

function FunctionName (ValueParameterList : Type) ;
```

Code example
```
procedure PrintMonth (month, year, dayForFirst: integer);
begin
    PrintHeading (month, year);
    PrintDates (dayForFirst, NumberOfDaysIn (month, year));
end;

procedure PrintMonth (month: integer; year: integer;
        dayForFirst: integer);

function Legal (year: integer): boolean;
```

Purpose
Parameters declared in a procedure or function heading define place holder names for quantities used within the procedure or function. Unless indicated otherwise, they are **value parameters**, which act as initialized local variables. When a subprogram is called, the argument expressions are evaluated and the values are copied into variables corresponding to the value parameters. This provides a way to protect information in the calling code.

See also procedure (p. 402), function (p. 408), var parameter (p. 415).

case Statement

Format
```
case SelectorExpression of
        ValueList1 : StatementForAlternative1 ;
        ValueList2 : StatementForAlternative2 ;

                    ⋮

end;
```

Code examples
```
case month of
    JAN, MAR, MAY, JUL, AUG, OCT, DEC:
        NumberOfDaysIn := 31;
    FEB:
        NumberOfDaysIn := 28 + LeapDay (year);
    APR, JUN, SEP, NOV:
        NumberOfDaysIn := 30;
end;

case letter of
    'P': DrawP(letterSize);
    'A': DrawA(letterSize);
    'S': DrawS(letterSize);
    'C': DrawC(letterSize);
    'L': DrawL(letterSize);
end;
```

Purpose The case statement evaluates the selector expression and executes the statement associated with the corresponding value. Commas separate values in a list with more than one value. Values must be constants, not variables. See also if (p. 397), const (p. 401).

for Statement

Format
```
for IntegerVariable := IntegerExpression1 to IntegerExpression2 do begin
    StatementSequence;
end;
```

Code example
```
for lineNum := 1 to height do begin
    for colNum := 1 to indentAmt do begin
        write(BLANK);
    end;
    for colNum := 1 to width do begin
        write('*')
    end;
end;

for date := startOfWeek to startOfWeek+6 do begin
    if (date>0) and (date<=monthLength) then begin
        write(date:3);
    end else begin
        write(BLANK:3);
    end;
    writeln;
end;
```

Purpose The for statement executes the **loop body**, the sequence of statements between the begin and the end, once for each integer value greater than or equal to the first integer expression and less than or equal to the second integer expression, inclusive. The named integer variable, referred to as the **loop variable**, is successively assigned each of these values. Thus the statement

```
for k := 3 to 5 do begin
    StatementSequence;
end;
```

has the effect of executing the given sequence of statements once with k having the value 3, once with k having the value 4, and once with k having the value 5. The for statement produces **definite iteration**, in which the number of repetitions of the loop are known (1 plus the difference of the two integer expression values).

The loop variable may not be changed by any of the statements in the loop body, since the incrementing of the loop variable happens automatically. If the value of the first integer expression is greater than the value of the second, the loop body is not executed. See also repeat (p. 409), while (p. 415).

Templates introduced or elaborated	Pascal constructs required	Pascal constructs introduced
Input and process until done		boolean type
Process in cycles		function declaration and use
		repeat statement
		boolean operators not, and, or

TEMPLATES **TEMPLATES**

TEMPLATES

Input and Process Until Done

Description and purpose

The action of this template is to repeat the process of getting a value and processing the value until some condition is met. This template elaborates the "input one, process one" template by adding the ability to continue until done.

As with "input one, process one," (p. 398) the processing can include output. For example, the input and process cycle might continue until all the values are entered or until a legal value is encountered. In Pascal this action is coded with a repeat or a while loop (the latter is introduced in *Roman Calculator Construction*).

Pseudocode

repeat the following until finished:
    read a value;
    process it;

while not finished, do the following:
    read a value;
    process it;

Pseudocode example

```
repeat
    ask the user for input;
    read values for variables;
    if not Legal (variables) then begin
        print an error message;
    end;
until Legal (variables);
```

Code examples

```
repeat
    write ('Please type the year for which you want a calendar: ');
    readln (year);
    if not Legal (year) then begin
        writeln ('Can''t make a calendar for that year.');
    end;
until Legal (year);

{from Roman Calculator Construction}
while not eoln do begin
    read(romanDigit);
    currentValue := DecimalTrans(romanDigit);
    if currentValue <= prevValue then begin
        sum := sum + currentValue;
    end else begin
        sum := sum + currentValue - prevValue - prevValue;
    end;
    prevValue := currentValue;
end;
```

Use in case studies

In *The Calendar Shop* and *Is It Legal?* "input and process until done" is used to read values and error check them until a legal value is read. *Is It Legal?* and subsequent case studies also apply the template to the problem of reading the characters on a line of input; here end-of-line, signalled by the eoln function, is the terminating condition.

In the driver program for *Space Text*, "input and process until done" is used to continue processing lines until there are no more lines to process. *Chess Challenges* uses it to read queens, terminating input when a **sentinel value** is read.

You Forgot What You Ate and *The Eating Club* apply this template to input from files (where "done" is signalled by the eof function) and to the process of reading and executing commands in the history editor (where "done" means that the user has typed a "quit" command).

Process in Cycles

Description and purpose

This template is used to perform some cyclic process. It incorporates a test within a loop, often involving the mod operator, to see if a cycle has been completed.

Pseudocode examples

for each date from 1 to the month length, do the following:
    print the date;
    if we're at the end of a week, print a carriage return;

for k := 1 to the number of blanks to insert, do the following:
    if k is more than the number of gaps in the line, set k to 1;
    add a blank to the kth gap in the line;

Code example

```
for date := 1 to monthLength do begin
    write (date: 3);
    if (date + dayForFirst) mod 7 = 0 then begin
        writeln;
    end;
end;
```

Use in case studies

In *The Calendar Shop*, the day-by-day version prints a carriage return every seventh date.

In the blank-by-blank *Space Text* program, an index variable cycles through the characters in the line array.

PASCAL **PASCAL**

boolean Type

Code examples

```
function Legal (year: integer): boolean;
begin
    Legal := (year>0);  {return true if year > 0, false otherwise}
end;

if not Legal (year) then begin
    writeln ('Can''t make a calendar for that year.');
end;

function IsInRange (n: integer): boolean;
begin
    {return true if n is one of 5, 6, ..., 23, 24, false otherwise}
    IsInRange := (n >= 5) and (n <= 24);
end;

{error is declared as a boolean variable}
repeat
    error := false;
    write('Type a size for the letters between 5 and 24 : ');
    ReadTrimmedLine(line, length);
    if (length = 0) or (length > LINELENGTH) then begin
        error := true;
    end else if not IsAllDigits(line, length) then begin
        error := true;
    end else begin
        n := IntegerValue(line, length);
        if not IsInRange(n) then begin
            error := true;
        end;
    end;
    if error then begin  {note: we didn't write "if error = true"}
        writeln('You must type an integer between 5 and 24.');
    end;
until not error;  {note: we didn't write "until error = false"}
```

Purpose Boolean variables represent yes-or-no quantities. They can take on just two values: true (yes) or false (no). The condition used in an if statement, a repeat statement, or a while statement is a boolean expression, which is one of the following: a boolean constant (true or false), a boolean variable, a comparison, or the combination of boolean expressions with the not, and, or or operators. See also if (p. 397), comparison operators (p. 394), repeat (p. 409), boolean operators (p. 410), while (p. 415).

Function Declaration and Use

Format
```
function FunctionName (ParameterList) : ReturnType;
{definitions and variable declarations may appear here}
begin
    StatementSequence;
end;

function FunctionName : ReturnType;
{definitions and variable declarations may appear here}
begin
    StatementSequence;
end;
```

Code examples
```
function NumberOfDaysIn (month, year: integer): integer;
begin
    case month of
        JAN, MAR, MAY, JUL, AUG, OCT, DEC:
            NumberOfDaysIn := 31;
        FEB:
            NumberOfDaysIn := 28 + LeapDay (year);
        APR, JUN, SEP, NOV:
            NumberOfDaysIn := 30;
    end;
end;

{example of a use of NumberOfDaysIn}
PrintDates (dayForFirst, NumberOfDaysIn(month, year));

function Legal (year: integer): boolean;
begin
    Legal := (year > 0);
end;

{example of a use of Legal}
if not Legal(year) then begin
    writeln ('Can''t make a calendar for that year.');
end;
```

Purpose A function is a subprogram that returns a value, as opposed to a procedure, which performs some action. The function heading indicates the type of the value to be returned. When the function is called, the statements executed in its body must include an assignment statement in which the name of the function appears to the left of the := symbol; this assignment provides the value that the function is to return.

By convention, a function has no effect on the program other than to compute the value it returns. Thus a function's parameters are almost always value parameters.

An integer function call may appear anywhere an integer expression may appear, for instance in a comparison or as an argument to another subprogram. More generally, a call to a function of any unstructured type may appear anywhere that an expression of that type may appear. Standard Pascal does not allow a function to return a structured value, such as an array or a record.

Pascal has many built-in functions; examples are ord, chr, sqr (square), trunc (truncated, with the integer part isolated), and abs (absolute value).

See also procedure (p. 402), value parameter (p. 403).

repeat Statement

Format
```
repeat
    StatementSequence;
until TerminatingCondition;
```

Code example
```
repeat
    write ('Please type the year for which you want a calendar: ');
    readln (year);
    if not Legal (year) then begin
        writeln ('Can''t make a calendar for that year.');
    end;
until Legal (year);
```

Purpose
The repeat statement executes the given sequence of statements and then tests to see if the terminating condition has been met. If the condition has not been met the statements are executed again, then the condition is tested again. The loop executes forever (subject to interruption by the user or the operating system) if the terminating condition is never met. The repeat statement provides an example of **indefinite iteration**, in which the number of loop repetitions is not necessarily known.

The body of a repeat loop is always executed at least once. In the case studies, repeat is only used to ask the user for input. In other situations appropriate for indefinite iteration, a while loop is used to handle more easily the condition where *no* loop iterations are desired.

See also for (p. 404), boolean (p. 407), while (p. 415).

Boolean Operators not, and, or

```
if not Legal (year) then begin
    writeln ('Can''t make a calendar for that year.');
end;

{from Is It Legal?}
if not ((line[k] >= '0') and (line[k] <= '9')) then begin
    IsAllDigits :false;
end;

if (year mod 4 = 0) and (year mod 100 <> 0) then begin
    LeapDay := 1;
end;

if (date > 0) and (date <= monthLength) then begin
    write (date:3);
end else begin
    write (BLANK:3);
end;

if (length = 0) or (length > LINELENGTH) then begin
    error := true;
end;
```

Purpose The boolean operator not, applied to a boolean value, returns the negation of that value. If the value is true, not returns false; if the value is false, not returns true. In the case studies, not most commonly is used in the condition for a while loop: while not done do ... . In general, if not is to be used with a complicated boolean expression, the expression should be coded as a boolean function to increase clarity.

The boolean operator and, applied to two boolean values, returns true if both values are true and false otherwise. The boolean operator or, applied to two boolean values, returns true if at least one of the values is true and false if both the values are false. If the operands of and or or are comparisons, they must be enclosed in parentheses. (Parentheses may also be used to clarify the order of evaluation, in the same way as in arithmetic expressions.)

Standard Pascal does not specify the order in which the operands to and and or are evaluated, and does not guarantee that evaluation will be terminated early if, for instance, the first operand of an or has value true. This usually requires that the conditions be tested in separate if conditions; for this reason, the or operator is used only once in all the case study programs.

See also comparison operators (p. 394), boolean (p. 407).

Templates introduced or elaborated	Pascal constructs required	Pascal constructs introduced
Accumulate values until done	type definition	var parameter
Fill an array	one-dimensional array declaration and use	while statement
		eoln function

TEMPLATES TEMPLATES

Accumulate Values Until Done

Description and purpose

This template implements the action of accumulating a result from a variety of values. A straightforward example would be to add up values as they are input. A more subtle example would be to identify the maximum value or the minimum value as values are input. This template is an extension of the "input and process until done" template (p. 405).

Pseudocode

initialize a variable in which the values will be accumulated (for example, set a "sum" variable to 0 or a "product" variable to 1);
repeat the following for each of the sequence of values:
    accumulate the value (add it to a sum, or multiply it by a product);

Pseudocode example

initialize a "sum" variable to 0;
repeat the following:
    read a Roman digit;
    add the decimal value of the Roman digit into the sum;
until the end of the line is encountered;

Code example

```
repeat
    read (romanDigit);
    if DecimalTrans (romanDigit) <= DecimalTrans (prevDigit) then begin
        sum := sum + DecimalTrans (romanDigit);
    end else begin
        sum := sum + DecimalTrans (romanDigit)
            - DecimalTrans (prevDigit) - DecimalTrans (prevDigit);
    end;
    prevDigit := romanDigit;
until eoln;
```

Use in case studies

In *Roman Calculator Construction* the value of a Roman number is accumulated by evaluating the values of each of the Roman digits and adding regular values or subtracting prefixes.

The "process every element of a one-dimensional array" template (p. 417) introduced in *Is It Legal?* is an extension of this template when the "process" involves accumulation.

Fill an Array

Description and purpose

The action of this template is to read values from the input and store them in sequence in an array. This template is an extension of the "input and process until done" template (p. 405). It is important to guard against assigning a value to a location outside the declared bounds of the array.

Reading values into an array and processing them afterward, rather than reading and evaluating the values one at a time, makes some operations more convenient. For example, storing the values makes it possible to review them in different ways. It is also easier to evaluate relationships among the values, such as determining whether or not a digit in a Roman numeral is a prefix.

Pseudocode

Pseudocode for the situation when a function like eoln or eof is used to indicate when to stop filling the array:

```
set an array index variable to 0;
while more input, do the following:
      read a value;
      add 1 to the array index;
      store the value into the indexed array location;
(if reading characters from a line) readln;
```

Pseudocode for the situation when a sentinel value is used to indicate when to stop filling the array:

```
set an array index variable to 0;
repeat
      read a value;
      if it's not the sentinel, then
            add 1 to the array index;
            store the value into the indexed array location;
until the sentinel is encountered;
```

In either case, the index variable contains the number of values stored in the array at the end of the loop.

Code example

```
writeln ('Type a Roman numeral followed by RETURN: ');
length := 0;
```

```
while not eoln do begin
    read (ch);
    length := length + 1;
    roman [length] := ch;
end;
readln;
```

Use in case studies   In the entire-numeral solution for *Roman Calculator Construction*, values are input into an array until all the Roman digits are read. Since the longest Roman numeral is known, the array is declared to handle Roman numerals up to the maximum length, and there is no need to worry about overflow.

In *Is It Legal?* values are read into an array of characters before they are checked for legality. To be sure not to overflow the array, the template is elaborated to check the length of the input against the length of the array.

In *You Are What You Eat, You Forgot What You Ate*, and *The Eating Club*, an array is filled with values from a file. The *Chess Challenges* program fills the board array with values from the user terminated by a sentinel. In *The Shuffler's Dilemma*, values from one array are used to fill another.

PASCAL **PASCAL**

type Definition

Format
```
type
    Name = OneType;
    AnotherName = AnotherType;
         .
         .
         .
```

Code example
```
type
    StringType = array [1..MAXSTRLEN] of char;

var
    roman: StringType;

{from Is It Legal?}
type
    DigitTable = array[1..4] of char;
    LineType = array[1..MAXSTRLEN] of char;
    StateType = integer;

var
    TENDIGITS, FIVEDIGITS: DigitTable;
    roman: LineType;
    state: StateType;
```

Purpose   Pascal allows the definition of new type names. Such names may merely provide better descriptions for already existing types, as does StateType above, or may provide abbreviations for structured types, as do StringType, DigitTable, and LineType.

The type of any subprogram parameter must be a type name, either a pre-defined type (integer, char, real, or boolean) or a name defined in a type definition.

See also integer (p. 392), real (p. 393), char (p. 393), boolean (p. 407), array (p. 414, p. 434), record (p. 426), file (p. 427), enumerated type (p. 430).

One-Dimensional Array Declaration and Use

Format

```
array [PositionOfFirst .. PositionOfLast] of ElementType
```

Code example

```
type
      StringType = array [1..MAXSTRLEN] of char;

var
      roman: StringType;  length: integer;
      DECIMALEQUIV: array['C'..'X'] of integer;

roman [length] := ch;
DECIMALEQUIV['M'] := 1000;
```

Purpose

The one-dimensional array is used to store a sequence of values—the **elements** of the array—all of the same type. The positions in the array are named by an **index range**, specified in brackets in the array type definition. Arrays may be indexed by integers (most common), characters, booleans, or enumerated type members. The code example gives examples of an array of characters indexed by integers and an array of integers indexed by characters.

An array is often diagrammed as a sequence of boxes, each accompanied by its index, as shown below.

The most common array error is the use of an index value that is outside the array's index range.

See also record (p. 426), file (p. 427), two-dimensional array (p. 434).

var Parameter

Format

```
procedure ProcedureName (var ValueParameterList:Type);
```

Code example

```
procedure ReadRoman (var roman: StringType; var length: integer);
```

Purpose

Parameters declared in a procedure heading (functions rarely have var parameters) with the word var act as renamed global variables. The argument corresponding to a var parameter must be a variable, not a constant or a more complicated expression; within the procedure, any reference to the parameter name constitutes a reference to the variable. In this way, results from a procedure are communicated back to the calling code.

Procedures with exactly one var parameter of type integer, char, or boolean are usually better coded as functions. An exception is an input procedure; most Pascal experts believe that functions should not include side effects such as reading values from the user.

A var parameter is also used to pass a structured value, to avoid the inefficiency of copying it. A file parameter must be a var parameter.

See also procedure (p. 402), value parameter (p. 403), function (p. 408).

while Statement

Format

```
while Condition do begin
     StatementSequence;
end;
```

Code example

```
while not eoln do begin
    read (ch);
    length := length + 1;
    roman [length] := ch;
end;

while not done do begin
    if pos > length then begin
        done := true;
    end else if line[pos] <> ch then begin
        done := true;
    end else begin
        pos := pos + 1;
    end;
end;
```

Purpose

The while statement provides another facility for indefinite iteration. Execution of the while statement starts by evaluating the condition; if it is true, the statements bracketed by begin and end are executed and the condition is tested again. This process is repeated as long as the condition evaluates to true. As with the repeat statement, there is a possibility of an infinite loop. A while statement is often used to implement the "input and process until done" template (p. 405) and other related templates.

The following code segments are exactly equivalent:

```
while Condition do begin              if Condition then begin
    StatementSequence;                    repeat
end;                                          StatementSequence;
                                          until not Condition;
                                      end;
```

See also for (p. 404), boolean (p. 407), repeat (p. 409).

eoln Function

Format
```
eoln
```
```
eoln(FileVariable)
```

Code example
```
while not eoln do begin
    read (ch);
    length := length + 1;
    roman [length] := ch;
end;
readln;
```

Purpose
The eoln function returns true exactly when the last character on the input line has been read. (A subsequent readln moves through the carriage return on that line and starts input on the line immediately following.) See also readln (p. 395), file (p. 427), eof (p. 429).

Templates introduced or elaborated	Pascal constructs required	Pascal constructs introduced
Process every element of a one-dimensional array		
Search a one-dimensional array		

TEMPLATES TEMPLATES

Process Every Element of a One-Dimensional Array

Description and purpose

This template is used to perform an action on each element of an array. The action may be simple, such as checking to see if the element is non-blank, adding the element to a running total, or comparing the element to the maximum value found so far, or the action may be complex, such as determining whether the value is a properly ordered component of a Roman numeral.

This template combines the actions described as "do something a specified number of times" (p. 399) and, in some situations, "accumulate values until done" (p. 411). When values are represented in an array, it makes sense to think of these specific actions as special cases of the more abstract action called "processing."

Since the number of elements in an array is known, this template is usually implemented with a for loop. The loop variable k is used in the examples below; other possibilities are pos (for "position") or index.

The template may also be applied to a section of an array, for instance when deleting an array element. All subsequent elements must be "processed" by being moved down one place in the array.

Pseudocode

```
for k := 1 to the array length do begin
    process element k of the array;
end;
```

```
for k := 1 to length do begin
    tally line[k] in the counts array;
end;

for k := 1 to length do begin
    if line[k+1] can't legally follow line[k], then IsLegalOrder := false;
end;
```

```
for k := 1 to length do begin
    value := value * 10 + DigitValue (line[k]);
end;

for k := pos+1 to length-1 do begin
    line[k] := line[k+1];
end;

for k := 1 to length do begin
    counts[line[k]] := counts[line[k]] + 1;
end;

{from Space Text}
for k := 1 to length-1 do begin
    if (line[k]<>BLANK) and (line[k+1]=BLANK) then begin
        numGaps := numGaps + 1;
    end;
end;
```

In *Is It Legal?* this template is used to check whether input elements are all digits or all characters from a specified list, to compute the integer value of a numeral, to shift array elements after deleting an element, to count the number of occurrences of each Roman digit, and to check that Roman digits are in the correct order. The template also supplies a starting point for the design of code that replaces each pair of Roman digits that starts with a prefix with a single new digit.

Space Text applies this template to print a line, to determine if a line contains a blank character, to count the gaps in the line, and to copy part of one array to another. In *You Art What You Eat* this template is used to compare strings, to compute the sum of array values, to graph each array value, and to write all the values of an array into a file.

In *Chess Challenges* this template is generalized to two-dimensional arrays. It is also used to print the array of queen positions and to process all pairs of queens in the array.

The Shuffler's Dilemma applies the template to each half of the deck to implement the perfect shuffle algorithm, and to the whole deck to implement the efficient selection shuffle.

Search a One-Dimensional Array

Description and purpose

This template searches a one-dimensional array for a specified value or condition and returns the location of the result of the search or indicates that the search was unsuccessful. It does not always examine every array element: it terminates the search when an appropriate element is found.

This template is an extension of "process every element in an array" (p. 417); the difference is the termination condition that says when to stop processing array elements. Instead of a for loop, it uses a while loop with a boolean done variable and explicit incrementing of the array index variable. It is also an extension of "process until done" to handle arrays.

Pseudocode

```
done := false;
k := 1;
while not done do begin
    if k > number of array elements then begin
        indicate search failure;
        done := true;
    end else if kth element satisfies search condition then begin
        indicate search success;
        done := true;
    end else begin
        k := k + 1;
    end;
end;
```

Code example

```
function Location (ch: char; str: LineType; length: integer): integer;
var
    k: integer;  done: boolean;
begin
    done := false;
    k := 1;
    while not done do begin
        if k > length then begin
            done := true;
            Location := 0;
        end else if line[k] = ch then begin
            done := true;
            Location := k;
        end else begin
            k := k + 1;
        end;
    end;
end;
```

Use in case studies

The rule-violation approach in *Is It Legal* uses the "search a one-dimensional array" template to find a Roman digit in an ordering array in order to check for legally ordered digit pairs. In the rule-confirmation approach, the template is used to find the end of a sequence of M's, C's, X's, or I's.

In *Space Text*, the line array is searched to find the next blank or the next nonblank. The first selection shuffle in *The Shuffler's Dilemma* searches for each randomly chosen card to make sure it has not yet been added to the shuffled deck.

In *You Are What You Eat* and *You Forgot What You Ate*, the "search a one-dimensional array" template is extended to files. *Chess Challenges* similarly extends this template to two-dimensional arrays in order to find a queen attacking a given position.

Templates introduced or elaborated	Pascal constructs required	Pascal constructs introduced
Insert into a one-dimensional array		
Copy a one-dimensional array		
Insert while copying a one-dimensional array		

TEMPLATES **TEMPLATES**

Insert Into a One-Dimensional Array

Description and purpose This template is used to add a single element anywhere in an array. The action is to locate the position for the new element or elements, move all the elements following that position over to make room for the new element, and add the new element at the located position.

One must, of course, make sure there is room in the array for the new element. Also, the element shifting must be done from right to left (using a for statement with downto). The programmer should be on the alert for off-by-one errors in the for statement.

Pseudocode
```
{a new value is to be inserted into array at position}
for k := length+1 downto position+1 do begin
    array[k] := array[k–1];
end;
array[position] := the new value;
add 1 to the number of array elements;
```

Code example
```
{inserting a blank at line[position]}
for k := length+1 downto position+1 do begin
    line[k] := line[k-1];
end;
line[position] := BLANK;
length := length + 1;
```

Use in case studies In *Space Text*, this template is used to insert a blank into a line.

You Forgot What You Ate extends this template to insertion into files. *The Eating Club* describes an insertion sort; revisions made to the history editor also involve array insertions. Shuffling by insertion is considered in study questions in *The Shuffler's Dilemma*.

Copy a One-Dimensional Array

Description and purpose

This template is used to create a new array or portion of an array that is a copy of an existing array or portion of an array. This is an extension of the "process every element of an array" template (p. 417).

The array segment to copy may be specified either by a start and end position or by a start position and the number of elements to copy. Failure to keep track of all the variables is the biggest pitfall associated with this template. A for statement is probably the best choice for the code, although use of a for statement rather than while or repeat causes the index variables used with the source and destination arrays to be treated differently.

Standard Pascal allows the entire contents of one array to be copied to another array of the same type with a single assignment statement.

Pseudocode

```
(using a start position and a number of elements to copy)
identify the index for the startCopying location in the source array;
identify the index for the startAdding location in the destination array;
determine numberToCopy, the number of elements to copy;
for index := 0 to numberToCopy-1 do begin
    newArray [startAdding+index] := originalArray [startCopying + index];
end;
```

Code example

```
{this approach uses start and end positions in source and destionation}
procedure CopySequence (source: StringType;
    sourceStart, sourceEnd: integer;
    var destination: StringType; var destPosition: integer);
var
    k: integer;
begin
    for k := sourceStart to sourceEnd do begin
        destination[destPosition] := source[k];
        destPosition := destPosition + 1;
    end;
end;
```

Use in case studies

In *Space Text*, sequences of nonblank characters are copied from one array to another. The efficient selection shuffle in *The Shuffler's Dilemma* involves copying elements into a new array while changing their order.

Insert While Copying a One-Dimensional Array

Description and purpose

When all insertions can be done at the end of an array, it is no longer necessary to shift elements. This template inserts values into an array by copying the elements of an array up to the insertion point, inserting the new elements into the new array at the insertion point, and then copying the remaining elements into the subsequent locations in the new array. This template combines the "copy a one-dimensional array" and the "insert into an array" templates (p. 421, p. 422).

As with the "insert into a one-dimensional array" template, it is important to guard against off-by-one errors and against index out-of-bounds errors.

Pseudocode

while not finished inserting, do the following:
    copy from the source array to the destination array,
      up to the next insertion point;
    add elements to be inserted at the end of the destination array;

Code example

```
for k := 1 to numGaps do begin
    gapPosition := NextGapPosition (line, length, currentPosition);
    CopySequence (line, currentPosition, gapPosition,
        newLine, newLinePosition);
    if k <= numExtras then begin
        AddBlanksToEnd (newLine, newLinePosition, numPerGap+1);
    end else begin
        AddBlanksToEnd (newLine, newLinePosition, numPerGap);
    end;
end;
```

Use in case studies

In *Space Text*, the "insert while copying a one-dimensional array" template is used to improve the gap-by-gap solution.

In *You Forgot What You Ate*, this template is extended to files.

Templates introduced or elaborated	Pascal constructs required	Pascal constructs introduced
Process elements in a file until done	file type	record type
Insert into a file		reset procedure
		rewrite procedure
		eof function

TEMPLATES **TEMPLATES**

Process Elements in a File Until Done

Description and purpose

This template processes elements in a file, performing some action on them and stopping at the end of the file or when some specified value or condition is met. This is similar to processing elements in an array except that locations in the file are not identified by an index. Copying or searching a file are special cases of "process elements in a file until done."

This template for processing a file addresses a range of activities such as copying and searching that were the subject of separate templates for arrays. Now that the similarities among these actions are clear, it is appropriate to group them in a single file template.

Note that input, the source of keyboard input, is a Pascal file. Thus processing elements in a file is similar to processing input values. The main difference is that one rarely needs to consider end-of-file with input from the terminal.

Pseudocode
```
done := false;
reset the file;
while not done do begin
    if eof (file) then begin
        done := true;
    end else begin
        read a file element;
        if the file element indicates that we're "done" then begin
            done := true;
        end else begin
```

```
                    process the file element;
                end;
            end;
        end;
```

Code example

```
{read up to HISTORYSIZE elements from historyFile into recentHistory}
done := false;  numEntries := 0;
reset (historyFile);
while not done do begin
    if eof(historyFile) then begin
        done := true;
    end else if numEntries = HISTORYSIZE then begin
        done := true;
    end else begin
        numEntries := numEntries + 1;
        readln (historyFile, recentHistory[numEntries].fat,
            recentHistory[numEntries].calories);
    end;
end;
```

Use in case studies

In *You Are What You Eat*, the "process a file" template is used to copy a file into a temporary file and to copy a temporary file back to the original file. In *You Forgot What You Ate*, this template is used for reading and writing files and for searching the food and history files.

Insert Into a File

Description and purpose

This template is used to add an element or elements to a file. The action is similar to that of inserting into an array except that there are constraints on file operations. It most closely resembles the "insert while copying" template (p. 423).

Since Pascal files cannot be open for reading and writing simultaneously, the original file must be copied to a temporary file, the new element inserted, the copying completed, and then the copy written back to the original file. (The insertion may be done in the write-back step instead of the copying step.)

Files are opened for writing with the rewrite procedure. Since the rewrite empties the file, writing starts with an empty file. Thus, inserting into an existing file involves first copying the existing file, then rewriting (emptying) the file, and finally writing the new and old values back to the file.

Pseudocode

```
rewrite (tempFile);
copy the contents of the data file to tempFile, up to the insertion point;
write the new element to tempFile;
copy the rest of the data file to tempFile;
rewrite (data file);
reset (tempFile);
copy tempFile to the data file;
```

```
rewrite (tempFile);
for k := 0 to HISTORYSIZE do begin
    writeln (tempFile, recentHistory[k].fat, recentHistory[k].calories);
end;
while not eof (historyFile) do begin
    readln (historyFile, fat, calories);
    writeln (tempFile, fat, calories);
end;
reset (tempFile);
rewrite (historyFile);
while not eof (historyFile) do begin
    readln (tempFile, fat, calories);
    writeln (historyFile, fat, calories);
end;
```

Use in case studies

In *You Are What You Eat*, the "insert into a file" template is used to add fat and calorie values to the file. (This is illustrated in the code example.) *You Forgot What You Ate* uses this template to add an entry to the history file.

PASCAL **PASCAL**

record Type

Format

```
record
    FieldName: FieldType;
    AnotherFieldName: AnotherType;
          ⋮
end;
```

Code example

```
type
    EntryType = record
        fat, calories: integer;
    end;
    HistoryType = array [0..HISTORYSIZE] of EntryType;
    LineType = record
        length: integer;
        chars: StringType;
    end;
var
    entry: EntryType;
    recentHistory: HistoryType;

line.length := 1;
line.chars[1] := ch;
while not eoln(inFile) do begin
    read (inFile, ch);
    if line.length < MAXLINELEN then begin
        line.length := line.length + 1;
        line.chars[line.length] := ch;
    end;
```

```
end;
readln (inFile);

for k := numEntries+1 to HISTORYSIZE do begin
    recentHistory[k].fat := 0;
    recentHistory[k].calories := 0;
end;
```

Purpose   The Pascal record type allows elements of differing types to be grouped. The components of a record are called its **fields**. Records are commonly used in combination with arrays, as shown in the code examples; especially common is the grouping of an array with an integer containing the number of elements that the array currently contains. See also array (p. 414, p. 434), file (p. 427).

file Type

Format   file of ElementType

Purpose   The Pascal file provides a way to access and store data *external* to a program. As with an array, a file's elements must be all one type; unlike arrays, files may contain any number of elements. A file's elements are stored sequentially in the order in which they are written to the file. In order to access a given element of a file, the elements preceding it must be read; a file is similar to a cassette tape in this way.

Within a program, one refers to a variable declared to be of type file. In Standard Pascal, each file variable must appear in the program heading; thus a file acts like a parameter passed from the outside environment into the Pascal program. A file variable is associated with an actual file on disk by using the reset or rewrite procedure. One must take care not to confuse the file variable name with the operating system's name of the external file.

The read and write procedures are used to read to and write from user-declared files just as they are used with terminal input and output. To read from a file, one adds the corresponding file variable as the first argument to read. Similarly, to write to a file, one adds the file variable as the first argument to write. The file variables input and output are predeclared in Pascal to refer to keyboard input and terminal output respectively; the statements

```
read(input, n);
```

and

```
read(n);
```

are equivalent, as are the statements

```
write(output, n);
```

and

```
write(n);
```

The type text is predefined in Pascal as essentially a file of characters. (The files input and output are text files.) The readln and writeln procedures and the eoln function may be used with text files. As with read and write, the file variable must be the first argument to readln, writeln, or eoln used with a file.

Any file parameter must be a var parameter.

A file may be **open** for reading; this means that a read from the file is permitted. A file may also be open for writing, but not at the same time as it is open for reading. The reset procedure is used to open a file for reading; rewrite is used to open a file for writing.

Pascal environments typically provide file operations beyond those specified in Standard Pascal. These may include random access operations that allow a file to be treated essentially as an array.

See also writeln (p. 395), readln (p. 395), write (p. 395), read (p. 396), array (p. 414, p. 434), var parameter (p. 415), eoln (p. 416), reset (p. 428), rewrite (p. 429), eof (p. 429).

reset Procedure

Format
```
reset (FileVariable);
```

Code example
```
reset (tempFile);
```

Purpose
The reset procedure opens its file argument for input. The first read from the file will read the file's first element. A file must be reset in order for its elements to be read (except that input is reset prior to the start of the program). Values are read sequentially; for example, to read the third file element, the program must first read the first and second.

Pascal environments often allow the reset procedure to take a second argument, a string that contains the external name of the file to which the given file variable is to be associated.

See also readln (p. 395), read (p. 396), eoln (p. 416), file (p. 427), rewrite (p. 429), eof (p. 429).

rewrite Procedure

Format `rewrite (FileVariable);`

Code example `rewrite (historyFile);`

Purpose The rewrite procedure opens a file for output. It also initializes the file to empty. A file must be rewritten in order for its elements to be written (except that output is rewritten prior to the start of the program). Values are written sequentially to a file; for example, the value written after the fourth element becomes the fifth element of the file.

Pascal environments often allow the rewrite procedure to take a second argument, a string that contains the external name of the file to which the given file variable is to be associated.

See also writeln (p. 395), write (p. 395), reset (p. 428), file (p. 427).

eof Function

Format `eof (FileVariable)`

Code example `while not eof (historyFile) do begin`

Purpose The eof function returns true exactly when the last element in the given file has been read. To reread elements of a file, the reset procedure must be called to reopen the file for input.

See also readln (p. 395), read (p. 396), eoln (p. 416), file (p. 427), reset (p. 428), eof (p. 429).

Templates introduced or elaborated	Pascal constructs required	Pascal constructs introduced
		enumerated type
		pred and succ functions

PASCAL **PASCAL**

Enumerated Type

Format
(TypeMember1, TypeMember2, ...)

Code example
```
type
     CommandType = (LISTCMD, ADDCMD, DELETECMD, HELPCMD, QUITCMD, UNKNOWN);
     StatusType = (SUCCESS, NOINPUT, LINETOOLONG, NODATE, WORDTOOLONG);

if status = SUCCESS then begin
     status := NODATE;
end;

case command of
     LISTCMD:    ExecuteList (line, history, status);
     ADDCMD:     ExecuteAdd (line, history, status);
     DELETECMD: ExecuteDelete (line, history, status);
     HELPCMD:    ExecuteHelp (line, history, status);
     QUITCMD:    ExecuteQuit (line, history, status);
end;
```

Purpose
An enumerated type is defined by enumerating its members—the constant values that variables of the type may contain—inside parentheses. (The order in which the members are listed is used with the pred and succ functions.) Enumerated type values may not be read or printed in Standard Pascal; they are meant for a program's internal use only. Defining a collection of constants as an enumerated type is more concise than defining them as separate named constants.

Enumerated types are mainly used to represent status values and to provide a more convenient way to store strings such as commands that will be used with the "select from alternatives" template.

In the case study programs, the names of members of enumerated types are written in all capital letters, like any other constants. See also const (p. 401), type (p. 413).

pred Function

Format `pred (EnumeratedTypeMember)`

Code example `prior.month := pred (current.month);`

Purpose The pred function returns the predecessor of the given enumerated type member, that is, the member that appears just prior to the given member in the parenthesized list. It is an error if the given member is first in the list. See also enumerated type (p. 430), succ (p. 431).

succ Function

Format `pred (EnumeratedTypeMember)`

Code example
```
if current.month < DECEMBER then begin
    next.month := succ (current.month);
end;
```

Purpose The succ function returns the successor of the given enumerated type member, that is, the member that appears just following the given member in the parenthesized list. It is an error if the given member is last in the list. See also enumerated type (p. 430), pred (p. 431).

Templates introduced or elaborated	Pascal constructs required	Pascal constructs introduced
Process elements in a two-dimensional array until done		two-dimensional array
Process the diagonal of a two-dimensional array		

TEMPLATES **TEMPLATES**

Process Elements Until Done in a Two-Dimensional Array

Description and purpose

Find the row and column position of a value in an array that satisfies specified conditions. This template processes elements in a two-dimensional array, performing some action on them and stopping at the end of the array or when some specified value or condition is met.

This is similar to processing elements in a one-dimensional array except that rows and columns must be considered. The template is constructed essentially by viewing a two-dimensional array as a one-dimensional array of rows, and viewing each row as a one-dimensional array of elements.

Pseudocode

When all elements of the array are to be processed:

```
for row := 1 to the number of rows do begin
    for col := 1 to the number of columns do begin
        process the [row, col]th element;
    end;
end;
```

When not all the elements are to be processed:

```
done := false;
row := 1;
while not done and (row <= number of rows) do begin
    col := 1;
    while not done and (col <= number of columns) do begin
        process the [row, col]th element, possibly setting done to true;
        col := col + 1;
```

```
          end;
          row := row + 1;
     end;
```

Code example

```
attacking := false;
queenRow := 1;
while not attacking and (queenRow <= 8) do begin
     queenCol := 1;
     while not attacking and (queenCol <= 8) do begin
          if board[queenRow, queenCol] then begin
               {check for other queens on the same row and column}
          end;
          queenCol := queenCol + 1;
     end;
     queenRow := queenRow + 1;
end;
```

Use in case studies

Chess Challenges describes the search for queens on a two-dimensional array representing a chess board.

Process the Diagonal of a Two-Dimensional Array

Description and purpose

Process values in an array by indexing both the row and the column to follow a diagonal.

Pseudocode

initialize row and column variables to the position of the first element of the diagonal;
while row and column variables are still in bounds, do the following:
    process the array element at position [row, column];
    update the row variable:
        row := row − 1 to go up ("northeast" or "northwest" in the array);
        row := row + 1 to go down ("southeast" or "southwest");
    update the column variable;
        column := column + 1 to go right ("northeast" or "southeast");
        column := column − 1 to go left ("northwest" or "southwest");

Code example

To print all the elements in the diagonal going up and to the right (northeast) from the element at row 6, column 1, in a 6-by-4 array called board:

```
row := 6;
col := 1;
while (row <= 6) and (row >= 1) and (col <= 4) and (col >= 1) do begin
     writeln (board[row, col]);
     row := row - 1;
     col := col + 1;
end;
```

Use in case studies

In *Chess Challenges*, the diagonals of the chess board are searched for multiple queens. (After some refinement it is possible to write a general program to search a row, a column, or a diagonal.)

Two-Dimensional Array Declaration and Use

Format
```
array [PositionOfFirstRow..PositionOfLastRow,
        PositionOfFirstColumn..PositionOfLastColumn] of ElementType
array [PositionOfFirstRow..PositionOfLastRow] of RowType
```

Code example
```
type
    BoardType = array [1..8, 1..8] of boolean;
    RowType = array [1..8] of boolean;
    DifferentBoardType = array [1..8] of RowType;

var
    board1: BoardType;
    board2: DifferentBoardType;
    row, column: integer;

write (board1[row, column]);
write (board2[row][column]);
```

Purpose
A two-dimensional array may be viewed either as an array of arrays or as an array with "width" as well as length. The two definitions are essentially equivalent in Pascal. The array-of-arrays definition is preferable in situations where rows are processed independent of the array that contains them, for instance by being passed as subprogram arguments. Where rows and columns are treated symmetrically, the width-plus-length definition is preferable. See also one-dimensional array (p. 414).

Note: No new templates or Pascal constructs are introduced in Chapter 10, *The Shuffler's Dilemma.*

Templates introduced or elaborated	Pascal constructs required	Pascal constructs introduced
Read forward, process backward		recursion

TEMPLATES **TEMPLATES**

Read Forward, Process Backward

Description and purpose The action of the "read forward, process backward" template is to read a series of values from the first to the last and to process them from the last to the first. This can be accomplished by calling the procedure for reading a value from inside itself. It is useful to think of these calls from inside the procedure as creating a copy of the procedure and executing the copy. When a copy of the procedure reads the last element, the procedure does not call itself again but instead processes this last element and returns control to the previous copy. The previous copy processes the next-to-last element, then returns. This continues until all the elements have been processed "backward" from last to first.

Pseudocode
if there are more values to read, then
　　read a value;
　　make a recursive call to read and process the remaining values;
　　process the value just read in this call;

Code example
```
read (romanDigit);
romanInt := Translation (romanDigit);
if eoln then begin
    lastRoman := romanDigit;
    valToReturn := romanInt;
end else begin
    ReadRoman (valToReturn, lastRoman);
    if romanInt < Translation (lastRoman) then begin
        valToReturn := valToReturn - romanInt;
    end else begin
```

```
              valToReturn := valToReturn + romanInt;
        end;
        lastRoman := romanDigit;
    end;
```

Use in case studies

In *Roman Calculator Repair*, Roman numerals are read from left to right and processed from right to left.

PASCAL PASCAL

Recursion

Code example

```
procedure WriteBackward;
var
    ch: char;
begin
    if not eoln then begin   {eoln is the base case}
        read (ch);
        {apply the same procedure to a line with 1 fewer character}
        WriteBackward;
        write (ch);
    end;
end;
```

Purpose

Recursion, in which a procedure or function includes a call to itself, allows programmers to define the solution of a problem in terms of itself. This is helpful when a solution can be naturally decomposed into solution of the same problem on smaller sets of data. A recursive subprogram includes one or more **base cases**, situations in which an answer can be immediately computed, and one or more **recursive cases**, which involve a recursive call.

It is useful to think of recursion as the process of executing a new copy of the procedure each time the procedure is called. Once the action of any copy of the procedure is completed, control over execution is returned to the procedure from which the copy was called. Recursion stops when a base case is encountered.

Templates introduced or elaborated	Pascal constructs required	Pascal constructs introduced
Divide and process elements		

TEMPLATES **TEMPLATES**

Divide and Process Elements

Description and purpose

This template recursively applies the process of dividing elements into groups and processing the groups. Processing each group can be thought of as creating a copy of the procedure and applying it to divide the elements into groups and process the groups. Groups are divided until they have a single element. As in "read forward, process backward" (p. 435), once a copy of the procedure is executed, control returns to the copy of the procedure that called it.

Pseudocode example

```
if zero elements remain, do something
else if one element remains, process it
else do the following:
        divide the elements into two groups;
        (depending on the application)
            either process each group with a recursive call,
            or choose one of the groups and make a recursive call with it
```

Code example

```
{search for value in positions low through high of list}
procedure Search (value: integer;
    var list: ListType; low, high: integer
    var position: integer; var found: boolean);
var
    middle: integer;
begin
    if high < low then begin
        found := false;
    end else begin
        middle := (low + high) div 2;
        if list[middle] = value then begin
            found := true;
            position := middle;
        end else if list[middle] < value then begin
```

```
              Search (value, list, middle+1, high, position, found);
          end else begin
              Search (value, list, low, middle-1, position, found);
          end;
      end;
  end;
```

Use in case studies The binary search algorithm described in *The Eating Club* is an application of this template, as is the Quicksort algorithm mentioned in a study question.

Chapter Illustration Credits

Chapter 1   Copiers courtesy of Xerox Corporation; ATM courtesy of Chemical Bank; lock courtesy of Unican.

Chapter 2   GIRAUDON/ART RESOURCE, NY. G28761. Egypt, 6th cent. B.C., ms. 3096, *Book of the Dead*, The Dead Soul Being Judged, Paris, Louvre.

Chapter 3   Courtesy of Amaze, Inc.

Chapter 4   SCALA/ART RESOURCE, NY. K64137. Sixth cent., *Roman Calendar*, Ravenna, Archbishop's Museum.

Chapter 5   Courtesy of Legal Seafoods, Inc.

Chapter 6   ET Archive, London.

Chapter 7   Courtesy of Green Market, Council on the Environment, New York City

Chapter 8   Drawing by Cheney; © 1989 The New Yorker Magazine, Inc.

Chapter 9   Courtesy of U.S. Chess Federation.

Chapter 10   Photo from the Irving Desfor Collection, from the American Museum of Magic, Marshall, Michigan.

Chapter 11   *Day and Night.* © 1938 M.C. Escher/Cordon Art-Baarn-Holland.

Chapter 12   Courtesy of IBM Archives.

Index

boolean 407

boolean expression 383, 394

bottom-up 35, 38, 201, 206, 383

boundary value 8, 15, 59, 227, 240, 252, 297, 377, 383

box, as a way to represent a variable 11

breakpoint 350, 354

brute force 121

brute force vs. elegance 253

brute force, benefit of 251

bug(s) 34, 53, 55, 81, 84, 161, 163, 202, 228, 239, 240, 260, 262, 302, 349–354, 356, 357, 373, 375, 379, 383, 386, 388

bug(s), anticipating 60, 241

bulk processing 27, 384, 390

call diagram 35, 38, 201, 220, 230, 366, 377, 384

CalorieAverage 195, 213, 367

CardType 336

case 29, 30, 51, 54, 80, 120, 403

case vs. if 51, 54, 64

case, test data for 60

case, used with status indicator 153

Change 16

char 393

char vs. integer 12, 98

char vs. real 98

character input 12, 98, 130

character sequence 13, 396

character-to-integer conversion 13, 98, 105, 131

CheckNoMore 277

chr 396

Clock Solitaire 335

clumsy code 27, 38, 115, 121

CmdWordType 253, 282

code reuse 256, 260, 375

command interpreter 222, 233, 260, 384, 399

command scanner 241

command scanning 242, 243, 253

commands, representation of 430

CommandType 244, 253, 271, 282

comment 392

comparing code 61, 64, 84, 256

comparison of records 239

comparison operators 394

compressing an array 332, 371

concise code 65, 79

condition 384, 394

confused user 130

consistency check 117

consistent coding 48, 58, 102, 110, 247, 250, 261

consistent design 50

const 401

constant array 85

ContainsBlank 179

contents 384, 392

ConvertRoman 90

ConvertToArgs 256, 284

ConvertToCommand 256, 283

ConvertToDate 256

copy an array 330, 334, 335, 422, 423

copying a file 237

CopySequence 169, 180

CopyThenCopyBack 237, 269

correctness, evidence of 59

correctness, insufficient evidence of 118

correctness, verification of 15

cyclic behavior, represented with mod 64

data structure 384

data type 384, 388, 413

data type design 187, 205, 233, 234, 290

data type operations 188, 234

date scanning 250

date, representation of 227

DateType 228, 263, 271

DayType 228, 263, 271

dead end 325

debugger 350, 354

debugging 8, 9, 34, 36, 38, 379

DEBUGGING constant 118, 202, 312, 315, 318

DEBUGGING constant, lack of 252, 260

DEBUGGING constants, multiple 230, 231, 260

debugging output 9, 12, 36, 39, 108, 118, 131, 153, 203, 206, 230, 231, 260, 324, 348

debugging output for state-based code 127

debugging variable 9, 12, 17, 18

debugging, reduced by template use 65

DebugPrint 312, 315, 318

DecimalTrans 77, 79, 80, 85, 90, 91

DecimalValue 82, 84, 85, 88, 91, 93

DeckType 337

declaration 384, 392

decomposing 24

decomposition 384

decomposition into template applications 131

decomposition, to ease reuse of code 106

default 364, 365, 384

definite iteration 384, 404

Delete 238, 270, 375

deletion from a file 238

deletion from an array 375, 417

deletion of a file element 236

deletion of array element 114

design 3–13, 24–34, 48–59, 61, 76–80, 82–85, 97–107, 109–127, 150–170, 186–201, 219–230, 232–239, 241–257, 290–297, 299–306, 321–324, 326–332, 364–375

design conflicts 50

design flaw 224, 228, 240, 260, 367, 375

design, maintaining consistency in 50

design, successful 375, 378

designing a data type 187, 205, 233, 234, 290

development 8, 9, 12, 14, 34, 36, 52, 53, 59-61, 80, 81, 83, 84, 101, 107, 108, 118, 127, 128, 151–154, 163, 164, 167, 170, 201–203, 224, 227, 228, 230, 231, 239, 240, 252, 253,